Fostoria

VOLUME II

IDENTIFICATION AND VALUE GUIDE
TO ETCHED, CARVED &
CUT DESIGNS

Ann Kerr

COLLECTOR BOOKS
A Division of Schroeder Publishing Co., Inc.

Searching For A Publisher?

We are always looking for knowledgeable people considered to be experts within their fields. If you feel that there is a real need for a book on your collectible subject and have a large comprehensive collection, contact Collector Books.

Cover design by Beth Summers
Book design by Kent Henry

Additional copies of this book may be ordered from:

COLLECTOR BOOKS
P.O. Box 3009
Paducah, Kentucky 42002-3009

or

Ann Kerr
P.O. Box 437
Sidney, Ohio 45365

@$24.95. Add $2.00 for postage and handling.

Contents

⇜ Dedication ⇝

It is with such pleasure that I dedicate this writing to my family: my husband Ralph, my daughters Ann and Susan, and my son David. From the time of my marriage, on every holiday, every special occasion, every time of rejoicing, our table would be set with my wedding crystal, Chintz. As our family grew and we had more occasions to celebrate — mine, theirs, and ours — Chintz was always on the table. For a time, before I knew of matching services and when our children were younger, we moved too many times and my Chintz goblets had dwindled down to a favorite few. I thought our tables had changed and might never be as lovely. However, in New York City, just as I was finding the collecting world, I looked "across a crowded room" to see eight Chintz goblets on a table of glass for sale. They added new life to my old pattern and we continue to believe that any celebration is more festive when our Chintz is on the table. May it be so for a long time.

⇜ In Gratitude ⇝

Many people helped in many ways as I have pieced together the two writings on Fostoria Glass and I remain very appreciative of the favors extended towards this project. Photograph preparation, pricing, and information shared have all added to the finished work. Contributions of busy researchers, busy glass dealers, photographers who bent their schedules to mine, and collectors whose observations added to printed records, these, too, have been important to my writing. I must again thank those whom I mentioned in Volume I, but I must add Gary Geiselman, Allyn Rosa, Joe Erickson, Donna Sperow, Jim Davis, Barbara Adt, Margaret and Kenn Whitmyer, Millicent Conley, Susan Mangus, Len and Arlyn Ols, Jerry Gallagher, and Randy Suplee.

I must single out the influences of Mike Baker in this project. Mike, an early Fostoria friend of mine, and a friend to all collectors of this glass, has served the Fostoria Glass Society as an officer since 1979 when the group was formed. He has shared his love of glass, his time, and his hard work with the membership for many years. He is my special friend and I have been able to accomplish this writing because of Mike's help and support. The depth of his recall and the extent of his kindness have counted for so much as I wrote. I could depend upon his cheerful voice on the phone when he *had* to know that this was Ann with another question, needing more information, more verification, more of his time. His friendship has been constant. The score between us leans heavily in my favor and I feel so privileged that I count him as my friend, He has several Fostoria books of his own "in his head," and collectors of this glass will hear from him, I am sure.

Plate given to the author on the occasion of retirement as president of the Fostoria Glass Society of America.

⊰⊱ General Remarks ⊰⊱

If this is your introduction to Fostoria Glass, welcome. This Volume II in the Fostoria series presents the detailed information covered in Fostoria's etched, carved, and cut designs, perhaps the most interesting, and certainly the lines most sought after by collectors today. It is a companion book to *Fostoria, An Identification and Value Guide of Pressed, Blown, and Hand Molded Shapes*, (Collector Books, 1994).

The Volume I updated information is intended to add to your understanding of the extensive, hundred year production Fostoria enjoyed. It adds important identification material, useful as we examine and understand Fostoria Glass. An acquaintance with these plain shapes will assist you as you identify Fostoria's work from that of other hand-made glass houses.

The designs listed in this Volume II of Fostoria's etched, carved, and cut patterns follow in alphabetical order and the attempt has been

made also to list the items in each pattern alphabetically. That has not always been possible. Logic, in some cases, is better determined by size and, in some instances, letters give way to numbers. A baseball philosopher, it has been said, told his players to "line up alphabetically according to your height." Those words took on added meaning as I formatted long lists of glass items, trying to keep order. Occasionally an identical item, produced over long periods of time, goes through a name change, but the number remains the same. In such instances, some items will be found duplicated in company lists, as well as lists here. Alphabetical listings, numerical listings, and ounces and inches are presented.

These writings are a study in numbers and I caution you not to be overwhelmed by them. Their order is confusing at first, but they take on meaning as we come to understand Fosto-

Metamorphosis
The Fostoria etching process. This complex operation actually required 10 separate steps to transform a crystal "blank" into a delicately patterned goblet.

Blown crystal blank to which a tissue will be applied, transferring the etching pattern in wax from an engraved plate.

Tissue has been removed, leaving pattern "printed" on the glass.

Stem and rim and inside of glass are coated with a wax masking composition.

After an acid bath, a delicate beauty emerges from its waxy cocoon.

ria's logical numbering system. The formula presented in the Update section applies also to designs shown here. (Refer to the clarification example given on page 344.) It is not unusual to find more than one shape of a particular item, each with its own number, used in the same pattern. This seems to be inefficient duplication, but is not. No less than three researchers have written that this was done to take advantage of patent time, using another shape for the same item, and so using remaining time on an existing patent while allowing a similar shape's patent to retire. Order and efficiency were the rule at Fostoria.

Such policy had a secondary benefit: product comparison could be achieved and, by the wise use of available patents, market research often determined the most popular shapes. Trends studied, usage examined, and sales recorded all allowed Fostoria management to make important adjustments. Diverse shapes assumed same prices in most instances, fortunately for collectors then and now. Fostoria maintained its leadership through these fine tuned, sensitive business practices.

Before leaving numbers, some words of encouragement: be generous with your own measurements and do not be discouraged if your figures and those given are a shade apart. Even the company noted very small differences and the addition of a handle or finial can confuse dimensions. Mold changes account for small variances also. An item made in a new mold was a bit smaller and more accurate than an item made in an old mold. Company listings

differ from time to time by fractional amounts and the company tended to improve and update their item listings and measurements as items were added or dropped. All this proves again that when lists and measurements were drawn, no one had any idea that collectors would make such a scrutinized study and hold lists accountable for accuracy. Every effort has been made to record all of Fostoria's identifying numbers but transcribing such extensive listings invites error in spite of good intentions.

Determining dates of production has not been an exact science and those who write about Fostoria have different frames of reference, with very similar findings. In most cases this writer has worked backward and taken the date of the first catalog in which a design did not appear as the ending date. The reasoning behind this has been that the company put out several supplemental catalogs a year and a line could reasonably have been produced for a portion of the preceding year, then dropped at the printing of the next yearly catalog. No attempt has been made to list the matching service years except for those lines included in Patterns of the Past and the Nostalgia programs. Matching service was available for most items for indefinite periods, determined by demand, not time. For the most part, matching service was limited to basic stems but, given time, the company accommodated customers and skilled workmen were called out of retirement to produce a few of this and a little of that. To include it here as extended production, however, would presume facts not known.

A study of these designs should point out that it was the usual policy to present a line for the first time with its largest component of items. That listing almost always became smaller as years passed and items were dropped, although, as we have seen, a duplicate item with time left on its patent often made a delayed debut. Stems were basic, in most cases, and they were usually available for the life of the design with serving items in diminished numbers as the product life continued. For that reason, a serving item may be considerably more rare than a goblet introduced at the same time. Color follows the same merchandising formula. If a design was made in colors, it was the usual (but not always) policy to offer the widest variety of colors at the outset, or very soon after the line was introduced. Crystal, with few exceptions, was basic, available for the duration of the design.

Formality, the order of the day in 1897, gave way many times, but informality, made popular after WWII, spawned a definite and permanent change in design and the company managed to make room for that while continuing delicate hand work, never compromising quality. A comparison of production amount indicates that growth periods for the company were greatest as the country moved from the Great Depression and after WWII when many new homemakers entered the buying market. Economic and social changes were important guides to Fostoria.

The terms *needle etching, master etching,* and *plate etching* have confused us. *Needle etching* is accomplished by covering a glass item with what is called "resist," through which a design could be traced with a stylus. Fostoria's early etchings were needle etchings. *Plate etching* is a hand process by which a design is made by pressing a special paper on a metal plate on which a design has been made and then transferred from the paper to glass. By use of an acid bath chemical process, the design is permanently etched into the glass and the paper is washed off when the design is complete. To assure that the etching followed the lines of the piece, a separate plate was made for each undecorated item until the process of photographic reduction was achieved. When that processing became available, it reduced the number of plates necessary to achieve the design on various sized pieces. *Master etching* was a term emphasizing the fact that the plate etchings were traced by master designers, carefully and artistically.

Cuttings were divided into two categories. A *gray crystal cutting* was cut, but left unpolished, taking on a gray cast, a frosted effect. These were comparable in price to plate etchings. *Rock crystal cuttings* were cuttings done on Rock Crystal Glass, not on the semi-precious stone.

The term was used to define Fostoria's finest polished cuttings. Some designs incorporate a combination of the two cuttings but the Fostoria company warned that such a combination was not to be called Rock Crystal, a term applied to a polished cutting only. All cuttings were done by holding a glass item against a revolving abrasive wheel. Workmen were so skilled that they could hold the piece of glass to the blade and duplicate the design again and again.

In spite of the delicate work and quality material involved in the cutting process, Fostoria was never able to make these cuttings as commercially successful as they had hoped. That was an industry-wide experience, unhappily, and these cuttings have not been favored by collectors today. Their values reflect that position. In spite of that, most collectors have seen items emerge into popularity after having been dismissed for a time, and there exists the possibility that Fostoria's cuttings may yet become important. Some of those who know Fostoria's work best believe that as collectors become better acquainted with these cuttings, they will be more valued. Certainly, seen in table settings, they are difficult to ignore.

Carvings, "rich, costly in appearance, and artistic in effect," were done on thick crystal. Tape was used to mask out all of the glass except that part on which the design was to be shown. Using compressed air, an abrasive was blown against the uncovered portion of the piece, causing it to gradually erode the design into a smooth frosty finish. Most of Fostoria's carvings are whimsical, informal, and rare.

Fostoria used a process called *Optic* to indicate a variance in plain crystal identified by shadowy self-shading of loops, ribs, or ridges. These are made visible by refraction and add beauty to a plain item, enhancing an etched design.

An explanatory word should be added to these remarks. Delicate etchings and detailed cuttings do not photograph well. In reviewing Fostoria's sales material, that fact stands out, unfortunately, and even company photographers suffered with pictures of beautiful etched and cut crystal showing less detail than all would like. Color pictures, presented here and photographed by professionals as well as those which appear in company advertising, come with fingers crossed. Fortunately, etched and cut details are more distinct in black and white prints, and for that reason, many of those have been included here, along with all line drawings and shape information available. We have used all avenues open to us for identification.

No discussion of this glass would near completion without the acknowledgment that the hand-made process invited experimentation. We have seen that lunch hour whimsies account for interesting rarities, particularly in hand molded items. The practice extended to the detailed designs covered here also. Given a bit of colored glass left over from a morning's pour, frugal and imaginative workers were sure to see how a design would look in a different color and it is conceivable that unnumbered variations and hand enameled etchings can been found, the work of very skilled workers, no doubt. Beautiful examples have been found in June and in Bouquet #207. There is no way one can account for what may be found as a result of such glass fantasies. It would be wrong, though, to be so absolute as to declare "this and no other," for all things are possible in hand-made glass. That is part of its beauty.

Some interesting original advertising is included here in spite of age, poor condition, and questionable reproduction. Reading between the lines adds to our understanding of Fostoria's advertising expertise and the support system which their customers enjoyed. Most of this material is to be found with the patterns to which it applied. Other advertising information is presented here, including advertisements referring to the 18th Amendment to our Constitution which prohibited the use of alcoholic beverages, passed on January 16, 1919, World War I years, when, some said, "the boys were away and could not vote." Fostoria Glass said little at the time, seemingly supportive in spite of their interest in the beverage business. On December 5, 1933, just as the Great Depression threw off its confines, the 21st Amendment repealing the 18th Amendment was ratified and Fostoria spoke to the point, even before passage, advertising proper usage for various spirits, prescribed amounts, and what, how, and when to serve them. These several pages of company text are timeless and describe uses which still apply.

From a little later time span, Horoscope/Zodiac flyers were give-aways at glass counters in shops. These interesting small cards told your future, gave you an unusual recipe, pointed to the glass pattern which could be used, and suggested servings hints. These flyers were pointed to a new market, the lady of the house, as the use of alcohol in the home was again appropriate, the bar, saloon, and restaurant no longer the only places where such beverages were served. Advertising appeared in nationally distributed magazines, appealing, once again, to the homemaker. In 1926, boom-times for the country, Fostoria ads were included in *Vanity Fair*, *Vogue*, *House and Garden*, and *Good Housekeeping*. In 1936, with the brunt of depression behind us, full page advertisements appeared in *The Woman's Home Companion*, *American Home*, *Time*, *The New Yorker*, *House and Garden*, and *House Beautiful*. No doubt they found a ready market as they carried the information that service for eight cost less than $12. Business was brisk.

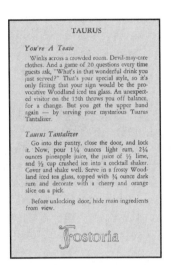

Production after 1985 has not been listed here. The designs from this period were imported by Fostoria and are outside the study of this work. They would include Bellwether, Athens, Alta, Vale, Northampton, and possibly more.

Permission to use pictures and line drawings presented in both these works was given to me by the late William B. Dalzell, former president of the Fostoria Company, and by David Gerlach, president of Lancaster Colony Company. Without such original records and the consent to use and reprint them, such a writing as this could not have been accomplished. Mr. Dalzell was especially kind to me as I have studied Fostoria production, and during his life he came to understand the collector syndrome. He took a personal interest in collectors' need-to-know, and his involvement with collectors' interests illustrated his generosity.

This writing is not meant to determine or to change pricing on items. Several researchers from around the country were willing to spend many hours of time and study in order to offer their well considered prices. These have not been arrived at easily, and averaging to determine final values to report was equally difficult. When one considers the thousands of items which Fostoria made, it is obvious that no one

person can be familiar with all of the items and their values. For that reason, some researchers could help pricing on some things, and some with others. In some cases wide variations were confusing. Advertised items in the trade papers also reflect wide differences and show prices tend to be lower. Pricing is not a science, certainly not an exact one. As you consult these averages, factor in your own experience. Half of us will think these prices too high, half will think them too low, but none of us would be pleased if prices were not included. They reflect mint condition crystal glass. Colored items should reflect a higher price. Green and Amber items should be valued at about 20% higher than crystal items. Add 30% for Azure, Dawn, and Pink items. Regal Blue and Empire Green usually add 40% to crystal values, and the difficult-to-find Wisteria items increase pricing about 70%. Exceptions to these percentages are noted in the listings. If you are selling, be aware that dealers can offer half of the value they ascribe to an item, that they hope you have a price at which you would like to sell and that you will be aware that their selling price reflects many business costs. Your considered judgment should be your most important reference in establishing values. Guides should help, but not establish prices.

An excellent reference source for Fostoria collectors is the Fostoria Glass Society of America, Box 826, Moundsville, WV 26041. This national group has several chapters around the country and holds regular meetings for members, issues a monthly publication, *The Facets*, and maintains a museum of Fostoria Glass in Moundsville. This writer had not visited the museum in some time and was pleased to find extensive research material available to the membership. Most of the information derives from company sales material, but it includes past issues of *The Facets* as well as cross referenced material pertaining to Fostoria Glass, published in other glass publications. The amount of information which the Society and the Museum owns is overwhelming, some very fragile and not all cataloged. I am told, however, that all information is becoming available to the membership as cataloging is accomplished. You are invited to join the Society and in doing so will find yourself part of a group with common interests, sharing the beauty of glass.

Common Terms

Terms used for item description need clarification. Some were established in early production of the late 19th century and are confusing to today's collectors. Others, only generationally removed, seem equally unfamiliar and still leave collectors guessing as to what they may be. Time and familiarity have left voids in our understanding. Early listings described various older items simply by the foods they might contain; "Egg," "Grapefruit," and "Oil" are typical.

The Fostoria Company recognized this problem and addressed it by including a list of lesser known terms in sales material sent to sales persons who were encouraged to study and use "the same language." Identity problems were very important and accuracy was imperative in communication between the factory and retail accounts. Here, no effort has been made to ascribe descriptions for items of undetermined size or shape. It would seem best to call an item what it was named in original catalogs and in common usage at the time when the article was first offered for sale. Uniformity, as was established by the glass houses, has become acceptable to collectors, though difficult to understand at times.

Terms which Fostoria standardized include:

A **Candelabra** is a decorative candlestick having two or more candleholders as well as boboches and prisms. Boboches were round pieces of glass placed at the base of the candle to catch drippings. Prisms were dangling pieces of faceted glass which reflected the candle glow.

A **Duo Candle Holder** has two branches or arms, usually of the same height with no boboches or prisms. A Trindle Candlestick, then, holds three candles. A Two Lite Candle Holder holds two candles while a Trio holds three.

A tall single candle holder, hung with prisms, is defined as a **Lustre**.

Candle Lamps were popular in older lines and involved a glass chimney, a lamp pot which held the candle, and chimney. Elaborate pieces, they are shown in a Fostoria 1913 catalog. They continued in popularity, however and we find them still advertised after 1950. A more familiar term would be a "Hurricane Lamp."

Though questionably accurate, Fostoria used the terms **Compote** and **Comport** as synonymous terms in sales literature. In such cases, it describes a footed or stemmed dish used for serving candy, jelly, nuts and the like, and may have been covered or open.

The French term **Coupette** identifies a stemmed glass used for individual portions of sea food or dessert. The center of the glass is deep, ascending to a flat shoulder and upturned edge as the word "coupe" has come to be understood.

Cruets are stoppered bottles used for oil, vinegar or salad dressings. Fostoria often used the word "Oil," leaving the reader to recognize the item.

After Dinner Cups and Saucers are small, usually footed cups used to serve espresso or cappuccino. Originally used in formal entertaining, these small cups and saucers have taken on a renewed popularity. They are also referred to as demi or demitasse cups and saucers. Fostoria paired individual cream pitchers and sugar bowls with a small tray for companion usage.

Another French term, **Epergne,** is used to describe a serving item which has several branches or arms. Originally used as a centerpiece, it evolved in usage to include candle holders, vases, and small dishes for candies and nuts. Fostoria's epergnes often had interchangeable units allowing a hostess to custom design her epergne to suit her own uses.

Yesterday's **Flower Block** is today's Flower Frog, a round, square, oval or oblong piece of glass with holes in it. By placing it inside a bowl filled with water, flowers could be made to stand upright or in an arranged position.

A **Banana Split Dish** is oblong, frequently rounded on one end with a handle at the other. Obviously, it held two long slices of banana and chilled dessert.

A **Bedroom Set** consisted of a glass carafe with a tumbler which fit over the top, sealing water for convenient use on a bedside table.

Fostoria used the term **Cheese and Cracker** to describe a flat cracker plate and a bowl or low footed plate upon which cheese could be served.

A **Console** usually indicated a set comprised of a large bowl, often with a foot, and a pair of candles for use on each side as a centerpiece unit. Frequently referred to as "Consoles," the term may indicate only the bowl. These were popular in the first part of this century, less so after the mid-century.

A **Jug**, in glass terminology, is a pitcher and

the terms are interchangeable. The #7 Jug appears repeatedly in Fostoria catalogs and was said to hold three pints. It has been reported that they held more nearly 40 ounces.

An **Ice Cream Set** consisted of a tray and several individual serving bowls.

The **Crescent Salad** is a later term for the older crescent-shaped piece found in glass and pottery. It nestled beside the dinner plate and, originally, had much the same multi-use the Bread and Butter plate has today. Perhaps out of fashion, the use of the lovely Crescent Salad adds a lot to the grace of a beautiful table.

A **Salver** is a flat cake plate on a pedestal. Hostesses, of course, found other uses for such handsome pieces.

Handled Cake Plates were slightly larger than dinner plates, with two flat handles. Yesterday's hostesses found this a versatile item but collectors often are confused as to primary usage. By recall of the size and handles, we are able to identify this item quickly.

A **Crushed Fruit** was a tall jar made to hold a fruit dessert which took extended time to ferment before serving.

Yesterday's **Nappies** are today's bowls with multiple uses, frequently sized for candy, nuts,

jelly, snacks of all sorts. Nappies were round, square, oval, three-cornered, heart-shaped, and handles could be used on any of these styles. In early lines the term "Nappy" included larger bowls and it appears that the word "Nappy," at the turn of the century was interchangeable with the term "Bowl," regardless of size.

A **Puff Box** was an early term for a powder box while a **Pomade** held other cosmetics. A **Hair Receiver** is a dresser top box with a hole in the top to hold loose hair.

Fostoria's **Sandwich Trays** were plates, a bit larger than a dinner plate, with a handle in the center of the plate. Servers could pass a Sandwich Tray easily and the tray could be arranged decoratively with finger sandwiches, a favorite with 1940s hostesses.

Shrimp Bowls were large serving bowls to hold shrimp with smaller bowls, sometimes referred to as "liners," centered for sauce.

A **Swung Vase** is best described as a tall vase with careful detail at the base, extending to a relaxed uneven top that shows less attention to the detail that accents its base.

Lily Ponds were used to float flowers or serve sweetmeats. They were ten inches or more in diameter with a cupped edge and deep enough to hold two inches or so of water.

The term **"Liner"** was used to refer to a piece of glass which was used inside another to hold two sorts of food separately while serving both. The familiar liner which holds sauce inside a bowl of ice and topped with seafood is an example of this practice. Such liners could be used to hold any chilled food. The same term often applies to an underplate upon which bowls or some stems were used. Salespeople were advised never to sell a sherbet or individual serving bowl without attempting to sell a "liner." In such instances, specific liners were indicated.

A versatile item, the **Torte Plate**, ranged in size from 12 to 20 inches and was used to serve cake (torte, is French for cake) or a variety of foods in quantity. The size allowed for ideal buffet purposes, easily passed from guest to guest for extra helpings. Usually, torte plates do not have handles.

Tumblers or Stems for alcoholic beverages were frequently called by the name of the beverage for which it was intended, but in some instances, wine glass names were specific. Champagnes, Clarets, and Rhine wines are examples of this. There are others.

Typically, **Footed Tumblers** were used for

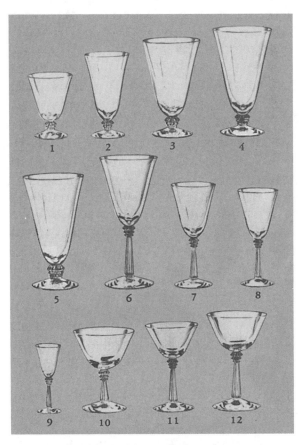

Footed Tumblers and Stemware

juice, water, iced tea, depending upon size, see illustration, page 11. A 4 oz. footed cocktail glass (1) may also be used for oysters while a 5 oz. footed glass (2), considered a juice glass, could also be used for parfaits or wine. A 9 oz. footed glass (3) holds water, a 12 oz. footed tumbler (4) is an iced tea glass, while a 14 oz. footed tumbler (5) was for "tall drinks," later adapted for chilled desserts. A goblet (6) has a tall stem and holds 9 or 10 ounces. It is used typically for water. A 4 oz. stem (7) is for claret while a 3 oz. stem (8) is for wine in older lines. Later wines were larger than the older 3 oz. A small ¾ oz. stem (9) is for liqueur or cordial, usually the most sought-after stem by collectors. A low sherbet (10) holds 6 oz. as does a saucer champagne (12). Both are stem pieces. The 3½ oz. cocktail glass (11), also a stem, is different from the 4 oz. footed cocktail mentioned above.

In **Plates**; generally, a 10" or 10½" plate is a dinner plate, and a slightly smaller one, 8½" or 9", may be a luncheon plate. A 7" plate is used for salads or desserts and a 6" plate is a bread and butter plate.

⊷⊶ Master Etchings ⊷⊶

In 1936, Fostoria launched an extensive advertising program directed at an economy which had just turned the corner from the Great Depression. Intensive market research, especially directed toward design, indicated which etchings had been especially popular with customers. Armed with the findings of that study while keeping a sharp eye on the buying power of those who were selecting crystal for the first time, Fostoria quickly took advantage of its leadership position in hand-made glass to promote old favorites in a new way, advertising these designs as Master Etchings. The term was new, the designs tested, and buyers overwhelmingly accepted the concept. So successful was the program that it remained a part of company advertising until 1972.

Starting with a limited number of etched designs, and used at first on the Baroque, Fairfax, and Pioneer shapes (see Update Information), the Master Etching listing grew to include many of Fostoria's most important etched patterns, used on favorite shapes and produced in an extensive assortment of items including a variety of stems as well as table service items. Most designs were full dinnerware lines with 50 or more pieces, but some designs were not so extensive. So great was public acceptance that the Master Etching program was accompanied by supportive sales materials and a book was given to retail customers with tips on "How to Sell Master Etchings." It was a classic merchandising manual and supported by a national advertising program, the Master Etching Designs became known as an artistic, hand-made group of glass designs, a very special presentation of the best glass made in America. That group includes at least the following:

Arcady	Bouquet	Buttercup
Camellia	Chateau	Chintz
Colonial Mirror	Corsage	Daisy
Florentine	Fuchsia	Heather
June	Legion	Lenox
Lido	Manor	Meadow Rose
Morning Glory	Midnight Rose	Mayflower
Navarre	Nectar	Plymouth
Rambler	Romance	Rosemary
Sampler	Sheraton	Shirley
Starflower	Springtime	Thistle
Trojan	Versailles	Vintage
Willow	Willowmere	

Later the Fostoria Company extended the life of its most popular patterns with the use of a merchandising program called Patterns of the Past. This program was quickly refined and renamed the Nostalgia Program. You will find designs included in these programs in the listings in this book. Not all Patterns of the Past designs were as popular as had been hoped and some were not included in the Nostalgia Program. For the most part, the important few stems of a design were the items selected for inclusion and neither of these later programs featured the full dinnerware lines which had been typical of the Master Etching Program.

Note: Background information on Master Etchings is taken from work done by Juanita Williams, Therese McIlrath, and Maryann Roberts. Their book is listed in the bibliography.

⊷⊶ Shape/Color/Design Summary ⊶⊷

Baroque #2496, 1936 – 1966
Colors: amber, azure, azure tint, burgundy, crystal, empire green, gold tint, green, ruby, topaz
Etchings: Chintz, Gold Lace, Lido, Meadow Rose, Navarre, Shirley

Century #2630, 1949 – 1985
Colors: crystal
Etchings: Bouquet, Camellia, Heather, Lacy Leaf, Milkweed, Starflower

Contour #2638, #6060, #2666 1955 – 1977
Colors: blue opalescent, crystal, green opalescent, pink opalescent
Etchings: Skyflower, Sylvan, Thistle

Coronet #2560, 1938 – 1960
Colors: crystal
Etchings: Mayflower, Willomere

Fairfax #2375, 1927 – 1960
Colors: amber, azure, crystal, ebony, green, orchid, rose, ruby, topaz
Etchings: Acanthus, June, Kashmir, Trojan, Versailles, Vernon, Verona

Lafayette #2440, 1931 – 1960
Colors: amber, burgundy, crystal, empire green, gold tint, green, regal blue, rose, topaz, wisteria
Etchings: Arcady, Chateau, Corsage, Flemish, Florentine, Fuchsia, Midnight Rose, Morning Glory, Navarre, Springtime

Mayfair #2419, 1930 – 1944
Colors: amber, azure, burgundy, crystal, empire green, gold tint, green, regal blue, rose, ruby, topaz, wisteria
Etchings: Fern, Fountain, Kashmir, Manor, Minuet, New Garland, Wildflower

Pioneer #2350, 1926 – 1960
Colors: amber, azure, burgundy, blue, crystal, empire green, green, orchid, regal blue, rose, ruby, wisteria
Etchings: Beverly, Royal, Seville, Vesper, Queen Anne

Raleigh #2574, 1939 – 1966
Colors: crystal
Etchings: Colonial Mirror, Plymouth, Sampler, Willow

#2383 Round Optic, Early Round Shape
Colors: amber, crystal, green, rose, orchid
Etchings: Brunswick, Camden, Delphian, Eileen, Fresno, Melrose, Mystic, Oak Leaf, Oak Wood, Richmond, Rogene, Sheraton, Sherman, Spartan, Virginia, Washington

#2364 Late Round Shape
Colors: crystal only
Etchings: Buttercup, Romance, Morning Glory

⊷⊶ Stem Shape/Etching Summary ⊶⊷

#660 1922–1929 Crystal
Etchings: Washington, Woodland

#661 1922–1929 Crystal
Etchings: Orient, Melrose, Virginia

#766 1913–1929 Crystal
Etchings: Lotus, Modern Vintage, Oriental, Victory

#802 1918–1928 Crystal
Etchings: Rosilyn

#858 1908–1929 Crystal
Etchings: Blackberry, Empire Etching #214, Etching #215, Florid, Lily of the Valley, New Adam, New Vintage

#863 1910–1928 Crystal
Etchings: Etching #210, Etching #214, Garland, New Vintage, Persian

#869 1925–1934 Amber, Blue, Crystal, Green
Etchings: Royal

#870 1926–1934 Solid Amber, Blue, Green, Rose
Etchings: Seville

#877 1927–1934 Amber, Azure, Empire Green, Green, Orchid, Royal Blue
Etchings: Cordelia, Oak Leaf, Oak Wood, Vernon

#879 1915–1928 Crystal
Etchings: Lily of the Valley

#880 1913–1928 Crystal
Etchings: Garland, Kornflower, New Vintage, Rosilyn

#882 1913–1926 Crystal
Etchings: Garland, Grille, Ivy

#890 1929–1932 Crystal, Green, Rose
Etchings: Verona

#891 1933–1944 Crystal, Topaz
Etchings: Springtime

#892 1939–1944 Crystal
Etchings: Rosemary

#4020 1929–1934 Amber, Green, Ebony Base, Topaz, Rose, Wisteria Bowl
Etchings: Fern, Fountain, Kashmir, Minuet, New Garland, Queen Anne

#4095 1923–1929 Crystal Solid Green, Amber, Green, Rose Bowl, Amber, Blue Green Base
Etchings: Melrose, Mystic, Rogene, Virginia, Washington

#5008 1925–1934
Etchings: Beverly, Royal, Vesper

#5008 1904–1928 Crystal
Etchings: Vintage

#5070 1913–1928 Crystal
Etchings: Lotus, Poupee

#5082 1913–1929 Azure, Crystal
Etchings: Delphian, Mystic, Rogene

#5084 1926–1934 Azure, Amber, Crystal, Green
Etchings: Seville

#5093 1926–1934 Crystal, Amber, Azure, Green
Etchings: Vesper

#5097 1927–1943 Amber, Azure, Crystal, Green
Etchings: Spartan, Berverly

#5293 1929–1931 Azure, Rose with Crystal Foot
Etchings: Avalon

#5297 1927–1943 Amber, Azure, Crystal, Green
Etchings: Beverly, Spartan

#5098 1928–1952 Amber, Azure, Green, Rose, Topaz, Wisteria Bowl
Etchings: Acanthus, Camden, Fern, June, Versailles

#5099 1928–1944 Azure, Green, Rise Topaz, Wisteria Bowl
Etchings: Kashmir, Trojan, Versailles

#6000 1933–1940 Solid Amber, Green, Topaz
Etchings: Legion

#6002 1931–1933 Rose, Topaz Bowl/Green, Ebony Foot
Etchings: Minuet, New Garland

#6003 1932–1943 Crystal, Green, Topaz, Wisteria with Crystal Foot
Etchings: Manor

#6004 1934–1943 Crystal, Wisteria Foot with Crystal Foot
Etchings: Fuchsia

#6005 1931–1943 Green, Topaz Foot
Etchings: Florentine, Mayday

#6007 1931–1943 Green, Topaz. Wisteria Bowl Amber Base
Etchings: Manor, Morning Glory

#6008 1933–1940 Crystal
Etchings: Chateau

#6009 1933–1957 Crystal
Etchings: Midnight Rose

#6010 1933–1939 Crystal
Etchings: Sheraton

#6011 1934–1964 Crystal
Etchings: Nectar

#6012 1933–1943 Crystal, Topaz
Etchings: Rambler, Springtime

#6013 1935–1944 Crystal
Etchings: Daisy

#6014 1935–1960 Crystal
Etchings: Arcady, Corsage

#6016 1936–1985 Crystal, Azure Bowl with Crystal Foot, Pink Bowl with Crystal Foot
Etchings: Meadow Rose, Navarre

#6017 1937–1976 Azure, Crystal, Azure with Crystal Foot
Etchings: Lenox, Lido, Romance, Shirley

#6020 1939–1954 Crystal
Etchings: Mayflower

#6023 1939–1945 Crystal
Etchings: Colonial Mirror, Willow

#6024 1938–1970 Crystal
Etchings: Willowmere

#6025 1939–1945 Crystal
Etchings: Plymouth, Sampler

#6026/2 1940–1973 Crystal
Etchings: Chintz

#6030 1941–1960 Crystal
Etchings: Buttercup

#6033 1949–1960 Crystal
Etchings: Bouquet

#6036 1952–1965 Crystal
Etchings: Camelia

#6037 1949–1972 Crystal
Etchings: Heather

#6052 1954–1970 Crystal
Etchings: Thistle

#6060 1955–1965 Crystal
Crystal Print: Sylvan

#6061 1955-1959 Crystal
Etchings: Skyflower

Misc. Carving Summary

Crystal unless noted, 1938 – 1944

Carving #1 – Waterfowl, single goose in various positions, gulls, ducks, swans. Various sized tumblers, decanter, ice tub, cigarette box, ash tray, plate. *See listings.*

Carving #2 – Ski, various positions in action, #4132 decanter, ice tub, various #4139 tumblers, #2391 cigarette box, ash tray, #2337 plate. *See listings.*

Carving #3 – Wave, #2561, bath bottles, $55.00.

Carving #4 – Band, #2562, bath bottles, $55.00.

Carving #5 – Colonial, #26/1, spread eagle flanked by a star, candle lamp with flame, candlestick, 2", $50.00.

Carving #6 – Aztec, #1895½, vase, 10", $40.00.

Carving #7 – Carnival, #4128½, vase, 5", $25.00.

Carving #8 – Yachting, #4132½, vase, 8", $30.00.

Carving #9 – Skater, #4132½, vase, 8", $30.00.

Carving #10 – Stallion, #2567, vase, 7½", $35.00.

Carving #11 – King George, #2421, plate, 12".

Carving #12 – Morning Glory. *See listings.*

Carving #13 – Brocade. *See listings.*

Carving #14 – Star, #2585, book-end.

Carving #15 – 19th Hole, golfer in various poses. *See listings.*

Carving #16 – Hollyhock. *See listings.*

Carving #17 – Narcissus. *See listings.*

Carving #18 – Tiger Lily. *See listings.*

Carving #19 – Lily of the Valley. *See listings.*

Carving #20 – Laurel, fount. No additional information.

Carving #21 – Pineapple, fount. No additional information

Carving #22 – Bird, fount. No additional information.

Carving #23 – Star, book-end, eagle with carved stars on base, lamp base with star detail.

Carving #24 – Archer, #315, bowl, 9", $35.00.

Carving #25 – Greyhound, #2577, vase, 5½", $20.00.

Carving #26 – Three Geese, #4132½, one over the other flying left, vase, 8", $25.00.

Carving #27 – Dolphin, #2557, vase, 8½", $30.00.

Carving #28 – Bubble Baby, #4116½, vase, ball shape, 5", $30.00.

Carving #29 – Polar Bear, #2577, vase, 6".

Carving #30 – Lyre, #2427, ash tray, 3½", $10.00; #2427, cigarette box, oblong, covered, 7", $20.00.

Carving #31 – Heron, #2591, vase, 15".

Carving #32 – Spread Eagle, #4132½, vases, footed, 6", 7½".

Carving #33 – Toy, various toys shown in decoration, #620, 5 enamel colors. *See listings.*

Carving #34 – Hunt, horn, cap, stirrup, whip, horseshoe. *See listings.*

Carving #35 – Horse #4148, ash tray, 2½", $10.00; #4148, cigarette holder, 2¼", $20.00.

Carving #36 – Elephant, #4148, ash tray, 2½", $10.00; #4148, cigarette holder, 2¼", $20.00.

Carving #37 – Rooster, #4148, ash tray, 2½", $10.00; #4148, cigarette holder, 2¼", $20.00.

Carving #38 – Oil/Vinegar, #2083, salad dressing bottle, carved "Oil," "Vinegar."

Carving #39 – Nightmare, grotesque animals in five enamel colors, decoration, #621, 1940. *See listings.*

Carving #40 – Thoroughbred, #2516, ash tray, round, 5", $8.00.

Carving #41 – Chanticleer, #2516, ash tray, round, 5", $8.00.

Carving #42 – Snow Crystal, #2427, ash tray, oblong, 3½", $8.00; #2427, cigarette box, covered, 7", $20.00.

Carving #43 – Gros Point, #2427, ash tray, 3½", $10.00; #2427, cigarette box, oblong, covered, 7", $20.00.

Carving #44 – Map of USA, #2577, vase, 6".

Carving #45 – Banner, #2577, vase, 8½".

Carving #46 – Cornucopia. *See listings.*

Carving #47 – Stars and Bars. *See listings.*

Carving #48 – Orchid. *See listings.*

Carving #49 – Dog Show, Various dogs on #4139 tumblers, #2427 ash tray, #4132 decanter.

Note: Much of the information above is detailed in the original documentation on Fostoria carvings done by Henry Liebman and published in his book Fostoria Glass Carvings. It is listed in the bibliography.

Master Carvings

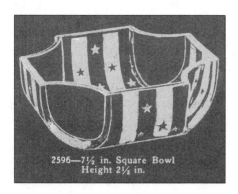

Carving #47 – Stars and Bars

2596—7½ in. Square Bowl
Height 2½ in.

2577—6 in. Vase
U.S.A. Map Carving 44

Carving #44 – Map of USA

2577—8½ in. Vase
Banner Carving 45

Carving #45 – Banner

**Carving #49
Dog Show Design**

**Carving #32
Spread Eagle**

Wonderful Colors

Grape #287 – Shallow bowl

Beverly #276 – Goblet

Heirloom #36 – Goblet

June #279 – Goblet

June #279 – High Sherbet

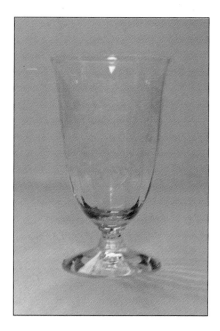

Meadow Rose #328 – Goblet

Mystic #270 – Footed jug and goblet

Mystic #270 – Place setting (5 pcs.)

19

Navarre #327 – Goblet (blue)

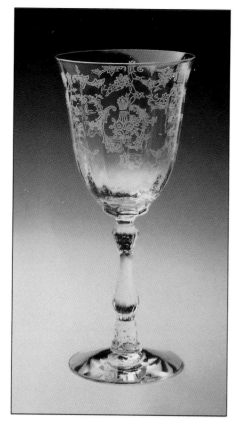

Navarre #327 – Goblet (pink)

Navarre #327 – Goblet

Nouveau #327 – Goblet

Oak Leaf Brocade #290
Oakwood Decoration #72 – 5 pc. place setting

Oakwood Decoration #72 – Window Vase with cover

Royal Plate Etching #273 – 11" Centerpiece (amber)

Royal Plate Etching #273 – 7" Comport (amber)

Royal Coronado #273 – Salad plate

Serenity #35 – Goblet

Serenity #35 – Goblet

Serenity Blue   Serenity Yellow

Serenity #35 – Goblets

Trojan #280 – Footed Sugar (topaz)

Vernon #277 – High Sherbet

Tara #34 – Goblet

Versailles #278 – Whip cream bowl and gravyboat (rose)

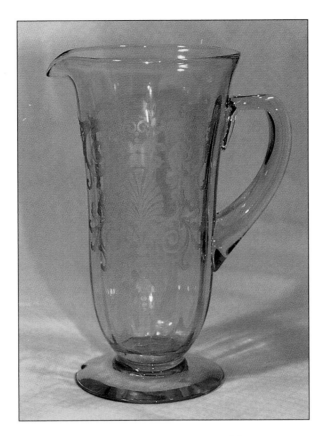

Versailles #278 – Footed jug

Vesper #275 – Small urn

Vesper #275 – Footed jug

306

549
550

137

681

679

650

567

500

448

648

344

622

620

707

Spartan #80 – Optic Goblet and Footed Tumbler

Camden #84 – Footed Tumbler

Greenfield #935 – Goblet

Kenmore #176 – Goblet and Wine

Poetry #2 – Sherbet/Dessert

Riviera Decoration #44 – Plate

29

Goblets

Navarre Crystal

**Chapel Bells – Cutting #888
(Vogue Pattern)**

**Bridal Belle – Decoration #639 Platinum
band with polished cutting (Celeste Pattern)**

**Carousel – Cutting #863 gray cutting
(Fascination Line)**

**Golden Lace – Decoration #645 crystal print
with gold band (Petite Pattern)**

**Westminster – Cutting #872
polished cutting (Embassy Pattern)**

**Holly – Decoration #815 combination
gray/polished cutting (Astrid Pattern)**

**Renaissance Gold – Decoration #678 crystal
print with gold band (Illusion Pattern)**

Patterns and Designs

⟿ ACANTHUS Plate Etching #282 ⟿

Dinnerware items Amber, Green Stemware Amber, Green with Crystal Base 1930 – 1933

#4095 Almond, Individual 6.00
#2350 Ash Tray, Small 10.00
#2375 Baker 9" 20.00
#2375 Bon Bon 18.00
#2375 Bouillon..20.00
#2375 Bowl 12" 30.00
#2394 Bowl, Footed 6" 16.00
     12" 35.00
#2395 Bowl 10" 30.00
#2430 Bowl 11" 30.00
#2375 Cake Plate 10" 26.00
#2375 Candlestick 3" ....pair 40.00
#2375½ Candlestick ....pair 36.00
#2394 Candlestick, Footed 2" ....pair 30.00
#2395½ Candlestick 5" ....pair 40.00
#2430 Candlestick 9½" ....pair 70.00
#2430 Candy Jar, Covered ½ lb. 20.00
#2375 Celery 11½" 16.00
#2375 Centerpiece 12" 35.00
#2375 Cereal 6" 18.00
#2375 Cheese, Footed 14.00
#2375 Chop Plate 13".................................30.00
#5098 Claret 32.00
#5098 Cocktail..22.00
#5098 Comport 6" 20.00
#5098 Cordial 60.00
#2375 Cracker Plate...................................40.00
#2375½ Cream, Footed 16.00
#2375½ Cream, Tea 15.00
#2375 Cream Soup 20.00
#2375½ Cream Soup Plate 16.00
#2375 Cup, After Dinner 12.00
#2375½ Cup, Footed 12.00
#2375 Dessert, Large 14.00
#869 Finger Bowl 10.00
#2375 Fruit 10.00
#5098 Goblet 24.00
#5082½ Grapefruit....................................30.00
#945 Grapefruit Liner.................................6.00
#2375 Grill Plate 10" 20.00
#2375 Ice Bucket 55.00
#2430 Jelly 7" 18.00
#5000 Jug 7...60.00
#2375 Lemon Dish 24.00

#2375 Mayonnaise 22.00
#2375 Mayonnaise Plate..........................18.00
#2430 Mint Dish 5½" 16.00
#2375 Oil, Footed...................................50.00
#5098 Oyster Cocktail 14.00
#5098 Parfait 24.00
#2375 Pickle Dish 8½" 18.00
#2283 Plate, Optic 6" 10.00
#4375 Plate
    6" 10.00
    7" 12.00
    8" 15.00
    9" 20.00
    10" 25.00
#2375 Platter
    12" 30.00
    15" 50.00
#2375 Relish 8½" 22.00
#2083 Salad Dressing Bottle 60.00
#2375 Sauce Boat 35.00
#2375 Sauce Boat Plate 20.00
#2375 Saucer...10.00
#2375 Saucer, After Dinner 10.00
#2375 Shaker, Footed ....pair 50.00
#5098 Sherbet
    High 24.00
    Low 16.00

#2375½ Sugar, After Dinner 18.00
#2375½ Sugar, Footed 16.00
#2375½ Sugar, Tea....................................16.00
#2375 Sweetmeat.....................................20.00
#5098 Tumbler, Footed
    2½ oz. 22.00
    5 oz. 16.00
    9 oz. 15.00
    12 oz. 22.00
#2375 Tray, Lunch, Handled 30.00
#2417 Vase, Optic 8" 45.00
#2430 Vase 8" 50.00
#4105 Vase, Optic 8" 50.00
#5098 Wine 26.00

⤛⇒ **AIRDALE Cutting #175** ⇐⤜

Crystal
1924 – 1928

#880 Almond 8.00
#880 Bon Bon, Footed 15.00
#2219 Candy Jar, Covered
    ¼ lb. 50.00
    ½ lb. 65.00
#2250 Candy Jar, Covered
    ¼ lb. 50.00
    ½ lb. 65.00
#1697 Carafe 20.00
#880 Champagne, Saucer 5½ oz. 8.00
#880 Cocktail..7.00
#2241 Cologne 65.00
#803 Comport 5" 12.00
#1712½ Cream...16.00
#1769 Finger Bowl 8.00
#880 Fruit, Footed 5½ oz.........................7.00

#880 Goblet 10 oz. 8.00
#945½ Grapefruit......................................40.00
#945½ Grapefruit Liner 18.00
#5039 Liner (Tumbler Shaped) 8.00
#303 Jug 7 ....30.00
#2040 Jug 3..35.00
#2082 Jug 7..35.00
#803 Nappy
    5" 8.00
    6" 10.00

⇨ AIRDALE Cutting #175 cont. ⇦

#837 Oyster Cocktail 6.00	#880 Sweetmeat.......................................22.00
#822 Parfait 8.00	#2194 Syrup 12 oz. 40.00
#701 Plate, Tumbler 5" 10.00	#2287 Tray, Lunch (fleur-de-lis) 26.00
#2283 Plate	#701 Tumbler 13 oz. 10.00
6" 14.00	#820 Tumbler 8.00
7" 18.00	#887 Tumbler 2½ oz. 8.00
11" 30.00	#889 Tumbler 5 oz. 6.00
#2290 Plate 8¼" 22.00	#4011 Tumbler, Handled 12 oz. 18.00
#2263 Salt Dip 10.00	#4023 Tumbler 6 oz. 8.00
#2235 Shaker, Glass Top.................pair 60.00	#880 Wine 2½ oz. 8.00

⇨ ALASKA Needle Etching #77 ⇦

Needle Etching #77
Decoration #54
White Gold Trim
1925 – 1931
SEE SHERMAN FOR LISTING

⇨ ALLEGRO Cutting #748 ⇦

Optic Pattern
Rock Crystal
1935 – 1943

#2533 Bowl, Handled 9" 30.00
#2533 Candlestick, Duo ....pair 40.00
#6013 Champagne, Saucer 6 oz. 19.00
#6013 Claret 4 oz. 28.00
#6013 Cocktail 3½ oz. 18.00
#6013 Comport 5" 20.00
#6013 Cordial 1 oz. 32.00
#766 Finger Bowl (not Optic) 12.00
#6013 Goblet
    High 10 oz. 22.00
    Low 9 oz. 20.00
#5000 Jug, Footed 100.00
#1184 Old Fashioned Cocktail
    7 oz. (not Optic) 8.00

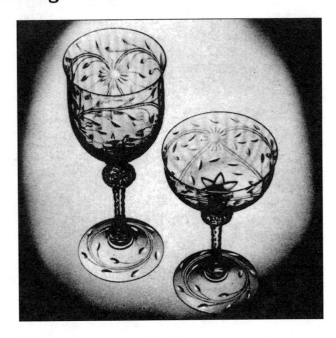

☞ ALLEGRO Cutting #748 cont. ☜

#6013 Oyster Cocktail 4 oz. 16.00
#2337 Plate
    6" 8.00
    7" 10.00
    8" 12.00
#6013 Sherbet, Low 5 oz. 18.00
#701 Tumbler, Sham (not Optic)
    10 oz. 10.00
    12 oz. 10.00
#6013 Tumbler, Footed
    5 oz. 16.00
    13 oz. 18.00
#6013 Wine 3 oz. 28.00

☞ ALOHA Cutting #805 ☜

Crystal
1940 – 1954

#6023 Candlestick, Duo ....pair 50.00
#6027 Champagne, Saucer 5½ oz. 16.00
#6027 Cocktail 3½ oz. 14.00
#6027 Cordial 1 oz. 27.00
#4021 Finger Bowl 12.00
#6027 Goblet 10 oz. 20.00
#6011 Jug, Footed 100.00
#2364 Lily Pond 12" 60.00
#6027 Oyster Cocktail 4 oz. 10.00
#2337 Plate, Plain
    7" 8.00
    8" 10.00
#6027 Sherbet, Low 5½ oz.......................12.00
#6027 Tumbler, Footed
    5 oz. 14.00
    12 oz. 18.00
#6027 Wine 4 oz. 20.00

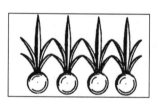

☞ ALTA Cutting #924 ☜

Crystal
1974 – 1975
**Alta was part of the Centennial II lead crystal
  collection.**

#2863/23 Double Old Fashioned
    11 oz. 4" 12.00
#2863/64 High Ball 13 oz. 5⅛"..................12.00

Gray Cutting
Crystal
1958 – 1962

#6077/20 Cocktail/Wine 4 oz. 4¼" 21.00
#6077/29 Cordial 1 oz. 3" 26.00
#6077/2 Goblet 10½ oz. 5⅝" 21.00

#6077/88 Juice, Footed 5½ oz. 4⅜" 16.00
#6077/63 Luncheon Goblet/Ice Tea 13 oz.
    5⅝" 20.00
#6077/11 Sherbet 7 oz. 18.00
#2337 Plate
    7" 10.00
    8" 10.00

1918 – 1929

#863 Almond 10.00
#880 Bon Bon 4½" 10.00
#1904 Bon Bon, Covered 30.00
#2136 Bon Bon, Covered 28.00
#896 Bowl, Covered, Footed 6" 18.00
#2199 Candy Jar, Covered
    ¼ lb. 20.00
    ½ lb. 44.00
    1 lb. 24.00
#1697 Carafe 25.00
#1697 Carafe with Tumbler–Bedroom Set ..35.00
#805 Champagne, Saucer 5 oz. 7.00
#863 Champagne, Saucer 5½ oz. 7.00
#1590 Cheese....................................10.00
#1590 Cheese Plate 6.00
#5051 Cheese, Footed 10.00
#5051 Cheese Plate 5" 6.00
#805 Cocktail...................................7.00
#863 Cocktail 3½ oz. 7.00
#2118 Cologne, 6 oz. 30.00
#2241 Cologne and Stopper 35.00
#803 Comport
    5" 10.00
    6" 10.00
#803 Comport, Footed 15.00
#1480 Cream 12.00
#1712½ Cream...................................12.00
#1598 Custard 6.00
#766 Finger Bowl 6.00
#769 Finger Bowl Plate 6".......................4.00
#863 Fruit 10.00
#1736 Fruit Plate 6" 4.00
#805 Goblet 9 oz. 7.00
#863 Goblet 9 oz. 7.00
#945½ Grapefruit 10.00
#945½ Grapefruit Liner 10.00
#766 Ice Tea, Footed, Handled 10.00
#300 Jug 7......................................45.00
#303 Jug 7......................................40.00
#1236 Jug 6....................................40.00
#2040 Jug 3....................................25.00
#2100 Jug 7, 9¾" 45.00
#2104 Jug and Tumbler, Punty 45.00
#1743 Jug, Covered 45.00
#1281 Lemon Dish 5" 8.00
#1733 Marmalade, Covered 18.00
#1831 Mayonnaise
    Bowl....................................18.00
    Plate...................................6.00
    Ladle...................................20.00

#1831 Mustard, Covered 16.00
#1227 Nappy
    4½ oz................................6.00
    8 oz.................................12.00
#453 Nappy, Handled 4½" 7.00
#803 Nappy, Footed
    5" 7.00
    6" 7.00
    7" 7.00
#803 Nappy, Footed, Covered 5" 15.00
#1465 Oil 5 oz. 35.00
#1465 Oil, Cut Neck, Cut Stopper 7 oz. 40.00
#805 Parfait 7.00
#2050 Plate, Cracker 9" 8.00
#1897 Plate, Salad 7" 8.00
#1848 Plate, Sandwich 9" 10.00
#1719 Plate, Sandwich 10½".....................12.00
#2135 Puff, Covered 30.00
#805 Salt Dip, Footed..........................14.00
#2022 Shaker, Glass Top 10.00
#805 Sherbet 6 oz. 7.00
#840 Sherbet Plate 4.00
#1480 Sugar....................................10.00
#1712 Sugar....................................10.00
#858 Sweetmeat 10.00
#2194 Syrup, Removable Nickel Top
    8 oz. 50.00
    12 oz. 52.00
#922 Toothpick 2½" 18.00
#820 Tumbler, Table............................7.00
#858 Tumbler, Table............................7.00
#4011½ Tumbler, Table 7.00

⊷ APPLE BLOSSOM Cutting #138 cont. ⊶

#701 Tumbler 14 oz. 10.00	#858 Tumbler, Table, Handled 14 oz. 12.00
#701 Tumbler Plate 5" 4.00	#4011 Tumbler, Table, Handled 12 oz. 12.00
#833 Tumbler 8 oz. 7.00	#865 Vase 7½" 22.00
#833 Tumbler, Sham, Punty 8 oz. 7.00	#1761 Vase, Cut Star Bottom 10½"...........25.00
#858 Tumbler 14 oz. 10.00	#4069 Vase 9 oz. 22.00
#889 Tumbler 5 oz. 7.00	#2137 Vase, Brush 22.00
#4011 Tumbler 12 oz. 8.00	#863 Wine 3 oz. 7.00
#127 Tumbler, Table, Handled 10.00	

⊷ APRIL LOVE Cutting #866 ⊶

Crystal
1958 – 1961

#6068/29 Cordial 1¼ oz. 3" 20.00
#6068/2 Goblet 10 oz. 5¾" 18.00
#6068/63 Ice Tea, Footed 13 oz. 5⅞" 16.00
#6068/88 Juice, Footed 5 oz. 4½".............14.00
#2337 Plate
    7" 10.00
    8" 10.00
#6068/11 Sherbet 6½ oz. 4⅝" 14.00
#6068/27 Wine/Cocktail 4¼ oz. 4½" 16.00

⭑⇒ ARBOR Cutting #185 ⇐⭑

Amber, Blue, Green
1926 – 1928
   Add 80% to values for Blue

#2324 Bowl, Footed 10" 45.00
#2297 Bowl, Deep 12" 40.00
#2297 Bowl, Shallow 10"
#2324 Candlestick
   4" ....pair 40.00
   9" ....pair 90.00
#2331 Candy Box, Covered 70.00
#2250 Candy Jar, Covered ½ lb. 80.00
#2329 Centerpiece
   11" 50.00
   13" 65.00
#816 Cocktail...18.00
#2317 Comport 7" 20.00
#2315 Cream 14.00
#869 Finger Bowl 12.00
#869 Goblet..18.00
#5100 Jug, Footed #7.............................125.00
#869 Oyster Cocktail 14.00
#869 Parfait 16.00
#2273 Plate
   6" 8.00
   7" 12.00
   8" 18.00
   13" 30.00
#869 Sherbet
   High 18.00

   Low 14.00
#2315 Sugar 20.00
#2287 Tray, Lunch, Handled 11" 28.00
#5100 Tumbler, Footed
   2½ oz. 22.00
   5 oz. 12.00
   9 oz. 12.00
   12 oz. 18.00
#2324 Urn, Small......................................60.00
#2292 Vase 8" 70.00
#4100 Vase 8" 80.00
#869 Wine 20.00

⭑⇒ ARCADY Plate Etching #326 ⇐⭑

Crystal
1936 – 1955

#2470½ Bowl 10½" 35.00
#2496 Bowl, Flared 12" 50.00
#2496 Bowl, Handled 10½".......................40.00
#2440 Cake Plate, 2-Handled 10½"...........40.00
#2472 Candlestick, Duo ....pair 70.00
#2495 Candlestick 5½" ....pair 45.00
#2496 Candlestick, Duo ....pair 70.00
#2496 Candlestick, Trindle ....pair 80.00
#2482 Candlestick, Trindle ....pair 80.00
#2440 Celery 11½" 20.00
#6014 Champagne, Saucer/High Sherbet
   5½ oz. 24.00
#6014 Claret 4 oz. 35.00

#6014 Cocktail 3½ oz. 22.00
#2440 Comport 6" 22.00

#6014 Cordial 1 oz. 50.00
#2440 Cream, Footed 18.00
#2440 Cup 10.00
#869 Finger Bowl 10.00
#2440 Finger Bowl 10.00
#6014 Goblet 9 oz. 26.00
#2375 Ice Bucket, Metal Tongs 6".............70.00
#5000 Jug, Footed 3 pint 60.00
#2375 Mayonnaise
    Bowl, Flared 20.00
    Plate 7" 14.00
    Ladle...20.00
#2496 Mayonnaise, 2 part 18.00
#6014 Oyster Cocktail 4 oz. 14.00
#2440 Pickle Dish 6½" 16.00
#2440 Plate
    6" 10.00
    7" 12.00
    8" 18.00
    9" 20.00
#2419 Relish, 5 part...............................40.00
#2496 Relish
    2 part 24.00
    3 part 32.00
#2496 Relish, 4 part...............................36.00
#2496 Sauce Dish, Oblong 6½"................18.00
#2440 Saucer...8.00
#2375 Shaker, Footed ....pair 60.00
#6014 Sherbet, Low 5½ oz. 18.00
#2440 Sugar, Footed 20.00
#2496 Sweetmeat 18.00
#2496 Torte Plate 14" 50.00
#2496 Tray, Oblong 8½" 35.00
#6014 Tumbler, Footed
    5 oz. 16.00
    9 oz. 18.00
    12 oz. 24.00
#2470 Vase 10"......................................90.00
#4121 Vase 5" 60.00
#4128 Vase 5" 60.00
#6014 Wine 3 oz. 35.00

⇒ ARIEL Crystal Tracing #93 ⇐

Crystal
1940 – 1944

#892 Champagne, Saucer 7 oz. 8.00
#892 Claret 4 oz. 8.00
#892 Cocktail 4 oz. 7.00
#1769 Finger Bowl 6.00
#892 Goblet 11 oz. 8.00
#892 Oyster Cocktail 4½ oz. 7.00
#2237 Plate 7" 8.00
#892 Sherbet, Low 6½ oz. 7.00
#892 Tumbler, Footed
    5 oz. 7.00
    12 oz. 8.00

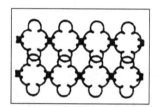

⇒ ARROW Cutting #142 ⇐

Rock Crystal
Crystal
1919 – 1925

#766 Bon Bon 5.00
#2219 Candy Jar, Covered
    ¼ lb. 20.00
    ½ lb. 24.00
    1 lb. 30.00
#1697 Carafe 4.00
#1697 Carafe Tumbler 10.00
#766 Champagne, Saucer 5 oz. 6.00
#766 Cocktail 3 oz. 6.00
#766 Comport
    5" 5.00
    6" 7.00
#2133 Cream 10.00
#2214 Cream, Covered 12.00
#2241 Cologne, Stoppered 35.00
#766 Finger Bowl 8.00
#766 Finger Bowl Plate..............................6.00
#766 Fruit, Footed 4½ oz..........................6.00
#766 Goblet 9 oz. 14.00
#766 Ice Tea, Footed, Handled
#300 Jug 7...12.00

#303 Jug 7..12.00
#2100 Jug 7..12.00
#1734 Jug, Covered 7...............................12.00

#2104 Jug and Tumbler, Punty..........set $20.00
#1733 Marmalade, Covered 24.00
#2138 Mayonnaise
    Bowl..18.00
    Plate..14.00
    Ladle 20.00
#1831 Mustard, Covered 24.00
#453 Nappy, Handled 4½" 5.00
#766 Nappy, Footed
    5" 5.00
    6" 5.00
    7" 8.00
#1464 Oil, Cut Neck 5 oz......................16.00
#1465 Oil, Cut Neck 7 oz......................20.00
#766 Parfait 8.00
#766½ Parfait..8.00

#1719 Plate 10½" 15.00
#2135 Puff Box, Covered 75.00
#2022 Sugar, Glass Top 20.00
#2133 Sugar 14.00
#2214 Sugar, Covered 16.00
#2194 Syrup, Moveable Nickel Top
    8 oz. 20.00
    12 oz. 30.00
#820 Tumbler, Table 6.00
#4011½ Tumbler, Table 10 oz. 8.00
#701 Tumbler 14 oz. 12.00
#4011 Tumbler 12 oz. 12.00
#4011 Tumbler, Handled 12 oz. 16.00
#701 Tumbler Plate 5" 8.00
#4069 Vase 9" 24.00

⇝ ARVIDA Cutting #185 ⇜

Amber, Blue, Green, Orchid
1927 – 1928

#2297 Bowl, Deep 12" 50.00
#2315 Bowl, Footed 10½" 45.00
#2331 Candy Box, Covered 70.00
#2234 Candlestick 4" ....pair 40.00
#2372 Candle Block 2" ....pair 30.00
#2329 Centerpiece
    11" 50.00
    13" 60.00
#2371 Centerpiece, Oval 65.00
#2368 Cheese & Plate 40.00
#2327 Comport 7".................................. 26.00
#2362 Comport 11½" 35.00
#2378 Ice Bucket, Nickel Handle 70.00
#2378 Ice Bucket, Nickel Handle 70.00
    Drainer, Tongs 40.00
#2350 Plate 13" 40.00
#2369 Vase, Footed, Optic 9" 70.00
#4100 Vase, Optic
    6" 50.00
    8" 70.00
    10" 90.00
    12" 110.00
#4103 Vase, Optic
    3" 40.00

4" 50.00
5" 70.00
6" 80.00
7" 100.00
9" 120.00

⇒ ATHENIAN Cutting #770 ⇐

Crystal
1937 – 1944

#6011 Champagne, Saucer 5½ oz. 14.00
#6011 Claret 4½ oz. 18.00
#6011 Cocktail 3 oz. 14.00
#6011 Cordial 1 oz. 22.00
#4132 Decanter, Stopper 50.00
#1769 Finger Bowl 8.00
#6011 Goblet 10 oz. 17.00
#4132 Ice Bowl.......................................30.00
#4132 Old Fashioned 7½ oz. 8.00
#6011 Oyster Cocktail 4 oz. 10.00
#2337 Plate 7" 8.00
#6011 Sherbet, Low 5½ oz........................12.00
#4132 Tumbler, Sham
    5 oz. 6.00
    9 oz. 8.00
    12 oz. 10.00
    14 oz. 10.00
#6011 Tumbler, Footed
    5 oz. 6.00
    10 oz. 8.00
    13 oz. 10.00
#4132 Whiskey, Sham 1½ oz......................8.00
#6011 Wine 3 oz. 18.00

⇒ ATLANTA #500 – Engraving #133 ⇐

Crystal
1895 – 1899
ATLANTA is easily identified by the lions' heads at the base of most pieces as well as finials on items with covers. It has a respected place in the ranks of old pattern glass. While no numbers were available to me, the names of some items are those frequently found in fine, old pattern glass.

Berry
    7" 10.00
    8" 10.00
    9" 12.00
Bowls, High Foot
    6" 12.00
    7" 12.00
    8" 18.00
    9" 20.00
    6" Covered 15.00

    7" Covered 25.00
    8" Covered 65.00
    9" Covered 75.00
Bowls, Low Foot
    7" 12.00

ATLANTA #500 – Engraving #133 cont.

8" 15.00
9" 18.00
7" Covered 22.00
8" Covered 60.00
9" Covered 70.00
Butter Dish 110.00
Celery Dish 32.00
Cream 24.00
Cruet 120.00
Egg...15.00
Goblet 15.00
Jelly 35.00
Jug, ½ gallon 100.00
Molasses Can 95.00
Mustard 25.00
Nappy
   4½" 12.00
   5" 12.00
Oblong
   7" 15.00
   8" 20.00
   9" 22.00
Oil 120.00

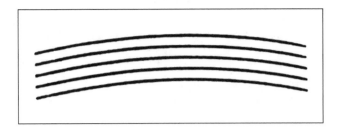

Pickle Dish.................................28.00
Salt Shaker ....pair 65.00
Salt, Table 20.00
Salt, Individual...........................10.00
Salver
   9" 125.00
   10" 150.00
Spoon...30.00
Sugar 75.00
Syrup...250.00
Toothpick...................................45.00
Tumbler 12.00

AUTUMN Cutting #850

Rock Crystal
Crystal
1957 – 1959

#6068 Cocktail/Wine/Seafood
   4¼ oz. 4½" 16.00
#6068 Cordial 1¼ oz. 3" 18.00
#6068 Goblet 10 oz. 5¾".............16.00
#6068 Ice Tea, Footed 13 oz. 5⅞" 16.00
#6068 Juice, Footed 5 oz. 4½" 12.00
#2337 Plate
   7" 8.00
   8" 10.00
#6068 Sherbet 6½ oz. 4⅝" 14.00

⇜ AVALON Needle Etching #85 ⇝

Rose, Azure with Crystal Foot
1929 – 1931
   Do not confuse with AVALON Cutting #832.

#5293 Claret 24.00
#5293 Cocktail...................................36.00
#5293 Cordial 32.00
#869 Finger Bowl................................8.00
#5293 Goblet 30.00
#5282½ Grapefruit.............................30.00
#945½ Grapefruit Liner 16.00
#500 Jug 7, Footed 65.00
#5200 Oyster Cocktail 10.00
#5293 Parfait 25.00
#2283 Plate
   7" 10.00
   8" 14.00
#5293 Sherbet
   Low 22.00
   High 24.00
#5200 Tumbler, Footed
   2½ oz..22.00
   5 oz. 25.00
   9 oz. 26.00
   12 oz. 28.00

⇜ AVALON Cutting #832 ⇝

Rock Crystal
Crystal
1952 – 1955
   Do not confuse with AVALON Needle Etching #85.

#6049 Champagne/High Sherbet
   7¼ oz. 5¼" 19.00
#6049 Claret 4 oz. 5⅛" 23.00
#6049 Cocktail 4 oz. 4⅞" 17.00
#6049 Cordial 1¼ oz. 3½".........................26.00
#6049 Goblet 11¼ oz. 7" 21.00
#6049 Ice Tea, Footed 15¼ oz. 6¼" 20.00
#6049 Juice, Footed 5¾ oz. 4⅞" 13.00
#6049 Oyster Cocktail 4½ oz. 4" 13.00
#6049 Parfait 6¾ oz. 6" 18.00
#2337 Plate
   7" 8.00
   8" 10.00
#6049 Sherbet, Low 7¼ oz. 4⅜" 16.00
#6049 Wine 4 oz. 5⅛" 23.00

⇜ **BALLERINA Cutting #900** ⇝

Gray Cutting
Crystal
1964 – 1967

#6103/31 Brandy 4½ oz. 20.00
#6103/25 Claret 7½ oz. 20.00
#6103/2 Goblet 12 oz. 20.00
#6103/63 Luncheon Goblet/Ice Tea
    14 oz. 20.00
#6103/26 Tulip Wine 7 oz. 20.00
#2337 Plate
    7" 10.00
    8" 10.00
#6103/11 Sherbet 8 oz. 20.00

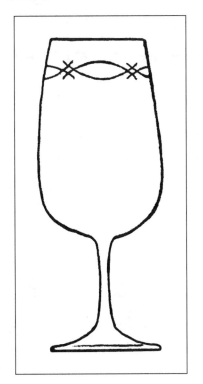

⇜ **BALLET Needle Etching #91** ⇝

Regular Optic
Crystal
1935 – 1944
  Do not confuse with BALLET Cutting #828.

#661 Champagne, Saucer/High Sherbet
    5½ oz. 6.00
#661½ Claret 4 oz. 6.00
#661 Cocktail 3 oz. 6.00
#661 Cordial ¾ oz. 7.00
#1769 Finger Bowl 5.00
#661 Goblet 9 oz. 8.00
#4095 Oyster Cocktail 6.00
#2337 Plate
    6" 6.00
    7" 6.00
    8" 8.00
#661 Sherbet, Low 5½ oz. 5.00
#4095 Tumbler, Footed
    5 oz. 6.00
    10 oz. 6.00
    13 oz. 8.00
#661 Wine 2¾ oz. 6.00

⇒ BALLET Cutting #828 ⇐

Rock Crystal
1952 – 1965
   Do not confuse with BALLET Needle Etching #91.

#6036/8 Champagne/High Sherbet
   6 oz. 4¾".....................................21.00
#6036/27 Claret/Wine 3¼ oz. 4¾" 26.00
#6036/21 Cocktail 3½ oz. 4⅛" 22.00
#6036/29 Cordial 1oz. 3¼".......................36.00

#6036/2 Goblet 9½ oz. 6⅞" 26.00
#6036/88 Juice, Footed 5 oz. 4⅝" 15.00
#6036/63 Luncheon Goblet/Ice Tea 12 oz.
   6⅛"..25.00
#6036/33 Oyster Cocktail 4 oz. 3¾" 15.00
#6036/18 Parfait 5½ oz. 5⅞" 28.00
#2337 Plate
   7" 10.00
   8" 12.00
#6036/11 Sherbet, Low 6 oz. 4⅛" 17.00

⤜ **BARCELONA Cutting #705** ⤛

Rose, Azure
1931 – 1933
   Do not confuse with BARCELONA Crystal Print #27.

#2375 Bon Bon 12.00
#2297 Bowl 12" 30.00
#2394 Bowl 6" 15.00
#2375 Cake Plate 10" 24.00
#2331 Candy Box, Covered 35.00
#2334 Candlestick 4" ....pair 36.00

#2374 Comport 7" 15.00
#2375 Cream, Footed 12.00
#2375 Dessert, Large 15.00
#2430 Jelly 7" 16.00
#2375 Lemon Dish 12.00
#2375 ½ Sugar, Footed..........................12.00
#2375 Sweetmeat 16.00
#2287 Tray, Lunch, Handled 26.00
#2430 Vase 8" 35.00
#4100 Vase 8" 40.00
#2375 Whip Cream 40.00

⤜ **BARCELONA Crystal Print #27** ⤛

Crystal
1971 – 1973
   Do not confuse with BARCELONA Cutting #705.

#6103/2 Goblet 12 oz. 20.00
#6103/63 Luncheon Goblet/Ice Tea
   14 oz. 18.00
#2337/549 Plate 7" 10.00
#6103/11 Sherbet/Dessert/Champagne
   8 oz. 18.00
#6103/26 Tulip Wine 7 oz. 20.00

⤙ BARONET Needle Etching #92 ⤚

Crystal
1936 – 1944
Do not confuse with BARONET Polished Cutting #847.

#870 Champagne, Saucer/High Sherbet
   6 oz. 9.00
#870 Claret 4½ oz. 9.00
#870 Cocktail 3 oz. 8.00
#870 Cordial ¾ oz. 10.00
#869 Finger Bowl 6.00
#870 Goblet 9 oz. 10.00

#5084 Oyster Cocktail 6.00
#2337 Plate
   6" 8.00
   7" 10.00
   8" 12.00
#870 Sherbet, Low 6 oz. 7.00
#5084 Tumbler, Footed
   5 oz. 6.00
   9 oz. 8.00
   12 oz. 10.00
#870 Wine 2¾ oz. 10.00

⤙ BARONET Polished Cutting #847 ⤚

Rock Crystal
Crystal
1956 – 1965
Do not confuse with BARONET Needle Etching #92.

#6065/21 Cocktail/Wine 4 oz. 26.00
#6065/29 Cordial 1 oz. 32.00

#6065/2 Goblet 11 oz. 24.00
#6065/88 Juice, Footed 6 oz. 20.00
#6065/63 Luncheon Goblet/Ice Tea
   12 oz. 22.00
#2337 Plate
   7" 10.00
   8" 10.00
#6065/7 Sherbet 7½ oz. 20.00

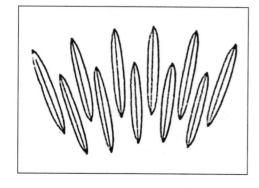
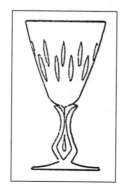
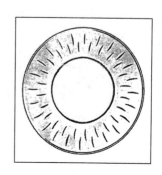

Rock Crystal
1937 – 1955

#2496 Bowl, Handled 10½".......................40.00
#2496 Bowl, Flared 12" 50.00
#2545 Bowl, "Flame", Oval 12½"...............45.00
#2496 Cake Plate, 2-Handled 10" 45.00
#2545 Candelabra, "Flame", 8 Prisms,
    2 Light.............................pair 100.00
#2545 Candlestick, "Flame", Duo ......pair 70.00
#2496 Candlestick
    4" ....pair 35.00
    5½" ....pair 50.00
    Duo ....pair 80.00
    Trindle............................pair 110.00
#2496 Celery Dish 11" 25.00
#6017 Champagne, Saucer 6 oz. 16.00
#2496 Cheese, Footed 20.00
#2496 Cheese & Cracker 40.00
#6017 Claret 4 oz. 23.00
#6017 Cocktail 3½ oz. 15.00
#2496 Comport
    Low 5½"...............................18.00
    High 6½"..............................22.00
#6017 Cordial ¾ oz. 30.00
#2496 Cracker Plate................................15.00
#2496 Cream, Footed 17.00
#2496 Cream, Individual 15.00
#4132 Decanter, Stopper 40.00
#766 Finger Bowl 8.00
#6017 Goblet 9 oz. 18.00
#4132 Ice Bowl..30.00
#2496 Ice Bucket, Gold Handle 50.00
#6011 Jug, Footed 60.00
#2496 Mayonnaise, 2 part 25.00
#2496½ Mayonnaise
    Bowl....................................15.00

Plate 10.00
Ladle 20.00
#4132 Old Fashioned Cocktail, Sham
    7½ oz....................................8.00
#6017 Oyster Cocktail 4 oz. 13.00
#2496 Pickle Dish 8" 18.00
#2337 Plate
    6" 8.00
    7" 8.00
    8" 10.00
#2496 Relish
    2 part 26.00
    3 part 32.00
#2496 Sauce Dish, Oblong 24.00
#2496 Serving Dish, 2-handled 8½" 26.00
#6017 Sherbet, Low 6 oz. 11.00
#2496 Sugar, Footed 18.00
#2496 Sugar, Individual 16.00
#2496 Sweetmeat....................................18.00
#2496 Torte Plate 14"..............................50.00
#2496 Tid Bit, 3 Toed, Flat.......................18.00
#2496 Tray, Oblong 8" 50.00
#2496½ Tray for Cream & Sugar 6½" 10.00
#4132 Tumbler, Sham
    4 oz. 6.00
    5 oz. 6.00
    7 oz. 8.00
    9 oz. 8.00
    12 oz. 10.00
    14 oz. 10.00
#6017 Tumbler, Footed
    5 oz. 11.00
    9 oz. 13.00
    12 oz. 18.00
    14 oz. 18.00
#4132 Whiskey, Sham 1½ oz.....................6.00
#6017 Wine 3 oz. 24.00

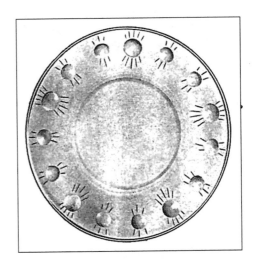

⋙ BEACON HILL Cutting #917 ⋘

Polished Cutting with Polished Cut Stem
Crystal
1968 – 1970

#6014½/25 Claret 7 oz. 22.00
#6014½/29 Cordial 1½ oz. 26.00
#4185/495 Dessert/Finger Bowl 12.00
#6014½/2 Goblet 11 oz. 25.00
#6014½/63 Luncheon Goblet/Ice Tea
    13½ oz. 22.00
#2574 Plate (not cut)
    7" 6.00
    8" 6.00
#6014½/11 Sherbet 9 oz. 21.00
#6014½/26 Wine 6 oz. 23.00

⋙ BERKELEY Cutting #903 ⋘

Crystal
1966 – 1967

#6106/25 Claret 8 oz. 18.00
#6106/2 Goblet 12 oz. 20.00
#6106/29 Liqueur 2 oz. 25.00
#6106/63 Luncheon Goblet/Ice Tea 14 oz...20.00
#2337 Plate
    7" 10.00
    8" 10.00
#6106/11 Sherbet 9 oz. 18.00
#6016/26 Tulip Wine 6½ oz......................22.00

**Green and Rose Bowls with Crystal Stem and
    Foot
1928 – 1929
BERRY is one of only two cuttings done on
    colored glass.**

#2394 Bowl
    9" 40.00
    12" 60.00
#2324 Candlestick 4" ....pair 40.00
#2394 Candlestick 2" ....pair 30.00
#2331 Candy Box, Covered.......................65.00
#2329 Centerpiece
    11" 50.00
    13" 65.00
#2368 Cheese, Footed 26.00
#5298 Cocktail...24.00
#2400 Comport 8" 36.00
#2368 Cracker Plate.................................18.00
#2350 Cream, Footed 14.00
#869 Finger Bowl 10.00
#5298 Goblet, Optic 10 oz. 26.00
#5288½ Grapefruit....................................30.00
#945½ Grapefruit Liner 12.00
#2378 Ice Bucket 85.00
#5000 Jug 7, Optic.................................140.00
#2315 Mayonnaise 22.00
#2375 Mayonnaise Ladle 25.00
#2394 Mint Dish, 3 Toed 4½" 24.00
#5298 Oyster Cocktail, Optic 5½ oz. 18.00
#5298 Parfait 26.00
#2283 Plate
    6" 8.00
    7" 12.00
    8" 20.00
#2315 Plate 13" 30.00
#2332 Plate 7" 14.00
#5298 Sherbet, Optic ....
    High 6 oz. 24.00
    Low 6 oz. 20.00
#2350½ Sugar, Footed 20.00
#2378 Sugar Pail 60.00
#2342 Tray, Lunch, Handled 30.00
#5298 Tumbler, Footed, Optic
    2½ oz. 24.00

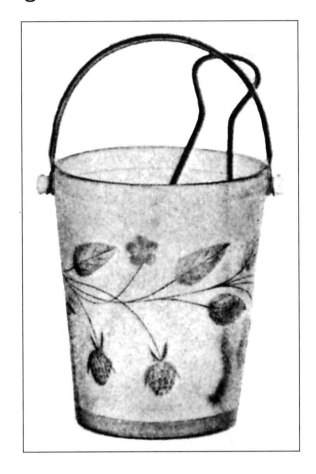

    5 oz. 16.00
    9 oz. 16.00
    12 oz. 26.00
#2369 Vase, Footed, Optic
    6" 50.00
    9" 80.00
#4100 Vase, Optic 8" 45.00
#4103 Vase, Optic 6" 45.00
#4105 Vase, Optic
    6" 50.00
    8" 70.00
#2373 Vase, Window, Covered
    Large 80.00
    Small 55.00
#2378 Whip Cream Pail 70.00

⊷ BEVERLY Plate Etching #276 ⊶

Optic Pattern
Crystal, Amber, Azure, Green, Orchid
1927 – 1934.
    Azure, 1928 – 1931; Amber, Green 1927 –
    1934; Orchid, 1927 – 1928; Amber and
    Green with Crystal Bowl, 1927 – 1934
See pricing in text for color values.

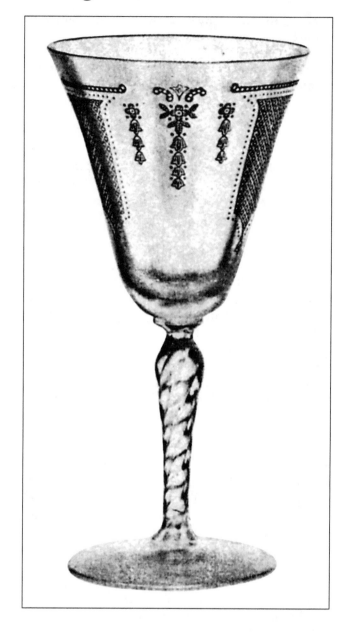

#2350 Ash Tray, Small 12.00
#2350 Baker, Oval
    9" 21.00
    10½" 38.00
#2350 Bouillon...22.00
#2350½ Bouillon, Footed 28.00
#2297 Bowl, Deep 12" 55.00
#2324 Bowl, Footed 10" 60.00
#2324 Candlestick
    4" ....pair 50.00
    6" ....pair 70.00
    9" ....pair 120.00
#2331 Candy Box, Covered 3" 90.00
#2350 Celery 24.00
#2329 Centerpiece
    11" 50.00
    13" 65.00
#2371 Centerpiece, Oval.........................70.00
#2350 Cereal Bowl 6" 24.00
#2368 Cheese, Footed 20.00
#2368 Cracker Plate................................24.00
#2368 Cheese and Cracker Plate 35.00
#2327 Comport 7" 30.00
#2350 Comport, Low 8" 35.00
#2350½ Cream...22.00
#2350 Cream Soup...................................28.00
#2350 Cream Soup Plate 16.00
#2350½ Cream Soup, Footed 30.00
#2350 Cup 16.00
#2350 Cup, After Dinner 26.00
#2350½ Cup, Footed 18.00
#2350 Egg Cup 50.00
#2350 Grapefruit (Mayonnaise) 24.00
#2379 Ice Bucket, Nickel Handle 75.00
#2379 Ice Bucket, Nickel Handle 75.00
    Drainer and Tongs Add 50.00
#5000 Jug 145.00
#2350 Nappy
    8" 35.00
    9" 40.00
#2350 Pickle Dish 26.00
#2350 Plate
    6" Bread and Butter 15.00
    7" Salad 18.00
    8" Salad 24.00
    9" Dinner 30.00
    10" Dinner 40.00
    13" Chop 55.00
#2350 Platter, Oval
    10½" 70.00
    12" 80.00
    15" 90.00
#2350 Salad Bowl 10" 50.00
#2350 Sauce Boat 70.00
#2350 Sauce Boat Plate 10.00
#2350 Saucer..10.00
#2350 Saucer, After Dinner 16.00
#5000 Shaker, Footed ....pair 125.00

BEVERLY Plate Etching #276 cont.

#2350 Soup 7" 24.00
#2350½ Sugar 22.00
#2350½ Sugar, Covered 50.00
#2311 Tray, Lunch 11".............................38.00
#2297 Vase 8" 110.00

BEVERLY Stemware made in Crystal, Green or Amber Bowl, Crystal Base

#5097 Claret 4 oz. 20.00
#5097 Cocktail 3 oz...................................14.00
#5097 Cordial ¾ oz. 25.00
#869 Finger Bowl 10.00
#2283 Finger Bowl Plate............................8.00
#5097 Goblet 9 oz. 18.00
#5097½ Grapefruit 24.00
#945½ Grapefruit Liner 16.00
#5000 Jug 7, Footed.................................240.00
#5000 Oyster Cocktail 4½ oz. 14.00
#5097 Parfait 5½ oz..................................18.00
#5097 Sherbet
    Low 5½ oz. 12.00
    High 5½ oz......................................18.00
#5000 Tumbler, Footed
    2½ oz..18.00

5 oz. 16.00
9 oz. 16.00
  12 oz. 20.00
#5097 Wine 2½ oz. 22.00

BEVERLY Stemware made in Crystal, Amber, Green only

#5297 Claret 20.00
#5297 Cocktail...15.00
#5297 Cordial 38.00
#5297 Goblet 20.00
#5297½ Grapefruit 30.00
#5200 Jug, Footed 250.00
#5200 Oyster Cocktail 18.00
#5297 Parfait 21.00
#5297 Sherbet, High/Saucer Champagne..18.00
#5297 Sherbet, Low/Fruit 15.00
#5200 Tumbler, Footed
    2 oz. 20.00
    5 oz. 16.00
    9 oz. 16.00
    12 oz. 20.00
#5297 Wine 25.00

BIANCA Crystal Print #22

1969 – 1970

#6102/31 Brandy 3 oz. 22.00
#6102/25 Claret 7½ oz. 23.00
#6102/2 Goblet 10 oz. 24.00
#6102/63 Luncheon Goblet/Ice Tea
    14 oz. 22.00
#2337 Plate
    7" 12.00
    8" 15.00
#6102/11 Sherbet 8 oz. 20.00
#6102/26 Tulip Wine 5½ oz. 22.00

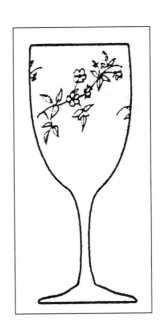

⊷ BILLOW PATTERN Cutting #118 ⊶

Crystal
1913 – 1918

#858 Ale, Bass 15.00
#863 Almond, Individual 10.00
#1904 Bon Bon, Covered 25.00
#1904 Bon Bon, Covered,
    Cut Star Bottom 30.00
#858 Brandy 1 oz. 10.00
#5058 Brandy 8.00
#793 Champagne, Hollow Stem 10.00
#858 Champagne, Hollow Stem 10.00
#863 Champagne, Hollow Stem 10.00
#825 Champagne, Saucer 8.00
#858 Champagne, Saucer
    5½ oz. 8.00
    7 oz. 8.00
#863 Champagne, Saucer 5½ oz. 8.00
#932 Champagne, Saucer 8.00
#858 Champagne, Tall 5½ oz. 15.00
#863 Champagne, Tall 5½ oz. 15.00
#5049 Cheese...............................12.00
#802 Claret 4½ oz. 8.00
#858 Claret
    4½ oz. 8.00
    6½ oz. 8.00
#863 Claret 4½ oz. 8.00
#858 Cocktail 3½ oz. 8.00
#853 Cocktail ....
    3 oz. 8.00
    3½ oz. 8.00
#952 Cocktail...............................8.00
#803 Comport
    5" 10.00
    6" 10.00
#858 Cordial 1 oz. 10.00
#863 Cordial 1¼ oz. 10.00
#863½ Cordial ¾ oz. 10.00
#858 Creme de Menthe 2½ oz. 10.00
#862 Creme de Menthe 2½ oz. 10.00
#1478 Cream 12.00
#1480 Cream 12.00
#1759 Cream 12.00
#1851 Cream 12.00
#1712½ Cream 12.00
#1931 Cream, Covered 15.00
#481 Custard...............................7.00
#858 Custard...............................7.00
#1598 Custard...............................7.00
#1598 Custard Plate...............................4.00
#300 Decanter, Cut Neck
    Pint 40.00

    Quart 50.00
#1195 Decanter, Cut Neck Large 40.00
#1464 Decanter, Cut Neck, Cut Flute
    10 oz. 40.00
    18 oz. 45.00
#315 Finger Bowl 6.00
#315 Finger Bowl Plate...............................4.00
#858 Finger Bowl 6.00
#858 Finger Bowl Plate...............................4.00
#1499 Finger Bowl 6.00
#1499 Finger Bowl Plate 4.00
#1769 Finger Bowl 6.00
#1769 Finger Bowl Plate 4.00
#863 Fruit 10.00
#858 Fruit Salad 10.00
#802 Goblet
    7 oz. 8.00
    10 oz. 8.00
#826 Goblet 9 oz. 8.00
#858 Goblet
    8 oz. 8.00
    9 oz. 8.00

10 oz. 10.00	#1465 Oil 40.00
11 oz. 10.00	#1465 Oil, Cut Stopper....................35.00
#863 Goblet	#1894 Oil 8 oz. 35.00
5 oz. 8.00	#858 Oyster Cocktail 8.00
7 oz. 8.00	#1389 Oyster Cocktail 8.00
9 oz. 8.00	#5049 Plate 10.00
10½ oz. 10.00	#1719 Plate, Sandwich 15.00
#863½ Goblet	#1848 Plate, Sandwich 15.00
7 oz. 8.00	#863 Pousse-Cafe 1½ oz. 10.00
9 oz. 8.00	#863½ Pousse-Cafe ¾ oz. 10.00
#945 Grapefruit 12.00	#1666 Puff Box, Covered, Cut Star
#945½ Grapefruit 12.00	on Cover 27.00
#945½ Grapefruit Liner 10.00	#1277 Punch Bowl with Stand 100.00
#1132 Horseradish....................20.00	#863 Rhine Wine 4½ oz. 8.00
#858 Ice Cream 4½" 10.00	**#863 Roemer**
#1713 Ice Tub 6" 20.00	4½ oz. 8.00
#303 Jug 7 One Band 40.00	5½ oz. 8.00
#724 Jug 7 One Band 40.00	#116554 Shaker, Silver-Plated Top....................12.00
#1478 Lavender Salts, Stoppered 25.00	#840 Sherbet 8.00
#1478 Lavender Salts, Cut Star Stopper....................30.00	#840 Sherbet Plate 4.00
#1281 Lemon Dish 10.00	#842 Sherbet 8.00
#1733 Marmalade, Covered, Notch in	#858 Sherbet 8.00
Cover 20.00	#846 Sherry 8.00
#1831 Mustard, Covered, Notch in Cover ..20.00	#858 Sherry 2 oz. 8.00
#315 Nappy	#863 Sherry 2 oz. 8.00
4½" 8.00	#858 Short Cake 8.00
5" 8.00	#1478 Sugar 12.00
6" 10.00	#1480 Sugar 12.00
7" 10.00	#1712½ Sugar 12.00
8" 15.00	#1759 Sugar 12.00
9" 14.00	#1851 Sugar 12.00
10" 20.00	#1931 Sugar, Covered 15.00
#453 Nappy, Handled	**#300 Tankard, Two Bands**
4½" 10.00	6 ....40.00
5" 12.00	7 ....45.00
6" 14.00	**#724 Tankard, Two Bands**
#803 Nappy	6....................50.00
4½ oz. 8.00	7 ....50.00
5" 8.00	#1761 Tankard Two Bands....................40.00
6" 10.00	#1787 Tankard Two Bands....................40.00
7" 12.00	#1852 Tankard 8 Two Bands 45.00
8" 15.00	#1743 Tankard 5 and Cover, Two Bands ..50.00
#1227 Nappy	#1741 Tea Caddy and Cover....................35.00
4½" 8.00	#922 Toothpick, Cut Flute 20.00
5" 8.00	**#701 Tumbler**
6" 10.00	12 oz. 10.00
7" 12.00	14 oz. 10.00
8" 15.00	#701 Tumbler Plate 4.00
#1848 Nappy, Deep 7" 18.00	#820 Tumbler....................10.00
#303½ Oil	#820 Tumbler, Half Sham....................10.00
Small 35.00	#833 Tumbler, Half Sham....................10.00
Large 40.00	#858 Tumbler 3½ oz. 6.00

BILLOW Pattern Cutting #118 cont.

#858 Tumbler, Table Sham
    8½ oz. 10.00
#858 Tumbler, Sham
    3 oz. 5.00
    4 oz. 5.00
    5 oz. 5.00
    6 oz. 6.00
    7½ oz. 8.00
    8 oz. 8.00
    10 oz. 8.00
    12 oz. 10.00
    14 oz. 10.00
    16 oz. 12.00
#858 8 oz. Tumbler, Sham
#858 Tumbler, Sham 8.00
#858 Tumbler Plate 4.00
#887 Tumbler 3 oz. 8.00
#889 Tumbler 5 oz. 10.00
#1297 Tumbler 7 oz. 10.00
#725 Vase, One Band
    8" 25.00

    10" 35.00
#1895 Vase, 2 Bands 10" 30.00
#160½ Water Bottle, Cut Neck 32.00
#1558 Water Bottle, Cut Neck....................35.00
#1697 Water Bottle.....................................35.00
#858 Whiskey 3½ oz. 8.00
#858 Wine
    2¾ oz. 8.00
    3½ oz. 8.00
#863 Wine 3 oz. 8.00
#902 Wine 2 oz. 8.00

BLACK BORDER Enamel Decoration #20

Enameled Flowers on Black Band
Gold Band on Rim and Foot
Crystal
1920

#858 Champagne, Saucer.........................30.00
#858 Cocktail...30.00
#858 Fruit 30.00

#858 Goblet 9 oz. 30.00
#858 Ice Tea, Footed, Handled 35.00
#2104 Jug 175.00
#1743 Jug, Covered 185.00
#858 Mug, Handled 35.00
#701 Tumbler...30.00
#820 Tumbler...30.00

⚞ **BLACKBERRY Deep Etching #205** ⚟

Blown Ware
Crystal
1908 – 1910

#858 Beer, Split 8 oz. 8.00
#858 Brandy 1 oz. 10.00
#5008 Champagne, Tall 6 oz. 12.00
#858 Champagne, Hollow Stem 10.00
#858 Champagne, Saucer 7 oz. 8.00
#932 Champagne, Saucer 8.00
#5008 Champagne, Saucer 6 oz. 8.00
#5008 Champagne, Tall 5½ oz................12.00
#1711 Cigar Jar, Cut Star 85.00
#858 Claret
     4½ oz...8.00
     6½ oz...8.00
#5008 Claret
     4½ oz...8.00
     6½ oz...8.00
#858 Cocktail 3½ oz. 8.00
#5008 Cocktail 3½ oz. 8.00
#858 Cordial 1 oz. 10.00
#5008 Cordial 1 oz. 10.00
#1478 Cream 12.00
#1480 Cream 12.00
#858 Creme de Menthe 2½ oz. 10.00
#5008 Creme de Menthe 2½ oz. 10.00
#858 Custard.......................................7.00
#858 Custard Plate 4.00
#300 Decanter, Cut Neck
     Pint 25.00
     Quart 30.00
#1128 Decanter 37 oz. 65.00
#1464 Decanter, Cut Neck
     10 oz. 30.00
     18 oz. 35.00
#1464 Decanter, Cut Neck, Cut Flute
     10 oz. 35.00
     18 oz. 40.00
#5000 Egg 7.00
#315 Finger Bowl 7.00
#858 Finger Bowl 7.00
#858 Finger Bowl Plate...........................4.00
#858 Goblet
     9 oz. 8.00
     10 oz. 10.00
     11 oz. 10.00
#5008 Goblet
     9 oz. 8.00
     10 oz. 10.00
     11 oz. 10.00
#858 Ice Cream 6.00

#303 Jug
     5.....................................25.00
     6.....................................30.00
     7.....................................38.00
#318 Jug, Optic 35.00
#1236 Jug
     5.....................................25.00
     6.....................................30.00
     7.....................................38.00
#858 Lemonade, Strained 10 oz. 10.00
#858 Lemonade 16 oz. 10.00
#858 Lemonade Plate 4.00
#858 Mineral 8.00
#315 Nappy
     4" 5.00

⚞ BLACKBERRY Deep Etching #205 cont. ⚟

4½"	5.00
5"	5.00
6"	6.00
7"	6.00
8"	8.00
9"	10.00

#300½ Oil, Cut Stopper

Small	35.00
Large	40.00
#5008 Pousse-Cafe 1 oz.	10.00
#1227 Punch Bowl and Foot	85.00
#1165 Shaker, Silver-Plated Top	12.00
#840 Sherbet	8.00
#5008 Sherbet	8.00
#858 Sherry 2 oz.	10.00
#5008 Sherry 2 oz.	10.00
#1478 Sugar	12.00
#1480 Sugar	12.00

#300 Tankard

5	25.00
6	30.00
7	35.00

#303 Tankard

5	25.00
6	30.00
7	35.00
#127 Tumbler	8.00
#820 Tumbler	8.00
#820½ Tumbler, Sham	10.00
#833 Tumbler, Sham 8 oz.	10.00
#858 Whiskey 3½ oz.	8.00
#858 Whiskey, Hot 4 oz.	10.00
#5008 Whiskey, Hot 4 oz.	10.00
#858 Wine 3½ oz.	8.00
#5008 Wine 3½ oz.	8.00

⚞ BLOCK Needle Etching #38½ ⚟

Blown Optic Pattern
Crystal
1915 – 1927

#863 Almond	6.00
#4065 Apollinaris, ½ Sham Cut #19	7.00
#4070 Bar Water ½ Sham Cut #19	7.00
#4065 Beer ½ Sham, Cut #19 12 oz.	7.00
#4065 Split Beer ½ Sham Cut #19 7 oz.	7.00
#4070 Split Beer ½ Sham Cut #19	7.00
#863 Champagne 5½ oz.	7.00
#863 Champagne, Hollow Stem	8.00
#863 Champagne, Saucer 5½ oz.	7.00
#879 Champagne, Saucer 5 oz.	7.00
#863 Claret 4½ oz.	7.00
#879 Claret 4½ oz.	7.00
#879 Cocktail 3 oz.	7.00
#863 Cocktail 3½ oz.	7.00

#803 Comport

5"	8.00
6"	10.00
#863 Cordial 1 oz.	10.00
#879 Cordial ¾ oz.	10.00
#1478 Cream	8.00
#863 Creme de Menthe 2½ oz.	10.00
#879 Creme de Menthe 2½ oz.	10.00
#1598 Custard	8.00
#200 Custard Plate 5"	4.00

#300 Decanter, Cut Neck, quart	32.00
#1769 Finger Bowl	7.00
#200 Finger Bowl Plate 6"	4.00

BLOCK Needle Etching #38½ cont.

#863 Fruit 5½ oz. 8.00
#4065 Gin Fizz ½ Sham Cut #19 8 oz. 7.00
#863 Goblet, Plain 10½ oz. 7.00
#863 Goblet 9 oz. 7.00
#879 Goblet 7.00
#945 Grapefruit 8.00
#945½ Grapefruit 8.00
#945½ Grapefruit Liner 7.00
#4070 Highball ½ Sham Cut #19 ....7.00

#4065 Ice Tea ½ Sham Cut #19 ....7.00
#303 Jug 7 ....40.00
#1236 Jug 6 ....40.00
#4061 Lemonade 7.00
#4065 Strained Lemonade ½ Sham, Cut #19
 12 oz. 8.00
#4070 Milk Punch ½ Sham Cut #19 12 oz....8.00
#4065 Mineral ½ Sham Cut #19 5 oz. 7.00
#4065 Wine ½ Sham Cut #19 4½ oz. 7.00

BLUE BORDER Decoration #19

**Blue Bands above and below enameled
 flowers at rim of bowl**
Crystal
1920

#858 Champagne, Saucer 5½ oz. 30.00
#858 Cocktail...30.00
#858 Fruit 25.00

#858 Goblet 9 oz. 30.00
#766 Ice Tea, Footed, Handled..................35.00
#2104 Jug 175.00
#1743 Jug, Covered 185.00
#127 Mug, Handled 35.00
#701 Tumbler..30.00
#820 Tumbler..30.00

BLUE MEADOW Crystal Print #8

Blue
1958 – 1962
**Tumblers produced to accompany similarly
 decorated melamine dinnerware.**

Juice Tumbler 7 oz. 10.00
Water Tumbler 12 oz. 10.00

⇒ BORDEAUX Cutting #758 ⇒

Regular Optic Pattern
Crystal
1936 – 1944

#2470½ Bowl 10½"....................................25.00
#2472 Candlestick, Duo 45.00
#6014 Champagne, Saucer 5½" 22.00
#6014 Claret 4 oz. 25.00
#6014 Cocktail 3½ oz. 20.00
#2400 Comport 6"................................... 30.00
#6014 Cordial 1 oz. 30.00
#869 Finger Bowl 15.00
#6014 Goblet 9 oz. 24.00

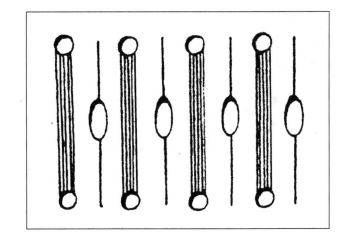

#2375 Ice Bucket 30.00
#2451 Ice Dish...20.00
#2451 Ice Dish Plate...............................25.00
#5000 Jug, Footed 150.00
#2337 Plate
     6"..8.00
     7"..10.00
     8"..12.00
#6014 Sherbet, Low 5½ oz......................16.00
#6014 Tumbler, Footed
     5 oz. 16.00
     9 oz. 16.00
     12 oz. 20.00
#2470 Vase 10" 75.00
#4121 Vase 5" 40.00
#4128 Vase 5" 40.00
#6014 Wine 3 oz. 24.00

⇒ BOUQUET Cutting #756 ⇐

Rock Crystal
Optic
1935 – 1938
  Do not confuse with BOUQUET Plate Etching #342.

#2527 Bowl, Footed 9"	25.00
#2527 Candelabra, 2 Light	40.00
#6013 Champagne, Saucer 6 oz.	10.00
#6013 Claret 4 oz.	12.00
#6013 Cocktail 3½ oz.	8.00
#6013 Comport 5"	20.00
#6013 Cordial 1 oz.	25.00
#766 Finger Bowl	8.00
#6013 Goblet	
9 oz.	13.00
10 oz.	15.00
#5000 Jug, Footed	50.00
#6013 Oyster Cocktail 4 oz.	8.00
#2337 Plate	
6"	6.00
7"	8.00
8"	10.00
#6013 Sherbet, Low 5 oz.	8.00
#6013 Tumbler, Footed	
5 oz.	6.00
13 oz.	8.00
#6013 Wine 3 oz.	10.00

⇒ BOUQUET Plate Etching #342 ⇐

Crystal
1949 – 1960
  Do not confuse with BOUQUET Cutting #756.

#2630 Basket, Reed Handled 10¼"	30.00
#2630 Bon Bon, 3 Toed 7¼"	18.00
#2630 Bowl, Flared	
8"	25.00
12"	30.00
#2630 Bowl, Footed, Flared 10¾"	30.00
#2630 Bowl, Footed, Rolled Edge 11"	35.00
#2630 Butter, Oblong, Covered 7½"	25.00
#2630 Cake Plate, 2 Handled	20.00
#2630 Cake Salver, Footed 12¼"	50.00
#2630 Candlestick	
4½"	20.00
Duo 7"	30.00
Trindle 7¾"	40.00
#2630 Candy Jar, Covered 7"	50.00
#2630 Cereal 6"	15.00
#6033 Champagne, Saucer 6 oz.	15.00
#2630 Cheese & Cracker	
Cheese, Footed 5⅜"	35.00
Plate 10¾"	18.00

#6033 Claret/Wine 4 oz............................22.00
#6033 Cocktail 4 oz.................................18.00
#2630 Comport 4⅜" 15.00
#6033 Cordial 1 oz. 30.00
#2630 Cream 4¼".....................................12.00
#2630 Cruet, Stopper
    Oil 5 oz. 40.00
    Vinegar 5 oz......................................30.00
    Tray for Vinegar & Oil........................15.00
#2630 Cup 10.00
#2630 Fruit 5" 8.00
#6033 Goblet 20.00
#2630 Ice Bucket, Chrome Handle & Tongs
    4⅞" 35.00
#2630 Jug, Ice 3 pint 9½"..........................70.00
#2630 Lily Pond 11¼"...............................60.00
#6033 Oyster Cocktail 4 oz. 13.00
#2630 Mayonnaise
    Bowl...15.00
    Plate...12.00
    Ladle 20.00
#2630 Mayonnaise, Footed, 2 part, Ladle
    3⅜"...16.00
#2630 Muffin Tray, Handled 9½" 25.00
#2630 Nappy, Round, Handled 4½" 10.00
#6033 Parfait 6 oz. 18.00
#2630 Party Plate, Cup Ring 8"................20.00
#2630 Pickle Dish 8¾"............................15.00
#2630 Pitcher, Cereal 6⅛" 30.00
#2630 Preserve, Covered 6" 22.00
#2630 Plate
    6" 8.00
    7" 12.00
    8" 15.00
    9" 18.00

#2630 Platter, Oval 12"............................25.00
#2630 Relish, Divided 7⅜" 20.00
#2630 Relish, Handled, 3 part 11⅛" 25.00
#2630 Salad Bowl 10½" 20.00
#2630 Salad Plate, Crescent 7½" 50.00
#2630 Saucer..6.00
#2630 Serving Dish, Handled 2½" high......15.00
#2630 Snack Bowl 3½" high 10.00
#2630 Sugar, Footed 4" 15.00
#2630 Shaker, Chrome Top ....pair 25.00
#6033 Sherbet, Low 6 oz. 14.00
#2630 Tid Bit, 3 Toed 8⅛" 16.00
#2630 Tid Bit, 2 Plates, Center Metal Handle
    10¼" 40.00
#2630 Tricorn, 3 Toed 7⅛" 18.00
#2630 Vegetable Dish, Oval 9½" 22.00
#2630 Torte Plate 14" 50.00
#2630 Tray, Sugar & Cream 7⅛" 20.00
#2630 Tray, Handled, Lunch 11¼" 30.00
#2l30 Tray, Snack 10½" 20.00
#6033 Tumbler, Footed
    5 oz. 18.00
    13 oz. 18.00
#2630 Utility Bowl, Handled 2⅞" high 10.00
#2630 Utility Tray, Handled 9⅛".................20.00
#2630 Vase, Bud, Footed 6" 25.00
#5092 Vase, Bud, Footed 8" 30.00
#6021 Vase, Bud, Footed 6" 25.00
#2470 Vase, Footed 10" 30.00
#4143 Vase, Footed 6" 40.00
#2630 Vase, 2-Handled 7½" 30.00
#2630 Vase, Oval 8½"...............................35.00
#2660 Vase, Flip 8" 40.00
#4121 Vase, Round 5" 30.00

⇒ BRACELET Cutting #838 ⇐

Rock Crystal
1953 – 1957

#6051 Claret/Wine 4 oz. 4½" 20.00
#6051 Cocktail 3¾ oz. 3⅞" 15.00
#6051 Cordial 1¼ oz. 3⅛" 25.00
#6051 Goblet 10½ oz. 6³⁄₁₆" 20.00

#6051 Ice Tea, Footed 12¼ oz. 6⅛" 20.00
#6051 Juice, 5 oz. 4" 12.00
#6051 Oyster Cocktail 4¼ oz. 3¾" 10.00
#2337 Plate
   7" 8.00
   8" 10.00
#6051 Sherbet 6½ oz. 4⅜" 18.00

⇒ BRIDAL BELLE Decoration #639 ⇐

Platinum Band with Polished Cutting
Crystal
1957 – 1973
Not originally listed as part of Patterns of the Past Program, BRIDAL BELLE was included in Nostalgia Program.

#6072/27 Cocktail/Wine 4½ oz. 22.00
#6072/29 Cordial 1 oz. 28.00
#4185/495 Dessert/Finger Bowl 12.00
#6072/2 Goblet 10 oz. 24.00
#6072/63 Luncheon Goblet/Ice Tea
   13 oz. 20.00
#6072/88 Juice, Footed 5¼ oz. 15.00
#2337 Plate
   7" 10.00
   8" 10.00
#6072/11 Sherbet 7¼ oz. 20.00

BRIDAL BELLE items included in Nostalgia Program

BR02/011 Dessert/Champagne 7¼ oz. 5" 20.00
BR02/002 Goblet 10 oz. 6⅜" 24.00
BR02/063 Luncheon Goblet/Ice Tea 13 oz.
   6⅜"...20.00
BR02/027 Cocktail/Wine 4½ oz. 6⅜" 22.00

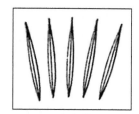 BRIDAL CROWN Polished Cutting #882

Rock Crystal
Crystal
1961 – 1965

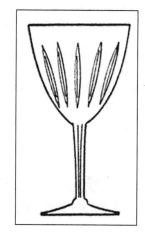

#6089/31 Brandy 1½ oz. 20.00
#6089/27 Cocktail/Wine 4½ oz. 20.00
#6089/2 Goblet 11½ oz. 20.00
#6089/88 Juice, Footed 5 oz. 14.00
#6089/63 Luncheon Goblet/Ice Tea
    13 oz. 18.00
#2337 Plate
    7" 10.00
    8" 10.00
#6089/11 Sherbet 7 oz. 18.00

BRIDAL SHOWER Cutting #897

Rock Crystal
Crystal
1963 – 1970
   Do not confuse with BRIDAL SHOWER Cut-
   ting #768.

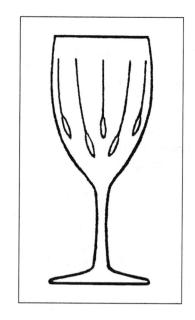

#6102/31 Brandy 3 oz. 23.00
#6102/25 Claret 7½ oz. 23.00
#4185/495 Dessert/Finger Bowl 12.00
#6102/2 Goblet 10 oz. 23.00
#6102/63 Luncheon Goblet/Ice Tea
    14 oz. 22.00
#2337 Plate
    7" 10.00
    8" 10.00
#6102/11 Sherbet 8 oz. 21.00
#6102/26 Tulip Wine 5½ oz. 21.00

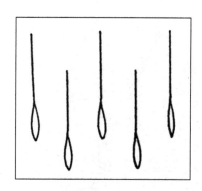

CRYSTAL
1937 – 1938
   Do not confuse with BRIDAL SHOWER Cutting #897.

#2545 Bowl, "Flame", Oval 12½".................70.00
#2545 Candelabra, "Flame", 2 Light ..pair 60.00
#2545 Candlestick "Flame", Duo ....pair 50.00
#6017 Champagne, Saucer 6 oz. 18.00
#6017 Claret 4 oz. 24.00
#6017 Cocktail 3½ oz. 18.00
#6017 Cordial ¾ oz. 28.00
#2350½ Cream, Footed............................20.00
#766 Finger Bowl 10.00
#6017 Goblet 9 oz. 20.00
#6011 Jug, Footed 120.00
#4132 Old Fashioned Cocktail, Sham
      7½ oz. 12.00
#6017 Oyster Cocktail 4 oz. 12.00
#2337 Plate
      6"..8.00
      7"..10.00
      8"..12.00
#6017 Sherbet, Low 6 oz. 15.00
#2350½ Sugar, Footed 20.00
#4132 Tumbler, Sham
      4 oz. 10.00
      5 oz. 10.00
      7 oz. 10.00
      9 oz. 10.00

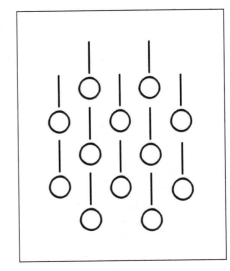

      12 oz. 10.00
      14 oz. 10.00
#6017 Tumbler, Footed
      5 oz. 14.00
      9 oz. 14.00
      12 oz. 18.00
      14 oz. 18.00
#4132 Whiskey, Sham 1½ oz. 10.00
#6017 Wine 3 oz. 22.00

Combination Gray and Polished Cutting
Rock Crystal
Crystal
1960 – 1965

#2630/137 Bon Bon, 3 Toed 7¼" 18.00
#2630/224 Bowl, Footed, Flared 10¾" 25.00
#2630/306 Cake Plate, Handled..............35.00
#2630/316 Candlestick 4½" ....pair 35.00
#2630/332 Candlestick Duo ....pair 50.00
#6049/8 Champagne/High Sherbet 7¼ oz.
   5¼" 21.00
#6049/25 Claret 5 oz. 5⅝" 26.00
#6049/21 Cocktail 4 oz. 4⅞" 17.00
#6049/29 Cordial 1¼ oz. 3½" 35.00
#2630/681 Cream, Footed 4¼"................18.00
#2630/688 Cream, Individual 12.00
#2630/396 Cup, Footed 8.00
#6049/2 Goblet 11¼ oz. 7".......................23.00
#6011 Jug 8⅞" 110.00
#6049/88 Juice, Footed 5¾ oz. 4⅞" 15.00
#6049/63 Luncheon Goblet/Ice Tea
   15¼ oz. 6¼" 21.00
#2630/237 Lily Pond 11¼" 65.00
#2630/477 Mayonnaise
   Bowl 12.00
   Plate 10.00

Ladle 20.00
#6049/33 Oyster Cocktail 4½ oz. 4" 15.00
#6049/18 Parfait 6¾ oz. 6"......................23.00
#2666/454 Pitcher, quart......................55.00
#2337 Plate
   7" 8.00
   8" 10.00
#2630/620 Relish 2 part 7⅜" 18.00
#2630/622 Relish 3 part 11⅛" 24.00
#2630/221 Salad Bowl 10½" 30.00
#2630/397 Saucer 6.00
#2630/654 Shaker, Chrome Top ....pair 30.00
#6049/11 Sherbet, Low 7¼ oz. 4⅜" 17.00
#2630/679 Sugar, Footed 4"....................20.00
#2630/687 Sugar, Individual 14.00
#2630/567 Torte Plate 14" 35.00
#2630 Tray, Cream & Sugar ....set 40.00
#2630/723 Tray, Lunch, Handled 11¼" 32.00
#6049/26 Wine 4 oz. 5⅛" 26.00

⤳ BRIDESMAID Decoration #658 ⤳

Platinum Band with Polished Cutting
Crystal
1962 – 1970

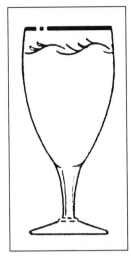

#6100/31 Brandy 1½ oz. 24.00
#6100/25 Claret 7½ oz. 24.00
#4185/495 Dessert/Finger Bowl 12.00
#6l00/2 Goblet 11 oz.............................22.00
#6100/63 Luncheon Goblet/Ice Tea
    14½ oz...24.00
#2337 Plate
    7" 12.00
    8" 12.00
#6100/11 Sherbet 7½ oz. 23.00
#6100/26 Tulip Wine 5½ oz. 24.00

⤳ BRIGHTON Cutting #801 ⤳

Rock Crystal
Crystal
1940 – 1955

#2574 Bowl, Handled 9½" 40.00
#2574 Candlestick, Duo ....pair 60.00
#6023 Champagne, Saucer 6 oz. 4⅞" 16.00
#6023 Claret/Wine 4 oz. 4¾" 20.00
#6023 Cocktail 3¾ oz. 4⅜" 14.00
#6023 Comport 5" 18.00
#6023 Cordial 1 oz. 3⅜" 26.00

#766 Finger Bowl 12.00
#6023 Goblet 9 oz. 6⅜".............................20.00
#6011 Jug, Footed 100.00
#6023 Juice, Footed 5 oz. 4½" 12.00
#6023 Ice Tea, Footed 12 oz. 5¾" 18.00
#6023 Oyster Cocktail 4 oz. 3⅝" 10.00
#2337 Plate
    7" 8.00
    8" 10.00
#6023 Sherbet, Low 6 oz.4⅛" 12.00
#6023 Water, Footed 9 oz. 5⅛" 12.00

BRISTOL Cutting #710

Rock Crystal
Crystal
1933 – 1939
Do not confuse with BRISTOL Cutting #880.

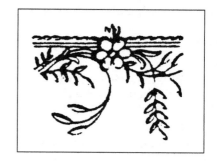

#2470½ Bowl 10½" 30.00
#2470 Bowl 12" 40.00
#2470 Cake Plate 10" 35.00
#2470½ Candlestick 5½" ....pair 35.00
#6007 Champagne, Saucer/High Sherbet
    5½ oz...16.00
#6007 Claret 4 oz. 22.00
#6007 Cocktail 3½ oz. 16.00
#2470 Comport, Tall 6" 25.00
#2470 Comport, Low 6" 20.00
#6007 Cordial 1 oz. 26.00
#869 Finger Bowl 8.00
#2283 Finger Bowl Plate............................6.00
#6007 Goblet 10 oz. 18.00
#2451 Ice Dish 15.00
#2451 Ice Dish Plate.................................10.00
#6007 Oyster Cocktail 4½ oz. 12.00
#2283 Plate
    6" 8.00
    7" 10.00
    8" 12.00
#6007 Sherbet, Low 5½ oz.........................10.00
#2440 Torte Plate 13" 40.00
#6007 Tumbler, Footed
    2 oz. 18.00
    5 oz. 10.00
    9 oz. 10.00
    12 oz. 16.00
#6007 Wine 3 oz. 23.00

⇒ BRISTOL Cutting #880 ⇐

Rock Crystal
Crystal
1960 – 1963
   Do not confuse with BRISTOL Cutting #710.

#6093/21 Cocktail 4 oz. 4⅜" 20.00
#7093/29 Cordial 1¼ oz. 3⅝" 30.00
#6093/2 Goblet 10¼ oz. 7³⁄₁₆" 22.00
#6093/63 Ice Tea, Footed 12 oz. 6⅞" 20.00
#6093/88 Juice, Footed 5 oz. 5¹⁄₁₆" 14.00
#2337 Plate
   7" 10.00
   8" 10.00
#6093/11 Sherbet 7 oz. 5½" 18.00
#6093/26 Wine 4½ oz. 5⁵⁄₁₆" 24.00

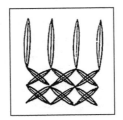

⇒ BROCADE Crystal Print #30 ⇐

Crystal
1971 – 1973
   Do not confuse with BROCADE Carving #13.

#6124/2 Goblet 10½ oz. 32.00
#6124/63 Luncheon Goblet/Ice Tea
   14 oz. 30.00
#2337/549 Plate 7" 15.00
#6124/11 Sherbet/Dessert/Champagne
   9 oz. 28.00
#6124/26 Tulip Wine 7 oz. 30.00

⇒ BROCADE Carving #13 ⇐

Crystal
1939 – 1944
   Do not confuse with BROCADE Crystal
   Print #30.

#2424 Ash Tray 3" 8.00
#2516 Ash Tray 5" 12.00
#2424 Bowl 8" 22.00
#2424 Bowl, Flared 9½" 25.00
#2424 Candlestick 3½" ....pair 70.00
#2424 Candlestick, Duo ....pair 120.00
#2424 Candy Jar, Covered 5½".................24.00
#2424 Comport 5" 10.00
#2424 Comport, Covered 5" 15.00
#2424 Mayonnaise
   Bowl 18.00
   Plate 12.00
   Ladle 20.00
#2424 Plate 12" 32.00
#2424 Sweetmeat 7"................................12.00

#2424 Urn, Footed
   5½" 40.00
   7½" 50.00
#2424 Urn, Footed, Flared
   5" 40.00
   6½" 60.00

⇒ BRUNSWICK Needle Etching #79 ⇐

Amber, Crystal, Green, Blue
1926 – 1933
   Amber, Crystal, Green, 1926 – 1933; Blue
   1926 – 1933

Also produced as MONARD, Decoration #60,
Yellow Gold Trim

#870 Champagne, Saucer.........................11.00
#870 Claret 11.00
#870 Cocktail...9.00
#870 Cordial 13.00
#869 Finger Bowl 10.00
#870 Fruit 10.00
#870 Goblet 12.00
#2270 Jug 7..80.00
#870 Oyster Cocktail 8.00
#870 Parfait 11.00
#2263 Plate 6" 6.00
#2283 Plate
   7" 8.00
   8" 8.00
#870 Sherbet
   Low 15.00
   High 16.00

#869 Tumbler, Table 8.00
#869 Tumbler
   2 oz. 7.00
   5 oz. 8.00
#5048 Tumbler, Footed
   2½ oz. 6.00
   5 oz. 8.00
   9 oz. 10.00
   12 oz. 10.00

⇒ BURGUNDY Cutting #878 ⇐

Combination Cutting and Crystal Print
Crystal
1960 – 1974

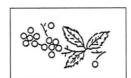

#6092/29 Cordial 1½ oz. 3½" 26.00
#2666/680 Cream 18.00
#6092/2 Goblet 10½ oz. 7 1/16" 22.00
#6092/63 Ice Tea, Footed 14 oz. 6⅜" 20.00
#6092/88 Juice, Footed 5½ oz. 4¾" 16.00
#2337 Plate
    7" 10.00
    8" 10.00
#2666 Relish
    /620 2 part..20.00
    /622 3 part..25.00
#2364/654 Shaker, Chrome Top ....pair 25.00
#6092/11 Sherbet 7 oz. 5 7/16" 18.00
#2666/677 Sugar....................................18.00
#2364/567 Torte Plate 14" 30.00
#6092/27 Wine/Cocktail 4 oz. 5¼" 22.00

⇒ BUCKINGHAM Cutting #721 ⇐

Rock Crystal
Regular Optic
Crystal
1933 – 1935

#2470½ Bowl 10½" 30.00
#2470½ Candlestick 5½" ....pair 45.00
#6009 Claret/Wine 3¾ oz. 5⅜" 25.00
#6009 Cocktail 3¾ oz. 4¾" 18.00
#2400 Comport 6" 20.00
#6009 Cordial 1 oz. 3¾" 30.00
#869 Finger Bowl 8.00
#6009 Goblet 9 oz. 7⅝"............................22.00
#6009 Oyster Cocktail 4¾ oz. 3¾" 12.00
#2337 Plate
    6" 6.00
    7" 8.00
    8" 10.00
#6009 Sherbet
    High 5½ oz. 5⅜" 18.00
    Low 5½ oz. 4⅜" 16.00
#6009 Tumbler, Footed
    5 oz. 4⅜"...12.00
    9 oz. 5¼"...12.00
    12 oz. 5⅞".......................................18.00
#4112 Vase 8½" 40.00

Crystal
1941 – 1960
BUTTERCUP Included in Patterns of the Past and Nostalgia Programs. Designed to coordinate with Gorham Silver Butter Cup and Spode Buttercup China Dinnerware.

#2364 Ash Tray, Individual 6.00
#2364 Bowl, Baked Apple 6" 6.00
#2364 Bowl, Flared 12" 30.00
#2594 Bowl, Handled 10" 25.00
#6023 Bowl, Footed 9 oz. 30.00
#2364 Candy Box, Covered......................30.00
#2324 Candlestick
    4" ....pair 40.00
    6" ....pair 50.00
#2594 Candlestick 5½" ....pair 60.00
#6023 Candlestick, Duo ....pair 60.00
#2594 Candlestick, Trindle ....pair 70.00
#6030 Champagne 6 oz. 5⅝" 20.00
#2364 Cigarette Holder............................30.00
#2350 Celery Dish 11".....................pair 18.00
#2364 Cheese, Footed 16.00
#2364 Cracker Plate 11" 20.00
#2364 Cheese & Cracker......................set 35.00
#6030 Claret/Wine 3½ oz. 6" 26.00
#6030 Cocktail 3½ oz. 15.00
#2364 Comport 8" 20.00
#6030 Comport 5" 18.00
#6030 Cordial 1 oz. 32.00
#2350½ Cream, Footed............................12.00
#2364 Crescent Plate 30.00
#2350½ Cup, Footed 20.00
#1769 Finger Bowl 10.00
#2364 Fruit Bowl 13" 45.00
#6030 Goblet 10 oz. 7⅞" 25.00
#6030 Goblet, Low 10 oz. 6⅜".................22.00
#6011 Jug, Footed 60.00
#2364 Lily Pond 12" 40.00
#2364 Mayonnaise
    Bowl...20.00
    Plate...15.00
    Ladle 20.00
#6030 Oyster Cocktail 4 oz. 14.00
#2350 Pickle Dish 8" 14.00
#2337 Plate
    6" 8.00
    7" 15.00
    8" 15.00
    9" 20.00
#2364 Relish
    2 part 20.00

    3 part 25.00
#2364 Salad Bowl
    9" 30.00
    10½"...40.00
#2083 Salad Dressing Bottle 75.00
#2364 Sandwich Plate 11" 50.00
#2350 Saucer...8.00
#2364 Shaker ....pair 36.00
#6030 Sherbet, Low 6 oz. 16.00
#2350½ Sugar, Footed 12.00
#2586 Syrup, Sani-Cut top.......................45.00
#2364 Torte Plate
    14" 50.00
    16" 60.00
#2364 Tray, Lunch, Handled 40.00
#6030 Tumbler, Footed
    5 oz. 16.00
    12 oz. 6" 22.00

#2614 Vase 10" 50.00
#4143 Vase, Footed
    6" 40.00
    7½" 60.00
#6021 Vase, Bud, Footed 6" 40.00
#6030 Wine.. 30.00

BUTTERCUP items included in Patterns of the Past and Nostalgia Programs

BU01/008 Champagne/High Dessert
    6 oz. 5⅝".....................................20.00
BU01/011 Champagne/Low Dessert
    6 oz. 4⅜"......................................18.00
BU01/027 Claret/Wine 3½ oz. 6" 30.00
BU01/002 Goblet 10 oz. 7⅞" 25.00
BU01/003 Goblet, Low 10 oz. 6⅜" 22.00
BU01/063 Luncheon Goblet/Ice Tea
    12 oz. 6" 20.00

~≈ **CADENCE Cutting #806** ≈~

Rock Crystal
1940 – 1944

#6023 Candlestick, Duo ....pair 55.00
#6027 Champagne, Saucer
    5½ oz..16.00
#6027 Cocktail 3½ oz. 15.00
#6027 Cordial 1 oz. 25.00
#4021 Finger Bowl 14.00
#6027 Goblet 10 oz. 20.00
#6011 Jug, Footed 100.00
#2364 Lily Pond 12" 65.00
#6027 Oyster Cocktail 4 oz. 10.00
#2337 Plate, Plain
    7" 9.00
    8" 12.00
#6027 Sherbet, Low 5½ oz.......................13.00
#6027 Tumbler, Footed

    5 oz. 13.00
    12 oz. 18.00
#6027 Wine 4 oz. 20.00

75

⇜ CAMDEN Needle Etching #84 ⇝

Amber, Green Bowl with Crystal Stem and Foot
1928 – 1931

Produced also as KINGSTON, Decoration #41 in Green Bowl with Coin Gold Band

#5298 Claret 4 oz. 18.00
#5298 Cocktail 3½ oz. 20.00
#5298 Comport 5" 16.00
#5298 Cordial 24.00
#869 Finger Bowl 12.00
#5298 Goblet 10 oz. 20.00
#5282½ Grapefruit 25.00
#945½ Grapefruit Liner 25.00
#5000 Jug 7, Footed...............................100.00
#5298 Nappy, Footed 6" 10.00
#5298 Oyster Cocktail 5½ oz. 13.00
#5298 Parfait 6 oz. 18.00
#2283 Plate
    7" 8.00
    8" 10.00
#5298 Sherbet
    Low 6 oz. 13.00
    High 6 oz. 17.00

#5298 Tumbler, Footed
    2½ oz...8.00
    5 oz. 8.00
    9 oz. 10.00
    12 oz. 10.00
#5298 Wine 3 oz. 20.00

⇜ CAMELLIA Plate Etching #344 ⇝

Crystal
1952 – 1965

#2630 Basket, Reed Handle 10¼" 30.00
#2630/137 Bon Bon, 3 Toed 7¼" 18.00
#2630/179 Bowl, Flared 8".....................25.00
#2630/249 Bowl, Flared 12"....................30.00
#2630/235 Bowl, Footed, Rolled Edge 11" 35.00
#2630/224 Bowl, Footed, Flared 10¾" 30.00
#2630/204 Bowl, Utility, Oval 15.00
#2630/300 Butter, Covered, Oblong 7½" ..25.00
#2630/306 Cake Plate, Handled................20.00
#2630/316 Candlestick 4½" ....pair 40.00
#2630/332 Candlestick, Duo ....pair 60.00
#2630/336 Candlestick, Trindle ....pair 80.00
#2630/350 Candy Jar, Covered 7" high 50.00
#2630/393 Cereal Bowl 6" 15.00
#6036/8 Champagne/High Sherbet 6 oz.
    4¾" 15.00
#6036/369 Cheese & Cracker
    Bowl, Footed 5⅜" 35.00

Plate 10¾" 15.00
#6036/27 Claret/Wine 3¼ oz. 4¾" 29.00
#6036/21 Cocktail 3½ oz. 4⅛"................. 20.00
#2630/388 Comport 4⅜" 15.00
#6036/29 Cordial 1 oz. 3¾" 32.00
#2630/681 Cream, Footed 4¼"..................15.00
#2630/688 Cream, Individual 12.00
#2630/396 Cup, Footed 6 oz. 10.00
#2630/421 Fruit Bowl 5" 8.00

#6036/2 Goblet 9½ oz. 6⅞" High 22.00
#2630/424 Ice Bucket, Chrome Handle, Tongs
    7⅜"...55.00
#2630/456 Jug 7, Ice 3 pint 18"................70.00
#6036/88 Juice, Footed 5 oz. 4⅝" 14.00
#2630/197 Lily Pond 9" 60.00
#2630/237 Lily Pond 11¼" 70.00
#6036/63 Luncheon Goblet/Ice Tea 12 oz.
    6⅛"...17.00
#2630/477 Mayonnaise
    Bowl 3½"high 15.00
    Plate..12.00
    Ladle 20.00
#2630 Mayonnaise, 2 part, 2 Ladles ....set 50.00
#2630/481 Mayonnaise, 2 part
    Bowl 3⅜" high.....................................15.00
    Plate..12.00
    Ladle 20.00
#2630/487 Mustard, Covered, Spoon
    4" high 40.00
#2630/499 Nappy, Handled 4½"................10.00
#2630/528 Oil, Stoppered 5 oz. 30.00
#6036/33 Oyster Cocktail 4 oz. 3¾" 14.00
#6036/18 Parfait 5½ oz. 5⅞" 18.00
#2630 Party Plate, Cup Indentation 8" 20.00
#2630/540 Pickle Dish 8¾" 16.00
#2630/453 Pitcher, Cereal, pint 6⅛".........30.00
#2630 Plate
    /548 6"...10.00
    /549 7"...12.00
    /550 8"...15.00
    /552 9"...20.00
    /554 10½" (Dinner Plate) 30.00
#2630/560 Platter, Oval 12".....................25.00

#2630/591 Preserve, Footed, Covered 6" ..22.00
#2630/620 Relish, 2 part 7⅜" 20.00
#2630/622 Relish, 3 part 11⅛" 26.00
#2630/190 Salad Bowl 8½" 20.00
#2630/221 Salad Bowl 10½" 30.00
#2630/579 Salad, Crescent 7½" 60.00
#2630/630 Salver, Footed 12¼", 2⅛" high ..45.00
#2630/397 Saucer 6.00
#2630/648 Serving Dish, Handled
    2½" high 15.00
#2630/654 Shaker, Chrome Top ....pair 25.00
#6036/11 Sherbet, Low 6 oz. 4⅛".............15.00
#2630/666 Snack Bowl 3½" high 10.00
#2630/679 Sugar, Footed 4".....................15.00
#2630/687 Sugar, Individual 12.00
#2630/707 Tid Bit, 3 Toed 8⅛" 16.00
#1630/583 Tid Bit, Metal Handle,
    Two Tiered 40.00
#2630/567 Torte Plate 14" 50.00
#2630/573 Torte Plate 16" 65.00
#2630/697 Tray, Cream & Sugar/Cruets
    7⅛"...120.00
#2630/723 Tray, Lunch, Handled 11¼" 30.00
#2630/726 Tray, Muffin, Handled 30.00
#2630/729 Tray, Snack 10½"....................20.00
#2630/732 Tray, Utility, Handled 9⅛" 20.00
#2630/734 Tricorn Bowl, 3 Toed, 7⅛" 18.00
#2470 Vase, Footed 10" 30.00
#2630 Vase, Handled 7½"..........................30.00
#2630 Vase, Oval 8½"...............................35.00
#2660 Vase, Flip 8" 40.00
#2657 Vase, Footed 10½"..........................30.00
#4121 Vase 5½" 30.00
#4143 Vase, Footed 6" 20.00
#6021 Vase, Bud, Footed 6" 18.00
#5092 Vase, Bud, Footed 18.00
#2630/836 Vegetable Dish, Oval 9½" 20.00

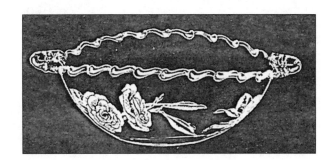

⚛ CAMEO Double Needle Etching #88 ⚛

Crystal
1934 – 1940
   Do not confuse with CAMEO Crystal Print #28.

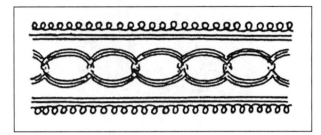

#6009 Claret 3¾ oz. 20.00
#6009 Champagne, Saucer/High Sherbet
   5½ oz..16.00
#6009 Cocktail 3½ oz. 16.00
#6009 Cordial 1 oz. 24.00
#869 Finger Bowl 8.00
#6009 Goblet 9 oz. 18.00
#1184 Old Fashioned Cocktail, Sham or Plain
   7 oz. 7.00
#6009 Oyster Cocktail 4¾ oz. 10.00
#6009 Sherbet, Low 5½ oz.......................14.00
#701 Tumbler, Sham or Plain
   10 oz. 6.00

   12 oz. 6.00
#6009 Tumbler, Footed
   5 oz. 10.00
   9 oz. 10.00
   12 oz. 15.00
#887 Whiskey, Sham or Plain 1¾ oz. 6.00
#4122 Whiskey, Sham 1½ oz......................6.00

⚛ CAMEO Crystal Print #28 ⚛

Green Mist Bowl with Crystal Base
1971 – 1982
   Do not confuse with CAMEO Needle Etching #88.

#6123/2 Goblet 8½ oz. 20.00
#6123/63 Luncheon Goblet/Ice Tea
   11½ oz...20.00
#2337/549 Plate, Green Mist 7" 15.00
#6123/11 Sherbet/Dessert/Champagne
   7½ oz..18.00
#6123/26 Wine 5½ oz. 20.00

CANTATA Cutting #907

Rock Crystal
Crystal
1965 – 1970

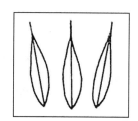

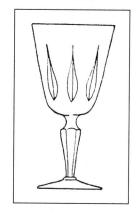

#6015/29 Cordial 1½ oz. 28.00
#6105/25 Claret 7 oz. 25.00
#6105/2 Goblet 11 oz. 25.00
#6105/63 Luncheon Goblet/Ice Tea
    13½ oz..23.00
#2337 Plate
    7" 10.00
    8" 10.00
#6105/11 Sherbet 22.00
#6105/26 Wine 6 oz. 25.00

CANTERBURY Cutting #716

Rock Crystal
Regular Optic
Crystal
1933 – 1936

#2470 Bon Bon 12.00
#2470½ Bowl 10½".................................30.00
#2481 Bowl, Oblong 11" 32.00
#2470 Cake Plate 35.00
#2430 Candy Dish, Covered ½ lb..............20.00
#2470½ Candlestick 5½" ....pair 40.00
#2472 Candlestick, Duo ....pair 50.00
#2482 Candlestick, Trindle ....pair 65.00
#6008 Claret 4 oz. 23.00
#6008 Cocktail 3½ oz. 18.00
#2400 Comport 6" 20.00
#6008 Cordial 1 oz. 28.00
#2440 Cream, Footed 15.00
#869 Finger Bowl 8.00
#1769 Finger Bowl 8.00
#2283 Finger Bowl Plate.........................6.00
#6008 Goblet 10 oz. 20.00
#2451 Ice Dish 15.00
#2451 Ice Dish Plate..............................10.00
#2470 Lemon Dish 12.00
#6008 Oyster Cocktail 4½ oz. 12.00
#2283 Plate
    7" 8.00
    8" 10.00

#2364 Plate 16" 35.00
#2419 Relish, 4 part...............................30.00
#6008 Sherbet
    High 5½ oz. 18.00
    Low 5½ oz. 14.00
#2440 Sugar, Footed 16.00
#2470 Sweetmeat 10.00
#2440 Torte Plate 13".............................40.00
#6008 Tumbler, Footed
    2 oz. 10.00
    5 oz. 12.00
    9 oz. 12.00
    12 oz. 16.00
#4107 Vase 7" 35.00
#6008 Wine 3 oz. 23.00

⊸ CARILLON Cutting #915 ⊷

Rock Crystal
Crystal
1967 – 1969

#6104/25 Claret 7 oz. 23.00
#6104/29 Cordial 1½ oz. 28.00
#6104/2 Goblet 11 oz. 25.00
#6104/63 Luncheon Goblet/Ice Tea
    13½ oz...22.00
#2337 Plate
    7" 8.00
    8" 10.00
#6104/11 Sherbet 9 oz. 23.00
#6104/26 Wine 6 oz. 24.00

⊸ CARLISLE Cutting #715 ⊷

Rock Crystal
Regular Optic
Crystal
1933 – 1936

#2470 Bon Bon 12.00
#2470½ Bowl 10½"................................30.00
#2481 Bowl, Oblong 11" 40.00
#2470 Cake Plate 35.00
#2430 Candy Dish, Covered ½ lb. 20.00
#2470½ Candlestick 5½" ....pair 40.00
#2472 Candlestick Duo ....pair 50.00
#2482 Candlestick, Trindle ....pair 65.00
#6008 Claret 4 oz. 23.00
#6008 Cocktail 3½ oz. 18.00
#2400 Comport 6" 22.00
#6008 Cordial 1 oz. 28.00
#2440 Cream, Footed 16.00
#869 Finger Bowl 8.00
#1769 Finger Bowl 8.00
#2283 Finger Bowl Plate 5.00
#6008 Goblet 10 oz. 20.00
#2451 Ice Dish 15.00
#2451 Ice Dish Plate..............................10.00
#2470 Lemon Dish 12.00
#6008 Oyster Cocktail 4½ oz. 12.00
#2283 Plate
    7" 8.00
    8" 10.00
#2419 Relish, 5 part..............................35.00
#6008 Sherbet
    High 5½ oz..................................18.00
    Low 5½ oz. 14.00
#2440 Sugar, Footed 16.00
#2470 Sweetmeat...................................10.00
#2440 Torte Plate 13" 40.00
#6008 Tumbler, Footed
    2 oz. 10.00
    5 oz. 12.00
    9 oz. 12.00
    12 oz. 16.00
#6008 Wine 3 oz. 23.00

CAROUSEL Cutting #863

Gray Cutting
Crystal
1958 – 1976
CAROUSEL included in Patterns of the Past Program, not in Nostalgia Program

#6080/25 Claret, Large 6 oz. 20.00
#6080/27 Claret/Wine 4 oz. 5⅛" 20.00
#6080/20 Cocktail 4 oz. 4⅜" 16.00
#6080/29 Cordial 1 oz. 3½" 23.00
#2666/680 Cream 20.00
#4185/495 Dessert/Finger Bowl 12.00
#6080/2 Goblet 10 oz. 6¾"........................18.00
#6080/88 Juice, Footed 5 oz. 4¼" 14.00
#6080/63 Luncheon Goblet/Ice Tea 13½ oz.
    5½"..16.00
#2337 Plate
    7" 10.00
    8" 10.00
#2666/620 Relish 2 part 20.00
#2666/622 Relish 3 part 20.00
#2364/654 Shaker, Chrome Top,
    Large ....pair 25.00
#6080/11 Sherbet/Dessert/Champagne 7 oz.
    4¾" 16.00
#2666/677 Sugar......................................20.00
#2364/567 Torte Plate 14" 30.00

CAROUSEL items included in Patterns of the Past Program

CA03/011 Champagne/Dessert 7 oz. 4¾"..16.00
CA03/025 Claret, Large 6 oz. 5¾".............20.00
CA03/027 Claret/Wine 4 oz. 5⅛" 20.00
CA03/002 Goblet 10 oz. 6¾" 18.00
CA03/063 Luncheon Goblet/Ice Tea 13½ oz.
    5½"..16.00

CASTLE Needle Etching #87

Optic
Crystal
1933 – 1943

#6007 Champagne, Saucer/High Sherbet
    5½ oz..16.00
#6007 Claret 4 oz. 23.00
#6007 Cocktail 3½ oz. 16.00
#6007 Cordial 1 oz. 26.00
#869 Finger Bowl 8.00
#6007 Goblet 10 oz. 18.00
#6007 Oyster Cocktail 4½ oz. 12.00
#2283 Plate
    6" 8.00
    7" 10.00
    8" 12.00
#6007 Sherbet, Low 5½ oz.......................12.00
#6007 Tumbler, Footed
    2 oz. 18.00

    5 oz. 10.00
    9 oz. 10.00
    12 oz. 16.00
#6007 Wine 3 oz. 22.00

⊷⇒ CATHEDRAL Cutting #792 ⇐⊷

Rock Crystal
Crystal
1939 – 1944

#6023 Bowl, Footed 20.00
#2324 Candlestick 6" ....pair 40.00
#6023 Champagne, Saucer 6 oz. 16.00
#6023 Claret/Wine 4 oz..........................20.00
#6023 Cocktail 3¾ oz. 14.00
#6023 Comport 5" 15.00
#6023 Cordial 1 oz. 26.00
#766 Finger Bowl 8.00
#6023 Goblet 9 oz. 20.00
#6011 Jug, Footed 50.00
#6023 Oyster Cocktail 4 oz. 10.00
#2337 Plate
    6" 6.00
    7" 8.00
    8" 10.00
#6023 Sherbet, Low 6 oz. 12.00

#6023 Tumbler, Footed
    5 oz. 12.00
    9 oz. 12.00
    12 oz. 18.00

⊷⇒ CAVENDISH Cutting #754 ⇐⊷

Regular Optic
Rock Crystal
Crystal
1935 – 1940

#2470½ Bowl 10½" 50.00
#2533 Bowl, Handled 9" 50.00
#2472 Candlestick, Duo ....pair 60.00
#2533 Candlestick, Duo ....pair 60.00
#6014 Champagne, Saucer 5½ oz. 22.00
#6014 Claret 4 oz. 25.00
#6014 Cocktail 3½ oz. 20.00
#6014 Cordial 1 oz. 30.00
#869 Finger Bowl 15.00

#6014 Goblet 9 oz. 22.00
#5000 Jug, Footed 150.00
#6014 Oyster Cocktail 4 oz. 16.00
#2337 Plate
    6" 8.00
    7" 10.00
    8" 12.00
#6014 Sherbet, Low 5½ oz.......................16.00
#6014 Tumbler, Footed
    5 oz. 16.00
    9 oz. 16.00
    12 oz. 20.00
#6014 Wine 3 oz. 25.00

⊶ CELEBRITY Cutting #749 ⊷

Rock Crystal
Crystal
1935 – 1944

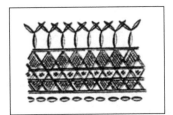

#2424 Bowl 8" 40.00
#2481 Candlestick 5" ....pair 60.00
#6000 Champagne, Saucer 6 oz. 12.00
#6000 Cocktail 3½ oz. 13.00
#869 Finger Bowl (Optic) 10.00
#6000 Goblet 10 oz. 15.00
#5000 Jug, Footed 100.00
#1185 Old Fashioned Cocktail, Plain
    7 oz. 12.00
#6000 Oyster Cocktail 4 oz. 8.00
#2337 Plate
    6" 6.00
    7" 8.00
    8" 10.00
#2337 Service Plate 11" 15.00
#6000 Sherbet, Low 6 oz. 10.00
#701 Tumbler, Sham or Plain 10 oz. 10.00
#6000 Tumbler, Footed
    5 oz. 11.00
    13 oz. 13.00
#6000 Wine 3 oz. 18.00

⊶ CELESTIAL Cutting #731 ⊷

Crystal
1934 – 1938

#4024 Bowl, Footed 10" 40.00
#6011 Brandy 1 oz. 22.00
#906 Brandy Inhaler 15.00
#4024 Candlestick 6" ....pair 30.00
#795 Champagne, Hollow Stem 5½ oz. 12.00
#863 Champagne, Hollow Stem, Cut Flute
    5 oz. 15.00
#6011 Champagne, Saucer 5½ oz. 14.00
#6011 Claret 4½ oz. 18.00
#6011 Cocktail 3 oz. 14.00
#6011 Cordial 1 oz. 22.00
#6011 Creme de Menthe 2 oz. 16.00
#6011 Decanter, Footed 70.00
#1769 Finger Bowl 8.00
#6011 Goblet 10 oz. 15.00
#6011 Jug, Footed 50.00
#1184 Old Fashioned Cocktail, Sham or Plain

    7 oz. 6.00
#6011 Oyster Cocktail 4 oz. 10.00
#2337 Plate
    6" 6.00
    7" 8.00
    8" 10.00
#6011 Rhine Wine 4½ oz. 18.00
#6011 Sherbet, Low 5½ oz. 12.00
#6011 Sherry 2 oz. 16.00
3701 Tumbler, Sham or Plain
    10 oz. 6.00
    12 oz. 5.00
#6011 Tumbler, Footed
    5 oz. 10.00
    10 oz. 8.00
    13 oz. 14.00
#887 Whiskey, Sham or Plain 1¾ oz. 6.00
#4122 Whiskey, Sham or Plain 1½ oz. 6.00
#6011 Whiskey, Footed 2 oz. 18.00
#6011 Wine 3 oz. 18.00

Blown Ware
Crystal
1898 – 1928

#880 Bon Bon 4½" 8.00
#766 Champagne, Saucer 5 oz. 7.00
#863 Champagne, Saucer 5½ oz. 7.00
#766 Claret 4½ oz. 7.00
#766 Cocktail...7.00
#863 Cocktail 3½ oz. 7.00
#803 Comport
    5" 8.00
    6" 8.00
#863 Cordial 1 oz. 10.00
#1478 Cream 8.00
#863 Creme de Menthe 2½ oz. 10.00
#481 Custard...7.00
#300 Decanter, Cut Neck, quart 35.00
#1769 Finger Bowl 6.00
#766 Fruit 6.00
#863 Fruit, Footed 5½ oz. 8.00
#1736 Fruit Plate 4.00
#766 Goblet 9 oz. 7.00
#863 Goblet
    9 oz. 7.00
    10 oz. 7.00
#766 Ice Tea, Footed, Handled
    12 oz. 8.00
#300 Jug 7..35.00
#318 Jug 7, Optic 7½" 38.00
#303 Jug 7..35.00
#1236 Jug 6...30.00
#803 Nappy, Footed
    5" 6.00
    6" 6.00
    7" 6.00
#1227 Nappy
    4½" 5.00
    8" 10.00
#300½ Oil, Small 20.00

#5054 Parfait 15.00
#863 Sherry 2 oz. 7.00
#1478 Sugar 8.00
#858 Sweetmeat 5".....................................8.00
#820 Tumbler, Table 7.00
#858 Tumbler, Table
    5 oz. 7.00
    8 oz. 7.00
    10 oz. 7.00
    12 oz. 7.00
    14 oz. 8.00
#4011½ Tumbler, Table 7.00
#701 Tumbler
    12 oz. 7.00
    14 oz. 10.00
#833 Tumbler, Sham 8 oz. 7.00
#833 Tumbler 8 oz. 7.00
#887 Tumbler 2 oz. 7.00
#889 Tumbler 5 oz. 7.00
#4011 Tumbler
    5 oz. 7.00
    8 oz. 7.00
#4011 Tumbler, Handled 12 oz. 10.00
#701 Tumbler Plate 5" 4.00
#863 Wine 3 oz. 7.00

⊶ CHALICE Cutting #812 ⊷

Crystal
1941 – 1944

#863 Champagne, Hollow Stem, Cut Flute
    2 oz. 20.00
#6029 Champagne, Saucer 6½ oz. 18.00
#6029 Claret 4 oz. 20.00
#6029 Cocktail 3½ oz. 15.00
#6029 Cordial 1 oz. 25.00
#766 Finger Bowl (Cut #786) 15.00
#6029 Goblet 9 oz. 20.00
#6029 Oyster Cocktail 4½ oz. 13.00
#846 Sherry (Cut #786) 2 oz. 15.00
#833 Tumbler (Cut #785)
    12 oz. 10.00
    14 oz. 12.00

⊶ CHAPEL BELLS Polished Cutting #888 ⊷

Rock Crystal
Crystal
1961 – 1974
CHAPEL BELLS included in Patterns of the
  Past Program

#6099/27 Cocktail/Wine 4½ oz.
    5⅛"..20.00
#6099/29 Cordial 1 oz. 25.00
#4185/495 Dessert/Finger Bowl 12.00
#6099/2 Goblet 11 oz. 6⅞"........................20.00
#6099/88 Juice, Footed 5½ oz. 15.00
#6099/63 Luncheon Goblet/Ice Tea
    14 oz. 6⅝"...20.00
#2337 Plate

7" 10.00
8" 10.00
#6099/11 Sherbet/Dessert/Champagne
    6½ oz. 5⅛" 18.00

CHAPEL BELLS items included in Patterns of
  the Past Program

CH 03/011 Dessert/Champagne
    6½ oz. 5⅛" 18.00
CH 03/002 Goblet 11 oz. 6⅞"...................20.00
CH 03/063 Luncheon Goblet/Ice Tea
    14 oz. 6⅝"...20.00
CH 03/027 Wine/Cocktail 4½ oz. 5⅛" 20.00

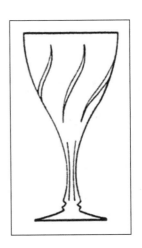

⇌ CHATEAU Plate Etching #315 ⇌

Crystal
1933 – 1940

#2470 Bon Bon 22.00
#2470½ Bowl 10½" 40.00
#2481 Bowl, Oblong 35.00
#2470 Cake Plate 30.00
#2470½ Candlestick 5½" ....pair 40.00
#2472 Candlestick, Duo ....pair 60.00
#2481 Candlestick 5" ....pair 50.00
#2482 Candlestick, Trindle ....pair 75.00
#2440 Celery 11½" 24.00
#6008 Champagne, Saucer/High Sherbet
   5½ oz. 18.00
#6008 Cocktail 3¼ oz. 18.00
#2470 Comport, Low 6" 30.00
#6008 Cordial 1 oz. 32.00
#2440 Cream, Footed 16.00
#2440 Cream Soup.................................200.00
#2440 Cup 12.00
#1769 Finger Bowl 8.00
#6008 Goblet 10 oz. 24.00
#2451 Ice Dish 30.00
#2451 Ice Dish Plate.............................14.00
#2470 Lemon Dish 26.00
#2440 Olive Dish 6½" 20.00
#6008 Oyster Cocktail 5 oz. 12.00
#2440 Pickle Dish 8½" 24.00
#2440 Plate
   6" 10.00
   7" 14.00
   8" 20.00
   9" 25.00

#2419 Relish, 4 part................................35.00
#2440 Saucer...8.00
#6008 Sherbet, Low 5½ oz.......................15.00
#2440 Sugar, Footed 22.00
#2470 Sweetmeat....................................20.00
#2440 Torte Plate 13" 40.00
#6008 Tumbler, Footed
   5 oz. 14.00
   9 oz. 12.00
   12 oz. 16.00
#2467 Vase 7½" 40.00
#6008 Wine 4 oz. 28.00

⇌ CHATHAM Cutting #829 ⇌

Rock Crystal
Crystal
1952 – 1960

#6036 Champagne/High Sherbet
   6 oz. 4¾"...20.00
#6036 Claret/Wine 3¼ oz. 4¾" 23.00
#6036 Cocktail 3½ oz. 4⅛" 19.00
#6036 Cordial 1 oz. 3¼" 27.00
#6036 Goblet 9½ oz. 6⅞" 23.00
#6036 Ice Tea, Footed 12 oz. 6⅛" 19.00
#6036 Juice, Footed 5 oz. 4⅝" 13.00
#6036 Oyster Cocktail 4 oz. 3¾"................11.00

#2337 Plate
   7" 8.00
   8" 10.00
#6036 Parfait 5½ oz. 5⅞" 21.00
#6036 Sherbet, Low 6 oz. 4⅛"...................15.00

➤ CHATTERIS Polished Cutting #197 ➤

Optic Pattern
Rock Crystal
Crystal
1929 – 1931

#2394 Bowl 12" 25.00
#877 Claret 11.00
#877 Cocktail...8.00
#877 Cordial 14.00
#2324 Candlestick 4" ....pair 50.00
#2394 Candlestick 2" ....pair 30.00
#2329 Centerpiece 11" 35.00
#2375 Cheese, Footed 18.00
#2375 Cracker Plate..............................20.00
#2375 Cheese & Cracker Set 35.00
#2400 Comport 6" 18.00
#2350½ Cream, Footed...........................15.00
#869 Finger Bowl 6.00
#877 Goblet 10.00
#2378 Ice Bucket, Nickel Plated Handle 35.00
#2375 Mayonnaise 20.00
#2332 Mayonnaise Plate 7"....................10.00
#877 Oyster Cocktail 7.00
#877 Parfait 10.00
#877 Sherbet
    High 9.00
    Low 6.00
#2350½ Sugar, Footed 14.00
#2383 Plate, Optic 6" 7.00

#2383 Plate
    7" 8.00
    8" 10.00
#2375 Tray, Lunch, Handled 18.00
#877 Tumbler, Footed
    2½ oz..8.00
    5 oz. 7.00
    9 oz. 7.00
    12 oz. 10.00
#2369 Vase 7" 20.00
#2417 Vase 8" 30.00
#4105 Vase 8" 30.00

➤ CHELSEA Cutting #783 ➤

Rock Crystal
Crystal
1938 – 1944

#4020 Champagne, Saucer 7 oz. 18.00
#4020 Claret 4 oz. 20.00
#4020 Cocktail 3½ oz. 16.00
#4020½ Cocktail 4 oz. 16.00
#4021 Finger Bowl 8.00
#4020 Goblet 11 oz. 20.00
#4020 Jug, Footed 60.00
#2419 Plate
    7" 10.00
    8" 10.00
#4020 Sherbet, Low
    5 oz. 16.00
    7 oz. 16.00

#4020 Whiskey 2 oz. 14.00
#4020 Wine 3 oz. 20.00

⇜ **CHINTZ Plate Etching #338** ⇝

Regular Optic
Crystal
1940 – 1973
CHINTZ was designed to accompany Spode China's Rosebud Chintz Dinnerware, an all-over floral pattern perfectly in keeping with the new 1940s functional design trends. NAVARRE, CHINTZ and MEADOW ROSE were the most popular of Fostoria's etchings.

CHINTZ included in Part of Patterns of the Past and Nostalgia Programs

#2496/137 Bon Bon, 3 Toed 26.00
#2484 Bowl, Handled 10" 36.00
#2496 Bowl, Handled 10½".......................50.00
#2496/249 Bowl, Flared 12".....................50.00
#6023 Bowl, Footed 55.00
#2496/306 Cake Plate, Handled 10".........40.00
#2496/315 Candlestick 4".................pair 55.00
#2496 Candlestick 5½" ....pair 60.00
#2496/332 Candlestick, Duo ....pair 80.00
#2496 Candlestick, Trindle ....pair 100.00
#6023 Candlestick, Duo ....pair 80.00
#2496 Candy Box, Covered, 3 part 6¼"......85.00
#2496 Celery 11" 18.00
#6026/8 Champagne/High Sherbet
    6 oz. 5½"...18.00
#2496 Cheese, Footed 7½ oz. 3¾"..............15.00
#2496 Cracker Plate.................................10.00
#6026/27 Claret 4½ oz. 5⅜".....................30.00
#6026/21 Cocktail 4 oz. 5" 22.00
#2496 Comport 5½" 35.00
#6026/29 Cordial 1 oz. 3⅞".......................65.00
#2496/681 Cream, Footed 3¾"..................16.00
#2496/688 Cream, Individual 4 oz. 3½" 15.00
#2496/396 Cup, Footed 15.00
#869 Finger Bowl 4½" 6.00
#2496 Fruit 5" 8.00
#6026/2 Goblet, High 9 oz. 7⅝" 25.00
#6026/3 Goblet, Low 9 oz. 6⅛".................22.00
#2496 Ice Bucket, Chrome Handle 4⅜"......60.00
#2496 Jelly 20.00
#2496 Jelly, Covered 7½" 35.00
#5000 Jug, Footed 3 pints, 9¾" 22.00
#6026/88 Juice, Footed 5 oz. 5¼" 20.00
#6026/60 Luncheon Goblet/Ice Tea
    13 oz. 6" 24.00
#2496½ Mayonnaise 3½" 20.00
#2574 Mayonnaise
    Bowl 18.00

    Plate 15.00
    Ladle 20.00
#2496 Mayonnaise, 2 part 40.00
#6026 Oyster Cocktail 13.00
#2496 Plate, Mayonnaise 15.00
#2496/500 Nappy, Handled, Flared 5" 16.00
#2496/501 Nappy, Handled, 3 Cornered
    4⅝"..15.00
#2496 Oil/Vinegar 3½ oz. 5½" ....pair 125.00
#6026/33 Oyster Cocktail 4 oz. 3⅝" 13.00
#2496 Pickle Dish 8" 18.00
#2666/454 Pitcher, quart.........................30.00
#2496 Plate
    6" 10.00
    7" 12.00
    8" 14.00
    9" 40.00
#2496 Platter, Oval 12".............................50.00
#2496/620 Relish 2 part Square 6" 22.00

#2496/622 Relish 3 part Oblong 10" 35.00
#2419 Relish, 5 part............................55.00
#2083 Salad Dressing Bottle 7 oz. 6½" 50.00
#2496 Sauce Dish, Oblong 25.00
#2496/397 Saucer 8.00
#2496 Serving Dish, Handled 8½" 25.00
#2364/655 Shaker, Chrome Top ....pair 40.00
#2496 Shaker 2¾"............................pair 100.00
#6026/11 Sherbet, Low 6 oz. 4⅜".............18.00
#2496 Soup, Cream 22.00
#2496 Plate, Cream Soup......................13.00
#2496/679 Sugar, Footed 3½" 20.00
#2496/687 Sugar, Individual 2⅞"..............45.00
#2596 Syrup, Sani-Cut top......................75.00

#2496/707 Tid Bit, 3 Toed 30.00
#2496/567 Torte Plate 14" 50.00
#2496/573 Torte Plate 16" 70.00
#2375/723 Tray, Handled, Lunch 11" 45.00
#2496/697 Tray, Cream & Sugar 6½" 15.00
#2496 Tray, Oblong 8" 45.00
#2496 Tray, Serving, Handled 40.00
#4128 Vase 5" 30.00
#2660 Vase, Flip 8" 40.00
#2470 Vase, Footed 10½" 85.00
#3143 Vase, Footed
    6" 45.00
    7½" 55.00
#2496 Vegetable Dish 9½" 30.00

⇜ CHIPPENDALE Cutting #788 ⇝

Rock Crystal
Crystal
1939 – 1943
   Do not confuse with CHIPPENDALE Etching CH05.

#6023 Bowl, Footed 20.00
#2324 Candlestick 6" ....pair 40.00
#6023 Champagne, Saucer 6 oz. 16.00
#6023 Claret/Wine 4 oz..........................20.00
#6023 Cocktail 3¾ oz. 15.00
#6023 Cordial 1 oz. 26.00
#766 Finger Bowl 8.00
#6023 Goblet 9 oz. 18.00
#6011 Jug, Footed 50.00
#6023 Oyster Cocktail 4 oz. 10.00
#2337 Plate
    6" 8.00
    7" 8.00
    8" 10.00
#6023 Sherbet, Low 6 oz. 12.00
#6023 Tumbler, Footed
    5 oz. 12.00
    9 oz. 10.00
    12 oz. 18.00

Crystal
1941 – 1969
CHRISTIANA included in part of Patterns of the Past and Nostalgia Programs

#6023 Bowl, Footed 9" 30.00
#6023 Candlestick, Duo ....pair 50.00
#6030/8 Champagne/High Sherbet
    6 oz. 5⅝"...22.00
#6030/27 Claret/Wine 3½ oz. 6" 26.00
#6030/21 Cocktail 3½ oz. 5¼" 24.00
#6030/29 Cordial 1 oz. 3⅞" 18.00
#769 Finger Bowl 12.00
#6030/2 Goblet 10 oz. 7⅞" 25.00
#6030/3 Goblet, Low 10 oz. 6⅜"...............20.00
#6011 Jug, Footed 120.00
#6031/88 Juice, Footed 5 oz. 4⅝" 15.00
#6030/63 Luncheon Goblet/Ice Tea
    12 oz. 6" 20.00
#6030/33 Oyster Cocktail 4 oz. 3¾" 15.00
#2337 Plate
    7" 8.00
    8" 10.00
#6030/11 Sherbet, Low 6 oz. 4⅜".............15.00

CHRISTIANA items included in Patterns of the Past and Nostalgia Programs

CH02/008 Champagne/High Dessert
    6 oz. 5⅝"..20.00
CH02/011 Champagne/Low Dessert
    6 oz. 4⅜"..15.00
CH02/027 Claret/Wine 3½ oz. 6" 26.00
CH02/002 Goblet 10 oz. 7⅞" 25.00
CH02/003 Goblet/Low 10 oz. 6⅜" 20.00
CH02/063 Luncheon Goblet/Ice Tea
    12 oz. 6" 20.00

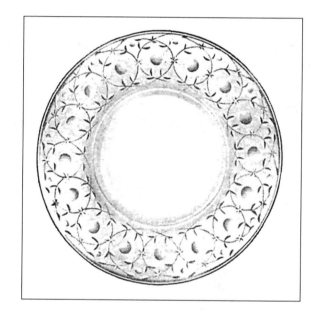

⊰≡ CHRISTINE Cutting #798 ≡⊱

Crystal
1940 – 1944

#6023 Bowl, Footed 25.00
#6023 Candlestick, Duo ....pair 50.00
#892 Champagne, Saucer 7 oz. 10.00
#892 Claret 4 oz. 12.00
#892 Cocktail 4 oz. 8.00
#892 Cordial 1 oz. 12.00
#1769 Finger Bowl 8.00
#892 Goblet 11 oz. 12.00
#6011 Jug, Footed 50.00
#892 Oyster Cocktail 4½ oz. 8.00
#2337 Plate
    7" 6.00
    8" 8.00
#892 Sherbet, Low 6½ oz. 8.00
#892 Tumbler, Footed

    5 oz. 6.00
    12 oz. 8.00
#892 Wine 3 oz. 10.00

⊰≡ CHRYSANTHEMUM Cutting #133 ≡⊱

Blown Ware
Crystal
1918 – 1929

#863 Almond 10.00
#880 Bon Bon 4½" 8.00
#863 Champagne, Saucer 5½ oz. 7.00
#863 Cocktail 3½ oz. 7.00
#803 Comport
    5" 10.00
    6" 10.00
#1480 Cream 12.00
#481 Custard 5½ oz. 6.00
#1769 Finger Bowl 6.00
#1769 Finger Bowl Plate 6" 4.00
#863 Fruit, Footed 5½ oz. 8.00
#840 Fruit Plate 5" 4.00
#863 Goblet 9 oz. 7.00
#4061 Ice Tea, Footed, Handled 10.00
#300 Jug 7 ....40.00
#303 Jug 7 ....40.00
#2100 Jug 7 ....35.00
#1733 Marmalade, Covered 18.00
#1831 Mustard, Covered 18.00
#803 Nappy, Footed
    5" 8.00
    6" 8.00
    7" 8.00
#1227 Nappy

    4½" 6.00
    8" 12.00
#1465 Oil 7 oz. 35.00
#2022 Shaker, Glass Top 12.00
#1480 Sugar 10.00
#2194 Syrup, Nickel Top
    8 oz. 32.00
    12 oz. 40.00
#820 Tumbler, Table 7.00
#701 Tumbler 14 oz. 10.00
#701 Tumbler Plate 5" 4.00
#833 Tumbler 8 oz. 7.00
#833 Tumbler, Sham, Punty 8 oz. 7.00
#889 Tumbler 5 oz. 7.00
#1694½ Vase
#1798 Vase 9" 18.00
#4069 Vase 9" 25.00
#869 Wine 3 oz. 7.00

Rock Crystal
Crystal
1954 – 1969

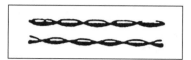

#2666/189 Bowl, Oval 8¼"........................30.00
#2666/309 Canape Plate 7⅜"....................15.00
#2666/311 Candlestick (Flora Candle) 6" ..18.00
#6055/27 Claret/Wine 4¼ oz. 4⅝" 20.00
#6055/20 Cocktail 3½ oz. 3⅞" 14.00
#6055/29 Cordial 1¼ oz. 3⁵⁄₁₆" 22.00
#2666/680 Cream 3½".............................15.00
#2666/688 Cream, Individual 12.00
#6055/2 Goblet 10 oz. 6⅛".......................16.00
#6055/60 Luncheon Goblet/Ice Tea, Footed
    12¼ oz. 6⅛" 16.00
#6055/88 Juice, Footed 5½ oz. 4⅞" 10.00
#2364/477 Mayonnaise
    Bowl 15.00
    Plate 12.00
    Ladle 20.00
#6055/33 Oyster Cocktail 4¾ oz. 4" 10.00
#2337 Plate
    7" 10.00
    8" 12.00
#2364 Relish
    2 part 8¼"...30.00
    3 part 10" 35.00
#2364/654 Shaker, Chrome Top
    Large...set 20.00
#6055/7 Sherbet 6 oz. 4½" 10.00
#2666/677 Sugar 2⅝" 15.00
#2666/687 Sugar, Individual 12.00
#2666/729 Snack Plate, Curved Handle
    10" 30.00
#2364/567 Torte Plate 14" 40.00
#2364/686 Tray, Cream & Sugar ....set 40.00

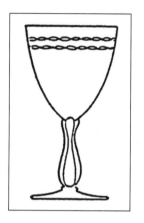

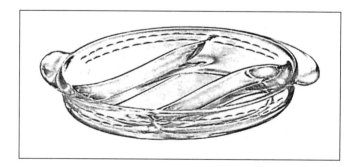

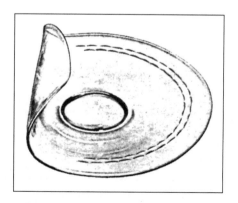

CLOVER Cutting #132

Crystal
1918 – 1928

#863 Almond 8.00
#880 Bon Bon 4½" 12.00
#2219 Candy Jar, Covered
    ¼ lb. 22.00
    ½ lb. 25.00
    1 lb. 30.00
#1697 Carafe 22.00
#863 Champagne, Saucer 5½ oz. 7.00
#863 Claret 3½ oz. 7.00
#863 Cocktail 3½ oz. 7.00
#803 Comport
    5" 10.00
    6" 10.00
#303 Cream 10.00
#1712½ Cream 10.00
#481 Custard..7.00
#766 Finger Bowl 7.00
#1769 Finger Bowl 7.00
#1769 Finger Bowl Plate 4.00
#863 Fruit, Footed 3½".............................8.00
#1736 Fruit Plate 6" 6.00
#863 Goblet 9 oz. 7.00
#825 Jelly, Covered 12.00
#303 Jug 7..35.00
#1124 Jug 7..35.00
#1236 Jug 6..30.00
#1793 Jug 35.00
#2040 Jug 3..25.00
#2082 Jug 5..35.00
#2104 Jug and Tumbler, Punty 45.00
#1733 Marmalade, Covered 16.00
#2138 Mayonnaise
    Bowl..12.00
    Plate..6.00
    Ladle 4.00
#1831 Mustard, Covered 3⅜" 14.00
#803 Nappy, Footed
    5" 8.00
    6" 9.00
    7" 10.00
#1227 Nappy
    4½ oz. 6.00
    8 oz. 14.00
#300½ Oil, Small 30.00
#1465 Oil, Cut Neck, Cut Stopper 7 oz. 35.00

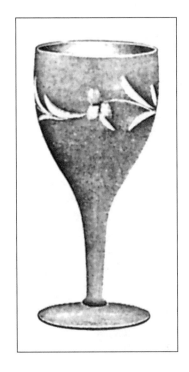

#837 Oyster Cocktail 7.00
#805 Parfait 5¾" 7.00
#880 Salt Dip 12.00
#2263 Salt, Individual 12.00
#2022 Shaker, Glass Top 12.00
#863 Sherry 2 oz. 7.00
#303 Sugar 10.00
#303 Sugar, Covered 12.00
#1712 Sugar, 2-handled 12.00
#2194 Syrup, Nickel Top
    8 oz. 42.00
    12 oz. 45.00
#922 Toothpick, Punty 15.00
#820 Tumbler, Table 7.00
#4011½ Tumbler, Table 7.00
#1697 Tumbler, Carafe 6 oz......................10.00
#701 Tumbler 14 oz. 10.00
#701 Tumbler Plate 4.00
#833 Tumbler 8 oz. 7.00
#833 Tumbler, Sham, Punty 8 oz 7.00
#889 Tumbler 5 oz. 7.00
#4011 Tumbler, Handled 12 oz. 7.00
#863 Wine 3 oz. 7.00
#2208 Vase, Sweet Pea 20.00
#4069 Vase 9" 20.00

\approx LARGE CLOVERLEAF Needle Etching #47 \approx

Crystal
Turn of the Century – 1920

#5001 Brandy ¾ oz. 8.00
#1697 Carafe 10.00
#1697 Carafe Tumbler 6 oz. 8.00
#1697 Carafe Whiskey 2½ oz. 6.00
#114 Champagne 8.00
#791 Champagne, Hollow Stem 10.00
#801 Champagne, Saucer 5½ oz. 8.00
#825 Champagne, Saucer 8.00
#858 Champagne, Saucer 5½ oz. 8.00
#863 Champagne, Hollow Stem 10.00
#932 Champagne, Saucer 8.00
#5001 Champagne, Tall 5¾ oz. 10.00
#5001 Champagne, Saucer 5 oz. 8.00
#5025 Champagne
    5½ oz. 8.00
    6½ oz. 10.00
#932 Champagne Plate...........................4.00
#448 Cheese, Covered
    8" 10.00
    9" 10.00
#1685 Cheese, Covered
    8" 10.00
    9" 10.00
#114 Claret 8.00
#801 Claret 5 oz. 8.00
#5001 Claret
    4¾ oz. 8.00
    5½ oz. 8.00
#5025 Claret 4¾ oz. 8.00
#852 Cocktail......................................8.00
#853 Cocktail......................................8.00
#952 Cocktail......................................8.00
#953 Cocktail......................................8.00
#5001 Cocktail
    2½ oz. 6.00
    3 oz. 6.00
    4 oz. 8.00
#114 Cordial 10.00
#801 Cordial
    ¾ oz. 10.00
    1 oz. 10.00
#5001 Cordial
    ¾ oz. 10.00
    1 oz. 10.00
#5025 Cordial ¾ oz. 10.00
#1227 Cream 5.00
#1478 Cream 5.00
#1480 Cream 5.00
#480 Custard 7.00

#481 Custard 7.00
#858 Custard 7.00
#1227 Custard 7.00
#1239 Custard 7.00
#1241 Custard 7.00
#1598 Custard 7.00
#300 Decanter, Cut Neck
    Pint 8.00
    Quart 10.00
#1195 Decanter, Cut Neck
    Small 6.00
    Medium 8.00
    Large 10.00
#192 Finger Bowl (Pressed).........................7.00
#315 Finger Bowl 7.00
#315 Finger Bowl Plate..............................4.00
#470 Finger Bowl 7.00
#858 Finger Bowl 7.00
#1192 Finger Bowl 7.00
#1349 Finger Bowl 7.00
#1449 Finger Bowl 7.00
#1449 Finger Bowl Plate 4.00
#1769 Finger Bowl 7.00
#1769 Finger Bowl Plate 6".........................4.00
#858 Fruit 5.00
#1736 Fruit Plate 6" 4.00
#114 Goblet 8.00
#801 Goblet
    9 oz. 10.00
    10 oz. 10.00
#826 Goblet 10.00
#991 Goblet 10.00
#5001 Goblet
    7½ oz. 8.00
    8¾ oz. 8.00
    11 oz. 10.00

#5025 Goblet

8 oz.	8.00
9 oz.	10.00
10 oz.	10.00

#945 Grapefruit 6.00
#945½ Grapefruit 6.00
#945½ Grapefruit Liner 6.00
#979 Horseradish 12.00
#4061 Ice Tea, Footed, Handled 10.00
#300 Jug

1	22.00
2	22.00
3	22.00
4	23.00
5	23.00
6	23.00
7	25.00
8	25.00

#300½ Jug #7 ......25.00
#303 Jug

4	22.00
5	22.00
6	23.00
7	27.00
8	28.00

#316 Jug 7 ......30.00
#317½ Jug 7 ......30.00
#3318 Jug

4	25.00
5	25.00
6	30.00
7	30.00

#1227 Jug 7 ......35.00
#1236 Jug

6	28.00
7	32.00

#1227 Jug

1	22.00
2	22.00
3	22.00
4	25.00
5	25.00
6	25.00

#1236 Pitcher

1	25.00
2	25.00
3	28.00
4	28.00
5	30.00

#2018 Jug 6 ......30.00
#801 Liquor ¾ oz. 10.00
#1733 Marmalade, Covered 15.00

#315 Nappy

4"	5.00
4½"	5.00
5"	5.00
6"	6.00
7"	6.00
8"	8.00

#1227 Nappy

4½"	5.00
8"	8.00

#300½ Oil

Small	25.00
Large	30.00

#312 Oil, Cut Stopper 35.00
#837 Oyster Cocktail 6.00
#1389 Oyster Cocktail 6.00
#805 Parfait 7.00
#822 Parfait 7.00
#5025 Pousse-Cafe ¾ oz. 10.00
#5001 Rhine Wine 4 oz. 8.00
#840 Sherbet 8.00
#840 Sherbet Plate 5" 4.00
#841 Sherbet 7.00
#846 Sherry 2 oz. 8.00
#849 Sherry 8.00
#5001 Sherry

1½ oz.	10.00
2 oz.	10.00

#1478 Sugar 7.00
#1480 Sugar 7.00
#858 Sweetmeat 10.00
#724 Tankard

6	35.00
7	35.00

#1224 Tankard

6	35.00
7	35.00

#820 Tumbler, Table 6.00
#858 Tumbler, Table 6.00
#701 Tumbler

7 oz.	6.00
8 oz.	6.00
10 oz.	7.00
12 oz.	7.00
14 oz.	8.00

#701 Tumbler, Straight

3 oz.	6.00
4 oz.	6.00
4½ oz.	6.00
5 oz.	6.00
6 oz.	6.00
6½ oz.	6.00

7½ oz. 7.00	#901 Tumbler 9 oz. 7.00
9 oz. 7.00	#4011 Tumbler 12 oz. 8.00
9½ oz. 7.00	#4011½ Tumbler, Table 10.00
10 oz. 7.00	#160½ Water Bottle, Cut Neck 28.00
#833 Tumbler 7.00	#304 Water Bottle, Cut Neck 30.00
#833 Tumbler, Sham 7.00	#1558 Water Bottle, Cut Neck.................30.00
#858 Tumbler	#1697 Water Bottle 22.00
8 oz. 7.00	#845 Whiskey, Hot 8.00
14 oz. 8.00	500 Wine
#883 Tumbler, Bell Top	Small 8.00
4 oz. 6.00	Large 8.00
5 oz. 6.00	#801 Wine
6 oz. 6.00	2 oz. 8.00
7 oz. 6.00	3 oz. 8.00
8 oz. 7.00	4 oz. 8.00
9 oz. 7.00	#847 Wine 8.00
10 oz. 8.00	#858 Wine 2¾ oz. 8.00
#701 Tumbler Plate 5" 4.00	#902 Wine
#887 Tumbler	3 oz. 8.00
2 oz. 6.00	4 oz. 8.00
2½ oz. 6.00	5 oz. 8.00
3 oz. 6.00	#5025 Wine
#889 Tumbler 5 oz. 6.00	2 oz. 8.00
	2¾ oz. 8.00

☞ COIN GOLD DECORATION #2 ☜

Etching #71
Gold Band Above and Below Etching Border
1906 – 1914

#858 Bass Ale 7 oz. 12.00	#858 Goblet
#858 Brandy 10.00	11 oz. 10.00
#858 Champagne, Hollow Stem 12.00	10 oz. 10.00
#858 Champagne, Saucer	9 oz. 8.00
7 oz. 12.00	8 oz. 8.00
#858 Champagne, Tall 5½ oz. 12.00	#303 Jug 100.00
#858 Claret	#858 Parfait 5½ oz. 8.00
4½ oz. 8.00	#863 Rhine Wine 8.00
6½ oz. 8.00	#858 Sherbet 8.00
#858 Cocktail...............................8.00	#858 Table Tumbler 8.00
#858 Cordial 12.00	#858 Hot Whiskey 8.00
#858 Fruit 8.00	#838 Wine
	2½ oz. 8.00
	3½ oz. 8.00

⊶ COIN GOLD BAND DECORATION #6 ⊷

Coin Gold Band at Bowl Rim and Foot
Crystal
1906 – 1929

#858 Bass Ale 7 oz. 12.00	#858 Fruit 8.00
#858 Brandy 8.00	#858 Goblet 8.00
#858 Champagne, Hollow Stem 12.00	#755 Grapefruit 20.00
#858 Champagne, Saucer 5½ oz. 12.00	#755 Grapefruit Liner............................20.00
#858 Champagne, Tall 5½ oz. 12.00	#303 Jug 85.00
#858 Claret 4½ oz. 8.00	#858 Parfait 5½ oz....................................8.00
#858 Cocktail..8.00	#858 Sherbet 8.00
#858 Creme de Menthe............................10.00	#858 Sherry 8.00
	#300 Tankard 15.00
	#858 Tumbler, Various Sizes 8.00
	#858 Wine 3½ oz. 8.00

⊶ COIN GOLD BAND DECORATION #7 ⊷

Wide Gold Band on Bowl, Gold Band on Foot
Optic
Crystal
1906 – 1928

	#858 Champagne, Saucer 5½ oz. 8.00
	#858 Fruit 7.00
	#858 Goblet 9 oz. 8.00
	#858 Oyster Cocktail 8.00
	#858 Wine 2½ oz. 8.00

⊶ COLONIAL MIRROR Plate Etching #334 ⊷

Crystal
1939 – 1945
A formal pattern, advertised as suited especially for Federal or Georgian type settings.

#2574 Bon Bon, 2-handled 5"....................14.00
#2574 Bowl, Flared 12" 30.00
#2574 Bowl, Handled 25.00
#6023 Bowl, Footed 30.00
#2574 Cake Plate, Handled 10" 22.00
#2574 Candlestick
    4" ....each 18.00
    6" ....each 22.00
#2574 Celery 10½" 18.00
#6023 Champagne, Saucer 6 oz. 12.00
#6023 Claret/Wine 4 oz. 14.00
#6023 Cocktail 3¾ oz. 8.00
#6023 Cordial 1 oz. 20.00
#1574 Comport 5" 14.00
#6023 Comport 5" 16.00
#2574 Cream, Footed 4¾" 15.00
#2574 Cream, Individual 14.00
#2574 Cup...8.00

#766 Finger Bowl 6.00
#2575 Fruit Bowl 13" 40.00

#6023 Goblet 9 oz. 14.00
#2574 Ice Tub 40.00
#6011 Jug, Footed 50.00
#2574 Lemon Dish, 2-handled 6½"............18.00
#2574 Mayonnaise
    Bowl...22.00
    Plate...18.00
    Ladle 20.00
#2574 Oil, Ground Stopper 4¼ oz. 5⅝"......30.00
#2574 Olive Dish 6" 15.00
#6023 Oyster Cocktail 4 oz. 8.00
#2574 Pickle Dish 8" 20.00
#2574 Plate
    6" 8.00
    7" 12.00
    8" 15.00

    9" 20.00
#2574 Relish, 3 Part 10".............................25.00
#2574 Saucer..8.00
#2574 Serving Dish, Deep, 2-handled 8½"..22.00
#2574 Shaker, Glass Top 2⅝" ....pair 35.00
#6023 Sherbet, Low 6 oz. 8.00
#2574 Sugar, Footed 15.00
#2574 Sugar, Individual 14.00
#2574 Sweetmeat Bowl, 2-handled 5¼" 15.00
#2574 Torte Plate 14".................................40.00
#6023 Tumbler, Footed
    5 oz. 8.00
    9 oz. 8.00
    12 oz. 12.00
#2574 Tray, Muffin, Handled 26.00
#2574 Whip Cream Bowl, Handled 5"........45.00

⋙ COMET Cutting #702 ⋘

Crystal
Crystal Bowl with Ebony Base 1930-1936
Crystal Bowl with Green Base 1934
1930 – 1943
*Crystal Bowl with Ebony Base

#4020 Champagne, Saucer/High Sherbet..24.00
#4020 Claret 4 oz. 24.00
#4020 Cocktail 3½ oz. 20.00
#4020½ Cocktail 4 oz. 20.00
#4120 Cocktail 3½ oz.*..............................20.00
#4020 Cream 12.00
#4120 Cream *..12.00
#2419 Cup, After Dinner 10.00
#2419 Cup, Footed......................................8.00
#4021 Finger Bowl 8.00
#4121 Finger Bowl * 8.00
#4020 Goblet 11 oz. 24.00
#4120 Goblet * 24.00
#4020 Jug, Footed 50.00
#4120 Jug, Footed* 50.00
#2419 Plate
    6" 8.00
    7" 10.00
    8" 12.00
#2419 Saucer...8.00
#2419 Saucer, After Dinner 6.00
#4020 Sherbet, High
    5 oz. 24.00
    7 oz. 24.00
#4020 Sherbet, Low

    5 oz. 20.00
    7 oz. 20.00
#4120 Sherbet, High*
    5 oz. 24.00
    7 oz. 24.00
#4120 Sherbet, Low
    5 oz. 20.00
    7 oz. 20.00
#4020 Sugar 15.00
#4120 Sugar * 15.00
#4020 Tumbler, Footed
    5 oz. 20.00
    10 oz. 20.00
    13 oz. 24.00
    16 oz. 24.00
#4120 Tumbler, Footed *
    5 oz. 20.00
    10 oz. 20.00
    13 oz. 24.00
    16 oz. 24.00
#2430 Vase 8" 40.00
#4020 Whiskey, Footed 2 oz. 20.00
#4120 Whiskey 2 oz. * 20.00
#4020 Wine 3 oz. 24.00

CORDELIA Needle Etching #82

Optic Pattern
Green 1927 – 1931; Orchid 1927 – 1928
1927 – 1931

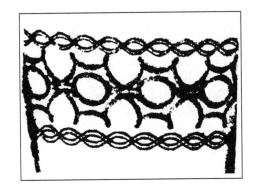

#877 Claret 4 oz.	17.00
#877 Cocktail 3½ oz.	10.00
#877 Cordial ¾ oz.	20.00
#869 Finger Bowl	10.00
#2283 Finger Bowl Plate 6"	10.00
#877 Goblet 10 oz.	15.00
#877 Grapefruit	15.00
#877 Grapefruit Liner	15.00
#5100 Jug 7 Footed	80.00
#877 Oyster Cocktail 4½ oz.	8.00
#877 Parfait 5½ oz.	13.00
#2283 Plate	
7"	8.00
8"	8.00
#877 Sherbet	
Low 6 oz.	11.00
High 6 oz.	13.00

#877 Tumbler, Footed	
2½ oz.	6.00
5 oz.	8.00
9 oz.	8.00
12 oz.	10.00
#877 Wine 2¾ oz.	16.00

CORNUCOPIA Carving #46

Crystal
1941 – 1944

#6023 Candlestick, Duo 5½"	pair 60.00
#2364 Fruit Bowl 13"	45.00
#2364 Lily Bowl 12"	50.00
#2364 Torte Plate	
14"	70.00
16"	80.00
#2577 Vase 8½"	100.00

CORONADO Plate Etching #273

Decoration #49
Blue with White or Yellow Gold Trim
1925 – 1927
SEE ROYAL FOR LISTING; Add 20% to prices.

CORONET Decoration #656

Platinum Band with Polished Cutting
Crystal
1962 – 1970

#6101/27 Cocktail/Wine 5 oz. 25.00
#6101/29 Cordial 1½ oz. 25.00
#4185/495 Dessert/Finger Bowl 12.00
#6101/2 Goblet 10 oz. 28.00

#6101/88 Juice, Footed 6 oz. 25.00
#6101/63 Luncheon Goblet/Ice Tea
   14 oz. 25.00
#2337 Plate
   7" 10.00
   8" 10.00
#6101/11 Sherbet 7 oz. 24.00

CORSAGE Plate Etching #325

Crystal
1935 – 1960
A delicate floral etching with a ribbon treatment suggesting a French interpretation.

CORSAGE included in Patterns of the Past and Nostalgia Program

#2496 Bon Bon, 3 Toed 16.00
#2484 Bowl, Handled 10" 30.00
#2496 Bowl, Footed 12" 45.00
#2527 Bowl, Footed 9" 40.00
#2536 Bowl, Handled 9" 35.00
#2545 Bowl, Oval 12½" 55.00
#2440 Cake Plate 10½".............................30.00
#2496 Cake Plate, Handled 10" 35.00
#2527 Candelabra 2 Light ....pair 50.00
#2496 Candlestick 5½" ....pair 40.00
#2545 Candlestick, Duo ....pair 50.00
#2496 Candlestick, Duo ....pair 50.00
#2496 Candlestick, Trindle ....pair 75.00
#2535 Candlestick 5½" ....pair 45.00
#2496 Candy Box, Covered 3 part 45.00
#2440 Celery 20.00
#6014 Champagne, Saucer/High Sherbet
   5½ oz. 22.00
#2496 Cheese & Cracker 30.00
#6014 Claret 4 oz. 30.00
#6014 Cocktail 3½ oz. 24.00
#2496 Comport 5½" 20.00
#6014 Cordial 1 oz. 45.00
#2440 Cream 16.00
#2440 Cup...12.00
#869 Finger Bowl 10.00
#6014 Goblet 9 oz. 22.00
#2496 Ice Bucket, Metal Handle 45.00
#5000 Jug, Footed 55.00
#2440 Mayonnaise, 2 part 20.00

#2496½ Mayonnaise
   Bowl...20.00
   Plate...16.00
   Ladle 20.00
#2496 Nappy, Handled, Flared 16.00
#2496 Nappy, 3 Cornered..........................18.00
#4119 Nappy, Footed 4" 16.00
#6014 Oyster Cocktail 4 oz. 16.00
#2440 Pickle Dish 14.00
#2666 Pitcher, quart.................................30.00
#2337 Plate
   6" 8.00
   7" 12.00
   8" 20.00
#2364 Plate 16" 50.00

⇜ CORSAGE Plate Etching #325 cont. ⇝

#2419 Relish
    4 part 30.00
    5 part 35.00
#2440 Relish
    2 part 20.00
    3 part 25.00
#2496 Relish
    2 part 20.00
    3 part 25.00
    4 part 30.00
#2440 Sauce Dish, Oval 6½" 22.00
#2440 Saucer....................................8.00
#6014 Sherbet, Low 5½ oz.....................18.00
#2440 Sugar 15.00
#2496 Tid Bit, 3 Toed....................................12.00
#2440 Torte Plate 13"....................................40.00
#2496 Tray for Cream & Sugar....................22.00
#2440 Tray, Oval 8½" 30.00
#6014 Tumbler, Footed
    5 oz. 14.00
    9 oz. 20.00
    12 oz. 22.00
#2470 Vase 10" 80.00
#5092 Vase, Bud 8" 60.00
#6014 Wine 3 oz. 30.00

CORSAGE items included in Patterns of the Past and Nostalgia Program

CO12/011 Champagne/Dessert 5½ oz.
    5¾" 22.00
CO12/025 Claret 4 oz. 5⅞"....................30.00
CO12/002 Goblet 9 oz. 7⅜" 22.00
CO12/063 Luncheon Goblet/Ice Tea 12 oz.
    6" 20.00

⇜ COTILLION Cutting #892 ⇝

Polished Cutting
Rock Crystal
Crystal
1962 – 1970

#6100/31 Brandy 1½ oz. 25.00
#6100/25 Claret 7½ oz. 25.00
#4185/495 Dessert/Finger Bowl 12.00
#6100/2 Goblet 11 oz. 25.00
#6100/63 Luncheon Goblet/Ice Tea
    14½ oz.....................25.00
#2337 Plate
    7" 10.00
    8" 10.00
#6100/11 Sherbet 7½ oz. 22.00
#6100/26 Tulip Wine 5½ oz. 25.00

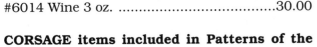

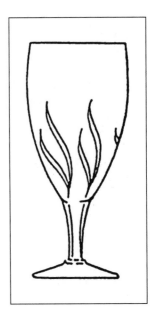

⇒ COVENTRY Cutting #807 ⇐

Rock Crystal
Crystal
1940 – 1944

#2596 Bowl, Oblong, Shallow 11" 30.00
#2596 Bowl, Square 7½" 35.00
#2324 Candlestick 6" ....pair 50.00
#2696 Candlestick 5" ....pair 50.00
#6023 Candlestick, Duo 60.00
#2364 Fruit Bowl 40.00
#2364 Lily Pond 12" 50.00
#2364 Salad Bowl 10½" 60.00
#2364 Torte Plate
   14" 40.00
   16" 70.00
#2567 Vase, Footed
   7½" 40.00
   8½" 70.00
#2577 Vase

   6" 40.00
   8½" 70.00
#4126½ Vase, Footed 11" 80.00
#4132½ Vase 8" 65.00
#4143½ Vase, Footed
   6" 40.00
   7½" 50.00

⇒ COUNTRY GARDEN Crystal Print #13 ⇐

Blue
1958 – 1962
Tumblers produced to accompany similarly decorated melamine dinnerware.

Juice Tumbler 7 oz. 10.00
Water Tumbler 12 oz. 10.00

⇒ CREST Cutting #843 ⇐

Gray Cutting
1955 – 1962

#2666/189 Bowl, Oval 40.00
#2666/311 Candlestick
   (Flora Candle) ....pair 50.00
#6061/21 Cocktail Wine 4 oz. 20.00
#6061/29 Cordial 1 oz. 22.00
#6061/2 Goblet 11 oz. 20.00
#6061/88 Juice, Footed 6 oz. 16.00
#6061/63 Luncheon Goblet/Ice Tea 12 oz. 18.00
#2337 Plate
   7" 8.00
   8" 10.00
#2364/557 Sandwich Plate 11" 12.00
#2364/567 Torte Plate 14" 30.00
#6061/11 Sherbet 7½ oz. 16.00

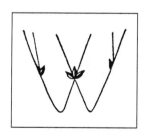 

↞ CUMBERLAND Cutting #762 ↠

Optic Pattern
Rock Crystal
Crystal
1936 – 1940

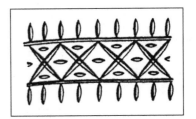

#2470½ Bowl 10½" 30.00
#2472 Candlestick, Duo ....pair 40.00
#6016 Champagne, Saucer 6 oz. 15.00
#6016 Claret 4½ oz. 20.00
#6016 Cocktail 3½ oz. 20.00
#2400 Comport 6" 18.00
#6016 Cordial ¾ oz. 25.00
#869 Finger Bowl 12.00
#6010 Goblet 10 oz. 20.00
#5000 Jug, Footed 100.00
#6016 Oyster Cocktail 4 oz. 15.00
#2337 Plate
    6" 8.00
    7" 10.00
    8" 15.00
#6016 Sherbet, Low 6 oz. 15.00
#6016 Tumbler, Footed
    5 oz. 8.00
    10 oz. 10.00
    13 oz. 15.00
#6016 Wine 3¾ oz. 20.00

↞ CUPID Plate Etching #288 ↠

Amber, Blue, Green, Ebony
1927 – 1929

#2297 Bowl, Deep 100.00
#2298 Candlestick ....pair 100.00
#2324 Candlestick 4" ....pair 120.00
#2329 Centerpiece
    11" 80.00
    13" 100.00
#2354 Cigarette Holder..........................125.00
#2298 Clock..300.00
#2298 Clock Set (Clock and Candles) 500.00
#2322 Cologne 100.00
#2359½ Puff Box, Covered 110.00
#2276 Vanity Set (Powder with Cologne part of
    Cover)..150.00

Blown Ware
Crystal
1904 – 1914

#858 Brandy 1 oz. 10.00
#858 Claret
     4½ oz. 8.00
     6½ oz. 8.00
#858 Champagne, Tall 5½ oz.....................10.00
#858 Champagne, Hollow Stem, Cut Flute 10.00
#858 Champagne, Long Stem 10.00
#858 Champagne, Saucer 7 oz. 8.00
#932 Champagne, Saucer 8.00
#801 Cordial ¾ oz. 10.00
#858 Cordial 1 oz. 10.00
#858 Cocktail 3½ oz. 8.00
#952 Cocktail 3 oz. 8.00
#1227 Custard 7.00
#1227 Cream 14.00
#1711 Cigar Jar, Covered 85.00
#858 Creme de Menthe 2½ oz. 10.00
#300 Decanter, Cut Neck, quart 45.00
#863 Fruit 12.00
#858 Fruit Salad 10.00
#315 Finger Bowl 7.00
#315 Finger Bowl Plate............................4.00
#858 Finger Bowl 7.00
#801 Goblet 10 oz. 8.00
#858 Goblet
     9 oz. 8.00
     10 oz. 10.00
     11 oz. 10.00
#858 Ice Cream 4½" 12.00
#801 Liquor ¾ oz. 10.00
#315 Nappy
     7" 20.00
     8" 25.00
#1227 Nappy 8" 25.00
#1227 Punch Bowl and Foot...................110.00
#1465 Oil, Cut Neck 55.00
#858 Sherry 2 oz. 8.00
#846 Sherry 8.00
#840 Sherbet 8.00
#843 Sherbet 8.00
#858 Sherbet 8.00
Various unlisted stemware may include:
     1 oz., 2 oz., 3 oz., 4 oz., 5 oz., 9 oz., 10 oz.,
     11 oz. 8.00-10.00

#1227 Sugar, Covered 22.00
#300 Tankard
     1...30.00
     2...30.00
     3...35.00
     3½ 35.00
     4...40.00
     5...40.00
     6...45.00
     7...45.00
#303 Tankard 7 ....45.00
#742 Tankard
     6...45.00
     7...45.00
#1236 Tankard 7 ....45.00
#1743 Tankard 5, Covered 60.00
#820 Tumbler..10.00
#833 Tumbler, Sham
     7 oz. 10.00
     10 oz. 10.00
#887 Tumbler 3 oz. 10.00
#889 Tumbler 5 oz. 10.00
#725 Vase
     8" 30.00
     10" 40.00
     12" 45.00
#1120 Vase 12" 50.00
#160½ Water Bottle, Cut Neck 38.00
#858 Whiskey, Hot 4 oz. 10.00
#858 Wine
     2¾ oz. 8.00
     3½ oz. 8.00

Blown Ware
Crystal
1908 – 1921

#315 Bitters Bottle, Cut Neck 30.00
#1904 Bon Bon, Covered 35.00
#858 Brandy 1 oz. 10.00
#822 Cafe Parfait 8.00
#701 Champagne, Hollow Stem 10.00
#702 Champagne, Hollow Stem Small 10.00
#703 Champagne, Hollow Stem Large.......10.00
#858 Champagne, Saucer 7 oz. 8.00
#858 Champagne, Hollow Stem, Cut
    Flute...10.00
#858 Champagne, Tall 5½ oz. 12.00
#932 Champagne, Saucer 8.00
#5051 Cheese and Cracker Plate 14.00
#300 Claret 8.00
#858 Claret
    4½ oz..8.00
    6½ oz..8.00
#858 Cocktail 3½ oz. 8.00
#932 Cocktail 8.00
#803 Comport, Footed
    5" 10.00
    6" 10.00
#858 Cordial 1 oz. 10.00
#1227 Cream 12.00
#1478 Cream 12.00
#1480 Cream 12.00
#1759 Cream 12.00
#858 Creme de Menthe 2½ oz. 10.00
#481 Custard 7.00
#858 Custard 7.00
#1241 Custard 7.00
#1508 Custard 7.00
#200 Custard Plate 7.00
#300 Decanter, Cut Neck
    Pint 35.00
    Quart 5.00
#315 Finger Bowl 7.00
#315 Finger Bowl Plate..............................4.00
#858 Finger Bowl 7.00
#858 Finger Bowl Plate..............................7.00
#1 Floating Island Flower Tray, Round 15.00
#823 Fruit
    4" 8.00
    5" 10.00
#858 Fruit Salad 10.00
#863 Fruit and Plate 5½ oz. 14.00
#826 Goblet
    7 oz. 8.00

    9 oz. 8.00
#858 Goblet
    9 oz. 8.00
    10 oz. 8.00
    11 oz. 10.00
#945 Grapefruit 12.00
#945½ Grapefruit and Footed Liner 18.00
#1132 Horseradish with Stopper 22.00
#858 Ice Cream 4½" 10.00
#701 Ice Tea, Crackeled Glass 14 oz. 12.00
#303 Jug 7..45.00
#303 Jug 8 Crackeled Glass 84 oz. 50.00
#303½ Jug 7 ....45.00
#318 Jug 7..45.00
#724 Jug 7..45.00
#1227 Jug 7..45.00
#315 Nappy
    4" 6.00
    4½"..6.00
    5" 7.00
    6" 8.00
    7" 10.00
    8" 12.00
    9" 12.00
    10" 14.00
#803 Nappy, Footed, Deep
    4" 8.00
    5" 9.00
    6" 9.00
    7" 10.00
#803 Nappy, Footed, Shallow
    4" 8.00
    5" 9.00
    6" 8.00
    7" 9.00
#1227 Nappy
    4½"..8.00
    8" 12.00

#1735 Oyster Cocktail 4 oz. 8.00
#300½ Oil, Cut Stopper
    Small 35.00
    Large 45.00
#312 Oil, Cut Stopper...........................45.00
#1465 Oil, Cut Neck, Cut Stopper 45.00
#1465 Oil 35.00
#837 Oyster Cocktail 8.00
#1666 Puff, Covered 45.00
#1227 Punch Bowl and Foot...................100.00
#1165 Shaker, Silver-Plated Top...............12.00
#840 Sherbet and Plate 12.00
#858 Sherbet 8.00
#930 Sherbet, Tall 9.00
#846 Sherry 8.00
#848 Sherry 2½ oz. 8.00
#858 Sherry 2 oz. 10.00
#2048 Stein 17 oz. 18.00
#2049 Stein 16 oz. 18.00
#1227 Sugar, Covered 15.00
#1478 Sugar, 2-handled 12.00
#1480 Sugar, 2-handled 12.00
#1759 Sugar 12.00
#300 Tankard Cut Star Bottom
    1..25.00
    2..25.00
    3..30.00
    3½..30.00
    4..40.00
    5..45.00
    6..45.00
    7..50.00
#724 Tankard 7 ....50.00
#858 Tumbler, Table 8.00
#858 Tumbler, Table, Sham, Cut #19
    3 oz. 6.00
    5 oz. 6.00
    6½ oz..6.00
    8 oz. 8.00

    10 oz. 8.00
    12 oz. 10.00
    14 oz. 12.00
    16 oz. 14.00
#74 Tumbler, Toddy 12.00
#701 Tumbler 12 oz. 10.00
#820 Tumbler 8.00
#820½ Tumbler, Sham 8.00
#833 Tumbler, Sham
    6 oz. 6.00
    8 oz. 8.00
#858 Tumbler
    3½ oz...6.00
    5 oz. 6.00
    6½ oz...6.00
    8 oz. 8.00
    10 oz. 8.00
    12 oz. 10.00
    14 oz. 12.00
    16 oz. 14.00
#887 Tumbler, Sham
    3 oz. 5.00
    5 oz. 6.00
#889 Tumbler 5 oz. 6.00
#837½ Tumbler, Footed 10 oz. 12.00
#858 Tumbler Plate 4.00
#725 Vase, Cut Top and Bottom
    8" 30.00
    10" 35.00
    12" 40.00
#160½ Water Bottle, Cut Neck 35.00
#1558 Water Bottle, Cut Neck...................35.00
#845 Whiskey, Hot 10.00
#858 Whiskey, Hot 4 oz. 10.00
#858 Whiskey, Sham 3 oz. 8.00
#858 Wine
    2¼ oz..8.00
    3½ oz..8.00

Blown Ware
Crystal
1913 – 1925

#863 Almond 4 Stars 12.00

#1163 Catsup, Cut Stopper, 4 Stars 45.00

#793 Champagne, Hollow Stem, Cut Flute,
    4 Stars 10.00

#794 Champagne, Hollow Stem, Cut Flute 10.00

#825 Champagne Saucer 7.00

#863 Champagne, Hollow Stem, Cut Flute,
    4 Stars 10.00

#863 Champagne, Saucer, 4 Stars 5½ oz.....7.00

#863 Champagne, Tall, 4 Stars 5½ oz. 10.00

#932 Champagne, Saucer, 3 Stars 7.00

#863 Claret, 4 Stars 4½ oz. 7.00

#863 Cocktail, 3 Stars 3½ oz. 7.00

#952 Cocktail, 3 Stars 7.00

#803 Comport
    5" 10.00
    6" 12.00

#863 Cordial, 3 Stars 1 oz. 10.00

#1473 Cream 10.00

#1480 Cream, Star Bottom, 4 Stars 12.00

#1720 Cream 10.00

#1759 Cream 10.00

#863 Creme de Menthe, 3 Stars 2½ oz. 7.00

#481 Custard, 3 Stars 6.00

#858 Custard, 3 Stars 6.00

#1241 Custard, 3 Stars 6.00

#1755 Custard, 4 Stars 6.00

#858 Custard Plate, 4 Stars 4.00

#300 Decanter, Cut Neck, Cut Stopper 6
    Stars, quart 35.00

#1464 Decanter, Cut Neck, Cut Flute, Cut
    Stopper 4 Stars 18 oz........................40.00

#315 Finger Bowl, 5 Stars 6.00

#315 Finger Bowl Plate..............................4.00

#858 Finger Bowl, 5 Stars 6.00

#1349 Finger Bowl, 4 Stars 6.00

#1499 Finger Bowl, 4 Stars 6.00

#1499 Finger Bowl Plate 4.00

#1769 Finger Bowl 6.00

#1769 Finger Bowl Plate 4.00

#858 Finger Bowl Plate..............................4.00

#823 Fruit, 4 Stars
    4½" 8.00
    5" 10.00

#863 Fruit 10.00

#826 Goblet 9 oz. 7.00

#863 Goblet
    7 oz. 4 Stars 7.00

    9 oz. 4 Stars 7.00
    10 oz. 4 Stars 8.00

#945½ Grapefruit with Footed Liner
    4 Stars 15.00

#1664 Horseradish, 4 Stars 20.00

#858 Ice Cream 10.00

#303 Jug
    2, 5 Stars 25.00
    3, 7 Stars 25.00
    4, 7 Stars 30.00
    5, 7 Stars 30.00
    6, 8 Stars 40.00
    7, 8 Stars 45.00
    8, 8 Stars 45.00

#317 Jug, Cut Neck 40.00

#1227 Jug, Cut Neck 7, 5 Stars on Body,
    2 Stars on Neck 50.00

#1227 Jug, 6 Stars on Body, 2 Stars on
    Neck 50.00

#1236 Jug
    6 oz. 30.00
    7 oz. 35.00

#315 Nappy
    4" 4 Stars 6.00
    4½" 4 Stars, Star Bottom 8.00
    5" 4 Stars 8.00
    6" 5 Stars 10.00
    7" 6 Stars 10.00
    8" 6 Stars 12.00
    9" 7 Stars 15.00
    10" 7 Stars 20.00

#1227 Nappy
    4½ oz...8.00
    8 oz. 15.00

#803 Nappy, Footed, Deep
    4½"...8.00
    5" 8.00

6" 10.00
7" 12.00
#803 Nappy, Footed, Shallow
    4½" 8.00
    5" 8.00
    6" 10.00
    7" 12.00
#300½ Oil, Cut Stopper, 4 Stars Small 45.00
#312 Oil, Cut Stopper, 4 Stars 45.00
#1164 Oil, Cut Stopper......................45.00
#1465 Oil, Cut Stopper, Cut Neck, Star
    Bottom 4 Stars 50.00
#863 Pousse-Cafe, 3 Stars ¾ oz. 7.00
#1227 Punch Bowl and Foot, Beaded Top..85.00
#863 Rhine Wine, 3 Stars 4½ oz. 7.00
#614 Shaker, Silver-Plated Top, 4 Stars 12.00
#1165 Shaker, Silver-Plated Top................12.00
#840 Sherbet, 3 Stars 7.00
#840 Sherbet Plate, 4 Stars 4.00
#843 Sherbet, 4 Stars 7.00
#846 Sherry, 3 Stars 2 oz. 7.00
#863 Sherry, 3 Stars 2 oz. 7.00
#1478 Sugar, Cut Star Bottom, 2-handled
    4 Stars 14.00
#1480 Sugar, 2-handled, 4 Stars 14.00
#1720 Sugar 12.00
#1759 Sugar 12.00
#300 Tankard
    1..25.00
    2..25.00
    3..25.00
    4..30.00
    5..30.00
    6..35.00
    7..40.00
    8..40.00
#330½ Tankard 7 ....40.00

#724 Tankard, 8 Stars
    6..35.00
    7..40.00
#858 Tumbler, Table, Cut #19
    3⅓" 7.00
    5" 3 Stars 7.00
    6½" 3 Stars 7.00
    8" 3 Stars 7.00
    10" 4 Stars 7.00
    12" 4 Stars 7.00
    14" 4 Stars 8.00
    16" 10.00
#701 Tumbler 14 oz. 10.00
#820 Tumbler, 4 Stars 8.00
#820½ Tumbler, 4 Stars Sham 8.00
#833 Tumbler 7.00
#833½ Tumbler, 3 Stars Sham 8.00
#858 Tumbler
    3½" 7.00
    5" 7.00
    6½" 7.00
    8" 7.00
    10" 7.00
    12" 7.00
    14" 8.00
#858 Tumbler Plate 4.00
#887 Tumbler, 3 Stars 3 oz. 7.00
#889 Tumbler, 3 Stars
    5 oz. 7.00
    8 oz. 7.00
    9 oz. 7.00
#725 Vase 8" 25.00
#160½ Water Bottle, Cut Neck, 6 Stars 35.00
#1558 Water Bottle, Cut Neck, Cut Star
    Bottom, 6 Stars 40.00
#801 Wine, 3 Stars 3 oz. 7.00
#863 Wine, 3 Stars 3 oz. 7.00

⇒ CUTTING #125 ⇐

Crystal
1915 – 1918

Item	Price
#863 Almond	12.00
#4065 Apollinaris Cut #19 6 oz.	7.00
#4070 Bar Water Cut #19 5½ oz.	7.00
#4065 Beer, Cut #19 10 oz.	7.00
#4065 Beer, Split, Cut #19 7 oz.	7.00
#4070 Beer, Split Cut #19 7 oz.	7.00
#863 Champagne, Hollow Stem	10.00
#766 Champagne, Saucer 5½ oz.	7.00
#863 Champagne, Saucer 5½ oz.	7.00
#932 Champagne, Saucer	7.00
#863 Champagne, Tall 5½ oz.	10.00
#863 Claret 4½ oz.	7.00
#863 Cocktail 3½ oz.	7.00
#803 Comport, Footed	
5 oz.	10.00
6 oz.	10.00
#863 Cordial ¾"	10.00
#863 Creme de Menthe 2½ oz.	7.00
#1478 Cream	10.00
#481 Custard	6.00
#481 Custard Plate	4.00
#300 Decanter, Cut Neck quart	35.00
#1769 Finger Bowl	7.00
#1769 Finger Bowl Plate	4.00
#766 Fruit	8.00
#823 Fruit	
4½"	8.00
5"	8.00
#863 Fruit, Footed 5½ oz.	9.00
#840 Fruit Plate 5"	4.00
#1465 Gin Fizz, Cut #19 8 oz.	7.00
#766 Goblet 9 oz.	7.00
#863 Goblet	
9 oz.	7.00
10½ oz.	7.00
#945½ Grapefruit	10.00
#945½ Grapefruit Liner	6.00
#4070 Highball, Cut #19 8 oz.	7.00
#766 Ice Tea, Footed, Handled	8.00
#4065 Ice Tea, Cut #19 14 oz.	10.00
#303 Jug 7	35.00
#4061 Lemonade	8.00
#4070 Milk Punch, Cut #19 12 oz.	8.00
#4065 Mineral, Cut #19 5 oz.	7.00
#803 Nappy, Deep	
5"	8.00
6"	10.00
7"	12.00
#1227 Nappy	

Item	Price
4½"	6.00
8"	12.00
#300½ Oil, Small	35.00
#4070 Old Fashioned, Cut #19 9 oz.	7.00
#899 Parfait, 6 oz.	7.00
#863 Pousse-Cafe ¾ oz.	8.00
#863 Rhine Wine 4 oz.	7.00
#1165 Shaker, Silver-Plated Top	12.00
#2022 Shaker, Glass Top	12.00
#840 Sherbet	7.00
#840 Sherbet Plate	4.00
#863 Sherbet	7.00
#846 Sherry	7.00
#863 Sherry	2 oz.
#4065 Strained Lemonade, Cut #19 12 oz.	7.00
#1478 Sugar	12.00
#300 Tankard 7	35.00
#4065 Tom Collins, Cut #19 16 oz.	10.00
#922 Toothpick, Cut Flute	20.00
#701 Tumbler	
5 oz.	7.00
8 oz.	7.00
14 oz.	10.00
#701 Tumbler Plate	4.00
#820 Tumbler	7.00
#820½ Tumbler, Sham	7.00
#833 Tumbler, Sham 8 oz.	7.00
#887 Tumbler 3 oz.	7.00
#889 Tumbler 5 oz.	7.00
#4077 Tumbler	
8 oz.	7.00
12 oz.	7.00
#160½ Water Bottle, Cut Neck	30.00
#4065 Whiskey, Cut #19 3 oz.	7.00
#4070 Whiskey, Cut #19	
2 oz.	7.00
2½ oz.	7.00
3 oz.	7.00
3½ oz.	7.00
#863 Wine 3 oz.	7.00

◦⇒ CUTTING #129 ⇐◦

Crystal
1918 – 1929

#863 Almond 10.00
#880 Almond 10.00
#880 Bon Bon 4½" 10.00
#2219 Candy Jar, Covered
    ¼ lb. 22.00
    ½ lb. 25.00
    1 lb. 30.00
#1697 Carafe 25.00
#1698 Carafe Tumbler 10.00
#5051 Cheese, Footed, Small 12.00
#2241 Cologne with Stopper.....................30.00
#2242 Cologne with Stopper.....................30.00
#825 Champagne, Saucer 7.00
#863 Champagne, Saucer 5½ oz. 7.00
#863 Claret 4½ oz. 7.00
#863 Cocktail 3½ oz. 7.00
#803 Comport
    5" 10.00
    6" 10.00
#803 Comport, Footed, Covered 5" 20.00
#303 Cream 4" 10.00
#1480 Cream 10.00
#1712½ Cream 2¾" 10.00
#1598 Custard 6.00
#858 Finger Bowl 7.00
#858 Finger Bowl Plate 6"..........................4.00
#1499 Finger Bowl 7.00
#863 Fruit 5½ oz. 10.00
#1763 Fruit Plate 6" 5.00
#863 Goblet 9 oz. 7.00
#945½ Grapefruit 10.00
#945½ Grapefruit Liner 8.00
#766 Ice Tea, Footed, Handled 10.00
#4061 Ice Tea, Footed, Handled 10.00
#825 Jelly, Covered 18.00
#300 Jug 7...40.00
#303 Jug 7...40.00
#1124 Jug 7...40.00
#1236 Jug 6...35.00
#2040 Jug 3...25.00
#2100 Jug 7...40.00
#1743 Jug and Cover 50.00
#2104 Jug and Tumbler, Punty 45.00
#1968 Marmalade, Covered 18.00
#2138 Mayonnaise
    Bowl...17.00
    Plate..7.00
    Ladle 4.00
#1831 Mustard, Covered 20.00

#803 Nappy, Footed
    5" 10.00
    6" 12.00
    7" 14.00
#503 Nappy, Footed, Covered 5" 18.00
#1227 Nappy
    4½" 8.00
    8" 14.00
#1590 Nappy
    4½" 8.00
#300½ Oil, Small 30.00
#1465 Oil, Cut Neck 7 oz.........................35.00
#837 Oyster Cocktail 7.00
#766½ Parfait 7.00
#805 Parfait 7.00
#822 Parfait 7.00
#1848 Plate, Sandwich 9" 12.00
#2263 Salt, Individual 15.00
#2022 Shaker, Glass Top 13.00
#840 Sherbet 5½ oz. 7.00
#830 Sherbet Plate 4.00
#303 Sugar 10.00
#1480 Sugar 10.00
#303 Sugar, Covered, 2-handled..............12.00
#1712 Sugar, 2 Handles 2½" 12.00
#2194 Syrup, Removable Nickel Top
    8 oz. 40.00
    12 oz. 45.00
#858 Sweetmeat......................................10.00
#922 Toothpick, Punty 20.00
#820 Tumbler, Table 7.00
#4011½ Tumbler, Table 7.00
#701 Tumbler 14 oz. 8.00
#701 Tumbler, Sham, Punty 14 oz...........10.00
#701 Tumbler Plate 7.00
#820 Tumbler 9 oz. 7.00
#820 Tumbler Sham, Punty 7.00
#833 Tumbler 8 oz. 7.00
#833 Tumbler, Sham, Punty 8 oz..............7.00
#858 Tumbler 14 oz. 10.00
#889 Tumbler 5 oz. 7.00
#4011 Tumbler, Handled 12 oz. 10.00
#4069 Vase 9" 25.00
#863 Wine 3 oz. 7.00

⊶⊷ CYNTHIA Cutting #170 ⊶⊷

Crystal
1924 – 1928
Do not confuse with CYNTHIA Cutting #785.

#1697 Bedroom Set (Carafe & Tumbler) 30.00
#2250 Candy Jar, Covered
    ¼ lb. 50.00
    ½ lb. 60.00
    1 lb. 80.00
#1697 Carafe 22.00
#4023 Carafe Tumbler 10.00
#661 Champagne, Saucer 6 oz. 10.00
#661 Cocktail 2½ oz. 10.00
#661 Cordial ¾ oz. 25.00
#5078 Comport
    5" 15.00
    6" 18.00
#5078 Comport, Covered
    5" 20.00
    6" 24.00
#2133 Cream 18.00
#300 Decanter, Cut Neck, quart 35.00
#1769 Finger Bowl 8.00
#661 Fruit, Footed 6 oz. 8.00
#661 Goblet 9 oz. 15.00
#945½ Grapefruit 40.00
#945½ Grapefruit Liner 18.00
#825 Jelly 20.00
#825 Jelly, Covered 30.00
#303 Jug 3..30.00
#724 Jug 7..30.00
#1852 Jug 6..35.00
#2270 Jug 30.00
#2270 Jug, Covered (Plain)......................50.00
#4087 Marmalade, Covered 30.00
#1769 Mayonnaise Set
    Bowl 18.00
    Plate 14.00
    Ladle 20.00
#5078 Nappy
    5" 10.00
    6" 10.00
#5078 Nappy, Covered
    5" 15.00
    6" 20.00

#1465 Oil, Cut Neck 5 oz..........................40.00
#837 Oyster Cocktail 8.00
#661 Parfait 5½ oz. 10.00
#1897 Plate 7" 12.00
#2282 Plate 6" 10.00
#2338 Plate
    7" 12.00
    8¼"...18.00
#1848 Plate, Sandwich 9" 20.00
#2235 Shaker, Glass Top...............pair 65.00
#2335 Shaker, Pearl Top ....pair 80.00
#2133 Sugar 24.00
#880 Sweetmeat.......................................20.00
#724 Tankard 7 ....32.00
#4085 Tumbler, Table 8.00
#4085 Tumbler
    2½ oz. 10.00
    6 oz. 8.00
    13 oz. 15.00
#4095 Tumbler, Footed
    2½ oz..10.00
    5 oz. 8.00
    10 oz. 6.00
    13 oz. 10.00
#4011 Tumbler, Handled 12 oz. 18.00
#4085 Tumbler, Handled 13 oz. 20.00
#661 Wine 2 oz. 10.00

⊰≍ CYNTHIA Cutting #785 ≍⊱

Gray Cutting
1918 – 1966
Do not confuse with CYNTHIA Cutting #170.

CYNTHIA included in Patterns of the Past and Nostalgia Programs

#2560 Bon Bon 20.00
#2560 Bon Bon, 3 Toed 7¼" 22.00
#2560/233 Bowl, Handled 11" 40.00
#2560 Bowl, Crimped 11½" 40.00
#2560/306 Cake Plate, Handled 10½" 35.00
#2560 Candlestick 4½" ....pair 40.00
#2560½ Candlestick 4" ....pair 36.00
#2560/332 Candlestick, Duo ....pair 60.00
#2560 Celery 11" 25.00
#6017/8 Champagne/High Sherbet
     6 oz. 5½"..20.00
#2560 Cheese...18.00
#2560 Cheese & Cracker 40.00
#6017/25 Claret 4 oz. 5⅞" 26.00
#6017/21 Cocktail 3½ oz. 4⅞" 21.00
#2460 Comport 6" 18.00
#6017/29 Cordial ¾ oz. 3⅞" 32.00
#2560 Cracker Plate................................22.00
#2560/681 Cream, Footed 7 oz. 4⅛"..........18.00
#2560 Cream, Individual 3¾" 14.00
#2560/396 Cup, Footed 10.00
#766 Finger Bowl 8.00
#2560 Fruit Bowl 13" 45.00
#6017/2 Goblet 9 oz. 7⅜".........................25.00
#2560 Ice Bucket, Chrome Handled 50.00
#6011 Jug, Footed 8⅞"..............................70.00
#6017/88 Juice, Footed 5 oz. 4¾" 13.00
#2560 Lemon Dish 15.00
#6017/63 Luncheon Goblet/Ice Tea
     12 oz. 6" 19.00
#2560 Mayonnaise
     Bowl..20.00
     Plate...15.00
     Ladle 20.00
#2560 Mayonnaise, 2 part 30.00
#2560 Muffin Tray, Handled.....................25.00
#2560 Oil, Footed, Stopper 3 oz................45.00
#2560 Olive Dish 6½"...............................16.00
#6017/33 Oyster Cocktail 4 oz. 3⅝" 13.00
#2560 Pickle Dish, Oval 8¾".....................18.00
#2666/454 Pitcher, quart.........................45.00
#2337 Plates
     6" 8.00
     7" 10.00
     8" 15.00

#2560 Relish 2 part 20.00
#2560/622 Relish 3 part 10" 25.00
#2560 Relish
     4 part 35.00
     5 part 40.00
#2560 Salad Bowl, 2 part 45.00
#2560/397 Saucer 8.00
#2560 Serving Dish 24.00
#6017/11 Sherbet, Low 6 oz. 4½".............17.00
#2560/679 Sugar, Footed 3½" 16.00
#2560 Sugar, Individual 3" 14.00
#2560 Sweetmeat, 2-handled 5½".............13.00
#2560 Tid Bit, 3 Toed...............................18.00
#2560 Torte Plate 14" 45.00
#2560/723 Tray, Lunch, Handled 11½" 32.00
#2567 Vase, Footed 7½" 40.00
#5100 Vase 10" 60.00
#6017/72 Water, Footed 9 oz. 5½" 12.00
#2560 Whip Cream 40.00
#6016/26 Wine 3 oz. 5½" 28.00

CYNTHIA items included in Patterns of the Past and Nostalgia Programs.

CY01/008 Champagne/High Dessert
     6 oz. 5½"..20.00
CY01/011 Champagne/Low Dessert
     6 oz. 4½"..17.00
CY01/027 Claret 4 oz. 5⅞" 26.00
CY01/002 Goblet 9 oz. 7⅜" 25.00
CY01/063 Luncheon Goblet/Ice Tea
     12 oz. 6" 19.00
CY01/026 Wine 3 oz. 5½".........................28.00

⇌ CYRENE Cutting #763 ⇌

Crystal
1937 – 1943

#2496 Bowl, Handled 10½".......................30.00
#2496 Candlestick 5½" ....pair 40.00
#6012 Champagne, Saucer 5½ oz. 20.00
#6012 Claret 4½ oz. 25.00
#6012 Cocktail 3 oz.................................20.00
#6012 Cordial 1 oz. 28.00
#2350½ Cream, Footed...........................15.00
#1769 Finger Bowl 13.00
#6012 Goblet 10 oz.................................22.00
#6011 Jug, Footed 120.00
#6012 Oyster Cocktail 14.00
#2337 Plate
    6"..8.00
    7"..10.00
    8"..15.00
#6012 Sherbet, Low 5½ oz. 15.00
#2350½ Sugar, Footed 20.00
#6012 Tumbler, Footed
    5 oz. 12.00
    10 oz. 10.00
    13 oz. 20.00
#6012 Wine 3 oz. 25.00

⇌ DAISY White Enamel Decoration #17 ⇌

Enamel and Cut Flowers, Gold Band on Brim
  and Base
1920

#858 Champagne, Saucer 5½ oz. 30.00
#858 Cocktail...30.00
#858 Fruit 5" 25.00

#858 Goblet 9 oz. 30.00
#724 Jug 175.00
#2104 Jug 175.00
#701 Juice, Footed 5 oz...........................30.00
#820 Water, Footed 10 oz. 30.00
#858 Wine 2½ oz. 30.00

Crystal
1935 – 1944

#2533 Bowl, Handled 9" 35.00
#2536 Bowl, Handled 9" 35.00
#2440 Cake Plate, Oval 10½" 40.00
#2535 Candlestick 5½" ....pair 40.00
#2533 Candlestick, Duo ....pair 70.00
#6013 Champagne, Saucer/High Sherbet
    6 oz. 20.00
#2535 Cheese & Cracker 40.00
#6013 Claret 4 oz. 30.00
#6013 Cocktail 3½ oz. 20.00
#2528 Cocktail Tray 35.00
#6013 Comport 5" 22.00
#6013 Cordial 1 oz. 45.00
#2350½ Cream, Footed............................10.00
#2450½ Cup, Footed 12.00
#766 Finger Bowl (Narrow Optic) 8.00
#6013 Goblet 10 oz. 26.00
#6013 Goblet, Low 9 oz. 20.00
#5000 Jug, Footed 80.00
#2375 Mayonnaise
    Bowl......................................18.00
    Plate......................................12.00
    Ladle (Plain)...........................20.00
#2440 Mayonnaise, Oval, 2 part 22.00
#1184 Old Fashioned Cocktail (Narrow Optic)
    7 oz. 12.00
#6013 Oyster Cocktail 4 oz. 16.00
#2337 Plate
    6"......................................10.00
    7"......................................14.00
    8"......................................20.00
#2364 Plate 16" 35.00
#2419 Relish, 4 part...............................30.00
#2440 Relish
    2 part 20.00
    3 part 26.00
#2514 Relish, 5 part...............................40.00

#2440 Sauce Dish, Oval 6½" 16.00
#2350 Saucer..10.00
#6013 Sherbet, Low 5 oz. 16.00
#2350½ Sugar, Footed 14.00
#2440 Torte Plate 13" 40.00
#2440 Tray, Oval 8½" 35.00
#701 Tumbler, Narrow Optic, Sham
    10 oz. 12.00
    12 oz. 15.00
#6013 Tumbler, Footed
    5 oz. 16.00
    13 oz. 20.00
#760 Vase 12" 100.00
#2470 Vase
    8"......................................70.00
    10"......................................90.00
#5090 Vase, Bud 8" 40.00
#5092 Vase, Bud 8" 40.00
#6013 Wine 3 oz. 30.00

✦— DAPHNE Cutting #797 —✦

Rock Crystal
Crystal
1939 – 1944

#2424 Ash Tray, Individual 3" 10.00
#2424 Bowl 8" 25.00
#2424 Bowl, Flared 9½" 30.00
#2424 Candlestick 3½" ....pair 30.00
#2424 Candy Jar, Covered 5½"...............30.00
#2424 Cigarette Box, Covered, 2 part 40.00
#2424 Fruit Bowl 11½" 30.00
#2424 Mayonnaise
    Bowl 15.00
    Plate 12.00
    Ladle 20.00
#2424 Plate 12" 15.00
#2424 Sweetmeat 7" 10.00

#2424 Urn, Footed 7½".............................30.00
#2424 Urn, Footed, Flared 6½".................30.00

✦— DEER Cutting —✦

Four Poses: A, B, C, D
1940 – 1944

Each Pose made in following items:

#4132 Decanter, Stopper 50.00
#4132 Ice Bowl...30.00
#4132 Old Fashioned 7½ oz. 10.00

#4132½ Scotch & Soda 9 oz. 10.00
#4132 Tumbler
    5 oz. 10.00
    9 oz. 10.00
    12 oz. 12.00
    14 oz. 15.00
#4132 Whiskey 1½ oz. 15.00

✦— DELPHIAN Plate Etching #272 —✦

Optic Pattern
Blue Stem and Foot
1925 – 1928

Also produced as DUCHESS, Decoration #51
Crystal Bowl, Blue Stem, Coin Gold Trim

*DUCHESS #51, Gold Trim
Do not confuse with DUCHESS Cutting #853.

#4095½ Candy Jar, Covered 95.00
#5082 Champagne, Saucer 5 oz. 25.00
#5082 Champagne, Saucer 5 oz. * 30.00
#5082 Cocktail 3 oz..................................22.00
#5082 Cocktail 3 oz. * 24.00

#5082 Cordial 45.00
#5082 Cordial * 48.00
#4095 Finger Bowl 8.00
#5082 Fruit, Footed 5 oz. 25.00
#5082 Goblet 9 oz. 30.00
#5082 Goblet 9 oz. * 30.00
#4095 Jug 7, Footed................................200.00
#4095 Jug 7, Footed * 225.00
#4095 Nappy
    5" 15.00
    6" 18.00
    7" 20.00
#4095 Nappy, Covered
    5" 30.00
    6" 35.00

⇜ DELPHIAN Plate Etching #272 cont. ⇝

7" 40.00
#5082 Parfait 6 oz. 30.00
#5082 Parfait 6 oz. * 30.00
#2283 Plate
    6" 8.00
    7" 12.00
    8" 18.00
#2283 Plate *
    6" 10.00
    7" 14.00
    8" 20.00
#4095 Oyster Cocktail 18.00
#4095 Oyster Cocktail * 18.00
#5082 Sherbet, Low 20.00
#5082 Sherbet, Low * 22.00
#4095 Tumbler
    2½ oz. 20.00
    5 oz. 10.00
    10 oz. 10.00
    13 oz. 18.00
#4095 Tumbler, Footed *
    2½ oz. 22.00
    5 oz. 15.00
    10 oz. 18.00
    13 oz. 22.00

#5082 Wine 2¾ oz. 34.00
#5082 Wine 2¾ oz. * 36.00
#4095½ Vase 8" 90.00

⇜ DELPHINE Cutting #199 ⇝

Crystal
1931 Only

#5098 Claret 25.00
#5098 Cocktail 20.00
#5098 Cordial 28.00
#5098 Goblet 22.00
#5098 Oyster Cocktail 16.00
#5098 Parfait 22.00
#2283 Plate, Optic 8" 12.00

#5098 Sherbet
    High 20.00
    Low 16.00
#5098 Tumbler, Footed
    2½ oz. 20.00
    5 oz. 15.00
    9 oz. 15.00
    12 oz. 20.00
#5098 Wine 25.00

⇜ DEVON Cutting #876 ⇝

Rock Crystal
Crystal
1960 – 1963

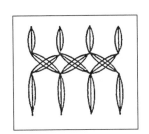 

#6089/31 Brandy 1½ oz. 4¹⁄₁₆" 20.00
#6089/2 Goblet 11½ oz. 6³⁄₁₆" 22.00
#6089/63 Ice Tea, Footed 13 oz. 6³⁄₁₆".......20.00
#6089/88 Juice, Footed 5 oz. 4¾" 16.00
#2337 Plate
    7" 10.00
    8" 10.00
#6089/11 Sherbet 7 oz. 5⁵⁄₁₆" 16.00
#6089/27 Wine/Cocktail 4½ oz. 5¼" 20.00

⇜ DIRECTOIRE Cutting #736 ⇝

Crystal
1934 – 1940

#319 Bar Bottle 15.00
#4013 Bowl, Footed 10" 18.00
#6011 Brandy 1 oz. 22.00
#906 Brandy Inhaler 15.00
#4024 Candlestick 6" ....pair 30.00
#4117 Candy Jar, Covered, Bubble Style ..20.00
#796 Champagne, Hollow Stem 12.00
#6011 Champagne, Saucer 5½ oz. 14.00
#6011 Claret 4½ oz. 18.00
#6011 Cocktail 3 oz. 14.00
#2525 ½ Cocktail Shaker 30 oz. 40.00
#2525 Cocktail Shaker 42 oz. 22.00
#6011 Cordial 1 oz. 22.00
#2400 Comport 6" 20.00
#2350 ½ Cream, Footed 15.00
#6011 Creme de Menthe 2 oz. 16.00
#2525 Decanter 30.00
#6011 Decanter, Footed 70.00
#1769 Finger Bowl 8.00
#6011 Goblet 10 oz. 16.00
#6011 Jug, Footed 50.00
#1185 Old Fashioned Cocktail, Sham..........6.00
#6011 Oyster Cocktail 4 oz. 10.00
#2337 Plate
    6" 6.00
    7" 7.00
    8" 8.00
    11" 12.00
#6011 Rhine Wine 4½ oz. 18.00

#2235 Shaker ....pair 30.00
#6011 Sherbet, Low 5½ oz........................12.00
#6011 Sherry 2 oz. 16.00
#2350 ½ Sugar, Footed............................15.00
#701 Tumbler, Sham
    10 oz. 6.00
    12 oz. 6.00
#6011 Tumbler, Footed
    5 oz. 8.00
    10 oz. 10.00
    13 oz. 12.00
#2518 Whiskey...6.00
#4122 Whiskey, Sham 6.00
#6011 Whiskey, Footed 2 oz. 18.00
#2518 Wine 5 oz. 12.00
#6011 Wine 3 oz. 18.00

DOLLY MADISON Cutting #786

Hand Cut Flutes at Bowl Base
Rock Crystal
Crystal
1939 – 1974

The cut design DOLLY MADISON matches Raleigh Pressed Tableware #2574 and they were sold as companion patterns.

DOLLY MADISON included in Patterns of the Past and Nostalgia Programs

#6023 Bowl, Footed 20.00
#2324/8 Candlestick 6" ....pair 60.00
#6023/8 Champagne/High Sherbet/Dessert
    6 oz. 4⅞".......................................16.00
#6023/27 Claret/Wine 4 oz. 4¾" 20.00
#6023/21 Cocktail 3¾ oz. 4⅜" 13.00
#6023 Comport 5" 18.00
#6023/29 Cordial 1 oz. 3⅜" 27.00
#4132 Decanter & Stopper 50.00
#4185/495 Dessert/Finger Bowl 8.00
#6023/2 Goblet 9 oz. 6⅜".........................22.00
#6011 Jug, Footed 65.00
#6023/88 Juice, Footed 5 oz. 13.00
#6323/63 Luncheon Goblet/Ice Tea
    12 oz. 18.00
#833½ Old Fashioned Cocktail, Sham
    7½ oz..10.00
#6023/33 Oyster Cocktail 4 oz. 3⅝" 10.00
#2666/454 Pitcher, quart.........................65.00
#2574 Plate (not Cut)
    6" 8.00
    7" 11.00
    8" 15.00
#6023/11 Sherbet/Low Dessert/Champagne
    6 oz. 4⅛".......................................12.00
#846 Sherry 2 oz. 6.00
#833½ Tumbler, Sham
    5 oz. 8.00
    8 oz. 8.00
    10 oz. 10.00
    12 oz. 10.00
    14 oz. 12.00
#6023 Water Tumbler, Footed
    5½ oz..12.00
    9 oz. 12.00
    12 oz. 18.00

DOLLY MADISON items included in Patterns of the Past and Nostalgia Programs

D001/008 Champagne/High Dessert
    6 oz. 4⅞"..16.00
D001/011 Champagne/Low Dessert
    6 oz. 4⅛"..14.00
D001/027 Claret/Wine 4 oz. 4¾" 20.00
D001/002 Goblet 9 oz. 6⅜" 19.00
D001/063 Luncheon Goblet/Ice Tea
    12 oz. 5¾"......................................22.00

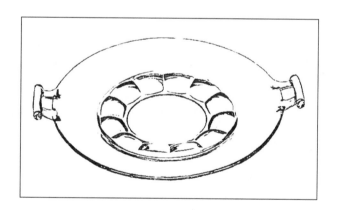

⤞ DONCASTER Cutting #718 ⤝

Rock Crystal
Crystal
1933 – 1944

#2470 ½ Bowl 10½" 30.00
#2470 ½ Candlestick 5½" ....pair 45.00
#6009 Champagne, Saucer 5½ oz. 18.00
#6009 Claret/Wine 3¾ oz. 25.00
#6009 Cocktail 3¾ oz. 18.00
#2400 Comport 6" 22.00
#6009 Cordial 1 oz. 30.00
#869 Finger Bowl 8.00
#6009 Goblet 9 oz. 22.00
#6009 Oyster Cocktail 4¾ oz. 12.00
#2337 Plate
    6" 6.00
    7" 8.00
    8" 10.00
#6009 Sherbet, Low 5½ oz.....................16.00
#2440 Torte Plate 13" 40.00
#6009 Tumbler, Footed
    5 oz. 12.00
    9 oz. 12.00
    12 oz. 18.00
#4112 Vase 8½" 50.00

⤞ DRAPE Cutting #784 ⤝

Rock Crystal
1938 – 1944

#6017 Champagne, Saucer 6 oz. 18.00
#6017 Claret 4 oz. 22.00
#6017 Cocktail 3½ oz. 16.00
#6017 Cordial ¾ oz. 26.00
#766 Finger Bowl 8.00
#6017 Goblet 9 oz. 20.00
#6011 Jug, Footed 70.00
#6017 Oyster Cocktail 4 oz. 10.00
#2337 Plate
    6" 8.00
    7" 8.00
    8" 10.00
#6017 Sherbet, Low 6 oz. 12.00
#6017 Tumbler, Footed
    5 oz. 10.00
    9 oz. 10.00
    12 oz. 15.00
#6017 Wine 3 oz. 20.00

⇒ DRESDEN Decoration #12 ⇐

Black Enamel Band with Floral Cutting
Gold Bands on Bowl and Foot
Crystal
1920

#858 Bass Ale 7 oz. 30.00
#858 Champagne, Saucer 5½ oz. 30.00
#858 Cocktail...30.00
#858 Claret 4½ oz. 30.00
#858 Fruit 30.00

#724 Jug, Handled 175.00
#1743 Jug, Covered 200.00
#858 Goblet 9 oz. 30.00
#858 Parfait 5½ oz. 30.00
#858 Wine 3½ oz. 30.00
#701 Tumbler...25.00
#820 Tumbler...25.00
#127 Tumbler, Handled 30.00
#4061 Tumbler, Handled 30.00

⇒ DRUM Cutting #781 ⇐

Crystal
1938 – 1944

#4139 Decanter 50.00
#4139 Ice Bowl..25.00
#4139 Old Fashioned 6.00
#4139 Tumbler
     5 oz. 4.00
     10 oz. 8.00
     12 oz. 8.00
     14 oz. 8.00
     16 oz. 8.00
#4139 Tumbler, Water 9 oz. 8.00
#4139 Whiskey...6.00

⇒ DUCHESS Plate Etching #272 ⇐

Decoration #51
Blue Base
1925 – 1927

Do not confuse with DUCHESS Cutting #853.

SEE DELPHIAN FOR LISTING AND PRICING

⇒ DUCHESS Cutting #853 ⇐

Rock Crystal
1957 – 1959
  Do not confuse with DUCHESS Etching #272.

#6068 Cocktail/Wine/Seafood
    4¼ oz. 4½" 15.00
#6068 Cordial 1¼ oz. 3" 18.00
#6068 Ice Tea, Footed 13 oz. 5⅞" 15.00
#6068 Juice, Footed 5 oz. 4½" 10.00
#6068 Goblet 10 oz. 5¾" 16.00
#2337 Plate
    7" 8.00
    8" 10.00
#6068 Sherbet 6½ oz. 4⅝" 12.00

⇒ EILEEN Needle Etching #83 ⇐

Optic Pattern
Crystal, Green, Rose, Azure with Crystal Foot
1928 – 1933

Add 15% for Rose and Azure

#5082 Claret 19.00
#5082 Cocktail 17.00
#5098 Comport 5" 16.00
#5082 Cordial 22.00
#869 Finger Bowl 10.00
#2283 Finger Bowl Plate 8.00
#5082 Goblet 20.00
#5082½ Grapefruit 25.00
#945½ Grapefruit Liner 25.00
#4095 Jug, Footed 100.00
#5298 Nappy 6" 10.00
#4295 Oyster Cocktail 16.00
#5082 Parfait 18.00
#2283 Plate
    7" 8.00
    8" 10.00
#5082 Sherbet
    Low 16.00

    High 14.00
#4095 Tumbler, Footed
    10 oz. 10.00
    13 oz. 10.00
#4295 Tumbler, Footed
    2½ oz. 8.00
    5 oz. 8.00
    9 oz. 10.00
#5082 Wine 18.00

⋙ ELSINORE Double Needle Etching #89 ⋘

Crystal
1934 – 1940

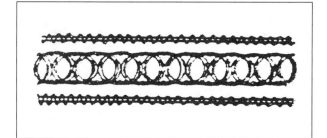

#4024 Champagne, Saucer 6 oz. 18.00
#4024 Claret 3½ oz. 18.00
#4024 Comport 5" 20.00
#4024 Cordial 1 oz. 20.00
#869 Finger Bowl 8.00
#4024 Goblet 10 oz. 18.00
#4024½ Goblet 11 oz. 18.00
#1184 Old Fashioned Cocktail, Sham 7 oz...6.00
#4024 Oyster Cocktail 4 oz. 12.00
#4024 Rhine Wine 3½ oz. 16.00
#4024 Sherbet 5½ oz. 15.00
#4024 Sherry 2 oz. 14.00
#701 Tumbler, Sham 10 oz. 6.00
#4024 Tumbler, Footed

5 oz. 12.00
8 oz. 12.00
12 oz. 18.00
3887 Whiskey, Sham 1¾ oz. 6.00
#4122 Whiskey, Sham 1½ oz. 6.00
#4024 Whiskey, Footed 2 oz. 20.00

⋙ EMBASSY Cutting #728 ⋘

Crystal
1933 – 1938

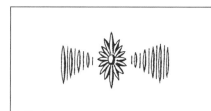

#4024 Bowl, Footed 10" 40.00
#4024 Candlestick 6" ....pair 30.00
#4024 Champagne, Saucer 6½ oz. 20.00
#4024 Cocktail 4 oz. 18.00
#4024 Comport 5" 15.00
#4024 Cordial 1 oz. 21.00
#6011 Decanter, Footed 70.00
#869 Finger Bowl 8.00
#4024 Goblet 10 oz. 20.00
#4024½ Goblet 11 oz. 20.00
#6011 Jug, Footed 50.00
#1184 Old Fashioned Cocktail, Sham or Plain
   7 oz. 6.00
#4024 Oyster Cocktail 4 oz. 12.00
#2337 Plate

   6" 6.00
   7" 8.00
   8" 10.00
   11" 15.00
#4024 Rhine Wine 3½ oz. 22.00
#4024 Sherbet 5½ oz. 18.00
#4024 Sherry 2 oz. 20.00
#701 Tumbler, Sham or Plain
   10 oz. 6.00
   12 oz. 6.00
#4024 Tumbler, Footed

5 oz. 12.00
8 oz. 12.00
12 oz. 20.00
#887 Whiskey 1¾ oz. 6.00
#4024 Wine 3½ oz. 22.00

⊸⇒ EMBRACE Cutting #887 ⇐⊷

Polished Cutting
Crystal
1961 – 1965

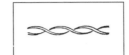

#6099/27 Cocktail/Wine 4½ oz. 20.00
#6099/29 Cordial 1 oz. 22.00
#6099/2 Goblet 11 oz. 20.00
#6099/88 Juice, Footed 5½ oz. 16.00
#6099/63 Luncheon Goblet/Ice Tea
    14 oz. 18.00
#2337 Plate
    7" 10.00
    8" 10.00
#6099/11 Sherbet 6½ oz. 16.00

⊸⇒ EMPIRE Deep Plate Etching #238 ⇐⊷

Optic Pattern
Crystal
1915 – 1928
  Do not confuse with EMPIRE Cutting #908.

#863 Almond 6.00
#858 Champagne, Saucer 5½ oz. 8.00
#803 Comport
    5" 10.00
    6" 10.00
#1480 Cream 8.00
#858 Custard 7 oz. 7.00
#858 Fruit 7.00
#858 Finger Bowl 7.00
#858 Finger Bowl Plate............................4.00
#858 Goblet
    9 oz. 8.00
    10 oz. 10.00
#945½ Grapefruit......................................9.00
#945½ Grapefruit Liner 7.00
#858 Ice Tea 14 oz....................................10.00
#4061 Ice Tea, Handled, Footed 12.00
#300 Jug 7 ....32.00
#303 Jug 7 ....32.00
#318 Jug 7 ....32.00
#1968 Marmalade, Covered 18.00
#1831 Mustard, Covered 15.00
#803 Nappy, Footed
    5" 7.00
    6" 7.00
    7" 8.00

#1227 Nappy
    4½ oz...7.00
    8 oz. 10.00
#300½ Oil, Small 25.00
#1465 Oil, Cut Neck 7 oz.........................35.00
#822 Parfait 8.00
#1848 Plate, Sandwich 9" 10.00
#840 Sherbet 8.00
#840 Sherbet Plate 5" 4.00
#1480 Sugar 8.00
#858 Sweetmeat......................................10.00
#820 Tumbler, Table 6.00
#858 Tumbler, Table 6.00
    5 oz. 4.00
    8 oz. 5.00
    10 oz. 7.00
    12 oz. 8.00
    14 oz. 10.00
#701 Tumbler 14 oz. 10.00
#833 Tumbler 8 oz. 8.00

⊶ EMPIRE Cutting #908 ⊷

Rock Crystal
Crystal
1966 – 1969
   Do not confuse with EMPIRE Etching #238.

#6106/25 Claret 8 oz. 23.00
#4185/495 Dessert/Finger Bowl 12.00
#6106/2 Goblet 12 oz. 25.00
#6106/29 Liqueur 2 oz. 28.00
#6106 Luncheon Goblet/Ice Tea 14 oz.......24.00
#2337 Plate
   7" 10.00
   8" 10.00
#6106/11 Sherbet 9 oz. 23.00
#6016 Tulip Wine 6½ oz. 23.00

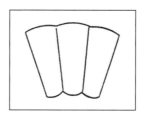

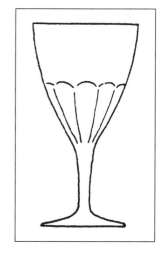

⊶ EMPRESS Cutting #861 ⊷

Crystal
1858 – 1970

#6079/27 Claret/Wine 4 oz. 20.00
#6079/29 Cordial 1 oz. 25.00
#6079/20 Cocktail 3½ oz. 16.00
#6079/2 Goblet 11 oz. 25.00
#6079/88 Juice, Footed 5½ oz. 14.00
#6079/63 Luncheon Goblet/Ice Tea
   13½ oz...20.00
#2337 Plate
   7" 8.00
   8" 8.00
#6079/11 Sherbet 6½ oz. 16.00

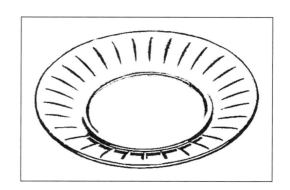

⊶ ENAMEL AND GOLD Decoration #21 ⊷

Gold and Enamel Floral Design, Gold Band on
   Rim and Foot
Crystal
1920

#858 Champagne, Saucer..........................30.00
#858 Fruit 30.00
#858 Goblet 9 oz. 30.00
#701 Tumbler..30.00
#820 Tumbler..30.00

⤐ ENCORE Cutting #860 ⤏

Rock Crystal
Crystal
1958 – 1961

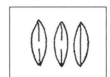

#6077/20 Cocktail/Wine 4 oz. 4¼"...........18.00
#6077 Cordial 1 oz. 3" 20.00
#6077/2 Goblet 10½ oz. 5⅝" 18.00
#6077/63 Ice Tea, Footed 13 oz. 5⅝" 18.00
#6077/88 Juice, Footed 5½ oz. 4⅜" 12.00
#2337 Plate
    7" 10.00
    8" 10.00
#6077/11 Sherbet 7 oz. 4¼"....................14.00

⤐ ENGRAVED #23 ⤏

Blown Ware
Crystal
Turn of the Century

#923 Champagne, Saucer 7.00
#801 Cocktail 3 oz...................................7.00
#952 Cocktail 3 oz...................................7.00
#801 Cordial ¾ oz. 7.00
#1227 Cream 10.00
#1478 Cream 10.00
#480 Custard...6.00
#481 Custard...6.00
#1136 Decanter, Cut Stopper 14.00
#315 Finger Bowl 10.00
Various Jugs which may include: 1, 2, 3, 3½, 4,
    5, 6, 7, ...each 60.00
#300 Jug, Claret 70.00
#801 Goblet 9 oz. 8.00
#801 Liquor ¾ oz......................................8.00
#300½ Oil, Cut Stopper, Large 25.00
#840 Sherbet 8.00
#846 Sherry 8.00
#801 Various Stems which may include:
    1 oz., 2 oz., 3 oz., 4 oz., 5 oz., 9 oz.,
    10 oz. ....each 6.00
#1227 Sugar, Covered 15.00
#1478 Sugar 15.00
#724 Tankard 6 ....10.00
#300 Tankard 7 ....10.00
#820 Tumbler 10 oz. 8.00
#833 Tumbler, Sham
    7 oz. 8.00
    8 oz. 8.00

    10 oz. 8.00
#887 Tumbler 3 oz. 6.00
#889 Tumbler 5 oz. 6.00
#160½ Water Bottle, Cut Neck, Cut Star
    Bottom 60.00
#845 Whiskey, Hot...................................8.00
#847 Wine 8.00

Blown Ware
Crystal
1910 – 1928

#863 Almond, Individual 6.00
#793 Champagne, Hollow Stem 8.00
#863 Champagne, Hollow Stem 8.00
#863 Champagne, Saucer 5½ oz. 7.00
#863 Champagne, Tall 5½ oz.....................7.00
#932 Champagne, Saucer 7.00
#300 Claret.. 7.00
#858 Claret
    4½ oz. 7.00
    6½ oz. 7.00
#863 Claret 4½ oz. 7.00
#863 Cocktail 3½ oz. 7.00
#863 Cordial 1 oz. 10.00
#803 Comport
    5" 8.00
    6" 8.00
#1478 Cream 8.00
#1480 Cream 8.00
#863 Creme de Menthe 2½ oz. 7.00
#481 Custard...5.00
#1241 Custard...5.00
#1598 Custard...5.00
#858 Custard...5.00
#858 Custard Plate 4.00
#300 Decanter, Cut Neck, quart 30.00
#1464 Decanter, Cut Neck, Cut Foot
    10 oz. 30.00
    18 oz. 40.00
#1491 Decanter, Cut Neck, Optic 25 oz. 40.00
#853 Finger Bowl 7.00
#853 Finger Bowl Plate............................4.00
#823 Fruit
    4½ " 6.00
    5" 7.00
#863 Fruit 6.00
#863 Goblet
    7 oz. 7.00
    9 oz. 7.00
    10½ oz. 7.00
#1132 Horseradish..................................18.00
#303 Jug
    6...30.00
    7...35.00
#317 Jug 7...32.00
#1227 Jug
    6...32.00
    7...32.00
#803 Nappy, Footed, Deep

    4½ oz...6.00
    5 oz..6.00
    6 oz..8.00
    7 oz..8.00
#315 Nappy
    4½ oz...5.00
    8 oz..12.00
#803 Nappy, Footed, Shallow
    4½ oz...6.00
    5 oz..6.00
    6 oz..8.00
    7 oz..10.00
#300½ Oil, Cut Stopper
    Small 25.00
    Large 30.00
#1465 Oil, Cut Stopper, Cut Neck.............35.00
#5039 Oyster Cocktail 7.00
#5039 Oyster Cocktail Liner 5.00
#863 Pousse-Cafe ¾ oz. 10.00
#863 Rhine Wine 4½ oz...........................7.00
#1165 Shaker, Silver-Plated Top..............12.00
#846 Sherry 7.00
#810 Sherbet 7.00
#840 Sherbet 7.00
#840 Sherbet Plate.................................4.00
#863 Sherry 2 oz.....................................7.00
#1478 Sugar 8.00
#1480 Sugar 8.00
#300 Tankard
    1..16.00
    2..20.00
    3..25.00
    5..30.00
    7..35.00
#724 Tankard

6...25.00
7...35.00
#858 Tumbler, Table Cut #19
    3½ oz. 7.00
    5 oz. 7.00
    6½ oz. 7.00
    8 oz. 7.00
    10 oz. 7.00
    12 oz. 8.00
    14 oz. 8.00
    16 oz. 8.00
#820 Tumbler 7.00

#820 ½ Tumbler, Sham....................7.00
#833 Tumbler
    7 oz. 7.00
    8 oz. 7.00
#833 Tumbler, Sham
    7 oz. 7.00
    8 oz. 7.00
#887 Tumbler 3 oz. 7.00
#889 Tumbler 5 oz. 7.00
#1558 Water Bottle, Cut Neck....................45.00
#863 Wine 3 oz. 8.00

⊷⊷ **ETCHING #212** ⊷⊷

Blown Ware
Crystal
1910 – 1929

#863 Almond, Individual 6.00
#793 Champagne, High Stem, Cut Foot 7.00
#825 Champagne, Saucer 7.00
#863 Champagne, Saucer 5½ oz. 7.00
#863 Champagne, High Stem, Cut Foot 7.00
#863 Champagne, Tall 5½ oz. 7.00
#932 Champagne, Saucer 7.00
#1686 Cheese and Cover 9" 35.00
#863 Claret 4½ oz. 7.00
#863 Cocktail 3½ oz. 7.00
#952 Cocktail..7.00
#803 Comport
    5" 8.00
    6" 8.00
#863 Cordial 1 oz. 10.00
#1478 Cream 8.00
#1480 Cream 8.00
#1759 Cream 8.00
#863 Creme de Menthe 2½ oz. 7.00
#480 Custard..5.00
#480 Custard Plate 4.00
#481 Custard..5.00
#858 Custard..5.00
#858 Custard Plate 4.00
#1598 Custard.......................................5.00
#300 Decanter, Cut Neck, quart 32.00
#1464 Decanter, Cut Neck, 18 oz..............38.00
#315 Finger Bowl 7.00
#315 Finger Bowl Plate............................4.00
#858 Finger Bowl 7.00

#858 Finger Bowl Plate.............................4.00
#1349 Finger Bowl 7.00
#823 Fruit
    4½"...5.00
    5" 5.00
#863 Fruit 4.00
#5013 Gin Rickey...................................7.00
#863 Goblet
    7 oz. 7.00
    9 oz. 7.00
    10 oz. 7.00
#1132 Horseradish................................18.00
#303 Jug 7...32.00
#318 Jug 7 Optic 35.00
#1236 Jug 6...30.00
#1743 Jug and Cover 5 ....35.00
#945 Grapefruit and Footed Liner.............15.00
#1733 Marmalade, Covered 16.00
#1831 Mustard, Covered 14.00

#315 Nappy
    4" 3.00
    4½" 4.00
    5" 4.00
    8" 10.00

#803 Nappy, Footed, Deep
    4½" 6.00
    5" 6.00
    6" 6.00
    7" 10.00

#803 Nappy, Footed, Shallow
    4½" 6.00
    5" 6.00
    6" 6.00
    7" 10.00

#1227 Nappy
    4½" 6.00
    8" 12.00

#300½ Oil, Cut Stopper
    Small 28.00
    Large 32.00

#312 Oil, Cut Stopper 35.00
#1465 Oil, Cut Stopper, Cut Neck.............35.00
#858 Oyster Cocktail 7.00
#5054 Parfait 7.00
#932 Plate 8.00
#863 Pousse-Cafe......................................10.00
#1227 Punch Bowl and Foot.....................85.00
#863 Rhine Wine 4½ oz. 7.00
#1719 Sandwich Plate 8.00
#840 Sherbet 7.00
#840 Sherbet Plate...................................4.00
#5036 Sherbet 7.00
#846 Sherry 2 oz. 7.00
#1478 Sugar 8.00
#1480 Sugar 8.00
#1759 Sugar 8.00

#858 Sweetmeat.......................................10.00
#1518 Syrup 8 oz. 35.00
#300 Tankard
    2...25.00
    7...35.00
    7 Cut Flute 38.00

#724 Tankard
    6...26.00
    7...30.00

#858 Tumbler, Table 7.00
#701 Tumbler 7.00
#701 Tumbler, Plate 4.00
#820 Tumbler 7.00
#820 Tumbler, Sham 7.00
#833 Tumbler, Sham
    6 oz. 7.00
    7 oz. 7.00
    8 oz. 7.00
    10 oz. 7.00

#858 Tumbler Cut #19
    3½ oz. 7.00
    5 oz. 7.00
    6½ oz. 7.00
    8 oz. 7.00
    10 oz. 7.00
    12 oz. 7.00
    14 oz. 10.00
    16 oz. 10.00

#858 Tumbler Plate 4.00
#885 Tumbler 2½ oz. 7.00
#887 Tumbler 3 oz. 7.00
#889 Tumbler 5 oz. 7.00
#837 Tumbler 9 oz. 7.00
#1462 Tumbler 7.00
#1558 Water Bottle, Cut Neck..................30.00
#863 Wine 3 oz. 7.00

Blown Ware
Crystal
1910 – 1928

#863 Almond, Individual 6.00
#793 Champagne, Hollow Stem, Cut Foot....8.00
#794 Champagne, Hollow Stem, Cut Foot....8.00
#863 Champagne, Saucer 5½ oz. 7.00
#863 Champagne, Tall 5½ oz. 8.00
#863 Champagne, Hollow Stem, Cut Foot....8.00
#932 Champagne, Saucer 7.00
#863 Claret 4½ oz. 7.00
#863 Cocktail 3½ oz. 7.00
#803 Comport, Footed
    5" 8.00
    6" 8.00
#863 Cordial 1 oz. 10.00
#1478 Cream 8.00
#1759 Cream 8.00
#863 Creme de Menthe 2½ oz. 7.00
#480 Custard 5.00
#481 Custard 5.00
#481 Custard Plate 4.00
#858 Custard 5.00
#858 Custard Plate 4.00
#300 Decanter, Cut Neck, quart 30.00
#1464 Decanter, Cut Neck, 18 oz. 35.00
#315 Finger Bowl 7.00
#315 Finger Bowl Plate............................4.00
#858 Finger Bowl 7.00
#858 Finger Bowl Plate............................4.00
#1499 Finger Bowl 7.00
#1499 Finger Bowl Plate..........................4.00
#823 Fruit
    4½" 6.00
    5" 6.00
#863 Fruit 7.00
#825 Goblet 9 oz. 7.00
#863 Goblet
    7 oz. 7.00
    9 oz. 7.00
    10½ oz. 7.00
#945 Grapefruit 8.00
#945½ Grapefruit and Footed Liner 15.00
#1132 Horseradish................................18.00
#303 Jug 7 ....32.00
#1111 Jug, Optic 35.00
#403 Mustard, Covered 20.00
#803 Nappy, Footed, Deep
    4½" 5.00
    5" 5.00
    6" 6.00

    7" 7.00
    8" 10.00
#803 Nappy, Footed, Shallow
    4½" 5.00
    5" 5.00
    6" 6.00
    7" 7.00
    8" 10.00
#1227 Nappy
    4½" 5.00
    8" 12.00
#312 Oil, Cut Stopper............................30.00
#1465 Oil, Cut Stopper, Cut Neck.............35.00
#932 Plate 7.00
#863 Pousse-Cafe ¾ oz. 10.00
#863 Rhine Wine 4½ oz. 7.00
#1165 Shaker, Silver-Plated Top................10.00
#840 Sherbet 7.00
#840 Sherbet Plate.................................4.00
#846 Sherry 7.00
#863 Sherry 2 oz. 7.00
#1478 Sugar 8.00
#1759 Sugar 8.00
#300 Tankard
    6...30.00
    7...35.00
#724 Tankard 7 ....32.00
#858 Tumbler, Table, Cut #19 ....7.00
#820 Tumbler 7.00

#820½ Tumbler, Sham 7.00
#833 Tumbler, Sham
    5 oz. 7.00
    7 oz. 7.00
    8 oz. 7.00
    9 oz. 7.00
#858 Tumbler Cut #19
    3½ oz. 7.00
    5 oz. 7.00
    6½ oz. 7.00
    8 oz. 7.00
    10 oz. 7.00
    12 oz. 8.00
    14 oz. 8.00

    16 oz. 8.00
#885 Tumbler
    2 oz. 7.00
    3 oz. 7.00
#887 Tumbler
    2 oz. 7.00
    3 oz. 7.00
#889 Tumbler
    5 oz. 7.00
    8 oz. 7.00
#858 Tumbler Plate 4.00
#160½ Water Bottle, Cut Neck 30.00
#1558 Water Bottle, Cut Neck...............32.00
#863 Wine 3 oz. 7.00

⇜ ETCHING #215 ⇝

Blown Ware
Crystal
1910 – 1928

#863 Almond 6.00
#858 Brandy 1 oz. 10.00
#858 Champagne, Hollow Stem 10.00
#825 Champagne, Saucer 8.00
#858 Champagne, Saucer 7 oz. 8.00
#858 Champagne, Tall 5½ oz. 12.00
#858 Champagne, Long Stem 12.00
#932 Champagne, Saucer 8.00
#858 Claret
    4½ oz. 8.00
    6½ oz. 8.00
#858 Cocktail 3½ oz. 8.00
#803 Comport
    5" 10.00
    6" 10.00
#858 Cordial 1 oz. 10.00
#1478 Cream, Cut Star Bottom 8.00
#1480 Cream 8.00
#1759 Cream 8.00
#858 Creme de Menthe 2½ oz. 10.00
#480 Custard 7.00
#480 Custard Plate 4.00
#481 Custard 7.00
#858 Custard 7.00
#858 Custard Plate 4.00
#300 Decanter, Cut Neck, quart 40.00
#1464 Decanter, Cut Neck 18 oz. 35.00
#315 Finger Bowl 7.00

#315 Finger Bowl Plate...............4.00
#858 Finger Bowl 7.00
#858 Finger Bowl Plate...............4.00
#1499 Finger Bowl 7.00
#1499 Finger Bowl Plate 4.00
#823 Fruit
    4½" 5.00
    5" 6.00
#963 Fruit
#963 Fruit Plate 4.00
#858 Fruit Salad 10.00
#858 Goblet
    9 oz. 8.00
    10 oz. 8.00

11 oz. 10.00
#945 Grapefruit 10.00
#945½ Grapefruit with Footed Liner 18.00
#945½ Grapefruit Plate...............................4.00
#1132 Horseradish, Stopper and Spoon 18.00
#303 Jug 7 ....35.00
#1111 Jug Optic 6 ....38.00
#1733 Marmalade and Cover 18.00
#1831 Mustard and Cover 16.00
#803 Nappy, Footed, Deep

    5 oz. 5.00
    5½ oz. 5.00
    6 oz. 7.00
    7 oz. 9.00

#803 Nappy, Footed, Shallow

    5 oz. 5.00
    5½ oz. 5.00
    6 oz. 7.00
    7 oz. 9.00

#1227 Nappy

    4½ oz. 5.00
    8 oz. 9.00

#312 Oil 25.00
#1465 Oil, Cut Neck, Cut Stopper 35.00
#5036 Parfait 8.00
#5054 Parfait 8.00
#932 Plate 5.00
#1165 Shaker.......................................12.00
#840 Sherbet 8.00
#840 Sherbet Plate..................................4.00
#858 Sherbet 8.00
#846 Sherry 8.00
#858 Sherry 2 oz. 10.00
#1478 Sugar 2-handled, Cut Star

    Bottom 10.00

#1480 Sugar 8.00
#1759 Sugar 8.00
#858 Sweetmeat....................................10.00
#300 Tankard

    6...28.00
    7...30.00

#724 Tankard 7 ....30.00
#858 Tumbler, Table 6.00
#701 Tumbler 14 oz. 8.00
#701 Tumbler Plate 4.00
#820 Tumbler 5.00
#820½ Tumbler, Sham 8.00
#833 Tumbler

    7 oz. 6.00
    8 oz. 6.00

#858 Tumbler

    3½ oz. 5.00
    5 oz. 5.00
    6½ oz. 6.00
    8 oz. 6.00
    10 oz. 8.00
    12 oz. 8.00
    14 oz. 8.00

#858 Tumbler Plate 6.00
#887 Tumbler 3 oz. 5.00
#889 Tumbler 5 oz. 6.00
#892 Tumbler 13 oz. 8.00
#1462 Tumbler..6.00
#160½ Water Bottle, Cut Neck 28.00
#1558 Water Bottle, Cut Neck.................30.00
#858 Whiskey, Hot 4 oz. ....8 .00
#858 Wine

    2¾ oz. 8.00
    3½ oz. 8.00

⇥ ETON Cutting #713 ⇤

Rock Crystal
Crystal
1933 – 1939

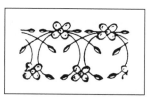

#2470 Bon Bon 12.00
#2470½ Bowl 10½" 30.00
#2481 Bowl, Oblong 11" 40.00
#2470 Cake Plate 35.00
#2430 Candy Dish, Covered ½ lb. 20.00
#2470½ Candlestick 5½" ....pair 45.00
#2472 Candlestick, Duo ....pair 60.00
#2482 Candlestick, Trindle....................75.00
#6007 Claret 4 oz. 23.00
#6007 Cocktail 3½ oz. 16.00
#2400 Comport 6" 20.00
#6007 Cordial 1 oz. 26.00
#2440 Cream, Footed 15.00
#869 Finger Bowl 8.00
#2283 Finger Bowl Plate 6.00
#6007 Goblet 10 oz. 18.00
#2451 Ice Dish 15.00
#2451 Ice Dish Plate..............................10.00
#2470 Lemon Dish 15.00
#6007 Oyster Cocktail 4½ oz. 12.00
#2283 Plate
   7" 8.00
   8" 10.00
#2419 Relish, 4 part.............................30.00

#6007 Sherbet
   High 5½ oz.....................................16.00
   Low 5½ oz. 10.00
#2440 Sugar, Footed 16.00
#2470 Sweetmeat 10.00
#2440 Torte Plate 13"............................40.00
#6007 Tumbler, Footed
   2 oz. 18.00
   5 oz. 10.00
   9 oz. 10.00
   12 oz. 16.00
#2440 Vase 7" 50.00
#6007 Wine 3 oz. 22.00

⇥ EVANGELINE Engraving #752 ⇤

Crystal
1935 – 1939

#2470½ Bowl 10½" 30.00
#2440 Cake Plate 20.00
#2472 Candlestick, Duo ....pair 40.00
#2482 Candlestick, Trindle ....pair 50.00
#2440 Celery Tray 16.00
#2440 Mayonnaise, 2 part 18.00
#2440 Pickle Dish 14.00
#2364 Plate 16" 30.00
#2419 Relish
   4 part 22.00
   5 part 28.00
#2440 Relish
   2 part 18.00
   3 part 24.00

#2514 Relish, 5 part................................35.00
#2440 Sauce Dish, Oval 6½" 18.00
#2440 Torte Plate 13" 35.00
#2440 Tray, Oval 8½"..............................18.00
#2470 Vase 10" 22.00
#2467 Vase 7½" 55.00

⊷ EVENING BREEZE Cutting #891 ⊶

Polished Cutting
Rock Crystal
Crystal
1962 – 1965

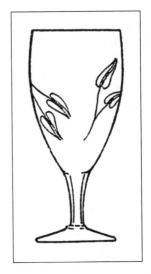

#6100/31 Brandy 1½ oz. 20.00
#6100/25 Claret 7½ oz. 20.00
#4185/495 Dessert/Finger Bowl 12.00
#6100/2 Goblet 11 oz. 22.00
#6100/63 Luncheon Goblet/Ice Tea, Footed
    14½ oz. 20.00
#2337 Plate
    7" 10.00
    8" 10.00
#6100/11 Sherbet 7½ oz. 18.00
#6100/26 Tulip Wine 5½ oz. 20.00

⊷ EVENING STAR Cutting #869 ⊶

Gray Cutting
Crystal
1959 – 1966

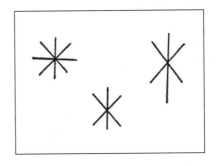

#6087/27 Cocktail/Wine 3¼ oz. 5¼" 25.00
#6087/29 Cordial 1¼ oz. 3½" 26.00
#4185/495 Dessert/Finger Bowl 10.00
#6087/2 Goblet 8¼ oz. 7".......................24.00
#6087/88 Juice, Footed 5 oz. 5" 16.00
#6087/63 Luncheon Goblet/Ice Tea
    11 oz. 6⅜"..22.00
#2337 Plate
    7" 10.00
    8" 10.00
#6087/11 Sherbet 6½ oz. 5⁷⁄₁₆" 16.00

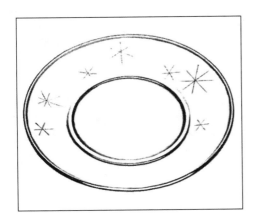

1922 – 1929
Do not confuse with FAIRFAX Pattern #2375.

#880 Bon Bon, Footed 14.00
#1697 Carafe 20.00
#4023 Carafe Tumbler 10.00
#2219 Candy Jar, Covered
    ¼ oz..40.00
    ½ lb..50.00
    1 lb..60.00
#863 Champagne, Saucer 5½ oz. 8.00
#863 Cocktail 3½ oz. 18.00
#803 Comport 5" 15.00
#803 Comport, Covered 5" 24.00
#803 Comport 6" 18.00
#1712½ Cream..12.00
#1769 Finger Bowl 6.00
#863 Fruit, Footed 5½ oz.........................8.00
#863 Goblet 9 oz. 10.00
#701 Ice Tea 12 oz....................................10.00
#4011 Ice Tea, Handled 12 oz. 18.00
#825 Jelly 12.00
#825 Jelly, Covered 18.00
#303 Jug 7..30.00
#2040 Jug 3...30.00
#2030 Jug 7, Covered..............................50.00
#2082 Jug 7 ....35.00
#1968 Marmalade, Covered 24.00
#2138 Mayonnaise
    Bowl...18.00
    Plate...12.00
    Ladle 20.00
#803 Nappy
    5" 10.00
    6" 10.00
    7" 14.00
#803 Nappy, Covered 5" 20.00
#300½ Oil, Small 50.00
#837 Oyster Cocktail 7.00
#661 Parfait 5½ oz. 8.00
#863 Parfait...8.00

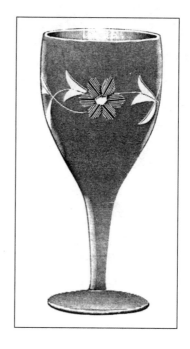

#2238 Plate, Salad 7.00
#840 Plate, Sherbet 6.00
#1736 Plate 6" 8.00
#880 Salt Dip, Footed..............................15.00
#2263 Salt, Individual 10.00
#2236 Shaker, Glass Top..................pair 80.00
#1712 Sugar 20.00
#1712 Sugar, Covered 30.00
#2194 Syrup, Nickel Plate Top
    8 oz. 30.00
    12 oz. 40.00
#820 Tumbler, Table 7.00
#4011½ Tumbler, Table 7.00
#701 Tumbler
    5 oz. 8.00
    14 oz. 10.00
#4011 Tumbler 12 oz. 10.00
#4069 Vase 9" 80.00
#863 Wine 3 oz. 8.00

⟨⚬═ FANTASY Crystal Print #17 ═⚬⟩

Crystal
1959 – 1965
Do not confuse with FANTASY Cutting #747.

#6086/27 Cocktail/Wine 5½ oz. 20.00
#6086/29 Cordial 1¼ oz. 23.00
#6086/2 Goblet 11¾ oz. 20.00
#6086/63 Ice Tea, Footed 13 oz. 18.00
#6086/88 Juice, Footed 5½ oz. 12.00
#2337 Plate
    7" 10.00
    8" 10.00
#6086/11 Sherbet 7½ oz. 18.00

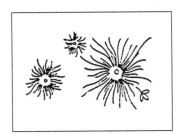

⟨⚬═ FANTASY Cutting #747 ═⚬⟩

Optic
Rock Crystal
Crystal
1935 – 1938
Do not confuse with FANTASY Crystal Print #17.

#2533 Bowl, Handled 9" 30.00
#2533 Candlestick, Duo ....pair 40.00
#6013 Champagne, Saucer 6 oz. 18.00
#6013 Claret 4 oz. 28.00
#6013 Cocktail 3½ oz. 18.00
#6013 Comport 5" 15.00
#6013 Cordial 1 oz. 30.00
#766 Finger Bowl (not Optic) 12.00
#6013 Goblet
    High 10 oz. 23.00
    Low 9 oz. 21.00
#5000 Jug, Footed 100.00
#1184 Old Fashioned Cocktail 7 oz.
    (not Optic) 10.00
#6013 Oyster Cocktail 4 oz. 15.00
#2337 Plate
    6" 8.00
    7" 10.00

    8" 12.00
#6013 Sherbet, Low 5 oz. 15.00
#701 Tumbler, Sham (not Optic)
    10 oz. 10.00
    12 oz. 10.00
#6013 Tumbler, Footed
    5 oz. 8.00
    13 oz. 12.00
#6013 Wine 3 oz. 27.00

FEDERAL Cutting #771

Crystal
1937 – 1944

#2430 Bowl 11"	30.00
#2496 Bowl, Handled 10½"	30.00
#2430 Candlestick 2"	pair 30.00
#2496 Candlestick 5½"	pair 50.00
#6019 Cocktail 3½ oz.	14.00
#4132 Decanter, with Stopper	60.00
#766 Finger Bowl	8.00
#6019 Goblet 10 oz.	18.00
#4132 Ice Bowl	25.00
#2430 Jelly 7"	18.00
#2430 Mint Dish 5½"	15.00
#4132 Old Fashioned Cocktail, Sham 7½ oz.	6.00
#6019 Oyster Cocktail 4¾ oz.	6.00
#6019 Parfait 6 oz.	15.00
#2337 Plate	
6"	8.00
7"	8.00
8"	10.00
#6019 Sherbet 6½ oz.	15.00
#4132 Tumbler, Sham	
5 oz.	7.00
9 oz.	8.00
12 oz.	8.00
14 oz.	10.00
#6019 Tumbler, Footed	
5 oz.	8.00
12 oz.	15.00
#4132 Whiskey, Sham 1½ oz.	6.00
#6019 Wine 3 oz.	18.00

FERN Plate Etching #305

Solid Crystal, Amber, Green, Rose, Crystal Bowl with Square Ebony Base, Rose Bowl with Crystal Base, Ebony with Gold Edge (Fern Design, Decoration #305)
1928 – 1934
Amber, Green 1931 – 1932; Crystal Bowl with Square Ebony Base 1929 – 1934; Ebony with Gold Edge (Decoration #305) 1929 – 1934; Rose 1928 – 1933

FERN items made in Amber, Crystal, Rose, Green

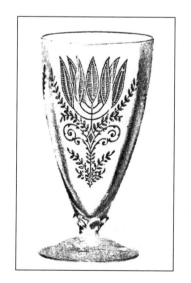

#2375 Bon Bon	18.00
#2297 Bowl 12"	50.00
#2395 Bowl 10"	45.00
#2375 Cake Plate 10"	22.00
#2324 Candlestick 4"	pair 40.00
#2395½ Candlestick 5"	pair 45.00
#5098 Claret	20.00
#4120 Cocktail 3 oz.	20.00
#5098 Cocktail	20.00
#2400 Comport 6"	35.00
#5098 Cordial	34.00

#2350 Cup, After Dinner 12.00
#2350½ Cup, Footed 8.00
#869 Finger Bowl 6.00
#4121 Finger Bowl 14.00
#4120 Goblet 25.00
#5098 Goblet 23.00
#5082½ Grapefruit 25.00
#945½ Grapefruit Liner 15.00
#5000 Jug 7, Footed.............................150.00
#2375 Lemon Dish 30.00
#5098 Oyster Cocktail 12.00
#5098 Parfait 24.00
#2283 Plate, Optic 6" 8.00
#2419 Plate, Square
    6" 10.00
    7" 12.00
    8" 20.00
#2419 Saucer......................................8.00
#2419 Saucer, After Dinner 8.00
#4120 Sherbet
    High 7 oz. 25.00
    Low 7 oz. 18.00
#5098 Sherbet
    High 22.00
    Low 17.00
#4120 Tumbler
    5 oz. 20.00
    10 oz. 18.00
    13 oz. 24.00
    17 oz. 24.00
#5098 Tumbler, Footed
    2½ oz. 23.00
    5 oz. 16.00
    9 oz. 15.00
    12 oz. 24.00
#4105 Vase, Optic 8" 60.00
#4120 Whiskey 2 oz. 18.00
#5098 Wine 20.00

FERN items made with Colored Bowls, Crystal Base

#5298 Claret 38.00
#5298 Cocktail...................................30.00
#5298 Cordial 50.00
#5298 Goblet 32.00
#5298½ Grapefruit 35.00
#5298 Oyster Cocktail 18.00
#5298 Parfait 30.00
#5298 Sherbet
    High 28.00

    Low 22.00
#5298 Tumbler, Footed
    2½ oz.......................................32.00
    5 oz.......................................20.00
    9 oz.......................................22.00
    12 oz.......................................30.00

FERN items made with Crystal Bowl, Square Ebony Base

#4020 Cocktail 3½ oz. 20.00
#4020½ Cocktail 4 oz. 20.00
#4020 Cream 12.00
#4020 Cream, Footed 15.00
#4120 Cream 18.00
#4121 Finger Bowl 10.00
#4020 Goblet 25.00
#4020 Jug, Footed 120.00
#4120 Jug, Footed 130.00
#2419 Plate 9"...................................24.00
#4020 Sherbet
    High 7 oz. 24.00
    Low 7 oz. 18.00
#4020 Sugar 15.00
#4020 Sugar, Footed 18.00
#4120 Sugar 16.00
#4020 Tumbler
    5 oz. 20.00
    10 oz. 18.00
    13 oz. 24.00
    16 oz. 24.00
#4020 Whiskey 2 oz. 18.00

FERN items made with Decoration #305, Ebony with Gold Edge

#2375 Bon Bon 32.00
#2297 Bowl 12" 65.00
#2395 Bowl 10" 50.00
#2415 Bowl, Combination 40.00
#2375 Cake Plate 10" 30.00
#2324 Candlestick 4" ....pair 50.00
#2395½ Candlestick 5" ....pair 60.00
#2427 Cigarette Box, Covered.....................50.00
#2400 Comport 6" 40.00
#2375 Lemon Dish 35.00
#2373 Vase, Window Large 65.00
#2485 Vase, Fan 8½" 110.00
#2409 Vase 7½" 80.00
#4105 Vase 8" 60.00

⤛ FESTIVAL Plate Etching #45 ⤜

Crystal
1981 – 1982

FE04/011 Champagne/Dessert 9 oz. 5" 20.00
FE04/002 Goblet 12 oz. 7⅜" 20.00
FE04/063 Luncheon Goblet/Ice Tea
    14 oz. 7" 20.00
FE04/025 Wine 9 oz. 6⅝" 20.00

⤛ FESTOON Cutting #738 ⤜

Cutting #738
Rock Crystal
Crystal
1934 – 1940

#319 Bar Bottle 15.00
#4024 Bowl, Footed 10" 40.00
#6012 Brandy 1 oz. 24.00
#4024 Candlestick 6" ....pair 30.00
#4117 Candy Jar, Covered, Bubble Style ..30.00
#863 Champagne, Hollow Stem 15.00
#6012 Champagne, Saucer 5½ oz. 16.00
#6012 Claret 4½ oz. 22.00
#6012 Cocktail 3 oz. 16.00
#2525 Cocktail Shaker 42 oz. 40.00
#2525 Cocktail Shaker 30 oz. 40.00
#2400 Comport 6" 20.00
#6012 Cordial 1 oz. 26.00
#2350½ Cream, Footed..............................15.00
#6012 Creme de Menthe 2 oz. 16.00
#2525 Decanter 25.00
#6011 Decanter, Footed 70.00
#1769 Finger Bowl 8.00
#6012 Goblet 10 oz. 20.00
#6011 Jug, Footed 50.00
#1185 Old Fashioned Cocktail, Sham..........6.00
#6012 Oyster Cocktail 4 oz. 14.00
#2337 Plate
    6" 6.00
    7" 7.00
    8" 8.00
#2364 Plate 16" 40.00
#2440 Plate 13" 35.00
#6012 Rhine Wine 4½ oz. 22.00
#6012 Sherbet, Low 5½ oz. 14.00
#6012 Sherry 2 oz. 16.00
#2350½ Sugar, Footed 15.00

#701 Tumbler, Sham
    10 oz. 6.00
    12 oz. 6.00
#6012 Tumbler, Footed
    5 oz. 12.00
    10 oz. 10.00
    13 oz. 16.00
#2470 Vase 10" 55.00
#4122 Whiskey, Sham 1½ oz. 6.00
#6012 Wine 3 oz. 22.00

⟞ 114 FIFTH AVENUE Needle Etching #32 and #46 ⟝

Crystal
Turn of the Century – 1929
  Items found with both etchings

#114 Champagne 6 oz. 8.00
#114 Claret 3¾ oz. 8.00
#114 Cordial 1 oz. 8.00
#114 Goblet 10 oz. 8.00
#114 Wine 3 oz. 8.00

⟞ FIRENZE Decoration #502 – Etching #218 ⟝

Topaz with Gold Edge
1931 – 1932

See VERONA #281 for design and additional
  items

#2375 Bon Bon 30.00
#2394 Bowl 12" 60.00
#2395 Bowl 10" 55.00
#2375 Cake Plate 10" 30.00
#2394 Candlestick 2" ....pair 42.00

#2395½ Candlestick 5" ....pair 60.00
#2375 Cheese, Footed 22.00
#2375 Cheese and Cracker........................30.00
#2427 Cigarette Box, Covered....................80.00
#2400 Comport 6" 45.00
#2375 Ice Bucket 75.00
#2375 Lemon Dish 20.00
#2375 Tray, Handled, Lunch 50.00
#2417 Vase 8" 100.00
#4105 Vase 8" 90.00

⟞ FIRST LOVE Cutting #918 ⟝

Rock Crystal
Crystal
1968 – 1970

#6111/25 Claret 7½ oz. 26.00
#6111/29 Cordial 2 oz. 26.00
#4185/495 Dessert/Finger Bowl 12.00
#6111/2 Goblet 12 oz. 28.00
#6111/63 Luncheon Goblet/Ice Tea
    15 oz. 26.00
#2337 Plate
    7" 10.00
    8" 10.00
#6111/11 Sherbet 9 oz. 25.00
#6111/26 Wine 7 oz. 26.00

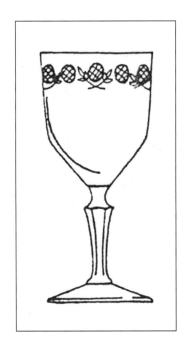

⊰⊱ FLEMISH Plate Etching #319 ⊰⊱

Crystal
1933 – 1939

#2440 Bon Bon, Handled 5" 10.00
#2440 Cake Plate, Oval 10½" 20.00
#4099 Candy Jar, Covered ½ lb. 22.00
#2440 Cream, Footed 12.00
#2440 Lemon Dish, Handled 5" 9.00
#2440 Mayonnaise, 2 part 6½" 18.00
#2440 Relish, Handled
    2 part 16.00
    3 part 20.00
#2440 Sauce Dish, Oval 6½" 16.00
#2440 Sugar, Footed 12.00
#2440 Sweetmeat, Handled 4½" 10.00
#2440 Tray, Oval 8½" 18.00
#2470 Tray for Sugar and Cream 14.00

⊰⊱ FLEURETTE Crystal Print #26 ⊰⊱

Crystal
1972 – 1974

#6102/2 Goblet 10 oz. 23.00
#6102/63 Luncheon Goblet/Ice Tea
    14 oz. 23.00
#2337/549 Plate 7" 10.00
#6102/11 Sherbet/Dessert/Champagne
    8 oz. 23.00
#6102/26 Tulip Wine 5½ oz. 23.00

⊰⊱ FLORENTINE Plate Etching #311 ⊰⊱

Crystal
Crystal Bowl, Topaz Base 1931 – 1938; Crystal Bowl, Gold Tint Base 1938 – 1942
1931 – 1944
FLORENTINE items made in Crystal, Gold Tint, Topaz; add 10% for Topaz, Gold Tint, or combinations.

***Not made in Topaz**

#2470 Bon Bon 18.00
#2470 Bowl 12" 40.00
#2470½ Bowl 10½" 35.00

#2470 Cake Plate 10" 30.00

#2470 Candlestick 5½" ....pair 60.00
#2470½ Candlestick 5½" ....pair 60.00
#2470 Comport
 Tall 6"..30.00
 Low 6" 20.00
#2440 Cream, Footed 14.00
#2440 Cup 10.00
#2470 Lemon Dish 24.00
#2440 Plate
 6" 8.00
 7" 12.00
 8" 18.00
 9" 24.00
#2470 Relish, Round, 3 part....................30.00
#2470 Relish, Oval, 4 part 32.00
#2440 Saucer 7.00
#2370 Service Dish 65.00
#2440 Sugar, Footed 20.00
#2470 Sweetmeat.....................................18.00
#2440 Torte Plate 13".............................40.00
#2470 Tray/Sugar and Cream 40.00

FLORENTINE items made in Solid Crystal, Gold Tint or Topaz with Crystal Base

#6005 Champagne, Saucer/High Sherbet
 5½ oz...18.00
#6005 Claret 5 oz. 26.00
#6005 Cocktail 4 oz.................................16.00
#6005 Cordial 1 oz. 28.00
#869 Finger Bowl (Crystal only) 14.00
#6005 Goblet 9 oz. 24.00
#6005 Oyster Cocktail 6 oz. 10.00

#6005 Parfait 6 oz. 22.00
#6005 Sherbet, Low 7 oz. 15.00
#2440 Torte Plate 13" (Crystal only) 40.00
#6005 Tumbler *
 2½ oz...18.00
 5 oz. 10.00
 9 oz. 10.00
 12 oz. 20.00
#6005 Tumbler, Footed
 2½ oz...20.00
 5 oz. 12.00
 9 oz. 12.00
 12 oz. 22.00
#6005 Wine 3 oz. 26.00

FLORID Deep Etching #256

Optic Pattern
Crystal
1920 – 1928

#880 Bon Bon 4½" 8.00
#896 Candy Bowl, Covered......................22.00
#2219 Candy Jar, Covered
 ¼ lb. 15.00
 ½ lb. 20.00
 1 lb. 22.00
#1697 Carafe 22.00
#1697 Carafe Tumbler 6 oz. 6.00
#858 Champagne, Saucer 5½ oz. 8.00

#858 Cocktail 3½ oz. 8.00
#803 Comport
 5" 10.00
 6" 10.00
#1478 Cream 8.00
#858 Fruit, Footed 5½ oz.........................7.00
#858 Finger Bowl 7.00
#858 Finger Bowl Plate 6".........................5.00
#858 Goblet 9 oz. 8.00
#845 Grapefruit 8.00
#945½ Grapefruit Liner 7.00
#4057 Grapefruit Liner.............................7.00

⊷ FLORID Deep Etching #256 cont. ⊶

#766 Ice Tea, Footed, Handled 10.00
#300 Jug 7...35.00
#303 Jug 7...35.00
#318 Jug 7...35.00
#317½ Jug, Covered 40.00
#1968 Marmalade, Covered 15.00
#2138 Mayonnaise
    Bowl 10.00
    Plate 7.00
    Ladle 20.00
#1831 Mustard, Covered 15.00
#803 Nappy
    5" 7.00
    6" 8.00
    7" 10.00
#1227 Nappy
    4½" 5.00
    8" 10.00
#1465 Oil, Cut Neck, Cut Stopper
    5 oz. 30.00

    7 oz. 35.00
#858 Oyster Cocktail 8.00
#805 Parfait 8.00
#1897 Plate, Salad 7" 7.00
#2238 Plate
    8¼" 8.00
    11" 10.00
#1719 Plate, Sandwich 10½" 10.00
#1848 Plate, Sandwich 9"..........................8.00
#2083 Salad Dressing Bottle 25.00
#2099 Sandwich Bowl, Covered 20.00
#2022 Shaker, Glass Top 12.00
#2023 Shaker, Glass Top 12.00
#858 Sherbet
    Low 8.00
    High 8.00
#858 Sherry 2 oz. 10.00
#1478 Sugar 8.00
#858 Sweetmeat.......................................10.00
#2094 Syrup, Nickel Top
    8 oz. 45.00
    12 oz. 50.00
#820 Tumbler, Table 6.00
#858 Tumbler, Table
    5 oz. 6.00
    8 oz. 7.00
    9 oz. 7.00
    12 oz. 8.00
    14 oz. 10.00
#701 Tumbler 14 oz. 10.00
#701 Tumbler Plate 5" 4.00
#833 Tumbler 8 oz. 8.00
#833 Tumbler, Sham, Punty 8 oz.................7.00
#4011 Tumbler, Handled 12 oz. 10.00
#766 Wine 2¾ oz. 8.00

⊷ FLOWER GIRL Decoration #659 ⊶

Gold Band with Polished Cutting
Crystal
1962 – 1967

FLOWER GIRL with silver band is BRIDES-
    MAID

#6100/31 Brandy 1½ oz. 24.00
#6100/25 Claret 7½ oz. 26.00
#4185/495 Dessert/Finger Bowl 10.00
#6100/2 Goblet 11 oz. 26.00
#6100/63 Goblet/Ice Tea 14½ oz. 24.00

#2337 Plate
    7" 10.00
    8" 10.00
#6100/11 Sherbet 7½ oz. 23.00
#6100/26 Tulip Wine 5½ oz. 26.00

❦ FLOWER SONG Cutting #894 ❦

Rock Crystal
Crystal
1962 – 1966

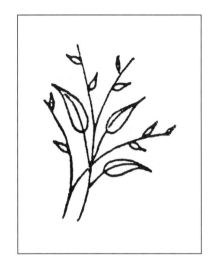

#6101/27 Cocktail/Wine 5 oz. 24.00
#6101/29 Cordial 1½ oz. 26.00
#4185/495 Dessert/Finger Bowl 12.00
#6101/2 Goblet 10 oz. 26.00
#6101/88 Juice, Footed 6 oz. 22.00
#6101/63 Luncheon Goblet/Ice Tea
  14 oz. 24.00
#2337 Plate
  7" 10.00
  8" 10.00
#6l01/11 Sherbet 7 oz. 23.00

❦ FOREVER Cutting #904 ❦

Gray Cutting
Crystal
1964 – 1965

#6103/31 Brandy 4½ oz. 20.00
#6103/25 Claret 7½ oz. 22.00
#6103/2 Goblet 12 oz. 23.00

#6103/63 Goblet/Ice Tea 14 oz. 21.00
#2337 Plate
  7" 10.00
  8" 10.00
#6103/11 Sherbet 8 oz. 20.00
#6103/26 Tulip Wine 7 oz. 22.00

❦ FORMAL Cutting #700 ❦

Square Base
Crystal, Crystal Bowl with Ebony Base
1930 – 1931

*Solid Crystal Only

#4020 Cocktail 3½ oz.*.............................18.00
#4120 Cocktail 3½ oz. 18.00
#2350½ Cup, Footed 8.00
#2350 Cup, After Dinner 10.00
#4121 Finger Bowl 8.00
#4020 Goblet* 24.00
#4120 Goblet 24.00
#2419 Plate, Square
  6" 8.00
  7" 10.00
  8" 12.00

☞ FORMAL Cutting #700 cont. ☜

#2419 Saucer..8.00	10 oz. 18.00
#2419 Saucer, After Dinner 6.00	13 oz. 24.00
#4020 Sherbet*	16 oz. 24.00
5 oz. 18.00	#4120 Tumbler, Footed
7 oz. 18.00	5 oz. 18.00
#4120 Sherbet	10 oz. 18.00
5 oz. 18.00	13 oz. 24.00
7 oz. 18.00	16 oz. 24.00
#4020 Tumbler, Footed*	#4020 Whiskey 2 oz.* 18.00
5 oz. 18.00	#4120 Whiskey 2 oz. 18.00

☞ FORMALITY Cutting #818 ☜

Crystal
1942 – 1952

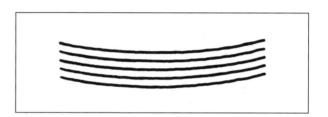

#2596 Bowl, Oblong, Shallow 11"..............35.00	
#1596 Candlestick 5" ....pair 50.00	
#6032 Champagne, Saucer 6 oz. 20.00	
#6032 Claret 4½ oz. 23.00	
#6032 Cocktail 3½ oz. 15.00	
#6032 Cordial 1 oz. 27.00	
#766 Finger Bowl 12.00	
#6032 Goblet 9 oz. 22.00	8" 12.00
#6011 Jug, Footed 100.00	#6032 Sherbet, Low 6 oz. 16.00
#6032 Oyster Cocktail 4 oz. 13.00	#6032 Tumbler, Footed
#2337 Plate	5 oz. 13.00
6" 8.00	13 oz. 18.00
7" 10.00	#6032 Wine 3½ oz. 25.00

☞ FOUNTAIN Plate Etching #307 ☜

Solid Crystal, Crystal Bowl with Green Foot
1929 – 1931
   Do not confuse with FOUNTAIN Cutting
   #901.

#4020 Cocktail 3½ oz. 18.00
#4120 Cocktail 3½ oz. 20.00
#4120 Cream 20.00
#2350 Cream Soup...................................30.00
#2350½ Cup, Footed 20.00
#2350 Cup, After Dinner 30.00
#4021 Finger Bowl 20.00
#4121 Finger Bowl 20.00

FOUNTAIN Plate Etching #307 cont.

#4020 Goblet 20.00
#4120 Goblet 24.00
#4120 Jug 400.00
#2350 Plate
    6" 12.00
    7" 15.00
    8" 20.00
#2419 Plate
    6" 12.00
    7" 15.00
    8" 22.00
#2350 Saucer...10.00
#2419 Saucer, After Dinner 15.00
#2350 Saucer, After Dinner 15.00
#4020 Sherbet
    High 20.00
    Low 5 oz. 18.00
    Low 7 oz. 18.00

#4121 Sherbet
    High 24.00
    Low 5 oz. 20.00
    Low 7 oz. 20.00
#4120 Sugar 35.00
#4020 Tumbler, Footed
    5 oz. 18.00
    10 oz. 18.00
    13 oz. 20.00
    16 oz. 20.00
#4120 Tumbler, Footed
    5 oz. 20.00
    10 oz. 20.00
    13 oz. 24.00
    15 oz. 24.00
#4020 Whiskey 2 oz. 16.00
#4120 Whiskey 2 oz. 18.00

FOUNTAIN Cutting #901

Gray Cutting
Crystal
1964 – 1965

#6103/31 Brandy 4½ oz. 20.00
#6103/25 Claret 7½ oz. 22.00
#6103/2 Goblet 12 oz. 22.00
#6103/63 Luncheon Goblet/Ice Tea
    14 oz. 22.00
#2337 Plate
    7" 10.00
    8" 10.00
#6103/11 Sherbet 8 oz. 18.00
#6103/26 Tulip Wine 7 oz. 22.00

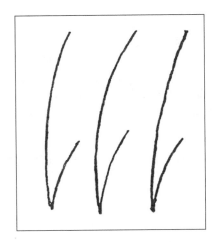

FOSTORIA WHEAT Cutting #837

Combination Rock Crystal and Gray Cutting
Crystal
1953 – 1973
Do not confuse with WHEAT Cutting #760.
   Late stems in this line were renumbered
   #6051½.
FOSTORIA WHEAT included in Patterns of
   the Past and Nostalgia Programs

#2666/136 Bon Bon 6⅞" 18.00
#2666/189 Bowl, Oval 8¼".......................22.00
#2666/300 Butter, Covered, Oblong 7"......30.00
#2666/311 Candlestick (Flora Candle) 6" ..16.00
#6051/27 Claret/Wine 4 oz. 4½" 24.00
#6051/20 Cocktail 3¼ oz. 3⅞" 18.00
#6051/29 Cordial 1¼ oz. 3⅛" 28.00

#2666/680 Cream 3½" 15.00
#2666/688 Cream, Individual 12.00
#2666/396 Cup 10.00
#4185/495 Dessert/Finger Bowl 10.00
#6051/2 Goblet 10½ oz. 6³⁄₁₆" 22.00
#6051/88 Juice, Footed 5 oz. 4" 15.00
#6051/60 Luncheon Goblet/Ice Tea
    12¼ oz. 6⅛" 20.00
#2666/477 Mayonnaise
    Bowl...15.00
    Plate...12.00
    Ladle 20.00
#6051/33 Oyster Cocktail 4¼ oz. 3¾".......14.00
#2666/454 Pitcher, quart........................40.00
#2337 Plate
    7" 7.00
    8" 8.00
#2666/620 Relish, 2 part 7⅜" 30.00
#2666/622 Relish, 3 part 10¾" 35.00
#2666/238 Salad Bowl 10½" 60.00
#2666/630 Salver, Footed 12¼" 70.00
#2666/397 Saucer 8.00
#2666/568 Serving Plate 14" 40.00
#2364/654 Shaker, Chrome Top
    Large ....pair 20.00
#6051/7 Sherbet/Dessert/Champagne
    6½ oz. 4⅜" 18.00
#2666/729 Snack Plate, Curved Handle
    10" 40.00
#2666/677 Sugar 2⅝" 15.00
#2666/687 Sugar, Individual 12.00

FOSTORIA WHEAT items included in Patterns of the Past and Nostalgia Programs

FO01/007 Champagne/Dessert
    6½ oz. 4⅜" 18.00
FO01/027 Claret/Wine 4 oz. 4½" 24.00
FO01/002 Goblet 10½ oz. 6¼" 20.00
FO01/060 Luncheon Goblet/Ice Tea
    12¼ oz. 6⅛" 20.00

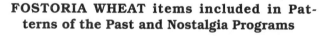

⟜⟞ **FRESNO Needle Etching #78** ⟜⟞

Crystal
1925 – 1931

#867½ Champagne, Saucer 5½ oz. 10.00
#867½ Cocktail 8.00
#866½ Fruit, Footed 5" 12 oz.....................8.00
#867½ Goblet 9 oz...................................10.00
#701 Jug 7...80.00
#701 Tumbler 13 oz. 8.00
#820 Tumbler 8.00
#4095 Tumbler, Footed 10 oz. 10.00

⁂ FRUIT Plate Etching #320 ⁂

1933 – 1939

#2440 Bon Bon, Handled 5" 10.00
#2440 Cake Plate, Oval 10½" 25.00
#4099 Candy Jar, Covered 22.00
#2440 Cream, Footed 14.00
#2440 Lemon Dish, Handled 5" 12.00
#2440 Mayonnaise, 2 part 6½" 20.00
#2449½ Plate, Crescent Salad...................18.00
#2337 Plate 8" 18.00
#2419 Relish, Handled 5 part 35.00
#2440 Relish, Handled
     2 part 18.00
     3 part 24.00
#2440 Sauce Dish, Oval 6½" 15.00
#2440 Sugar, Footed 15.00
#2440 Sweetmeat, Handled 4½" 12.00
#2440 Torte Plate 13" 35.00
#2440 Tray, Oval 8½" 15.00
#2470 Tray, Cream & Sugar.....................10.00

⁂ FUCHSIA Plate Etching #310 ⁂

Crystal 1931 – 1944
Crystal Bowl with Wisteria Base 1933 – 1935
1931 – 1944

***WISTERIA items; double values for Wisteria
  items.**

#2470 Bon Bon 18.00
#2395 Bowl 10" 40.00
#2470 Bowl 12"*......................................55.00
#2440½ Bowl 10½" 40.00
#2470½ Bowl 10½" 45.00
#2470 Cake Plate 10" 30.00
#2375 Candlestick 3" ....pair 50.00
#2395½ Candlestick 5" ....pair 60.00
#2470 Candlestick 5½"* ....pair 60.00
#2470½ Candlestick 5½" ....pair 60.00
#6004 Champagne, Saucer/High Sherbet
     5½ oz.* 18.00
#6004 Claret 4 oz.*..................................30.00
#6004 Cocktail 3 oz.* 20.00
#6004 Cordial ¾ oz.* 48.00
#2470 Comport
     Tall 6"* 30.00
     Low 6"* 20.00
#2440 Cream, Footed 14.00

FUCHSIA Plate Etching #310 cont.

#2440 Cup 10.00
#869 Finger Bowl 8.00
#6004 Goblet 9 oz. 24.00
#2470 Lemon Dish 24.00
#6004 Oyster Cocktail 4½ oz.* 15.00
#6004 Parfait 5½ oz.* 25.00
#2440 Plate
   6" 8.00
   7" 12.00
   8" 18.00
   9" 26.00
#2440 Saucer....................................7.00
#6004 Sherbet, Low 5½ oz.* 15.00

#2440 Sugar, Footed 20.00
#2470 Sweetmeat 20.00
#833 Tumbler
   2 oz. 10.00
   5 oz. 8.00
   8 oz. 8.00
   12 oz. 12.00
#6004 Tumbler, Footed
   2½ oz.* 28.00
   5 oz.* 16.00
   9 oz.* 14.00
   12 oz. 22.00
#6004 Wine 2½ oz.* 30.00

GADROON Cutting #816

Gray Cutting
Crystal
1941 – 1957

#6023 Bowl, Footed 9" 30.00
#6023 Candlestick, Duo ....pair 50.00
#6030 Champagne/High Sherbet
   6 oz. 5⅝"...............................18.00
#6030 Claret/Wine 3½ oz. 6" 25.00
#6030 Cocktail 3½ oz. 5¼" 12.00
#6030 Cordial 1 oz. 3⅞" 30.00
#769 Finger Bowl 13.00
#6030 Goblet 10 oz. 7⅞" 22.00
#6030 Goblet, Low 10 oz. 6⅜"..................20.00
#6030 Ice Tea, Footed 12 oz. 6" 20.00
#6011 Jug, Footed 100.00
#6030 Juice, Footed 5 oz. 4⅝" 12.00
#6030 Oyster Cocktail 4 oz. 3¾" 10.00
#2337 Plate
   7" 8.00
   8" 12.00
#6030 Sherbet, Low 6 oz. 13.00

GARLAND Deep Plate Etching #237

Crystal
1915 – 1928
Do not confuse with GARLAND, Cutting #859.

#863 Almond 6.00
#5051 Almond Small 1¾" high 6.00
#5051 Almond Large 3½" high 6.00
#1918 Bar Bottle, Cut Neck 30.00
#1918 Bitters Bottle with Tube Cut Neck ..30.00
#880 Bon Bon 4½" 7.00
#899 Cafe Parfait 6¾".........................8.00
#2219 Candy Jar and Cover
  ¼ lb. 20.00
  ½ lb. 22.00
  1 lb. 28.00
#1697 Carafe 20.00
#1697 Carafe Tumbler 6 oz. 7.00
#1697 Carafe Whiskey 2½ oz. 7.00
#825 Champagne, Saucer 7.00
#863 Champagne, Hollow Stem 7.00
#880 Champagne, Hollow Stem 4½ oz. 7.00
#863 Champagne, Saucer 5½ oz. 7.00
#880 Champagne, Saucer 5 oz. 7.00
#932 Champagne, Saucer 7.00
#863 Champagne, Tall 5 oz. 8.00
#863 Champagne, Tall 5½ oz....................8.00
#932 Champagne Plate..........................4.00
#1918 Cherry Jar, Cut Neck 28.00
#863 Claret 4½ oz. 7.00
#880 Claret 4½ oz. 7.00
#963 Cocktail 3½ oz. 7.00
#880 Cocktail 3½ oz. 7.00
#952 Cocktail...............................7.00
#766 Comport
  5" 8.00
  6" 8.00
#803 Comport
  5" 8.00
  6" 8.00
#803 Comport, Footed, Covered 20.00
#863 Cordial ¾ oz. 10.00
#880 Cordial 1 oz. 10.00
#863 Creme de Menthe 2½ oz. ..8.00
#880 Creme de Menthe 2½ oz. ..8.00
#1478 Cream 6 oz. 8.00
#1480 Cream 8.00
#481 Custard...............................5.00
#481 Custard Plate 4.00
#300 Decanter, Cut Neck, quart 35.00
#1918 Decanter, Cut Neck 30.00
#1769 Finger Bowl 7.00

#1769 Finger Bowl Plate..........................4.00
#863 Fruit 5½ oz. 6.00
#863 Goblet
  9 oz. 7.00
  10½ oz. 7.00
#880 Goblet 10 oz. 7.00
#880 Grapefruit 8.00
#880 Grapefruit Liner..........................7.00
#880½ Grapefruit and Liner 15.00
#880½ Grapefruit Liner 7.00
#979 Horseradish...........................18.00
#763 Ice Tea, Footed, Handled 10.00
#1401 Ice Tea 14 oz. 8.00
#1401 Ice Tea, Handled 14 oz. 10.00
#4061 Ice Tea, Footed, Handled 10.00
#1225 Jelly, Covered 18.00
#300 Jug 7...............................30.00
#300 Jug, Cut Flute 35.00
#303 Jug 7...............................30.00
#317½ Jug, Covered 40.00
#318 Jug 7...............................30.00
#724 Jug 30.00
#1236 Jug
  6...................................30.00
  7...................................30.00
#1761 Jug, Claret...........................40.00
#2018 Jug, Cut Neck 33.00
#2104 Jug and Tumbler, Punty 40.00
#1461 Lemonade, Handled 10.00
#2138 Mayonnaise
  Bowl...............................15.00
  Plate...............................6.00

149

Ladle 20.00
#1968 Marmalade, Covered 20.00
#2017 Molasses Can, Metal Handle 38.00
#1831 Mustard, Covered 18.00
#766 Nappy, Footed
    5" 8.00
    6" 9.00
    7" 10.00
#803 Nappy, Footed
    4½" 8.00
    5" 8.00
    6" 9.00
    7" 10.00
#803 Nappy, Footed, Covered 16.00
#1227 Nappy
    4½ oz. 6.00
    8 oz. 10.00
#1465 Oil, Small 25.00
#1465 Oil, Cut Neck
    5 oz. 30.00
    7 oz. 35.00
#1897 Plate 7" 7.00
#2238 Plate
    8¼" 8.00
    11" 12.00
#1719 Plate, Sandwich 10.00
#1848 Plate, Sandwich 9" 10.00
#863 Pousse-Cafe ¾ oz. 7.00
#880 Pousse-Cafe 1 oz. 7.00
#1227 Punch Bowl and Foot.....................55.00
#863 Rhine Wine 4 oz. 8.00
#880 Rhine Wine 4 oz. 8.00
#2083 Salad Dressing Bottle 50.00
#2169 Salad Dressing Bottle 50.00
#880 Salt, Footed 12.00
#1165½ Shaker, Pearl Top....................30.00 pr.
#1165 Shaker, Silver-Plated Top ....20.00 pr.
#2022 Shaker, F. Glass Top....................40.00 pr.
#2223 Shaker, F. Glass Top....................40.00 pr.
#840 Sherbet 6.00
#863 Sherbet 6.00
#880 Sherbet 5½ oz....................................6.00
#840 Sherbet Plate 6.00
#820 Sherry 2 oz. 8.00
#863 Sherry 2 oz. 8.00
#880 Sherry 2 oz. 8.00
#1478 Sugar, 2-handled 8 oz......................85.00
#1480 Sugar 8.00
#2017 Sugar Duster...............................18.00
#2194 Syrup, Nickel Top
    8 oz. 35.00
    12 oz. 35.00

#300 Tankard 7 ....30.00
#724 Tankard 7 ....30.00
#1761 Tankard, Claret 40.00
#1787 Tankard 6 ....30.00
#922 Toothpick 18.00
#4011½ Tumbler, Table 7.00
#701 Tumbler
    8 oz. 7.00
    14 oz. 8.00
#701 Tumbler, Handled 14 oz. 10.00
#820 Tumbler 7.00
#820½ Tumbler, Cut #19 ....7.00
#833 Tumbler 8 oz. 7.00
#833 Tumbler, Sham 7.00
#870 Tumbler, Sham, Punty 2½ oz. 7.00
#887 Tumbler, Whiskey 3 oz. 7.00
#889 Tumbler 5 oz. 7.00
#4011 Tumbler
    3 oz. 7.00
    5 oz. 7.00
    8 oz. 7.00
    12 oz. 8.00
    15 oz. 10.00
#4011 Tumbler, Handled 12 oz. 10.00
#4065 Tumbler Cut #19
    8 oz. 7.00
    14 oz. 10.00
#4077 Tumbler
    9½ oz. 7.00
    15 oz. 10.00
#160½ Water Bottle, Cut Neck 30.00
#863 Wine 3 oz. 7.00
#880 Wine 2¾ oz. 7.00

══ GARLAND Cutting #859 ══

Combination Gray and Rock Crystal Cutting
Crystal
1958 – 1959
  Do not confuse with GARLAND #237.

#6077/20 Cocktail/Wine 4 oz. 4¼"............18.00
#6077/29 Cordial 1 oz. 3" 18.00
#6077/2 Goblet 10½ oz. 5⅝" 18.00
#6077/88 Juice 5½ oz. 4⅜" 14.00
#6077/63 Luncheon Goblet/Ice Tea
    13 oz. 5⅝" 18.00
#2337 Plate
    7" 10.00
    8" 10.00
#6077/11 Sherbet 7 oz. 4¼" 16.00

══ GARTER Needle Etching #44 ══

Optic
Crystal
1898 – 1928

#863 Almond, Footed 1¾"............................6.00
#880 Bon Bon, Footed 5½" 10.00
#805 Champagne, Saucer 5 oz. 8.00
#805 Claret 4½ oz. 7.00
#805 Cocktail...7.00
#805 Cordial 10.00
#803 Comport
    5" 12.00
    6" 15.00
#1478 Cream 4" 12.00
#766 Finger Bowl 2" 8.00
#768 Finger Bowl Plate.................................6.00
#805 Goblet 9 oz. 8.00
#300 Jug 7 ....40.00
#303 Jug 7 ....50.00
#318 Jug 7 ....60.00
#1236 Jug 6 ....70.00
#803 Nappy, Footed
    5" 6.00
    6" 7.00
    7" 8.00
#300½ Oil, Small 10.00
#837 Oyster Cocktail 3¼" 8.00
#805 Sherbet 6 oz. 6.00
#805 Sherry 2 oz. 7.00
#1478 Sugar 3⅛" 14.00

#858 Sweetmeat...10.00
#820 Tumbler, Table 6.00
#858 Table Tumbler
    3 oz. 6.00
    5 oz. 6.00
    8 oz. 6.00
    12 oz. 8.00
    14 oz. 8.00
#701 Tumbler 14 oz. 10.00
#833 Tumbler 8 oz. 8.00
#833 Tumbler, Sham 8 oz. 8.00
#889 Tumbler 5 oz. 6.00
#4011 Tumbler, Handled 12 oz. 12.00
#701 Tumbler Plate 5" 6.00
#805 Wine 2¾ oz. 8.00

GENEVA Cutting #135

Crystal
1918 – 1926

#880 Bon Bon 4½" 10.00
#863 Champagne, Saucer 5½ oz. 7.00
#880 Champagne, Saucer 5½ oz. 7.00
#880 Cocktail 3 oz. 7.00
#803 Comport
    5" 10.00
    6" 10.00
#2133 Cream 12.00
#481 Custard 5½ oz. 6.00
#1769 Finger Bowl 7.00
#1769 Finger Bowl Plate 4.00
#863 Fruit Footed 5½ oz. 8.00
#863 Goblet 9 oz. 7.00
#880 Goblet 9 oz. 7.00
#4061 Ice Tea, Footed, Handled 10.00
#303 Jug 7...45.00
#724 Jug 7...45.00
#1968 Marmalade, Covered 18.00
#2138 Mayonnaise
    Bowl 20.00
    Plate 10.00
    Ladle 20.00
#1831 Mustard, Covered 18.00
#1227 Nappy
    4½ oz. 6.00
    8 oz. 15.00
#803 Nappy, Footed
    5" 10.00
    6" 10.00

    7" 12.00
#1465 Oil, Cut Neck 7 oz.........................38.00
#822 Parfait 6 oz.......................................7.00
#1848 Plate, Sandwich 9".......................12.00
#880 Salt Dip, Footed..............................14.00
#2022 Shaker, Glass Top 12.00
#880 Sherbet 5½ oz..................................7.00
#2133 Sugar, 2-handled 12.00
#922 Toothpick, Punty 15.00
#820 Tumbler, Table 7.00
#4011½ Tumbler, Table 7.00
#791 Tumbler 14 oz. 10.00
#4011 Tumbler 12 oz. 7.00
#833 Tumbler, Sham, Punty.....................7.00
#701 Tumbler Plate 5" 4.00
#4069 Vase 9" 28.00

GEORGETOWN Cutting #906

Rock Crystal
Crystal
1965 – 1973

#6105/25 Claret 7 oz. 25.00
#6105/29 Cordial 1½ oz. 28.00
#6105/2 Goblet 11 oz. 25.00
#6105/63 Luncheon Goblet/Ice Tea
    13½ oz..24.00
#2337 Plate
    7" 10.00
    8" 10.00
#6105/11 Sherbet/Dessert/Champagne
    9 oz. 22.00
#6105/26 Wine 6 oz. 23.00

❧ GEORGIAN Cutting #791 ❧

Rock Crystal
Crystal
Cut Flutes at Base of Bowl
1939 – 1944
  Do not confuse with GEORGIAN Cutting #885.

#6023 Bowl, Footed 20.00
#6025 Claret/Wine 4 oz............................20.00
#6025 Cocktail 3½ oz. 14.00
#6025 Cordial 1 oz. 25.00
#1769 Finger Bowl 8.00
#6025 Goblet 18.00
#6011 Jug, Footed 50.00
#6025 Oyster Cocktail 4 oz. 10.00
#2574 Plate, not Cut
    6" 6.00
    7" 8.00
    8" 10.00

#6025 Sherbet 6 oz. 14.00
#6025 Tumbler, Footed
    5 oz. 12.00
    9 oz. 10.00
    12 oz. 16.00

❧ GEORGIAN Cutting #885 ❧

Rock Crystal
Crystal
Hand Cut Flutes on Base of Bowl
1961 – 1982
  Do not confuse with GEORGIAN Cutting #791.

#6097/27 Cocktail/Wine 3½ oz. 22.00
#6097/29 Cordial...................................25.00
#833½ Double Old Fashioned Cocktail
    13 oz. 20.00
#6097/2 Goblet 10 oz. 22.00
#833½ Highball 14 oz. 20.00
#6097/63 Ice Tea, Footed 12 oz................20.00
#6097/88 Juice, Footed 5 oz. 16.00
#2574 Plate
    7" (not Cut)...............................8.00
    8" (not Cut)...............................8.00
#6097/11 Sherbet 7 oz. 16.00

GLENDALE Cutting #919

Rock Crystal
Crystal
1967 – 1972

#4185/495 Dessert/Finger Bowl 10.00
#6110/2 Goblet 11 oz. 25.00
#6110/29 Liqueur 2 oz. 23.00
#6110/63 Luncheon Goblet/Ice Tea
    14 oz. 25.00
#2337 Plate
    7" 10.00

    8" 10.00
#6110/11 Sherbet 7 oz. 20.00
#6110/26 Wine 7 oz. 25.00

GLOUCESTER Cutting #898

Rock Crystal
Crystal
1963 – 1969

#6097/27 Cocktail/Wine 3½ oz. 23.00
#6097/29 Cordial 1 oz..............................25.00
#4185/497 Dessert/Finger Bowl 12.00
#6097/2 Goblet 10 oz. 22.00
#6097/88 Juice, Footed 5 oz. 18.00
#6097/63 Luncheon Goblet/Ice Tea
    12 oz. 22.00
#2337 Plate
    7" 10.00
    8" 10.00
#6097/11 Sherbet 7 oz. 18.00

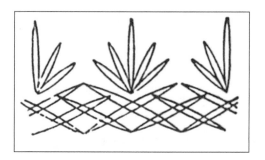

GOLD LACE Decoration #514

Etching with Gold Edge
1938 – 1944
   Do not confuse with GOLDEN LACE Decoration #645.

Also produced as ITALIAN LACE, Decoration #514 with Gold Edge.

#2496 Bowl, Flared 12" 50.00
#2545 Bowl, "Flame", Oval 12½"...............55.00
#2496 Cake Plate, Handled 10" 32.00
#2496 Candlestick 5½" ....pair 35.00
#2496 Candlestick, Duo ....pair 50.00
#2545 Candlestick "Flame" 4½".........pair 40.00

#2545 Candlestick "Flame," Duo ....pair 60.00
#2496 Candy Box, Covered, 3 part 75.00
#2496 Celery 11" 20.00
#2496 Cheese & Cracker 40.00
#2496 Comport 5½" 22.00
#2496 Cream, Footed 15.00
#2496 Mayonnaise
    Bowl 15.00
    Plate 10.00
    Ladle 20.00
#2496 Mayonnaise, 2 part 30.00
#2496 Nappy, Handled
    Flared......................................12.00
    Square 12.00

⌐══ GOLD LACE Decoration #514 cont. ══⌐

3 Cornered 15.00
#2496 Pickle Dish 8" 15.00
#2496 Relish
    2 part 25.00
    3 part 30.00
#2496 Sauce Dish 6½" 18.00

#2496 Sugar, Footed 15.00
#2496 Sweetmeat 20.00
#2496 Torte Plate 14" 50.00
#2496 Tray, Oblong 8" 30.00
#2467 Vase 7½" 45.00
#2545 Vase 10" 60.00

⌐══ GOLDEN GARLAND Decoration #664 ══⌐

Crystal Print with Gold Band on Bowl
Crystal
1964 – 1967

#6102/31 Brandy 4 oz. 30.00
#6102/25 Claret 7½ oz. 30.00
#4185/495 Dessert/Finger Bowl 15.00
#6102/2 Goblet 10 oz. 30.00
#6102/63 Luncheon Goblet/Ice Tea
    14 oz. 28.00
#2337 Plate
    7" 10.00

    8" 10.00
#6102/11 Sherbet 8 oz. 28.00
#6102/26 Tulip Wine 5½ oz. 28.00

⌐══ GOLDEN LACE Decoration #645 ══⌐

Crystal Print with Gold Band on Bowl
Crystal
1959 – 1974

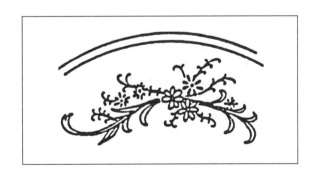

#6085/27 Cocktail/Wine 4¼ oz. 5" 26.00
#6085/29 Cordial 1¼ oz. 3½" 30.00
#6085/2 Goblet 8¾ oz. 6½" 24.00
#6085/88 Juice, Footed 5½ oz. 4⁹⁄₁₆".........24.00
#6085/63 Luncheon Goblet/Ice Tea
    11¾ oz. 6³⁄₁₆" 24.00
#2337 Plate
    7" 10.00
    8" 10.00
#6085/11 Sherbet/Dessert/Champagne
    6 oz. 5³⁄₁₆" 22.00

⚜ GOLDEN LOVE Decoration #640 ⚜

Gold Band with Rock Crystal Cutting
Rock Crystal
Crystal
1958 – 1966

#6074/20 Cocktail/Wine 4 oz. 5" 23.00
#6074/29 Cordial 1 oz. 3¼" 28.00
#4185/495 Dessert/Finger Bowl 12.00
#6074/2 Goblet 9½ oz. 6¼" 25.00
#6074/88 Juice, Footed 5 oz. 4¾" 16.00
#6074/63 Luncheon Goblet/Ice Tea
    13 oz. 6⅜"...................................24.00
#2337 Plate
    7" 10.00
    8" 10.00
#6074/11 Sherbet 6 oz. 4¾".....................20.00

⚜ GOLDEN SONG Decoration #662 ⚜

Gold Band with Polished Cutting
Crystal
1964 – 1968

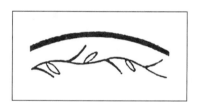

#6099/27 Cocktail/Wine 4½ oz. 24.00
#6099/29 Cordial 1 oz. 30.00
#4185/495 Dessert/Finger Bowl 12.00
#6099/2 Goblet 11 oz. 24.00
#6099/88 Juice, Footed 5½ oz. 20.00
#6099/63 Luncheon Goblet/Ice Tea
    14 oz. 24.00

#2337 Plate
    7" 10.00
    8" 10.00
#6099/11 Sherbet 6½ oz. 20.00

⚜ GOLDEN SWIRL Cutting #730 ⚜

Decoration #614
Crystal with Gold Trim on Bowl
1935 – 1938

#6011 Brandy 1 oz. 20.00
#906 Brandy Inhaler 15.00
#4116 Bubble Ball
    4" 20.00
    5" 25.00
    6" 25.00
    7" 25.00
#4117 Candy Jar, Covered, Bubble Style ..20.00

⊷⊜ GOLDEN SWIRL Cutting #730 cont. ⊜⊷

#795 Champagne, Hollow Stem 20.00
#6011 Champagne, Saucer 5½ oz. 15.00
#6011 Claret 4½ oz. 20.00
#6011 Cocktail 3 oz.................................15.00
#2525 Cocktail Shaker 100.00
#6011 Cordial 1 oz. 22.00
#6011 Creme de Menthe 2 oz. 16.00
#2525 Decanter 70.00
#6011 Decanter, Footed 85.00
#6011 Goblet 10 oz. 17.00
#1184 Old Fashioned Cocktail, Sham........12.00
#2337 Plate
    6" 8.00

    7" 10.00
    11" 12.00
#6011 Rhine Wine 4½ oz. 20.00
#6011 Sherbet, Low 5½ oz.......................13.00
#701 Tumbler, Sham
    10 oz. 10.00
    12 oz. 10.00
#6011 Tumbler, Footed
    10 oz. 10.00
    12 oz. 15.00
#4122 Whiskey, Sham 10.00
#6011 Whiskey, Footed 2 oz. 17.00
#6011 Wine 3 oz. 20.00

⊷⊜ GOLDEN TWILIGHT Crystal Print #12 ⊜⊷

Fawn
1958 – 1962
Tumblers produced to accompany similarly
  decorated melamine dinnerware.

Juice Tumbler 7 oz. 10.00
Water Tumbler 12 oz. 10.00

⊷⊜ GOLDWOOD Etching #264 ⊜⊷

Decoration #50
Crystal with Gold Band on Foot and Rim
1922 – 1929

SEE WOODLAND; Add 20% to values for pricing.

157

☞ GOSSAMER Cutting #746 ☜

Crystal
1935 – 1940
Do not confuse with GOSSAMER Cutting #852.

#2536 Bowl, Handled 9" 30.00
#6012 Brandy 1 oz. 28.00
#2536 Candlestick 5½" ....pair 40.00
#6012 Champagne, Saucer 5½ oz. 21.00
#6012 Claret 4½ oz. 26.00
#6012 Cocktail 3 oz. 21.00
#2400 Comport 6" 25.00
#6012 Cordial 1 oz. 30.00
#6012 Creme de Menthe 2 oz. 20.00
#1769 Finger Bowl 12.00
#6012 Goblet 10 oz. 24.00
#6011 Jug, Footed 100.00
#1185 Old Fashioned Cocktail, Plain 7 oz. ..8.00
#6012 Oyster Cocktail 4 oz. 15.00
#2337 Plate
    6" 8.00
    7" 10.00
    8" 12.00

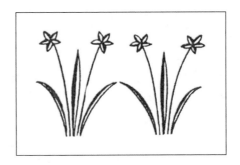

#6012 Rhine Wine 4 oz. 26.00
#6012 Sherbet, Low 5½ oz.........................16.00
#6012 Sherry 2 oz. 21.00
#701 Tumbler, Sham or Plain 12 oz...........10.00
#6012 Tumbler, Footed
    5 oz. 10.00
    10 oz. 10.00
    13 oz. 12.00
#6012 Wine 3 oz. 26.00

☞ GOSSAMER Cutting #852 ☜

Gray Cutting
Crystal
1957 – 1962
Do not confuse with GOSSAMER Cutting #746.

#2666/136 Bon Bon 6⅞" 18.00
#6068/27 Cocktail/Wine/Seafood
    4¼ oz. 4½" 15.00
#6068/29 Cordial 1¼ oz. 3" 18.00
#2666/680 Cream 3½"...............................12.00
#6068/2 Goblet 10 oz. 5¾".........................18.00
#6068/88 Juice, Footed 5 oz. 4½" 10.00
#6068/63 Luncheon Goblet/Ice Tea
    13 oz. 5⅞"...15.00
#2337 Plate
    7" 8.00
    8" 10.00
#2364/620 Relish, 2 part 8¼" 15.00
#2364/622 Relish, 3 part 10" 18.00
#6068/11 Sherbet 6½ oz. 4⅝" 13.00
#6068/677 Sugar 2⅝" 18.00
#2364/567 Torte Plate 14" 25.00

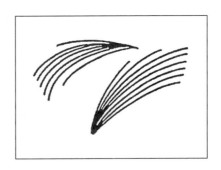

GOTHIC Cutting #744

Regular Optic
Rock Crystal
Crystal
1938 – 1944

#2430 Bowl 11" 30.00
#2580 Bowl, Handled 25.00
#2430 Candlestick 2" ....pair 30.00
#2560 Candlestick 4½" ....pair 40.00
#2560 Candlestick, Duo ....pair 50.00
#6020 Champagne, Saucer......................18.00
#6020 Claret 4½ oz. 24.00
#6020 Cocktail 3½ oz. 18.00
#2400 Comport 6" 20.00
#6020 Cordial 1 oz. 26.00
#2560 Cream, Footed 14.00
#869 Finger Bowl 6.00
#6020 Goblet 9 oz. 20.00
#5000 Jug 7, Footed................................14.00
#6020 Oyster Cocktail 4 oz. 10.00
#6020 Parfait 5½ oz................................19.00
#2337 Plate (Optic)
    6" 8.00
    7" 8.00
    8" 10.00
#6020 Sherbet, Low 6 oz. 15.00

#2560 Sugar, Footed 15.00
#6020 Tumbler, Footed
    5 oz. 14.00
    9 oz. 12.00
    12 oz. 18.00
#6020 Wine 3½ oz. 24.00

GRANADA Cutting #923

Gray Cutting
Crystal
1971 – 1972

#6124/2 Goblet 10½ oz. 32.00
#6124/63 Luncheon Goblet/Ice Tea
    14 oz. 30.00
#2337/549 Plate 7" 15.00
#6124/11 Sherbet 9 oz. 28.00
#6124/26 Wine 7 oz. 30.00

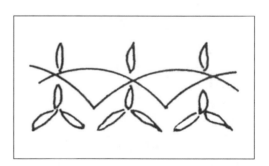

GRAND MAJESTY Etching GR03 and GR04

Crystal, Blue Bowl with Crystal Base
1979 – 1980

Add 25% for Blue items.

GRAND MAJESTY included in Patterns of the Past Program, not part of the Nostalgia Program.

#011 Dessert/Champagne 9 oz. 6⅜"..........18.00
#002 Goblet 13 oz. 8³⁄₁₆" 20.00
#063 Luncheon Goblet/Ice Tea
    16 oz. 6¾"...20.00
#035 Magnum 16 oz. 7¾".........................30.00
#025 Wine 9 oz. 7⅜"................................25.00

GRAPE Plate Etching #287

Blue, Green, Orchid
Blue, Orchid 1927 – 1927; Green 1927 – 1930
1927 – 1930

*Items produced in Green Only

#2375 Bon Bon*..30.00
#2297 Bowl
    10½"...65.00
    12" 90.00
#2297 Bowl, Deep 80.00
#2339 Bowl, Deep 7½" 70.00
#2362 Bowl, Low 12" 70.00
#2331 Candy Box......................................90.00
#2324 Candlestick 4" ....pair 50.00
#2362 Candlestick 3" ....pair 40.00
#2372 Candlestick 2" ....pair 40.00
#2329 Centerpiece
    11" 60.00
    13" 80.00
#2371 Centerpiece, Oval..........................75.00
#2317 Comport 7" 40.00
#2362 Comport, Footed 11" 75.00
#2378 Ice Bucket, Nickel Plate Handle 65.00
#2378 Ice Bucket, Nickel Plate Handle 65.00
    Drainer, Tongs Add............................50.00
#2375 Lemon Dish* 25.00
#2375 Sweetmeat* 15.00

#2287 Tray, Handled, Lunch 45.00
#2342 Tray, Lunch....................................36.00
#2292 Vase 8" 70.00
#2369 Vase
    7" 60.00
    9" 90.00
#4100 Vase, Optic
    6" 60.00
    8" 80.00
#4103 Vase, Optic
    3" 40.00
    4" 50.00
    5" 60.00
    6" 70.00
#2375 Whip Cream* 48.00

❧ GREEK Needle Etching #45 ❧

Narrow Optic
Amber, Green, Rose Bowls with Crystal Base
1930 – 1933

SEE NEEDLE ETCHING #45 FOR LISTING

❧ GREEK KEY Cutting #819 ❧

Crystal
1942 – 1944

#2596 Bowl, Oblong, Shallow 11" 35.00
#1596 Candlestick 5" ....pair 50.00
#6032 Champagne, Saucer 6 oz. 20.00
#6032 Claret 4½ oz. 24.00
#6032 Cocktail 3½ oz. 16.00
#6032 Cordial 1 oz. 30.00
#766 Finger Bowl 10.00
#6032 Goblet 9 oz. 22.00
#6011 Jug, Footed 90.00
#6032 Oyster Cocktail 4 oz. 15.00
#2337 Plate
    6" 8.00
    7" 10.00
    8" 12.00
#6032 Sherbet, Low 6 oz. 14.00

#6032 Tumbler, Footed
    5 oz. 14.00
    13 oz. 20.00
#6032 Wine 3½ oz. 22.00

❧ GREENBRIAR Crystal Print #14 ❧

Green
1958 – 1962
Tumblers produced to accompany similarly decorated melamine dinnerware.

Juice Tumbler 7 oz. 10.00
Water Tumbler 12 oz. 10.00

GREENFIELD Cutting #916

Rock Crystal
Crystal
1967 – 1968
Do not confuse with GREENFIELD Cutting #935.

#6110/2 Goblet 11 oz. 7⁵⁄₁₆" 25.00
#6110/29 Liqueur 2 oz. 23.00
#6110/63 Luncheon Goblet/Ice Tea
   14 oz. 23.00
#2337 Plate
   7" 10.00
   8" 10.00

#6110/11 Sherbet/Dessert/Champagne
   7 oz 23.00
#6110/26 Wine 7 oz. 24.00

GREENFIELD Polished Cutting #935

Lead Crystal
1976 – 1982
GREENFIELD was Fostoria's first 24% lead crystal cutting. Do not confuse with GREENFIELD Cutting #916.

#2916/29 Cordial 2 oz. 3⅜" 20.00

#2916/11 Dessert/Champagne
   9 oz. 5¹¹⁄₁₆"................................18.00
#2916/2 Goblet 11 oz. 7⁵⁄₁₆" 20.00
#2916/63 Luncheon Goblet/Ice Tea
   14 oz. 6⅝"................................22.00
#2916/26 Wine 6½ oz. 6³⁄₁₆" 24.00

GRILLE Etching #236

Crystal
1913 – 1925

#882 Ale, Tall 6½ oz. 8.00
#863 Almond 4.00
#882 Bon Bon 4½" 10.00
#882 Champagne, Hollow Stem, Cut Flute
   4½ oz..8.00
#882 Champagne, Saucer
   5 oz. 8.00
   7 oz. 8.00
#882 Champagne, Tall 5 oz. 8.00
#882 Claret
   4½ oz...8.00
   6½ oz. 8.00
#882 Cocktail
   3 oz. 7.00
   3½ oz. 7.00

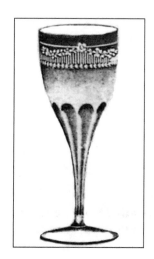

#882 Cordial
   ¾ oz. 10.00
   1 oz. 10.00

⊸⊶ GRILLE PATTERN Etching #236 cont. ⊷⊸

#803 Comport 5" 6.00
#882 Creme de Menthe 2½ oz. 7.00
#882 Custard, Cut Flute 5.00
#300 Decanter, Cut Neck, quart 20.00
#300 Decanter, Cut Neck, Handled, quart..30.00
#882 Finger Bowl, Cut Flute.....................5.00
#1499 Finger Bowl 5.00
#1769 Finger Bowl 5.00
#1499 Finger Bowl Plate 4.00
#1769 Finger Bowl Plate 4.00
#882 Goblet
    8 oz. 7.00
    9 oz. 7.00
    10 oz. 8.00
    11 oz. 8.00
#882 Grapefruit 10.00
#882½ Grapefruit 10.00
#882 Grapefruit Liner...............................6.00
#882½ Grapefruit Liner 6.00
#1464 Decanter, Cut Neck 18 oz. 20.00
#803 Nappy, Deep

5" 5.00
7" 5.00
#300½ Oil, Small 16.00
#1465 Oil, Cut Neck 7 oz.....................20.00
#801 Oyster Cocktail 6.00
#882 Pousse-Cafe
    ¾ oz. 10.00
    1 oz. 10.00
#882 Rhine Wine 4 oz. 8.00
#882 Sherbet 7.00
#882 Sherbet Plate 6.00
#882 Sherry 2 oz. 7.00
#300 Tankard 7, Cut Flute 6.00
#701 Tumbler, Cut B, Punty 24 oz.............6.00
#820 Tumbler, Cut B, Punty.....................6.00
#887 Tumbler, Cut B, Punty 3 oz.............6.00
#833 Tumbler, Cut B, Punty 8 oz.............6.00
#882 Whiskey, Hot 4½ oz. 7.00
#882 Wine
    2¾ oz..8.00
    3½ oz..8.00

⊸⊶ HAWTHORNE Cutting #790 ⊷⊸

Rock Crystal
Crystal
1939 – 1944

#6023 Bowl, Footed 20.00
#6025 Claret/Wine 4 oz.........................16.00
#6025 Cocktail 3½ oz. 10.00
#6025 Cordial 1 oz. 20.00
#1769 Finger Bowl 8.00
#6025 Goblet 16.00
#6011 Jug, Footed 55.00
#6025 Oyster Cocktail 4 oz. 8.00
#2574 Plate, not Cut
    6" 7.00
    7" 8.00
    8" 10.00
#6025 Sherbet 6 oz. 10.00
#6025 Tumbler, Footed
    5 oz. 8.00
    9 oz. 8.00
    12 oz. 14.00

**Optic
Crystal
1949 – 1972**

**HEATHER included in Patterns of the Past
and Nostalgia Programs**

#2630 Basket, Reed Handle 10¼" 40.00
#2630/137 Bon Bon, 3 Toed 7¼" 23.00
#2630/179 Bowl, Flared, Deep 8" 25.00
#2630/249 Bowl, Flared 12" 30.00
#2630/224 Bowl, Footed, Flared 10¾" 42.00
#2630/235 Bowl, Footed, Rolled Edge 11" 50.00
#2630/300 Butter, Covered, Oblong 7½" ..35.00
#2630/306 Cake Plate, Handled 30.00
#2630/316 Candlestick 4½" ....pair 35.00
#2630/332 Candlestick, Duo ....pair 60.00
#2630/336 Candlestick, Trindle ....pair 70.00
#2630/350 Candy Jar, Covered 7" 55.00
#2630/393 Cereal 6" 20.00
#6037/8 Champagne/High Sherbet
    7 oz. 6" high 20.00
#2630/369 Cheese & Cracker
    Cheese Bowl, Footed 5⅜" 35.00
    Plate 10¾" 15.00
#6037/27 Claret/Wine 4 oz. 6" high 28.00
#6037/21 Cocktail 4 oz. 5" high 24.00
#2630/388 Comport 4⅜" 25.00
#6037/29 Cordial 1 oz. 4" high...............40.00
#2630/681 Cream, Footed 4¼".................15.00
#2630/688 Cream, Individual 18.00
#2630/396 Cup, Footed 6 oz. 12.00
#2630/421 Fruit 5" 12.00
#6037/2 Goblet 9 oz. 7⅞" high 23.00
#6037/3 Goblet 9 oz. 6⅜" low................22.00
#2630/424 Ice Bucket, Chrome Handle/Tongs
    7⅜" 50.00
#2630/456 Ice Jug, 3 pint 9½" 120.00
#6037/88 Juice, Footed 5 oz. 15.00
#2630/197 Lily Pond 9" 70.00
#2630/237 Lily Pond 11¼" 85.00
#6037/63 Luncheon Goblet/Ice Tea
    12 oz. 23.00
#2630/480 Mayonnaise, 2 part, 2 Ladle 45.00
#2630/477 Mayonnaise
    Bowl...20.00
    Plate 15.00
    Ladle 20.00
#2630/481 Mayonnaise, 2 part
    Bowl 3⅜" high.......................................15.00
    Plate 10.00
    Ladle 20.00

#2630/487 Mustard, Covered and Spoon
    4" 50.00
#2630/499 Nappy, Round, Handled 4½" ..12.00
#2630/528 Oil, Stoppered 5 oz. 40.00
#6037/33 Oyster Cocktail 4½ oz. 4" high ..15.00
#6037/18 Parfait 6 oz. 6⅛".......................28.00

#6037/21 Parfait 4 oz. 28.00
#2630 Party Plate, Cup Indentation 8" 20.00
#2630/540 Pickle Dish 8¾" 16.00
#2630/453 Pitcher, Cereal, pint 6⅛".........35.00
#2630 Plate
    /548 6"...10.00
    /549 7"...10.00
    /550 8"...15.00
    /552 9"...25.00
    /554 10½" (Dinner Plate) 30.00
#2630/560 Platter, Oval 12" 40.00
#2630/591 Preserve, Covered 6"..............65.00
#1630/620 Relish, 2 part 7⅜" 25.00
#1630/622 Relish, 3 part 11⅛" 35.00
#2630/190 Salad Bowl 8½" 30.00
#2630/221 Salad Bowl 10½" 40.00
#2630/579 Salad, Crescent 7½" 60.00
#2630/630 Salver, 12¼" 65.00
#2630/397 Saucer 8.00
#2630/648 Serving Dish 2½" high 18.00
#2630/654 Shaker, Chrome Top ....pair 35.00
#6037/11 Sherbet, Low 9 oz. 4¾" high 16.00
#2630/666 Snack Bowl 3½" high 13.00
#2630/679 Sugar, Footed 4".....................16.00
#2630/687 Sugar, Individual 17.00
#2630/707 Tid Bit, 3 Toed 8⅛" 22.00
#2630/583 Tid Bit, Metal Handle,
    2-Tiered 50.00
#2630/567 Torte Plate 14" 50.00
#2630/573 Torte Plate 16" 65.00
#2630/723 Tray, Handled, Lunch 11¼" 35.00
#2630/726 Tray, Muffin, Handled 30.00

#2630/729 Tray, Snack 10½"....................30.00
#2630/697 Tray, Sugar & Cream/Cruets
    7⅛"...120.00
#2630/732 Tray, Utility Handled 9⅛"........35.00
#2630/734 Tricorne Bowl, 3 Toed 7⅛" 30.00
#6037 Tumbler
    5 oz. 25.00
    12 oz. 35.00
#2630/204 Utility Bowl, Oval 2⅞" high......12.00
#2630 Vase, Bud, Footed 6" 30.00
#2630 Vase, Oval 8½" 80.00
#2630 Vase, Handled 7½" 60.00
#2470 Vase, Footed 10" 50.00
#2660 Vase, Flip 8" 45.00
#4121 Vase 5" 35.00
#4143 Vase, Footed 6" 40.00
#5092 Vase, Bud, Footed 8" 35.00
#6021 Vase, Bud, Footed 6" 35.00
#2630/836 Vegetable Dish, Oval 9½" 20.00

HEATHER items included in Patterns of the Past and Nostalgia Programs

HE01/008 Champagne/High Dessert
    7 oz. 6" 22.00
HE01/011 Champagne, Low Dessert
    7 oz. 4¾"..18.00
HE01/027 Claret/Wine 4 oz. 6" 30.00
HE01/002 Goblet 9 oz. 7⅞" 26.00
HE01/003 Goblet, Low 9 oz. 6⅜" 22.00
HE01/063 Luncheon Goblet/Ice Tea
    12 oz. 6⅛"..24.00

❧ HEIRLOOM Plate Etching #36 ❧

1976 – 1982
Do not confuse with HEIRLOOM Cutting #751.

#6128/25 Claret 7 oz. 6⅛" 20.00
#6128/11 Dessert/Champagne
    7 oz. 5⁷⁄₁₆" 20.00
#6128/2 Goblet 10 oz. 6¾"........................20.00
#6128/63 Luncheon Goblet/Ice Tea
    14 oz. 6¹¹⁄₁₆"...20.00

⊷⊶ HEIRLOOM Cutting #751 ⊶⊷

Rock Crystal
Crystal
1935 – 1939
Do not confuse with HEIRLOOM Etching #36
Fancy Gift Items

#2394 Bowl, 3 Toed 12" 16.00
#2527 Candelabra, 2 Light ....pair 44.00
#2447 Candlestick, Duo ....pair 60.00
#2440 Mayonnaise, Oval, 2 part 20.00
#2364 Plate 16" 45.00
#2440 Relish
    2 part 20.00
    3 part 30.00
#2514 Relish, 5 part..................................18.00
#2440 Sauce Dish, Oval, Handled 18.00

#2440 Torte Plate 13" 30.00
#2440 Tray, Oval 22.00
#2470 Vase, Footed 10" 50.00

⊷⊶ HERALDRY Cutting #743 ⊶⊷

Gray Cutting
Crystal
1935 – 1970

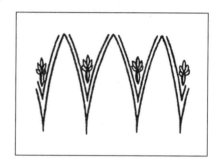

#2364/249 Bowl, Flared 12".....................30.00
#6012 Brandy 1 oz. 28.00
#2324/315 Candlestick 4"................pair 32.00
#6023/332 Candlestick, Duo ....pair 44.00
#6012/8 Champagne/High Sherbet
    5½ oz. ....15.00 – 20.00
#6012/25 Claret 4½ oz. 25.00
#6012/21 Cocktail 3 oz. 17.00
#2400 Comport 6" 24.00
#6012/29 Cordial 1 oz. 30.00
#2666/680 Cream 15.00
#2666/688 Cream, Individual 12.00
#6012 Creme de Menthe 2 oz. 20.00
#2666/396 Cup 10.00
#4185/495 Dessert/Finger Bowl 10.00
#1769 Finger Bowl 8.00
#6012/2 Goblet 10 oz. 20.00
#6011 Jug, Footed 40.00
#6012/88 Juice, Footed 5 oz. 12.00
#6012/60 Luncheon Goblet/Ice Tea
    13 oz. 5¾"...20.00
#2364/251 Lily Pond 12" 35.00
#2364/457 Mayonnaise
    Bowl...12.00
    Plate 10.00

    Ladle 20.00
#1185 Old Fashioned Cocktail, Plain 7 oz. 10.00
#6012/33 Oyster Cocktail 4 oz. 12.00
#2666/453 Pitcher, pint 30.00
#2666/454 Pitcher, quart.........................40.00
#2666/455 Pitcher, 3 pints.......................50.00
#2337 Plate
    6" 6.00
    7" 7.00
    8" 8.00
#2364/620 Relish 2 part 22.00
#2364/622 Relish 3 part 30.00
#6012 Rhine Wine 4½ oz. 25.00
#2364/195 Salad Bowl 9".........................40.00
#2364/557 Sandwich Plate 11" 35.00
#2350/397 Saucer 8.00
#2364/655 Shaker, Chrome Top 35.00
#6012 Sherry 2 oz. 20.00

✎ HERALDRY Cutting #743 cont. ✎

#2666/677 Sugar..15.00
#2666/687 Individual Sugar 16.00
#2364/567 Torte Plate 14" 35.00
#2364/723 Tray, Lunch, Handled 25.00
#2666/686 Tray for Cream & Sugar 20.00
#701 Tumbler, Sham or Plain
    10 oz. 6.00
    12 oz. 6.00
#6012 Tumbler, Footed
    10 oz. 10.00
    13 oz. 12.00
#6012/72 Water, Footed 10 oz. 5⅜" 12.00
#6012/26 Wine 3 oz. 25.00

✎ HERITAGE Cutting #849 ✎

Rock Crystal
1956 – 1957

#6065/21 Cocktail/Wine 4 oz. 4⅝"............25.00
#6065/29 Cordial 1 oz. 3⅛" 40.00
#6065/2 Goblet 11 oz. 6⅛"........................20.00
#6065/3 Ice Tea, Footed 12 oz. 6⅜" 22.00
#6065/8 Juice, Footed 6 oz. 4⅞" 18.00
#2337 Plate
    7" 8.00
    8" 8.00
#6065/7 Sherbet 7½ oz. 4¾" 18.00

✎ HOLLY Cutting #815 ✎

Combination Gray and Polished Cutting
Rock Crystal
Crystal
1942 – 1980

HOLLY included in Patterns of the Past and
  Nostalgia Programs

#2364 Ash Tray, Individual, Blown 2⅝" 10.00
#2364 Baked Apple Bowl 20.00
#2364/249 Bowl, Flared 12".......................50.00
#6023/315 Bowl, Footed 9" 60.00
#2324/315 Candlestick 4".................pair 40.00
#6023/332 Candlestick, Duo ....pair 55.00

#2364 Celery 11" 25.00
#6030/8 Champagne/Dessert/High Sherbet
    6 oz. 5⅝"..19.00
#2364 Cheese, Footed 20.00
#2364 Cigarette Holder, Blown 2" 40.00
#6030/27 Claret/Wine 3½ oz. 6" 30.00
#6030/21 Cocktail 3½ oz. 5¼" 19.00
#2364 Comport 8" 25.00
#6030 Comport 5" 16.00
#6030/29 Cordial 1 oz. 3⅞" 40.00
#2364 Cracker Plate.................................18.00
#2350/681 ½ Cream, Footed 3¼" 15.00
#2666/688 Cream, Individual 15.00
#4185/495 Dessert/Finger Bowl 10.00
#1769 Finger Bowl 15.00
#2364 Fruit 5" 10.00
#2364/259 Fruit Bowl 13" 45.00
#6030/2 Goblet 10 oz. 7⅞" 25.00
#6030/3 Goblet, Low 10 oz. 8⅜" 18.00
#6011 Jug, Footed 8⅞" 70.00
#6030/88 Juice, Footed 5 oz. 4⅝" 15.00
#2364/251 Lily Pond 12" 50.00
#6030/63 Luncheon Goblet/Ice Tea
    12 oz. 6" 20.00
#2364/477 Mayonnaise
    Bowl 15.00
    Plate 15.00
    Ladle 20.00
#6030/33 Oyster Cocktail 4 oz. 3¾" 14.00
#2364 Pickle Dish, Oval 8" 25.00
#2666/454 Pitcher, quart.........................50.00
#2337 Plate
    6" 8.00
    7" 10.00
    8" 12.00
#2364 Plate, Dinner 9" 20.00
#2364/620 Relish 2 part 8¼" 25.00
#2364/622 Relish 3 part 10" 32.00
#2364/195 Salad Bowl 9".........................50.00
#2364 Salad Bowl 10½" 65.00
#2364/557 Sandwich Plate 11" 60.00
#2350/397 Saucer 10.00
#2364/654 Shaker, Chrome Top, Large
    3¼" ....pair 40.00
#2364/655 Shaker, Chrome Top 2⅝"..pair 40.00
#6030/11 Sherbet/Low Dessert/Champagne
    6 oz. 4⅜"..16.00
#2364 Soup, Rim 8" 25.00
#2350/679 ½ Sugar, Footed 3⅛" 18.00
#1666/687 Sugar, Individual 16.00

#2364/567 Torte Plate 14" 45.00
#2364 Torte Plate 16" 65.00
#2364/686 Tray, Cream & Sugar, not Cut 10.00
#2364/723 Tray, Lunch, Handled 11¼" 35.00
#2619½ Vase, Ground Bottom
    6" 40.00
    7½" 50.00
    9½" 70.00

**HOLLY items included in Patterns of the Past
and Nostalgia Programs**

HO01/008 Champagne/High Dessert
    6 oz. 5⅝"...19.00
HO01/011 Champagne/Low Dessert
    6 oz. 4⅜"...16.00
HO01/027 Claret/Wine 3½ oz. 6" 30.00
HO01/002 Goblet 10 oz. 7⅞" 25.00
HO01/003 Goblet, Low 9 oz. 6⅜" 18.00
HO01/063 Luncheon Goblet/Ice Tea
    12 oz. 6" 20.00

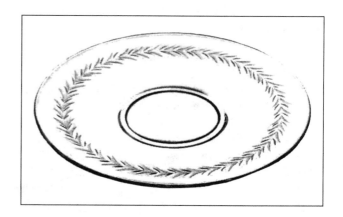

⊰≅ HOLLYHOCK Carving #16 ≅⊱

Crystal
1940 – 1944

#1895½ Vase 10" 100.00
#4126½ Vase 11" 100.00
#5100 Vase 10" 100.00

⊰≅ HUNT Carving #34 ≅⊱

Crystal
1940 – 1944

#4146 Ash Trays, Nesting
    2¾" 10.00
    3" 12.00
    3½" 15.00
#4146 Cocktail 4 oz. (Rider's Clothing) 15.00
#4146 Cordial 1 oz. (Horse) 18.00
#4146 Scotch & Soda 9 oz. (Hunter's
    Horn) 15.00

⊰≅ ICICLE Carving #59 ≅⊱

Blue Bowl, Blue Frosted Base
Crystal Bowl, Crystal Frosted Base
Yellow Bowl, Yellow Frosted Base
1982 Only

#6147 IC/011 Champagne/Dessert
    9 oz. 5" 18.00
#6147 IC/002 Goblet 12 oz. 7⅜"...............18.00
#6147 IC/063 Ice Tea 14 oz. 7" 18.00
#6147 IC/025 Wine 9 oz. 6⅝" 18.00

⊰≅ INGRID Cutting #794 ≅⊱

Combination Rock Crystal and Gray Cutting
Crystal
1939 – 1944
  Do not confuse with INGRID Cutting #836.

#6023 Bowl, Footed 25.00
#2324 Candlestick 6" ....pair 40.00
#892 Champagne, Saucer 7 oz. 10.00
#892 Claret 4 oz. 12.00
#892 Cocktail 4 oz.....................................8.00

#892 Cordial 1 oz. 15.00
#1759 Finger Bowl 8.00
#892 Goblet 11 oz. 12.00
#6011 Jug, Footed 50.00
#892 Oyster Cocktail 4½ oz. 8.00
#2337 Plate
    6" 6.00

7" 8.00
8" 10.00
#892 Sherbet, Low 6 oz. 8.00
#892 Tumbler, Footed
    5 oz. 6.00
    12 oz. 8.00
#892 Wine 3 oz. 10.00

INGRID Cutting #836

**Combination Rock Crystal and Gray Cutting
Crystal**
1953 – 1970
  Do not confuse with INGRID Cutting #794.

#2666/189 Bowl, Oval 8¼".......................25.00
#2666/311 Candlestick (Flora Candle)
    6" ....pair 30.00
#6052/27 Claret/Wine 4¼ oz. 4⅜" 26.00
#6052/20 Cocktail 3¾ oz. 3⅞" 16.00
#6052/29 Cordial 1¼ oz. 3⅛" 27.00
#2666/680 Cream 3½" 16.00
#2666/688 Cream, Individual 12.00
#6052/2 Goblet 9¾ oz. 5⅞" 20.00
#6052/88 Juice, Footed 5½ oz. 4⅞" 12.00
#6052/63 Luncheon Goblet/Ice Tea
    13 oz. 9⅛"...20.00
#2364/477 Mayonnaise

    Bowl...12.00
    Plate...10.00
    Ladle 20.00
#6052/33 Oyster Cocktail 4½ oz. 13.00
#2337 Plate
    7" 8.00
    8" 10.00
#2364/620 Relish 2 part 8¼" 16.00
#2364/622 Relish 3 part 10" 20.00
#2364/654 Shaker, Chrome Top
    Large ....pair 40.00
#6052/7 Sherbet 6½ oz. 4⅜" 17.00
#2666/729 Snack Plate, Curved Handle
    10" 15.00
#2666/677 Sugar 2⅝" 20.00
#2666/687 Sugar, Individual 14.00
#6052/567 Torte Plate 14" 35.00
#2666/686 Tray, Cream & Sugar ....set 40.00

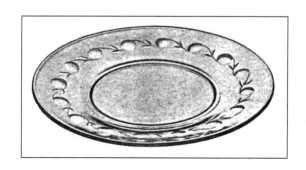

✒ INTIMATE Crystal Print #31 ✒

Blue Bowl with Crystal Base
1971 – 1974

#6123/2 Goblet 8½ oz. 20.00
#6123/63 Luncheon Goblet/Ice Tea
    11½ oz..20.00
#6123/11 Sherbet 7½ oz. 20.00
#6123/26 Wine 5½ oz. 20.00

✒ INVERNESS Cutting #711 ✒

Rock Crystal
Crystal
1933 – 1936

#2470 Bowl 12" 40.00
#2470 Cake Plate 35.00
#2470 Candlestick 5½" ....pair 45.00
#6007 Claret 4 oz. 23.00
#6007 Cocktail 3½ oz. 16.00
#2470 Comport, Tall 6" 25.00
#6007 Cordial 1 oz. 26.00
#869 Finger Bowl 8.00
#2283 Finger Bowl Plate..........................6.00
#6007 Goblet 10 oz. 18.00
#2451 Ice Dish 15.00
#2451 Ice Dish Plate..............................10.00
#6007 Oyster Cocktail 4½ oz. 12.00
#2283 Plate
    7" 8.00
    8" 10.00
#6007 Wine 3 oz. 23.00

#6007 Sherbet
    High 5½ oz..16.00
    Low 5½ oz. 10.00
#2470 Torte Plate 13".............................40.00
#6007 Tumbler, Footed
    2 oz. 18.00
    5 oz. 10.00
    9 oz. 10.00
    12 oz. 16.00

✒ IRISH LACE Needle Etching #36 ✒

Optic Pattern
Crystal
1916 – 1928

#766 Almond 6.00
#5051 Almond, Footed Small 1¾"...............7.00
#5051 Almond, Footed Large 3⁷⁄₁₆" 8.00
#880 Bon Bon 5½" 12.00
#5054 Cafe Parfait 5½ oz.........................14.00
#766 Champagne, Saucer 5 oz. 9.00

#879 Champagne, Saucer 5 oz. 10.00
#880 Champagne, Saucer 5 oz. 11.00
#880 Claret 4½ oz. 11.00
#880 Cocktail 3½ oz. 10.00
#766 Cocktail 3 oz..................................9.00
#803 Comport
    5 oz. 8.00
    6 oz. 8.00
#880 Cordial 1 oz. 12.00
#1440 Cream 14.00

#880 Creme de Menthe 2½ oz. 9.00
#810 Custard 5.00
#300 Decanter, Cut Neck, quart 30.00
#766 Fruit 4½ oz. 7.00
#879 Fruit 7.00
#810 Finger Bowl 6.00
#810 Finger Bowl Plate 6"...........................5.00
#766 Goblet 9 oz. 10.00
#879 Goblet 9 oz. 10.00
#880 Goblet 10 oz. 12.00
#890 Goblet 9 oz. 10.00
#895 Goblet 9 oz. 10.00
#880½ Grapefruit 10.00
#880½ Grapefruit Liner 12.00
#766 Ice Tea, Footed, Handled 10.00
#4061 Ice Tea, Footed, Handled 16.00
#300 Jug 7...18.00
#317½ Jug, Plain Cover 20.00
#724 Jug 7...20.00
#303 Jug 7...20.00
#318 Jug 7...20.00
#1236 Jug 6...20.00
#803 Nappy, Footed
    5" 5.00
    6" 5.00
    7" 8.00
#1227 Nappy 4½" 5.00
#1127 Nappy 8" 12.00
#300½ Oil, Large 30.00
#300½ Oil, Small 20.00
#1465 Oil, Cut Neck..................................20.00
#837 Oyster Cocktail 8.00
#766 Parfait 10.00
#701 Plate for Tumbler 5"..........................10.00
#840 Plate 10.00
#1897 Plate 7" 10.00
#766 Sherbet 8.00
#879 Sherbet 5 oz. 8.00
#880 Sherbet 5½ oz...................................8.00
#880 Sherry 2 oz. 9.00
#1480 Sugar 14.00
#858 Sweetmeat.......................................12.00
#1165½ Shaker, Pearl Top.................pair 40.00
#858 Tumbler, Table
    1¾ oz. 6.00
    3½ oz. 6.00
    5 oz. 6.00
    6½ oz. 8.00

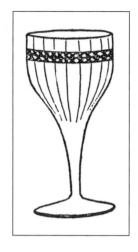

    8 oz. 8.00
    10 oz. 10.00
    12 oz. 12.00
    14 oz. 12.00
#4011½ Tumbler, Table 8.00
#4077 Tumbler, Table
    5½ oz. 9.00
    8 oz. 8.00
    12½ oz. 10.00
#701 Tumbler
    8 oz. 8.00
    10 oz. 8.00
    12 oz. 12.00
    14 oz. 14.00
#820 Tumbler 6.00
#833 Tumbler 8 oz. 6.00
#833 Tumbler 8 oz. Sham Bottom 8.00
#887 Tumbler 2½ oz. 10.00
#899 Tumbler 5 oz. 8.00
#4011 Tumbler, Handled 12 oz. 18.00
#4011 Tumbler
    5 oz. 8.00
    8 oz. 6.00
    10 oz. 8.00
    12 oz. 10.00
    15 oz. 14.00
#922 Toothpick 18.00
#766 Wine 2¾ oz. 10.00
#880 Wine 2½ oz. 11.00

⇒ ITALIAN LACE Decoration #514 ⇐

Gold Edge
1938 – 1944

SEE GOLD LACE FOR LISTING

⇒ IVY Cutting #745 ⇐

Rock Crystal
Crystal
1935 – 1944
   Do not confuse with IVY Etching #235.

#2536 Bowl, Handled 9" 30.00
#6012 Brandy 1 oz. 30.00
#2535 Candlestick 5½" ....pair 40.00
#6012 Champagne, Saucer 5½ oz. 21.00
#6012 Claret 4½ oz. 26.00
#6012 Cocktail 3 oz. 21.00
#2400 Comport 6" 25.00
#6012 Cordial 1 oz. 32.00
#6012 Creme de Menthe 2 oz. 21.00
#1769 Finger Bowl 12.00
#6012 Goblet 10 oz. 24.00
#6011 Jug, Footed 90.00
#1185 Old Fashioned Cocktail, Plain 7 oz. 10.00
#6012 Oyster Cocktail 4 oz. 13.00
#2337 Plate
     6" 8.00
     7" 10.00
     8" 12.00

#6012 Rhine Wine 4½ oz. 26.00
#6012 Sherbet, Low 5½ oz. 17.00
#6012 Sherry 2 oz. 21.00
#701 Tumbler, Sham or Plain
     10 oz. 10.00
     12 oz. 10.00
#6012 Tumbler, Footed
     5 oz. 10.00
     10 oz. 10.00
     13 oz. 10.00
#6012 Wine 3 oz. 25.00

⇒ IVY Deep Plate Etching #235 ⇐

Crystal
1913 – 1918
   Do not confuse with IVY Cutting #745.

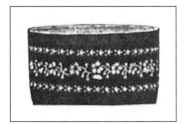

#882 Ale, Tall 6½ oz. 8.00
#882 Bon Bon 4½" 10.00
#882 Champagne, Hollow Stem, Cut Flute
     4½ oz...8.00
#882 Champagne, Saucer 8.00

#882 Champagne, Tall
    5 oz. 8.00
    7 oz. 8.00
#882 Claret
    4½ oz. 8.00
    6½ oz. 8.00
#882 Cocktail
    3 oz. 7.00
    3½ oz. 7.00
#882 Cordial
    ¾ oz. 10.00
    1 oz. 10.00
#882 Creme de Menthe 2½ oz. 7.00
#882 Custard, Cut Flute 6.00
#300 Decanter, Cut Neck, quart 20.00
#1464 Decanter, Cut Neck 18 oz. 25.00
#882 Finger Bowl, Cut Flute.......................5.00
#882 Goblet
    8 oz. 7.00
    9 oz. 7.00
    10 oz. 8.00
    11 oz. 8.00
#882 Grapefruit 10.00
#882½ Grapefruit 10.00
#882 Grapefruit Liner................................6.00
#882½ Grapefruit Liner 6.00
#1465 Oil, Cut Neck, Cut Stopper 20.00

#882 Pousse-Cafe
    ¾ oz. 10.00
    1 oz. 10.00
#882 Rhine Wine 4 oz. 8.00
#882 Sherbet 7.00
#882 Sherry 2 oz. 7.00
#300 Tankard 7 oz. 10.00
#701 Tumbler, Cut B
    5 oz. 8.00
    8 oz. 6.00
    10 oz. 8.00
#858 Tumbler, Cut #19
    3 oz. 8.00
    4 oz. 6.00
    6 oz. 6.00
    7½ oz. 8.00
    9 oz. 10.00
    11 oz. 12.00
    13 oz. 12.00
    15 oz. 12.00
#887 Tumbler, Cut B 3 oz. 8.00
#1568 Water Bottle, Cut Neck...................18.00
#882 Whiskey, Hot 4½ oz. 7.00
#882 Wine
    2¾ oz...8.00
    3½ oz...8.00

JULIET Cutting #865

Gray Cutting
Crystal
1959 – 1970

#6085/27 Cocktail/Wine 4½ oz. 5" 22.00
#6085/29 Cordial 1¼ oz. 3½" 25.00
#4185/495 Dessert/Finger Bowl 12.00
#6085/2 Goblet 8¾ oz. 6½" 22.00
#6085/88 Juice, Footed 5½ oz. 4⁹⁄₁₆"..........16.00
#6085/63 Luncheon Goblet/Ice Tea
    13¼ oz. 6³⁄₁₆" 22.00
#2337 Plate
    7" 10.00
    8" 10.00
#6085/11 Sherbet 6 oz. 5³⁄₁₆" 16.00

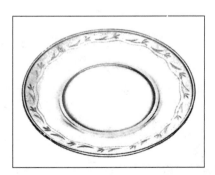

JUNE Plate Etching #279

Crystal
Azure, Gold Tint, Green, Rose, Topaz with Crystal Base

1928 – 1952
Azure 1928 – 1944; Crystal 1928 – 1951; Green 1928 – 1936; Rose 1928 – 1940; Gold Tint 1938 – 1944; Topaz 1929 – 1938; Colors with Crystal Base 1929 – 1944

JUNE is another of America's favorite etching designs. Ribboned garlands of small flowers tied with bows are altered in size to meet the shape of the item on which the etching was used. Sometimes confused with ROMANCE, a quick check shows a horseshoe type band encircles the JUNE etching. This is not found on ROMANCE.

JUNE items included in Patterns of the Past and Nostalgia Programs
*Items not produced in Crystal.
Add 30% to values for Rose, Topaz, Gold Tint and Green, 40% FOR Azure.

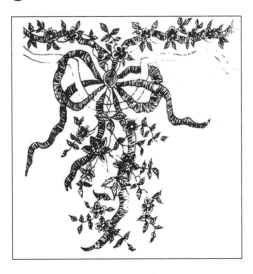

#2350 Ash Tray (not made in Rose, Azure, GT)
   Small 30.00
   Large 35.00
#2375 Baker 9" 30.00
#2375 Bon Bon (not made in Rose, Azure) 16.00
#2375 Bouillon, Footed 15.00
#2394 Bowl
   6" 18.00
   12" 40.00
#2375 Bowl 12" 35.00
#2395 Bowl 10" 30.00
#2375 Cake Plate 10" 28.00
#2375 Canapé Plate 15.00
#2375 Candlestick 3" ....pair 35.00
#2375½ Candlestick (Crystal only)......pair 30.00
#2394 Candlestick 2" ....pair 30.00
#2395½ Candlestick 5"*....................pair 50.00
#2331 Candy Box, Covered* 100.00
#2394 Candy Jar, Covered 150.00
#2375 Celery 11½" (not made in Rose) 30.00
#2375 Centerpiece
   11" 45.00
   12" (Crystal only) 50.00
#2375½ Centerpiece, Oval 13" 40.00
#2375 Chop Plate 13" (not made in Azure)
#2368 Cheese, Footed 30.00
#2375 Cheese, Footed (not made in Rose, Azure)...30.00

#2368 Cheese and Cracker........................50.00
#2375 Chop Plate 13" (not made in Azure) 35.00
#5098 Claret 4 oz. 6" 35.00
#5098 Cocktail 3 oz.................................25.00
#5098 Cordial ¾ oz. 55.00
#2375 Comport 7"*...................................50.00
#2400 Comport
   6" (not made in Crystal, Rose) 50.00
   8"* 60.00
#5098 Comport 5" 45.00
#2368 Cracker Plate................................20.00
#2375 Cracker Plate (not made in Rose, Azure)..20.00
#2375½ Cream, Footed...............................27.00
#2375½ Cream, Tea (not made in Rose, Azure)..30.00
#2375 Cream Soup, Footed 20.00
#2375 Cream Soup Plate 12.00
#2375½ Cup, Footed 20.00
#2375 Cup, After Dinner 25.00
#2439 Decanter 300.00
#2375 Dessert, Large (Crystal only) 50.00
#2375 Fruit 5" 15.00
#5098 Goblet 9 oz. 8¼".............................30.00
#5082½ Grapefruit (Crystal only)..........set 75.00
#2375 Grill Plate 25.00
#2451 Ice Dish (not made in Rose) 50.00
#2451 Ice Dish Plate................................20.00
#2375 Ice Bucket, Nickel Plate Handle 80.00
#5000 Jug, 7 Footed................................350.00
#2375 Ladle 25.00
#2375 Lemon Dish (not made in Rose, Azure)..20.00
#2375 Mayonnaise (not made in Rose, Azure)..32.00

#2375 Mayonnaise Plate (not made in Rose,
  Azure) 12.00
#2394 Mint Dish* 22.00
#2375 Nappy, Round 7" (Crystal only) 35.00
#5098 Nappy, Footed 6" 30.00
#2375 Oil, Footed (Crystal only) 300.00
#5098 Oyster Cocktail 5 oz. 20.00
#5098 Parfait 6 oz. 25.00
#2375 Plate
  6" 8.00
  7" 10.00
  8" 15.00
  9" 20.00
  10" 50.00
#2375 Platter
  12" 45.00
  15" 75.00
#2375 Relish, Divided 8½" (not made in
  Azure) 20.00
#2375 Salad Dressing Bottle (not made in Rose,
  Azure) 80.00
#2083 Salad Dressing Bottle 80.00
#2375 Sauce Boat 90.00
#2375 Sauce Boat Plate 30.00
#2375 Saucer 8.00
#2375 Saucer, After Dinner 12.00
#2375 Shaker, Footed ....pair 165.00
#5098 Sherbet 6 oz. 6"
  High 6 oz. 24.00
  Low 6 oz. 20.00
#2375 Soup 7" (Crystal only) 40.00
#2375½ Sugar, Footed 25.00
#2375½ Sugar, Footed, Covered 85.00
#2375½ Sugar, Tea (not made in Rose,
  Azure) 35.00
#2378 Sugar Pail 100.00
#2375 Sweetmeat (not made in Rose,
  Azure) 25.00
#2440 Torte Plate 13" (not made in Topaz, Gold
  Tint) 45.00
#2375 Tray, Handled, Lunch (not made in
  Azure) 45.00
#2394 Tray, Service/Lemon 60.00
#2429 Tray, Service 70.00
#5098 Tumbler, Footed
  2½ oz. 25.00
  5 oz. 18.00
  9 oz. 18.00
  12 oz. (Luncheon Goblet/Ice Tea) 6" 30.00
#2385 Vase, Footed, Fan
  5½" 70.00
  8½"* 80.00

#4100 Vase 8"* 85.00
#2375 Whip Cream (not made in Rose,
  Azure) 25.00
#2378 Whip Cream Pail 90.00
#5098 Wine 2½ oz. 30.00

JUNE stemware made in Azure, Crystal, Gold Tint, Rose, Topaz with Crystal Base

#5098 Champagne, Saucer/High Sherbet
  6 oz. 32.00
#5098 Claret 4 oz. 60.00
#5298 Claret 58.00
#5098 Cocktail 3 oz. 45.00
#5298 Cocktail 45.00
#5298 Comport 5" 40.00
#5098 Cordial ¾ oz. 90.00
#5298 Cordial 95.00
#869 Finger Bowl 20.00
#2283 Finger Bowl Plate 6" 10.00
#5098 Goblet 9 oz. 38.00
#5298 Goblet 10 oz. 40.00
#5282½ Grapefruit (Crystal only) ....set 65.00
#945½ Grapefruit Liner (Crystal only) 25.00
#5000 Jug 7, Footed, Optic 300.00
#5298 Nappy, Footed 6" 50.00
#5098 Oyster Cocktail 5½ oz. 28.00
#5298 Oyster Cocktail 5½ oz. 24.00
#5098 Parfait 6 oz. 65.00

↜═ JUNE Plate Etching #279 cont. ═↝

#5298 Parfait 54.00
#2283 Plate, Optic 6" 10.00
#5298 Sherbet 6 oz.
    High 28.00
    Low 24.00
#5098 Tumbler, Footed
    2½ oz. 50.00
    5 oz. 28.00
    9 oz. 28.00
#5298 Tumbler, Footed, Optic
    2½ oz. 42.00
    5 oz. 24.00
    9 oz. 24.00
    12 oz. 34.00
#5098 Whiskey............................30.00

#5098 Wine 2½ oz. 58.00
#5298 Wine 38.00

JUNE items included in Patterns of the Past and Nostalgia Programs
Crystal, Blue, Yellow only. Be aware that these colors are variants, not the original colors.

JU 011 Champagne/High Dessert 6 oz. 6" 28.00
JU 025 Claret 4 oz. 6" 34.00
JU 002 Goblet 9 oz. 8¼" 26.00
JU 063 Luncheon Goblet/Ice Tea
    12 oz. 6" 26.00

↜═ KASHMIR DESIGN Plate Etching #281 ═↝

Crystal, Azure, Topaz, Green 1930 – 1934;
1930 – 1934
Crystal Bowl with Azure Base 1931 – 1934;
  Crystal Bowl with Green Base 1931 – 1934;
  Crystal Bowl with Topaz Base 1931 – 1934;
  Kashmir Dinnerware made in Green

#2350 Cup, After Dinner 20.00
#2350½ Cup, Footed 18.00
#2419 Plate
    6" 12.00
    7" 20.00
    8" 24.00
#2419 Saucer..............................12.00
#2350 Saucer, After Dinner 12.00

Kashmir Dinnerware made in Azure and Topaz

#2350 Ash Tray, Small 15.00
#2375 Baker 9" 55.00
#2375 Bon Bon 35.00
#2375 Bouillon............................25.00
#2394 Bowl
    6" 30.00
    12" 60.00

#2375 Bowl 12" 60.00
#2395 Bowl 10" 65.00
#2430 Bowl 11" 70.00
#2375 Cake Plate 10" 40.00
#2430 Candy Jar, Covered ½ lb. 90.00
#2375 Candlestick 3" ....pair 45.00
#2375½ Candlestick ....pair 50.00
#2394 Candlestick, Footed 2" .....pair 40.00
#2395½ Candlestick 5" ....pair 60.00
#2430 Candlestick 9½" ....pair 125.00
#2375 Celery 11½" 26.00
#2375 Centerpiece 12" 65.00
#2375 Cereal 6" 15.00
#2375½ Cheese, Footed 30.00
#2375 Chop Plate 13".................86.00
#5299 Comport 6" 25.00
#2375 Cracker Plate 20.00

#2375½ Cream, Footed..............................22.00
#2375½ Cream, Tea 20.00
#2375½ Cream Soup 30.00
#2375 Cream Soup Plate 12.00
#2375½ Cup, After Dinner 18.00
#2375½ Cup, Footed 30.00
#2375 Dessert, Large 20.00
#2375 Fruit 5" 15.00
#2375 Grill Plate 10" 35.00
#2375 Ice Bucket 70.00
#2430 Jelly 7" 25.00
#2375 Lemon Dish 20.00
#2375 Mayonnaise 25.00
#2375 Mayonnaise Plate 15.00
#2350 Mint Dish 5½" 20.00
#2375 Oil, Footed...................................65.00
#2375 Pickle Dish 8½" 20.00
#2375 Plate

    6" 15.00
    7" 20.00
    8" 24.00
    9" 30.00
    10" 40.00

#2375 Platter

    12" 50.00
    15" 70.00

#2375 Relish 8½" 60.00
#2375 Sauce Boat 75.00
#2375 Sauce Boat Plate 30.00
#2375 Saucer, After Dinner 16.00
#2375 Saucer...12.00
#2375 Shaker, Footed ....pair 100.00
#2375 Soup 7" 26.00
#2375½ Sugar, Footed 40.00
#2375½ Sugar, Tea..................................35.00
#2375 Sweetmeat....................................35.00
#2375 Tray, Lunch, Handled 45.00
#2417 Vase 8" 110.00
#2430 Vase, Footed 8" 125.00
#4105 Vase 8" 110.00

Kashmir Stemware made in Azure or Topaz
  Bowl with Crystal Base
  Add 25% for Azure.

#5099 Claret 4 oz. 40.00
#5099 Cocktail 3 oz.................................35.00
#5099 Comport 6" 35.00
#5099 Cordial ¾ oz. 100.00
#5099 Goblet 9 oz. 35.00
#5082½ Grapefruit 40.00

#945½ Grapefruit Liner 20.00
#5000 Jug 7, Footed..............................300.00
#5099 Oyster Cocktail 4½ oz. 25.00
#5099 Parfait 5½ oz................................35.00
#5099 Sherbet

    High 6 oz. 32.00
    Low 6 oz. 30.00

#5099 Tumbler, Footed

    2½ oz...35.00
    5 oz. 30.00
    9 oz. 32.00
    12 oz. 35.00

Kashmir Stemware made in Crystal Bowl
  with Green Base

#4020 Cocktail 3½ oz. 28.00
#4020½ Cocktail 4 oz. 30.00
#4020 Goblet 11oz. 38.00
#4020 Jug, Footed 300.00
#4020 Sherbet

    High 34.00
    Low 5 oz. 28.00
    Low 7 oz. 28.00

#4020 Tumbler, Footed

    5 oz. 25.00
    10 oz. 24.00
    13 oz. 35.00
    16 oz. 35.00

#4020 Whiskey 2 oz. 30.00

✒️ KENMORE Cutting #176 ✒️

Optic Pattern
Crystal with Blue Foot
1925 – 1928

#4095 Candy Jar, Covered	55.00
#5082 Champagne, Saucer 5 oz.	22.00
#1693½ Coaster	4.00
#5082 Cocktail 3 oz.	20.00
#2315 Cream	18.00
#4095 Finger Bowl	10.00
#1769 Finger Bowl	10.00
#1769 Finger Bowl Plate	8.00
#5082 Fruit, Footed 5 oz.	18.00
#5082 Goblet 9 oz.	24.00
#303 Jug 7	35.00
#2082 Jug 7	35.00
#2315 Mayonnaise	18.00
#2315 Mayonnaise Plate 7"	14.00
#4095 Oyster Cocktail	14.00
#5082 Parfait 6 oz.	24.00
#2237 Plate	
7"	12.00
8"	20.00
#2283 Plate (Blue)	
6"	18.00
8"	30.00
#2283 Plate 13"	35.00
#2287 Relish Set (7 Pieces, Tray 13")	130.00
#2315 Sugar	22.00
#2287 Tray, Lunch	20.00

#820 Tumbler, Table	12.00
#701 Tumbler 13 oz.	16.00
#887 Tumbler 2½ oz.	20.00
#889 Tumbler 5 oz.	16.00
#4095 Tumbler	
5 oz.	16.00
10 oz.	18.00
13 oz.	20.00
#4011 Tumbler, Handled 12 oz.	32.00
#5082 Wine 2¾ oz.	24.00

✒️ KIMBERLEY Cutting #775 ✒️

Rock Crystal
Optic
Crystal
1938 – 1944
Do not confuse with KIMBERLY, Cutting #855.

#2560 Bowl, Handled	30.00
#2430 Bowl 11"	35.00
#2496 Bowl, Flared 12"	40.00
#2496 Bowl, Handled 10½"	35.00
#2545 Bowl, "Flame," Oval 12½"	45.00
#2496 Cake Plate, 2-handled 10"	30.00
#2545 Candelabra, 8 Prism, 2 Light	each 45.00
#2430 Candlestick 2"	each 20.00
#2545 Candlestick "Flame," Duo	each 25.00

179

#2560 Candlestick 4½" ....each 18.00
#2496 Candlestick
    4" ....each 20.00
    5½" ....each 25.00
#2496 Candlestick
    Duo ....each 30.00
    Trindle ....each 35.00
#2560 Candlestick, Duo ....each 25.00
#2496 Celery Dish 11" 24.00
#6020 Champagne, Saucer 6 oz. 18.00
#2496 Cheese, Footed 16.00
#2496 Cheese and Cracker.....................35.00
#6020 Claret 4½ oz. 24.00
#6020 Cocktail 3½ oz. 16.00
#2400 Comport 6" 18.00
#2496 Comport 5½" 20.00
#2496 Comport, Tall 6½" 20.00
#6020 Cordial 1 oz. 28.00
#2496 Cracker Plate................................20.00
#2496 Cream, Footed 16.00
#2560 Cream, Footed 14.00
#2496 Cream, Individual 14.00
#4132 Decanter, Stopper 45.00
#766 Finger Bowl 10.00
#869 Finger Bowl 10.00
#6020 Goblet 20.00
#4132 Ice Bowl...35.00
#2496 Ice Bucket, Chrome Handle 55.00
#6011 Jug, Footed 50.00
#5000 Jug 7, Footed................................60.00
#2496½ Mayonnaise
    Bowl 20.00

Plate 16.00
Ladle 20.00
#2496 Mayonnaise, 2 part 24.00
#4132 Old Fashioned Cocktail, Sham
    7½ oz..12.00
#6020 Oyster Cocktail 4 oz. 11.00
#6020 Parfait 5½ oz................................17.00
#2496 Pickle Dish 8" 18.00
#2337 Plate (Optic)
    6" 8.00
    7" 10.00
    8" 12.00
#2496 Relish
    2 part 26.00
    3 part 30.00
#2496 Sauce Dish, Oblong 24.00
#2496 Serving Dish, 2-handled 8½" 30.00
#6020 Sherbet, Low 6 oz. 15.00
#2496 Sugar, Footed 18.00
#2496 Sugar, Individual 14.00
#2560 Sugar, Footed 16.00
#2496 Sweetmeat.....................................14.00
#2496 Tid Bit, 3 Toed, Flat......................16.00
#2496 Torte Plate 14"..............................50.00
#6020 Tumbler, Footed
    5 oz. 12.00
    9 oz. 12.00
    12 oz. 18.00
#2496 Tray, Oblong 8" 40.00
#2496½ Tray for Cream and Sugar 35.00
#4132 Whiskey, Sham 1½ oz. 10.00
#6020 Wine 3½ oz. 24.00

⇝ **KIMBERLY Cutting #855** ⇜

Rock Crystal
Crystal
1957 – 1965
  Do not confuse with KIMBERLEY Cutting #775.

#6071/27 Cocktail/Wine/Seafood 4½ oz.
    5" 20.00
#6071/29 Cordial 1 oz. 3¼" 25.00
#2574/681 Cream, Footed 4" 15.00
#6071/2 Goblet 11½ oz. 6⅜" 18.00
#6071/88 Juice, Footed 5¼ oz. 4½" 12.00
#6071/63 Luncheon Goblet/Ice Tea
    13 oz. 6" 18.00

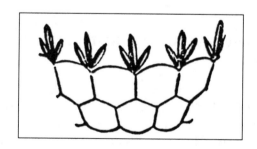

#2574 Plate
    7" 10.00
    8" 10.00
#2574/622 Relish 3 part 10" 18.00

◆══ KIMBERLY Cutting #855 cont. ══◆

#6071/11 Sherbet 7 oz. 4¾" 15.00
#2574/679 Sugar, Footed 3¾" 20.00
#2574/567 Torte Plate 14" 25.00

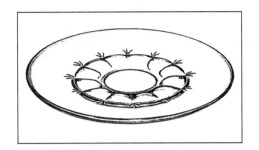

◆══ KINGSLEY DESIGN Polished Cutting #192 ══◆

**Azure, Crystal Rose
1929 – 1930**

#2297 Bowl, Deep 12" 50.00
#2342 Bowl 12" 45.00
#2324 Candlestick 4" ....pair 50.00
#2375 Candlestick 3" ....pair 48.00
#2321 Candy Box, Covered........................70.00
#2329 Centerpiece
    11" 50.00
    14" (not made in Azure)........................60.00
#2368 Cheese and Cracker ....set 35.00
#2400 Comport
    6" 24.00
    8" 30.00
#2378 Ice Bucket, Nickel Plated Handle 60.00
#2332 Mayonnaise 22.00
#2332 Mayonnaise Plate 7"........................14.00
#2342 Tray, Lunch, Handled 26.00

#2292 Vase 8" 85.00
#2369 Vase
    7" 70.00
    9" 100.00
#4105 Vase 8" 90.00
#2373 Vase, Window, Covered
    Large 90.00
    Small 60.00

◆══ KINGSTON PATTERN Needle Etching #84 ══◆

**Decoration #41
Green Bowl, Coin Glass Band
1928 – 1929**

SEE CAMDEN FOR LISTINGS

⊷≕ KISMET Crystal Print #10 ≕⊶

Blue
1958 – 1962
Tumblers produced to accompany similarly decorated melamine dinnerware.

Juice Tumbler 7 oz. 10.00
Water Tumbler 12 oz. 10.00

⊷≕ KORNFLOWER Etching #234 ≕⊶

Crystal
1913 – 1918

#880 Ale, Tall 6½ oz. 14.00
#863 Almond 4.00
#880 Bon Bon 4½ oz. 12.00
#880 Champagne, Hollow Stem, Cut Flute
    4½ oz...8.00
#880 Champagne, Saucer
    5 oz. 7.00
    7 oz. 7.00
#880 Champagne, Tall 5 oz. 8.00
#880 Claret
    4½ oz...7.00
    6½ oz...7.00
#880 Cocktail
    3 oz. 6.00
    3½ oz. 6.00
#803 Comport
    5" 5.00
    6" 6.00
#880 Cordial
    ¾ oz. 10.00
    1 oz. 10.00
#1478 Cream 10.00
#880 Creme de Menthe 2½ oz. 8.00
#300 Decanter, Cut Neck, quart 20.00
#863 Fruit 5.00
#1499 Finger Bowl 5.00
#1769 Finger Bowl 5.00
#1867 Finger Bowl 5.00
#1499 Finger Bowl Plate...........................6.00
#1769 Finger Bowl Plate 6.00
#1867 Finger Bowl Plate 6.00
#880 Goblet
    8 oz. 7.00
    9 oz. 7.00
    10 oz. 8.00

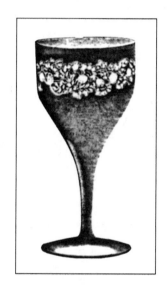

    11 oz. 10.00
#880 Grapefruit 12.00
#880½ Grapefruit and Liner ....set 15.00
#880 Grapefruit Liner...............................7.00
#880½ Grapefruit Liner.......................set 15.00
#303 Jug
    6...5.00
    7...6.00
#803 Nappy, Deep
    5" 5.00
    6" 6.00
    7" 7.00
#1236 Pitcher #6 ....20.00
#840 Plate 4.00
#880 Pousse-Cafe
    ¾ oz. 7.00
    1 oz. 7.00
#880 Rhine Wine 4 oz. 8.00
#810 Sherbet 6.00

KORNFLOWER Etching #234 cont.

#880 Sherbet 6.00	5 oz. 6.00
#880 Sherry 2 oz. 7.00	6½ oz. 6.00
#1478 Sugar 10.00	8 oz. 6.00
#858 Sweetmeat..............................8.00	10 oz. 8.00
#858 Tumbler, Table 6.00	12 oz. 10.00
#701 Tumbler	14 oz. 10.00
5 oz. 6.00	16 oz. 10.00
8 oz. 6.00	#885 Tumbler 3 oz. 8.00
10 oz. 8.00	#880 Whiskey, Hot 4½ oz. 8.00
#820 Tumbler 6.00	#880 Wine
#858 Tumbler	2¾ oz. 8.00
3½ oz...8.00	3½ oz. 8.00

LACE WORK Plate Etching #201

Blown Ware
Crystal
1904 – 1910

#480 Custard 8.00	
#481 Custard 8.00	
#1227 Custard 6.00	
#1239 Custard 6.00	
#1241 Custard 6.00	
#315 Finger Bowl 8.00	
#1281 Ice Cream Nappy 5" 8.00	
#315 Nappy	
4" 7.00	7" 12.00
4½" 7.00	8" 15.00
5" 8.00	#820 Tumbler 6.00
6" 10.00	#820½ Tumbler, Sham 6.00

LACY LEAF Crystal Print #6

Crystal
1937 – 1960

#2630 Bon Bon, 3 Toed 7¼" 20.00	
#2630 Bowl, Flared 12" 65.00	
#2630 Butter, Covered, Oblong 7½" 85.00	
#2630 Cake Plate, Handled 50.00	
#2630 Candlestick 4½" ....pair 50.00	
#2630 Candlestick, Duo ....pair 85.00	
#2630 Cream, Footed 4¼" 15.00	#2630 Lily Pond 9" 55.00
#2630 Cream, Individual 15.00	#2630 Mayonnaise
#2630 Jug, Ice 3 pint 7⅛".............275.00	Bowl...24.00

⇒ LACY LEAF Crystal Print #6 cont. ⇐

Plate 10.00
Ladle 20.00
#2630 Nappy, Handled, Round 4½" 16.00
#2630 Pickle Dish 8¾" 30.00
#2630 Relish
    2 part 7⅜"...35.00
    3 part 11⅛"..45.00
#2630 Salad Bowl 10½" 65.00
#2630 Shaker, Chrome Top ....pair 65.00
#2630 Sugar, Footed 4" 15.00
#2630 Sugar, Individual 15.00
#2630 Tid Bit, 3 Toed 8⅛" 25.00
#2630 Tricorn Bowl 7⅛"..........................35.00
#1630 Tray, Handled, Lunch 11¼" 50.00
#2630 Tray for Sugar & Cream.................18.00

#2630 Torte Plate 14"................................75.00

⇒ LANCASTER Cutting #719 ⇐

Rock Crystal
Crystal
1933 – 1936

#2470½ Bowl 10½" 30.00
#2470½ Candlestick 5½" ....pair 45.00
#6009 Champagne, Saucer 5½ oz. 18.00
#6009 Claret/Wine 3¾ oz. 24.00
#6009 Cocktail 3¾ oz. 18.00
#2400 Comport 6" 22.00
#6009 Cordial 1 oz. 30.00
#869 Finger Bowl 8.00
#6009 Goblet 9 oz. 22.00
#6009 Oyster Cocktail 4¾ oz. 12.00
#2337 Plate
    6" 6.00
    7" 8.00
    8" 10.00
#6009 Sherbet
    High 5½ oz...18.00
    Low 5½ oz. 16.00
#2440 Torte Plate 13" 40.00

#6009 Tumbler, Footed
    5 oz. 12.00
    9 oz. 12.00
    12 oz. 18.00
#4112 Vase 8½" 50.00

Blown Ware
Crystal
1904 – 1928

#880 Ale, Tall 6½ oz. 11.00
#863 Almond 10.00
#880 Bon Bon 4½" 12.00
#810 Brandy 1 oz. 10.00
#858 Brandy 1 oz. 10.00
#1697 Carafe 18.00
#1163 Catsup, Cut Stopper 40.00
#791 Champagne, Hollow Stem, Cut Flute ..10.00
#792 Champagne, Hollow Stem, Cut Flute ..10.00
#793 Champagne, Hollow Stem, Cut Flute ..10.00
#810 Champagne 6 oz. 7.00
#810 Champagne, Saucer
    5½ oz...7.00
    7 oz. 7.00
#825 Champagne 7.00
#825 Champagne, Saucer 7.00
#858 Champagne, Cut Flute.......................7.00
#858 Champagne, Long Stem.....................7.00
#858 Champagne, Saucer 7 oz. 7.00
#858 Champagne, Tall 5½ oz.....................7.00
#862 Champagne, Saucer 5½ oz. 7.00
#863 Champagne, Hollow Stem 10.00
#863 Champagne, Tall 5½ oz.....................7.00
#880 Champagne, Hollow Stem 4½ oz. 10.00
#880 Champagne, Saucer
    5 oz. 7.00
    7 oz. 7.00
#880 Champagne, Tall 8.00
#932 Champagne 7.00
#932 Champagne, Saucer 7.00
#5008 Champagne, Saucer 6 oz. 7.00
#5008 Champagne, Tall 5½ oz....................8.00
#300 Claret 7.00
#810 Claret
    4½ oz. 7.00
    5½ oz. 7.00
#858 Claret
    4½ oz. 7.00
    6½ oz. 7.00
#880 Claret
    4½ oz. 7.00
    6½ oz. 7.00
#863 Claret 4½ oz. 7.00
#5008 Claret
    4½ oz. 7.00
    6½ oz. 7.00
#810 Cocktail 3½ oz. 7.00
#863 Cocktail 3½ oz. 7.00

#858 Cocktail 3½ oz. 7.00
#880 Cocktail
    3 oz. 7.00
    3½ oz. 7.00
#952 Cocktail..7.00
#5008 Cocktail 3½ oz. 7.00
#803 Comport
    5" 8.00
    6" 10.00
#503 Comport, Footed, Covered 5" 18.00
#801 Cordial ¾ oz. 10.00
#810 Cordial 1 oz. 10.00
#858 Cordial 1 oz. 10.00
#863 Cordial 1 oz. 10.00
#880 Cordial
    ¾ oz...10.00
    1 oz. 12.00
#5008 Cordial 1 oz. 10.00
#1061 Cracker Jar, Covered 50.00
#1227 Cream 12.00
#1478 Cream 12.00
#1480 Cream 12.00
#1712 Cream 12.00
#1720 Cream 12.00
#1759 Cream 12.00
#810 Creme de Menthe 2½ oz. 7.00
#858 Creme de Menthe 2½ oz. 7.00
#863 Creme de Menthe 2½ oz. 7.00
#880 Creme de Menthe 2½ oz. 7.00

#5008 Creme de Menthe 2½ oz. 7.00
#481 Custard 6.00
#810 Custard 6.00
#858 Custard 6.00
#858 Custard Plate 4.00
#200 Custard Plate 4.00
#300 Decanter, Cut Neck, Cut Stopper
    Pint 35.00
    Quart 40.00
#1136 Decanter, Cut Stopper 40.00
#1195 Decanter, Cut Neck, Cut Stopper
    Small 35.00
    Medium 40.00
    Large 45.00
#1464 Decanter, Cut Stopper, Cut Neck
    10 oz. 40.00
    18 oz. 45.00
#1491 Decanter, Optic, Cut Neck 25 oz. 40.00
#1483 Decanter, Individual 22.00
#1483 Decanter, Individual, Cut Neck 30.00
#5008 Egg 13.00
#315 Finger Bowl 6.00
#315 Finger Bowl Plate............................4.00
#810 Finger Bowl 6.00
#858 Finger Bowl 6.00
#858 Finger Bowl Plate 6"........................4.00
#1349 Finger Bowl 6.00
#1499 Finger Bowl 6.00
#1499 Finger Bowl Plate...........................4.00
#823 Fruit
    4½"...8.00
    5" 8.00
#863 Fruit 8.00
#1736 Fruit Plate 6" 5.00
#858 Fruit Salad 10.00
#5013 Gin Rickey.......................................7.00
#810 Goblet 9 oz. 6.00
#801 Goblet
    1 oz. 10.00
    2 oz. 7.00
    3 oz. 7.00
    4 oz. 7.00
    5 oz. 7.00
    9 oz. 7.00
    10 oz. 7.00
    11 oz. 10.00
#826 Goblet 9 oz. 7.00
#858 Goblet
    9 oz. 7.00
    10 oz. 7.00
    11 oz. 8.00
#863 Goblet

    7 oz. 7.00
    9 oz. 7.00
    10 oz. 7.00
    10½ oz. 8.00
#5008 Goblet
    9 oz. 7.00
    10 oz. 8.00
    11 oz. 10.00
#880 Grapefruit 10.00
#880 Grapefruit Liner..............................4.00
#880½ Grapefruit 10.00
#880½ Grapefruit Liner...........................4.00
#945 Grapefruit 10.00
#945½ Grapefruit 10.00
#945½ Grapefruit Liner 4.00
#4024 Highball..7.00
#1132 Horseradish...................................22.00
#858 Ice Cream 4½" 10.00
#858 Ice Tea with Plate............................12.00
#825 Jelly, Covered 20.00
#303 Jug
    2..28.00
    3..20.00
    4..25.00
    5..25.00
    6..30.00
    7..30.00
    8..40.00
#303 Jug 7, Small Stars 50.00
#303 Jug 7, Large Stars 50.00
#724 Jug 7, Small Stars 50.00
#724 Jug 7, Large Stars 50.00
#1227 Jug 7...45.00
#1227 Jug 7, Cut Neck.............................50.00
#1227 Jug 7, 5 Stars on Bottom,
    2 on Neck 50.00
#1236 Jug, 6 Large Stars 45.00
#801 Liquor ¾ oz......................................10.00
#738 Marmalade, Covered 20.00
#858 Mineral Tumbler 5 oz. 7.00
#403 Mustard, Covered 20.00
#1831 Mustard, Covered 20.00
#314 Nappy 4" 6.00
#315 Nappy
    4½"...6.00
    5" 6.00
    6" 7.00
    7" 10.00
    8" 15.00
    9" 20.00
    10" 20.00
#803 Nappy, Footed, Deep 4½" 10.00

#803 Nappy, Footed, Shallow
    6" 10.00
    7" 14.00
    8" 16.00

#803 Nappy, Footed, Covered
    5" 18.00
    6" 18.00

#1227 Nappy
    4½" 6.00
    5" 6.00
    6" 7.00
    8" 10.00
    9" 10.00

#312 Oil, Cut Stopper.............................40.00
#900½ Oil, Small 40.00
#1164 Oil, Cut Stopper.............................45.00
#1465 Oil, Cut Neck 7 oz..........................45.00
#1389 Oyster Cocktail 7.00
#1542 Oyster Cocktail 7.00
#766½ Parfait...7.00
#863 Pousse-Cafe ¾ oz. 8.00

#880 Pousse-Cafe
    ¾ oz..8.00
    1 oz..8.00

#5008 Pousse-Cafe 1 oz..........................8.00
#1227 Punch Bowl with Foot 110.00
#2263 Salt, Individual 12.00
#601 Shaker, Silver-Plated Top.............12.00
#614 Shaker, Pearl Top 12.00
#1165 Shaker, Silver-Plated Top............12.00
#1165½ Shaker, Pearl Top 12.00
#810 Sherbet 7.00
#840 Sherbet 7.00
#840 Sherbet Plate...................................4.00
#842 Sherbet 7.00
#843 Sherbet 7.00
#858 Sherbet 7.00
#880 Sherbet 7.00
#830 Sherbet, Tall 5 oz............................8.00
#5008 Sherbet 7.00
#810 Sherry 2 oz. 7.00
#846 Sherry 2 oz. 7.00
#858 Sherry 2 oz. 7.00
#863 Sherry 2 oz. 7.00
#880 Sherry 2 oz. 7.00
#5008 Sherry 2 oz. 7.00
#315 Straw Jar, Covered 55.00
#1227 Sugar, Open 13.00
#1227 Sugar, Covered 15.00
#1478 Sugar, 2 Handles...........................12.00
#1480 Sugar, 2 Handles...........................12.00
#1712 Sugar 12.00

#1720 Sugar 12.00
#1759 Sugar 12.00
#858 Sweetmeat 12.00

#2194 Syrup, Nickel Top
    8 oz. 50.00
    12 oz. 50.00

#300 Tankard Cut Star Bottom
    1...25.00
    2...25.00
    3...30.00
    3½...30.00
    4...40.00
    5...40.00
    7...45.00
    7½...45.00
    8...50.00

#300 Tankard, Medium Stars
    6...40.00
    7...45.00

#300 Tankard, Large Stars 45.00

#724 Tankard
    6...40.00
    7...45.00

#403 Toothpick 25.00
#922 Toothpick, Cut Flute 25.00
#820 Tumbler, Table 7.00
#820 Tumbler, Table, Sham 7.00
#4011½ Tumbler, Table 7.00

#858 Tumbler, Table
    6½ oz. 7.00
    8 oz. 7.00
    10 oz. 7.00
    12 oz. 8.00
    14 oz. 8.00
    16 oz. 8.00

#701 Tumbler 13 oz. 10.00
#701 Tumbler Plate 4.00
#820½ Tumbler, Star Bottom 10.00
#833 Tumbler, Sham 8 oz. 7.00

#833 Tumbler, Sham, Cut Star Bottom
    8 oz. 10.00

#880 Tumbler
    8 oz. 7.00
    9 oz. 7.00
    10 oz. 8.00
    11 oz. 8.00

#889 Tumbler 5 oz. 7.00
#1697 Tumbler, Carafe 6 oz.....................7.00
#923 Tumbler, Handled 10.00
#4011 Tumbler 12 oz. 8.00
#4011 Tumbler, Handled 12 oz. 10.00
#858 Tumbler Plate 4.00

⇒ LARGE SUNBURST STAR Cutting #81 cont. ⇐

#1120 Vase	
12" 22.00	
15" 30.00	
#1694 Vase 8" 15.00	
#4069 Vase 9" 20.00	
#160½ Water Bottle, Cut Neck 35.00	
#304 Water Bottle, Cut Neck 35.00	
#1558 Water Bottle, Cut Neck..................35.00	
#858 Whiskey 7.00	
#844 Whiskey, Hot 8.00	
#845 Whiskey, Hot.........................8.00	
#858 Whiskey, Hot.........................8.00	

#5008 Whiskey, Hot 4 oz. 8.00
#810 Wine 3 oz. 7.00
#847 Wine 7.00
#858 Wine 7.00
   2¾ oz. 7.00
   3½ oz. 7.00
#863 Wine 3 oz. 7.00
#863 Wine, Rhine 4½ oz. 7.00
#880 Wine
   2¾ oz. 7.00
   3½ oz. 7.00
#5008 Wine 3½ oz. 7.00

⇒ LATTICE Cutting #196 ⇐

Optic
Crystal
1929 – 1930

#2394 Bowl 12" 20.00
#2394 Candlestick 2" ....pair 30.00
#877 Claret 12.00
#877 Cocktail...7.00
#877 Cordial 12.00
#869 Finger Bowl 8.00
#877 Goblet 9.00
#877 Oyster Cocktail 7.00
#877 Parfait 9.00
#2283 Plate, Optic
   6" 7.00
   7" 10.00
   8" 12.00
#877 Sherbet
   High 10.00

   Low 6.00
#877 Tumbler, Footed
   2½ oz. 8.00
   5 oz. 8.00
   9 oz. 8.00
   12 oz. 10.00
#877 Wine 12.00

⇒ LAUREL Cutting #776 ⇐

Crystal
1938 – 1960

LAUREL included in Patterns of the Past and Nostalgia Programs

Traditional in style, LAUREL is equally suited in modern table settings.

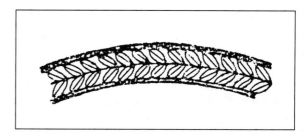

#4148 Ash Tray, Individual 2½" 8.00
#2574 Bon Bon 16.00
#2527 Bowl, Footed 9" 35.00
#2574 Bowl, Handled 9½" 35.00
#6023 Bowl, Footed 20.00
#2574 Cake Plate 30.00
#2527 Candelabra, 2 Light ....pair 64.00
#2324 Candlestick 6" ....pair 50.00
#2574 Candlestick 4" ....pair 40.00
#2574 Celery Dish 18.00
#6017 Champagne, Saucer 6 oz. 15.00
#4148 Cigarette Holder 2½" 30.00
#6017 Claret 4 oz. 25.00
#6019 Claret 4½ oz. 25.00
#6017 Cocktail 3½ oz. 16.00
#6019 Cocktail 3½ oz. 16.00
#2574 Comport 5".............................. 18.00
#6017 Cordial ¾ oz. 30.00
#2574 Cream, Footed 15.00
#2574 Cream, Individual 12.00
#766 Finger Bowl 8.00
#6017 Goblet 9 oz. 22.00
#6019 Goblet 10 oz. 22.00
#2451 Ice Dish.....................................20.00
#2574 Ice Tub 45.00
#6011 Jug, Footed 60.00
#2574 Lemon Dish 18.00
#2574 Mayonnaise
    Bowl...15.00
    Plate..12.00
    Ladle 20.00
#2574 Olive Dish 14.00
#6017 Oyster Cocktail 4 oz. 12.00
#6019 Oyster Cocktail 4¾ oz. 12.00
#6019 Parfait 6 oz. 15.00
#2574 Pickle Dish 16.00
#2337 Plate
    6" 8.00
    7" 8.00
    8" 10.00
#2574 Relish, 3 part..............................24.00
#2574 Serving Dish 22.00
#6017 Sherbet, Low 6 oz. 14.00
#6019 Sherbet 6½ oz.............................14.00
#2575 Sugar, Footed 18.00

#2574 Sugar, Individual 15.00
#2574 Sweetmeat...................................16.00
#2586 Syrup Server, Sani-Cut top 45.00
#6017 Tumbler, Footed
    5 oz. 10.00
    9 oz. 12.00
    12 oz. 16.00
#6019 Tumbler, Footed
    5 oz. 10.00
    12 oz. 16.00
#2574 Whip Cream 40.00
#6017 Wine 3 oz. 24.00
#6019 Wine 3½ oz. 24.00

LAUREL items included in Patterns of the Past and Nostalgia Programs

LA01/008 Champagne/High Dessert 6 oz.
    5½"...18.00
LA01/011 Champagne/Low Dessert 6 oz.
    4½"...14.00
LA01/025 Claret 4 oz. 5⅞" 25.00
LA01/002 Goblet 9 oz. 7⅜"......................22.00
LA01/063 Luncheon Goblet/Ice Tea 12 oz.
    6" 15.00
LA01/026 Wine 3 oz. 5½" 24.00

⤙ **LEGION Plate Etching #309** ⤚

Crystal, Rose, Topaz
Rose, Topaz 1931 – 1935
1931 – 1940

LEGION items made in Crystal

#2440 Bowl 10½" 35.00
#2374 Candlestick 3" ....pair 40.00
#6000 Champagne, Saucer/High Sherbet
    6 oz. 12.00
#6000 Cocktail 3½ oz. 12.00
#2375½ Cream, Footed......................18.00
#2375½ Cup, Footed 17.00
#6000 Goblet 10 oz. 14.00
#6000 Oyster Cocktail 4 oz. 8.00
#2375 Plate
    6" 10.00
    7" 10.00
    8" 15.00
    9" 20.00
#2440 Salad Bowl 12" 45.00
#2375 Saucer....................................8.00
#6000 Sherbet, Low 6 oz. 10.00
#2375½ Sugar, Footed 22.00
#2440 Torte Plate 13"...........................40.00
#887 Tumbler 2½ oz. 10.00
#889 Tumbler
    5 oz. 6.00
    13 oz. 10.00
#4076 Tumbler 9 oz. 8.00
#6000 Tumbler, Footed
    5 oz. 12.00
    13 oz. 14.00
#2440 Vase 7" 75.00
#6000 Wine 3 oz. 18.00

LEGION items made in Crystal, Rose and Topaz; add 20% to these values for Rose and Topaz.

#2470 Bon Bon 18.00
#2424 Bowl 8" 30.00
#2470 Bowl 12" 45.00

#2470½ Bowl 10½"....................................40.00
#2470 Cake Plate 10" 32.00
#2375 Candlestick 3" ....pair 50.00
#2470 Candlestick 5½" ....pair 60.00
#2470½ Candlestick 5½" ....pair 60.00
#2456 Candy Jar, Covered ½ lb. 70.00
#2419 Comport 6" 34.00
#2470 Comport
    High 6" 40.00
    Low 6" 30.00
#2470 Lemon Dish 26.00
#2470 Relish, 3 part, Round....................40.00
#2470 Relish, 4 part, Oval 50.00
#2440 Salad Bowl 12" 40.00
#2470 Service Dish 9" 30.00
#2470 Sweetmeat....................................26.00
#2440 Torte Plate 13"..............................45.00
#2470 Tray, Sugar and Cream.................. 70.00
#2440 Vase 7" 80.00
#2454 Vase 8" 100.00

LEICESTER Cutting #722½

Rock Crystal
Cut Bowl
Crystal
1933 – 1935
See WELLINGTON for pattern; LEICESTER has plain stem.

#2470½ Bowl 10½" 30.00
#2470½ Candlestick 5½" ....pair 45.00
#6010 Claret/Wine 4 oz...........................25.00
#6010 Cocktail 4 oz. 18.00
#2400 Comport 6" 20.00
#6010 Cordial 1 oz. 30.00
#869 Finger Bowl 8.00

#6010 Goblet 9 oz. 22.00
#6010 Oyster Cocktail 5½ oz. 12.00
#2337 Plate
    6" 6.00
    7" 8.00
    8" 10.00
#6010 Sherbet
    High 5½ oz. 18.00
    Low 5½ oz. 16.00
#6010 Tumbler, Footed
    5 oz. 12.00
    9 oz. 12.00
    12 oz. 20.00
#2470 Vase 10" 50.00

LENORE Needle Etching #73

Optic Pattern
Crystal
1923 – 1931

#858 Champagne, Saucer 8.00
#858 Claret 4½ oz. 8.00
#858 Cocktail 3½ oz. 8.00
#5078 Comport
    5" 10.00
    6" 10.00
#858 Cordial 1 oz. 10.00
#2333 Cream 8.00
#858 Finger Bowl 7.00
#2283 Finger Bowl Plate 6".........................4.00
#858 Fruit 7.00
#858 Goblet 9 oz. 10.00
#945½ Grapefruit 8.00
#945½ Grapefruit Liner 4.00
#701 Ice Tea 12 oz. 10.00
#303 Jug 7...28.00
#318 Jug 7...28.00
#1236 Jug 6...26.00
#2270 Jug, Covered 32.00
#858 Mayonnaise
    Bowl 6.00
    Plate 4.00
    Ladle 20.00
#5078 Nappy
    5" 5.00
    6" 5.00
    7" 6.00
#312 Oil 32.00

#858 Parfait 5½ oz. 8.00

#2283 Plate 5" 5.00
#858 Sherbet 8.00
#2133 Sugar 8.00
#858 Sweetmeat....................................10.00
#880 Sweetmeat....................................10.00
#300 Tankard 7 ....25.00
#820 Tumbler, Table 6.00
#858 Tumbler, Table 6.00
#858 Tumbler
    3 oz. 6.00
    5½ oz. 6.00
    8 oz. 8.00
    12 oz. 10.00
    14 oz. 10.00
#869 Tumbler, Handled 12.00
#701 Tumbler, Plate 5"..............................4.00
#858 Wine 2¾ oz. 8.00

⌐═ LENOX Plate Etching #330 ═⌐

Crystal
1937 – 1944

#6017 Champagne, Saucer/High Sherbet		
6 oz.	18.00	
#6017 Claret 4 oz.	22.00	
#6017 Cocktail 3½ oz.	18.00	
#6017 Cordial ¾ oz.	30.00	
#2350½ Cream, Footed	18.00	
#766 Finger Bowl	10.00	
#6017 Goblet 9 oz.	22.00	
#6011 Jug, Footed	70.00	
#4132 Old Fashioned Cocktail, Sham		
7½ oz.	12.00	
#6017 Oyster Cocktail 4 oz.	14.00	
#2337 Plate		
6"	10.00	
7"	14.00	
8"	20.00	
#6017 Sherbet, Low 6 oz.	15.00	
#2350½ Sugar, Footed	17.00	
#4132 Tumbler, Sham		
5 oz.	6.00	
7 oz.	8.00	
9 oz.	10.00	
12 oz.	10.00	

14 oz.	12.00
#6017 Tumbler, Footed	
5 oz.	14.00
9 oz.	12.00
12 oz.	16.00
14 oz.	18.00
#4132 Whiskey, Sham 1½ oz.	10.00
#4132 Whiskey Sour, Sham 4 oz.	10.00
#6017 Wine 3 oz.	23.00

⌐═ LIDO Plate Etching #329 ═⌐

Crystal
Azure Bowl with Crystal Base 1937 – 1943
1937 – 1955

Atune with the times, Fostoria suggested that
LIDO would compliment a modern table – a
Swedish Modern table. In 1937 the American furniture manufacturers had not incorporated modernism into their products.

*Stemware made with Azure Bowl. Tableware
made in Azure.

#2496 Bon Bon 3 Toed*	22.00
#2496 Bowl, Handled 10½"	45.00
#2496 Bowl, Flared 12"*	60.00
#2545 Bowl, "Flame," Oval 12½"	55.00
#2496 Cake Plate, 2-Handled 10"	35.00
#2496 Candy Box, Covered, 3 part*	60.00
#2496 Candlestick 4"*	pair 50.00

#2496 Candlestick 5½"*	pair 60.00
#2496 Candlestick, Duo*	pair 70.00
#2545 Candlestick, "Flame," Duo	pair 80.00
#2545 Candelabra, "Flame," Prisms	
2 Light*	pair 140.00
#2545 Lustre Candleholder	pair 100.00
#2496 Celery 11"	22.00

#6017 Champagne, Saucer/High
    Sherbet* 18.00
#2496 Cheese & Cracker (Bowl 5½",
    Plate 11") 40.00
#6017 Claret 4 oz.*................................18.00
#6017 Cocktail 3½ oz.*...........................18.00
#2496 Comport 5½" 25.00
#2496 Comport, Tall 6½" 30.00
#6017 Cordial ¾ oz.* 32.00
#2496 Cream, Footed* 18.00
#2496 Cream, Individual*.........................15.00
#2496 Cup, Footed* 10.00
#766 Finger Bowl* 8.00
#6017 Goblet 9 oz.* 20.00
#2496 Jelly, Covered 25.00
#6011 Jug, Footed 75.00
#2496 Ice Bucket, Gold Handled*..............65.00
#2545 Lustre* 35.00
#2496 Mayonnaise, 2 part 6½" 30.00
#2496½ Mayonnaise
    Bowl 20.00
    Plate 15.00
    Ladle 20.00
#2496 Nappy, Handled
    Regular.............................16.00
    Flared..............................16.00
    Square 18.00
    3 Cornered 16.00
#2496 Nut Bowl, 3 Toed, Cupped 18.00
#2496 Oil, Crystal Stopper 3½ oz. 70.00
#4132 Old Fashioned Cocktail 7½ oz. 16.00
#6017 Oyster Cocktail 4 oz.* 14.00
#2496 Pickle Dish 8" 14.00
#2337 Plate 7" 15.00
#2496 Plate *
    6" 10.00
    7" 15.00

    8" 20.00
    9" 30.00
#2419 Relish, 4 part (Crystal only) 45.00
#2496 Relish
    2 part 30.00
    3 part*............................35.00
#2496 Sauce Dish, Oblong 6½" 25.00
#2496 Saucer* 10.00
#2496 Serving Dish, Deep, 2-handled
    8½"..............................35.00
#2496 Shaker, Glass Top.................pair 60.00
#6017 Sherbet, Low 6 oz.* 12.00
#2496 Sugar, Footed* 18.00
#2496 Sugar, Individual* 16.00
#2496 Sweetmeat.................................14.00
#2496 Tid Bit, 3 Toed, Flat 8¼" 18.00
#2496 Torte Plate 14" 60.00
#2496 Tray, Oblong 8" 40.00
#2496½ Tray for Cream & Sugar 6½" 30.00
#4132 Tumbler, Sham
    4 oz. 8.00
    5 oz. 10.00
    7 oz. 10.00
    9 oz. 10.00
    12 oz. 12.00
    14 oz. 12.00
#6017 Tumbler, Footed *
    5 oz. 12.00
    9 oz. 14.00
    12 oz. 18.00
    14 oz. 20.00
#2470 Vase 10"*..................................80.00
#2496 Vase 8" 70.00
#4128 Vase 5"*....................................60.00
#4138 Whiskey, Sham 1½ oz. 10.00
#6017 Wine 3 oz. 23.00

⋙ LILY OF THE VALLEY Carving #19 ⋘

Crystal
1940 – 1944
Do not confuse with LILY OF THE VALLEY
Deep Plate Etching #241.

#2568 Vase, Footed 9" 100.00
#4132½ Vase 8" 100.00
#4132½ Vase, Footed 6" 60.00
#4132½ Vase, Footed 7½" 80.00

⋙ LILY OF THE VALLEY Deep Plate Etching #241 ⋘

Narrow Optic Pattern
Crystal
1915 – 1928
Do not confuse with LILY OF THE VALLEY
Carving #19.

#863 Almond 6.00
#1697 Carafe 20.00
#858 Champagne, Hollow Stem 10.00
#858 Champagne, Saucer 5 oz. 8.00
#858 Champagne, Tall 5½ oz. 12.00
#879 Champagne, Saucer 5 oz. 8.00
#858 Claret 4½ oz. 8.00
#879 Claret 4½ oz. 8.00
#858 Cocktail 3½ oz. 8.00
#879 Cocktail 3 oz. 8.00
#803 Comport
    5" 10.00
    6" 10.00
#858 Cordial 1 oz. 10.00
#879 Cordial ¾ oz. 10.00
#1480 Cream 8.00
#858 Creme de Menthe 2½ oz. 10.00
#879 Creme de Menthe 2½ oz. 10.00
#810 Custard..7.00
#810 Custard Plate 4.00
#858 Custard 7.00
#858 Custard Plate 4.00
#300 Decanter, Cut Neck, quart 50.00
#1464 Decanter, Cut Neck 18 oz. 45.00
#810 Finger Bowl 7.00
#810 Finger Bowl Plate..............................4.00
#858 Finger Bowl 7.00
#858 Finger Bowl Plate..............................4.00
#858 Fruit Salad 10.00
#858 Goblet 10 oz. 8.00

#873 Goblet 9 oz. 8.00
#945 Grapefruit 7.00
#4077 Grapefruit 7.00
#945 Grapefruit 7.00
#945½ Grapefruit 7.00
#945½ Grapefruit Liner 4.00
#4061 Ice Tea, Footed, Handled 10.00
#4077 Ice Tea 15 oz..................................10.00
#303 Jug 7..32.00
#318 Jug 7..32.00
#4061 Lemonade 8.00
#1968 Marmalade, Covered 18.00
#4077 Mineral Water 5½ oz. 6.00
#1831 Mustard, Covered 18.00
#803 Nappy, Deep
    4½"...6.00
    5" 6.00
    6" 7.00
    7" 10.00
#1227 Nappy

4½ oz.	6.00
8 oz.	10.00
#803 Nappy, Footed 8 oz.	10.00
#300½ Oil	
Small	25.00
Large	30.00
#1465 Oil, Cut Neck Large	35.00
#822 Parfait	8.00
#1719 Plate, Sandwich 10½"	12.00
#1848 Plate, Sandwich 9"	10.00
#858 Pousse-Cafe 1 oz.	10.00
#879 Pousse-Cafe ¾ oz.	10.00
#2083 Salad Dressing Bottle	22.00
#1165 Shaker	12.00
#858 Sherbet	8.00
#879 Sherbet	8.00
#840 Sherbet Plate	4.00
#858 Sherry 2 oz.	10.00
#879 Sherry 2 oz.	10.00
#858 Shortcake	6.00
#1480 Sugar	8.00
#858 Sweetmeat	10.00
#300 Tankard 7	32.00
#724 Tankard 7	32.00
#922 Toothpick	18.00
#858 Tumbler, Table	8.00
#4077 Tumbler, Table 9½ oz.	8.00
#820 Tumbler	6.00

#820½ Tumbler, Punty	8.00
#833 Tumbler 8 oz.	6.00
#858 Tumbler	
3½ oz.	4.00
3 oz.	4.00
5 oz.	4.00
6½ oz.	5.00
8 oz.	5.00
10 oz.	7.00
12 oz.	7.00
14 oz.	8.00
16 oz.	10.00
#858 Tumbler, Cut #19	
8 oz.	6.00
14 oz.	10.00
#887 Tumbler 3 oz.	4.00
#889 Tumbler 5 oz.	5.00
#1701 Tumbler 14 oz.	10.00
#4065 Tumbler, Sham, Cut #19	
2½ oz.	5.00
5 oz.	5.00
8 oz.	6.00
10 oz.	8.00
14 oz.	10.00
#1697 Tumbler, Carafe 6 oz.	8.00
#1558 Water Bottle, Cut Neck	30.00
#858 Wine 2¾ oz.	8.00
#879 Wine 2¾ oz.	8.00

⤚⊸ LINEAL Cutting #899 ⊶⤙

Gray Cutting
Crystal
1963 – 1965

#6102/31 Brandy 4 oz.	24.00
#6102/25 Claret 7½ oz.	26.00
#4185/495 Dessert/Finger Bowl	12.00
#6102/2 Goblet 10 oz.	26.00
#6102/63 Luncheon Goblet/Ice Tea 14 oz.	25.00
#2337 Plate	
7"	10.00
8"	10.00
#6102/11 Sherbet 8 oz.	24.00
#6102/26 Tulip Wine 5½ oz.	24.00

⇒ LIVING ROSE Crystal Print #5 ⇐

Crystal
1956 – 1958

Cocktail/Wine 4 oz. 4⅝" 28.00
Cordial 1 oz. 3⅛" 30.00
Goblet 11 oz. 6¼" 25.00
Ice Tea/Footed 12 oz. 6⅜" 25.00
Juice, Footed 6 oz. 4⅞".............................20.00
Plate
    7" 8.00
    8" 8.00
Sherbet 7½ oz. 4¾"..................................20.00

⇒ LOTUS Etching #232 ⇐

Crystal
1913 – 1928

#766 Almond 4.00
#863 Almond 4.00
#766 Bon Bon 10.00
#1490 Candlestick ....pair 20.00
#766 Champagne, Saucer 5 oz. 7.00
#5070 Champagne, Optic, Hollow Stem
    4½ oz..8.00
#5070 Champagne, Optic, Saucer 5½ oz. 7.00
#5070 Champagne, Optic, Tall 5½ oz. 7.00
#766 Claret 4½ oz. 8.00
#5070 Claret, Optic
    4½ oz. 8.00
    6 oz. 8.00
#766 Cocktail 3 oz. 7.00
#5070 Cocktail, Optic
    3 oz. 6.00
    3½ oz..6.00
#766 Comport
    5" 5.00
    6" 6.00
#803 Comport
    5" 5.00
    6" 5.00
#766 Cordial ¾ oz. 10.00
#5070 Cordial, Optic
    ¾ oz. 10.00
    1 oz. 10.00
#1478 Cream 12.00
#5070 Creme de Menthe, Optic 2½ oz. 7.00
#481 Custard, Optic...................................5.00
#766 Custard 5.00

#1195 Decanter, Cut Neck, Large 25.00
#1452 Decanter, Handled 35.00
#766 Finger Bowl 5.00
#1499 Finger Bowl 5.00
#1769 Finger Bowl 5.00
#766 Finger Bowl Plate 6".........................5.00
#1499 Finger Bowl Plate 5.00
#1769 Finger Bowl Plate 5.00
#766 Fruit 5.00
#766 Goblet 9 oz. 8.00
#5070 Goblet, Optic
    8 oz. 7.00
    9 oz. 7.00
    10 oz. 8.00
#766 Grapefruit 12.00–14.00

#766 Grapefruit and Liner 12.00	#5070 Sherry, Optic 8.00
#945½ Grapefruit and Liner 14.00	#1478 Sugar 10.00
#766 Ice Tea, Footed, Handled 14.00	#858 Sweetmeat......................................10.00
#4061 Ice Tea, Footed, Handled 15.00	#300 Tankard
#303 Jug 7...20.00	4 oz. 20.00
#1733 Marmalade, Covered, Notched 25.00	7 oz. 20.00
#803 Nappy 8" 6.00	#300 Tankard, Claret 20.00
#803 Nappy, Deep	#318 Tankard, Optic 7 ....7.00
5" 5.00	#922 Toothpick 18.00
6" 5.00	#4011½ Tumbler, Table 6.00
7" 8.00	#858 Tumbler, Table 6.00
#766 Nappy, Footed	#820 Tumbler, Optic 6.00
4½" 5.00	#858 Tumbler 14 oz. 10.00
5" 5.00	#887 Tumbler, 3 oz. 8.00
6" 5.00	#889 Tumbler
7" 5.00	5 oz. 6.00
#803 Nappy, Footed	7 oz. 6.00
5" 5.00	8 oz. 8.00
6" 5.00	10 oz. 10.00
7" 5.00	#4011 Tumbler
#1227 Nappy	3 oz. 8.00
4½"..5.00	5 oz. 6.00
8" 10.00	8 oz. 6.00
#300½ Oil, Cut Neck, Cut Stopper 25.00	10 oz. 8.00
#312 Oil...20.00	12 oz. 10.00
#1465 Oil, Cut Neck, Cut Stopper 20.00	15 oz. 12.00
#837 Oyster Cocktail 6.00	#4015 Tumbler 14 oz. 12.00
#766 Parfait.......................................7.00	#858 Tumbler Plate 12.00
#766½ Parfait.....................................7.00	#701 Tumbler Plate 10.00
#822 Parfait.......................................8.00	#1895 Vase 8" 30.00
#858 Plate 5.00	#1948 Vase
#5070 Pousse-Cafe, Optic	5" 30.00
¾ oz. 10.00	8" 40.00
1 oz. 10.00	10" 70.00
#5070 Rhine Wine, Optic 4½ oz. 8.00	12½"...80.00
#1165½ Shaker, Silver-Plated Top........set 20.00	#160½ Water Bottle, Cut Neck 25.00
#766 Sherbet 6.00	#1558 Water Bottle, Cut Neck...................20.00
#840 Sherbet 6.00	#5070 Whiskey, Hot, Optic 4 oz..................6.00
#840 Sherbet Plate................................6.00	#766 Wine 2¾ oz. 8.00
#5070 Sherbet, Optic 6.00	#5070 Wine, Optic 3 oz. 8.00
#766 Sherry 2 oz. 7.00	

⇜ LOVE SONG Decoration #655 ⇝

Platinum Band with Polished Cutting
Crystal
1961 – 1973

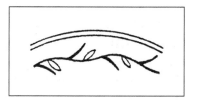

LOVE SONG included in Patterns of the Past Program, not included in Nostalgia Program

#6099/27 Cocktail/Wine 4½ oz. 24.00
#6099/29 Cordial 1 oz. 28.00
#4185/495 Dessert/Finger Bowl 12.00
#6099/2 Goblet 11 oz. 26.00
#6099/88 Juice, Footed 5½ oz. 18.00
#6099/63 Luncheon Goblet/Ice Tea
    14 oz. 24.00
#2337 Plate
    7" 10.00
    8" 10.00
#6099/11 Sherbet/Dessert/Champagne
    6½ oz. 22.00

LOVE SONG items included in Patterns of the Past Program

L002/01 Champagne/Dessert 6½ oz. 5⅛"..22.00
L002/027 Cocktail/Wine 4½ oz. 5⅛" 24.00
L002/002 Goblet 11 oz. 6⅞" 26.00
L002/063 Luncheon Goblet/Ice Tea
    14 oz. 6⅝"..24.00

⇜ LOUISA Cutting #168 ⇝

Crystal
1922 – 1928

#880 Bon Bon 12.00
#2250 Candy Jar, Covered
    ¼ lb. 40.00
    ½ lb. 50.00
    1 lb. 60.00
#1697 Carafe 20.00
#4023 Carafe Tumbler 10.00
#661 Champagne, Saucer 6 oz. 10.00
#661 Cocktail...10.00
#2241 Cologne, Stopper 70.00
#803 Comport
    5" 15.00
    6" 20.00
#803 Comport, Covered 24.00
#1480 Cream 14.00

#1769 Finger Bowl 8.00
#661 Fruit, Footed 6 oz. 8.00

➤ LOUISA Cutting #168 cont. ➤

#661 Goblet 9 oz. 10.00
#945½ Grapefruit 30.00
#945½ Grapefruit Liner 18.00
#825 Jelly, Footed 8 oz. 22.00
#825 Jelly, Covered 8 oz. 22.00
#303 Jug 7 ....30.00
#317 Jug, Cut Neck 34.00
#317½ Jug & Cover 50.00
#1852 Jug 6...30.00
#4087 Marmalade, Covered 10 oz. 30.00
#2138 Mayonnaise
    Bowl 18.00
    Plate 12.00
    Ladle 20.00
#803 Nappy
    5" 10.00
    6" 10.00
    7" 14.00
#803 Nappy, Covered 5" 20.00
#1465 Oil, Cut Neck

    5 oz. 40.00
    7 oz. 50.00
#661 Parfait 5½ oz. 10.00
#840 Plate 5" 8.00
#1736 Plate 6" 8.00
#2238 Plate
    8¼"..15.00
    11"...20.00
#2263 Salt, Individual 10.00
#2235 Salt, Glass Top ....pair 80.00
#2235 Salt, Pearl Top ....pair 100.00
#1480 Sugar 24.00
#2194 Syrup, Nickel Top
    6 oz. 25.00
    8 oz. 30.00
#4085 Tumbler, Table 9½ oz. 10.00
#4085 Tumbler 13 oz. 12.00
#4085 Tumbler, Handled 12 oz. 18.00
#2209 Vase 9" 80.00
#661 Wine 2 oz. 12.00

➤ LUCERNE Cutting #778 ➤

Rock Crystal
Crystal
1938 – 1939

#6017 Champagne, Saucer 5 oz. 17.00
#6017 Claret 4 oz. 24.00
#6017 Cocktail 3½ oz. 17.00
#6017 Cordial ¾ oz. 26.00
#4132 Decanter 60.00
#766 Finger Bowl 8.00
#6017 Goblet 9 oz. 22.00
#4132 Ice Bowl...25.00
#6011 Jug, Footed 70.00
#4132 Old Fashioned Cocktail, Sham
    7½ oz. 6.00
#6017 Oyster Cocktail 4 oz. 20.00
#6017 Sherbet, Low 6 oz. 12.00
#4132 Tumbler, Sham
    5 oz. 6.00
    9 oz. 8.00
    12 oz. 8.00
#6017 Tumbler, Footed
    5 oz. 10.00

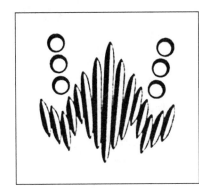

    9 oz. 10.00
    12 oz. 16.00
#2337 Plate
    6" 8.00
    7" 8.00
    8" 10.00
#4132 Whiskey, Sham 5 oz. 6.00
#6017 Wine 3 oz. 22.00

⊷ LYNN Cutting #180 ⊶

Crystal
1925 – 1928

#5083 Champagne, Saucer 5½ oz. 16.00
#5083 Cocktail 14.00
#2327 Comport 7" 30.00
#2315 Cream 18.00
#1769 Finger Bowl 8.00
#1769 Finger Bowl Plate 6" 6.00
#5083 Fruit, Footed 5½ oz. 13.00
#5083 Goblet 9 oz. 16.00
#2222 Grapefruit 20.00
#2222 Grapefruit Plate 10.00
#2332 Grapefruit 20.00
#2332 Grapefruit Plate 10.00
#2040 Jug 3 ....30.00
#2082 Jug 7 ....30.00
#2315 Mayonnaise 18.00
#2315 Mayonnaise Plate 7" 14.00
#2222 Plate
   7" 10.00
   8" 12.00
   10" 20.00

#2321 Plate 22.00
#2321 Sherbet 14.00
#820 Tumbler, Table 10.00
#701 Tumbler 13 oz. 12.00
#889 Tumbler 5 oz. 10.00
#4011 Tumbler, Handled 12 oz. 20.00
#5083 Wine 18.00

⊷ LYNWOOD Crystal Print #4 ⊶

Crystal
1956 – 1965

#6065/21 Cocktail/Wine 4 oz. 26.00
#6065/29 Cordial 1 oz. 35.00
#6065/2 Goblet 11 oz. 25.00
#6065/88 Juice, Footed 5 oz. 20.00
#6065/63 Luncheon Goblet/Ice Tea
   12 oz. 23.00
#2337 Plate
   7" 10.00
   8" 10.00
#6065/7 Sherbet 7½ oz. 21.00

LYRIC Cutting #796

Combination Rock Crystal and Gray Cutting
Crystal
1939 – 1944

#6023 Bowl, Footed 20.00
#2324 Candlestick 6" ....pair 40.00
#892 Champagne, Saucer 7 oz. 10.00
#892 Claret 4 oz. 12.00
#892 Cocktail 4 oz.....................................8.00
#892 Cordial 1 oz. 12.00
#1759 Finger Bowl 8.00
#892 Goblet 11 oz. 12.00
#6011 Jug, Footed 50.00
#892 Oyster Cocktail 4½ oz. 8.00
#2337 Plate
    6" 8.00
    7" 8.00
    8" 10.00
#892 Sherbet, Low 6 oz. 8.00

#892 Tumbler, Footed
    5 oz. 6.00
    12 oz. 8.00
#892 Wine 3 oz. 10.00

MANHATTAN Cutting #725

Rock Crystal
Crystal
1933 – 1939

#4024 Bowl, Footed 10" 40.00
#4024 Candlestick 6" ....pair 30.00
#4024 Champagne, Saucer 6½ oz. 20.00
#4024 Cocktail 4 oz....................................18.00
#4024 Comport 5" 15.00
#4024 Cordial 1 oz. 21.00
#6011 Decanter, Footed 70.00
#869 Finger Bowl 8.00
#4024 Goblet 10 oz. 20.00
#4024½ Goblet 11 oz. 20.00
#6011 Jug, Footed 50.00
#1184 Old Fashioned Cocktail, Sham or Plain
    7 oz. 6.00
#4024 Oyster Cocktail 4 oz. 15.00
#2337 Plate
    6" 6.00
    7" 8.00
    8" 10.00
    11 oz. 15.00

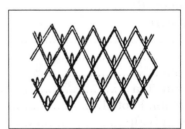

#4024 Rhine Wine 3½ oz. 20.00
#4024 Sherbet 5½ oz. 18.00
#4024 Sherry 2 oz. 18.00
#701 Tumbler, Sham or Plain
    10 oz. 5.00
    12 oz. 6.00
#4024 Tumbler, Footed
    5 oz. 15.00
    8 oz. 15.00
    12 oz. 20.00
#887 Whiskey, Sham or Plain 1¾ oz. 6.00
#4024 Wine 3½ oz. 15.00

⊰ MANOR Plate Etching #286 ⊱

1931 – 1944
Crystal 1931 – 1944; Green 1931 – 1935;
Topaz 1931 – 1938; Green Bowl, Crystal
Base 1931 – 1935; Topaz Bowl, Crystal Base
1931 – 1937; Crystal Bowl, Wisteria Base
1931 – 1935

MANOR Dinnerware made in Crystal, Green, Topaz; ADD 20% TO VALUES FOR GREEN AND TOPAZ

#4020 Almond, Individual	8.00
#2419 Ash Tray	18.00
#2419 Baker 10"	30.00
#2419 Bon Bon	24.00
#2433 Bowl 12"	40.00
#2443 Bowl, Oval 10"	38.00
#2394 Bowl 12"	40.00
#2470½ Bowl 10½"	34.00
#2419 Cake Plate	30.00
#2433 Candlestick 3"	pair 40.00
#2443 Candlestick 3"	pair 40.00
#2470½ Candlestick 5½"	pair 50.00
#2394 Candlestick 2"	pair 35.00
#2430 Candy Jar,, Covered ½ lb.	75.00
#2419 Celery 11"	26.00
#2419 Cereal 6"	20.00
#2419 Comport 6"	30.00
#2433 Comport	
Tall 6"	35.00
Low 6"	30.00
#2419 Cream	18.00
#2419 Cream, Tea	22.00
#2419½ Cream, Footed	18.00
#2419 Cream Soup	26.00
#2419 Cup, Footed	10.00
#2419 Cup, After Dinner	20.00
#4020 Decanter, Footed	150.00
#2419 Fruit 5"	8.00
#2451 Fruit Cocktail	8.00
#2451 Ice Dish	60.00
#2451 Ice Dish Plate	35.00
#2443 Ice Tub 6"	80.00
#2419 Jelly	20.00
#2419 Lemon Dish	28.00
#2419 Mayonnaise	26.00
#2419 Pickle 8½"	20.00
#2419 Plate	
6"	10.00
7"	14.00
8"	20.00
9"	30.00
#2419 Platter	
12"	40.00
15"	50.00
#2419 Relish 8½"	20.00
#2419 Relish 4 part	38.00
#2419 Sauce Boat with Stand	70.00
#2419 Saucer	6.00
#2419 Saucer, After Dinner	12.00
#2419 Shaker	pair 100.00
#4020 Shaker, Footed	pair 120.00
#2419 Soup 7"	24.00
#2419 Sugar	30.00
#2419 Sugar. Tea	30.00
#2419½ Sugar, Footed	34.00
#2419 Syrup, Covered	40.00
#2419 Syrup Saucer	20.00
#2440 Torte Plate 13"	40.00
#2419 Tray, Lunch, Handled	34.00
#4106 Vase 7"	60.00
#4107 Vase 9"	90.00
#4108 Vase	
5"	60.00
6"	70.00
7"	90.00
8"	110.00

MANOR stemware made in Crystal, Green, Topaz and Wisteria with Crystal Base; ADD 20% TO VALUES FOR GREEN AND TOPAZ, DOUBLE PRICE FOR WISTERIA

MANOR Plate Etching #286 cont.

#6003 Claret 4½ oz. 26.00
#6003 Champagne, Saucer/High Sherbet
    6 oz. 26.00
#6003 Cocktail 3½ oz. 25.00
#6003 Cordial 1¼ oz. (not made in Topaz) 36.00
#4021 Finger Bowl 8.00
#6003 Goblet 10 oz. 28.00
#4020 Jug, Footed (not made in Wisteria)..170.00
#6003 Oyster Cocktail 4½ oz. 18.00
#6003 Sherbet, Low 6 oz. 20.00
#6003 Tumbler, Footed
    2½ oz. (not made in Topaz) 24.00
    5 oz. 18.00
    9 oz. 18.00
    12 oz. 25.00

MANOR Stemware made in Solid Crystal
#6007 Champagne, Saucer/High Sherbet
    5½ oz...20.00
#6007 Claret 4 oz. 28.00
#6007 Cocktail 3½ oz. 20.00
#6007 Cordial 1 oz. 40.00
#6007 Goblet 10 oz. 25.00
#6007 Oyster Cocktail 4½ oz. 15.00
#6007 Sherbet, Low 5½ oz.........................20.00
#6007 Tumbler, Footed
    2 oz. 26.00
    5 oz. 14.00
    9 oz. 14.00
    12 oz. 24.00
#6007 Wine 3 oz. 28.00

MARDI GRAS Cutting #765

Rock Crystal
Crystal
1937 – 1944

#6011 Champagne, Saucer 5½ oz. 14.00
#6011 Claret 4½ oz. 20.00
#6011 Cocktail 3 oz.....................................15.00
#6011 Cordial 1 oz. 20.00
#1769 Finger Bowl 10.00
#6011 Goblet 10 oz. 18.00
#6011 Jug, Footed 100.00
#6011 Oyster Cocktail 4 oz. 10.00
#2337 Plate
    6" 8.00
    7" 10.00
    8" 12.00
#6011 Sherbet, Low 5½ oz.........................12.00
#6011 Tumbler, Footed
    5 oz. 10.00
    10 oz. 10.00
    13 oz. 13.00
#6011 Wine 3 oz. 18.00

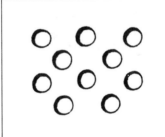

⋙ MARLBORO Cutting #717 ⋘

Rock Crystal
Regular Optic
Crystal
1933 – 1939

#2470 Bon Bon 12.00
#2470½ Bowl 10½" 30.00
#2470 Cake Plate 35.00
#2470½ Candlestick 5½" ....pair 35.00
#2472 Candlestick, Duo ....pair 50.00
#2482 Candlestick, Trindle ....pair 70.00
#6008 Champagne, Saucer/High Sherbet
    5½ oz. 18.00
#6008 Cocktail 3½" 18.00
#2400 Comport 6" 22.00
#6008 Cordial 1 oz. 28.00
#2440 Cream, Footed 15.00
#869 Finger Bowl 8.00
#1769 Finger Bowl 8.00
#2283 Finger Bowl Plate 6.00
#6008 Goblet 10 oz. 20.00
#2451 Ice Dish 15.00
#2451 Ice Dish Plate 10.00
#2470 Lemon Dish 14.00
#6008 Oyster Cocktail 5 oz. 12.00

#2283 Plate
    7" 8.00
    8" 10.00
#2264 Plate 16" 35.00
#6008 Sherbet, Low 5½ oz. 14.00
#2440 Sugar, Footed 15.00
#2470 Sweetmeat 10.00
#6008 Tumbler, Footed
    5 oz. 12.00
    9 oz. 12.00
    12 oz. 16.00
#2440 Vase 7" 50.00
#4107 Vase 9" 50.00
#6008 Wine 4 oz. 23.00

⋙ MARQUETTE Cutting #733 ⋘

Rock Crystal
Crystal
1934 – 1936

#4024 Bowl, Footed 10" 40.00
#906 Brandy Inhaler 15.00
#4024 Candlestick 6" ....pair 30.00
#795 Champagne, Hollow Stem 5½ oz. 12.00
#863 Champagne, Hollow Stem 5 oz. 15.00
#4024 Champagne, Saucer 6 oz. 20.00
#4024 Claret 3½ oz. 20.00
#4024 Cocktail 4 oz. 18.00
#4024 Comport 5" 20.00
#4024 Cordial 1 oz. 22.00
#6011 Decanter, Footed 70.00
#869 Finger Bowl 8.00
#4024 Goblet 10 oz. 20.00
#4024½ Goblet 11 oz. 20.00
#6011 Jug, Footed 50.00
#1184 Old Fashioned Cocktail 4 oz. 6.00
#4024 Oyster Cocktail 4 oz. 15.00

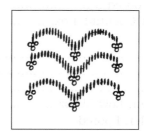

#2337 Plate
6" 6.00
7" 7.00
8" 8.00
#4024 Rhine Wine 3½ oz. 20.00
#4024 Sherbet 5½ oz. 18.00
#4024 Sherry 2 oz. 18.00
#701 Tumbler, Sham or Plain

10 oz. 6.00
12 oz. 6.00
#4024 Tumbler, Footed
5 oz. 15.00
8 oz. 15.00
12 oz. 20.00
#4024 Whiskey, Footed 2 oz. 15.00
#4122 Whiskey, Sham or Plain 1½ oz. 6.00

☞ MARQUIS Decoration #692 ☜

Crystal Print with Platinum Band on Bowl
Crystal
1971 – 1974
  Do not confuse with MARQUIS Cutting #831.

#6123/2 Goblet 8½ oz. 20.00
#6123/63 Luncheon Goblet/Ice Tea
11½ oz. 20.00
#2337/549 Plate 7" 12.00
#6123/11 Sherbet/Dessert/Champagne

7½ oz. 18.00
#6123/26 Wine 5½ oz. 20.00

☞ MARQUIS Cutting #831 ☜

Rock Crystal
Crystal
1952 – 1955
  Do not confuse with MARQUIS Decoration #692.

#6045 Claret/Wine 4¾ oz. 4" 21.00
#6045 Cocktail 4¾ oz. 3" 19.00
#6045 Cordial 1½ oz. 2⅝" 23.00
#6045 Goblet 15¾ oz. 5⅞" 21.00
#6045 Ice Tea, Footed 16 oz. 6⅛" 21.00
#6045 Juice, Footed 7¼ oz. 4⅝" 18.00
#2337 Plate 8" 10.00
#6045 Sherbet 9 oz. 3¾" 19.00

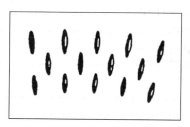

☜ MATRIMONY Cutting #910 ☞

Rock Crystal
Crystal
1966 – 1969

#6107/25 Claret 7½ oz. 23.00
#4185/495 Dessert/Finger Bowl 12.00
#6107/2 Goblet 11 oz. 25.00
#6107/29 Liqueur 2 oz. 28.00
#6107/63 Luncheon Goblet/Ice Tea
    14 oz. 23.00
#2337 Plate
    7" 10.00

8" 10.00
#6107/11 Sherbet 9 oz. 22.00
#6107/26 Tulip Wine 6½ oz. 25.00

☜ MAYDAY Plate Etching #312 ☞

Crystal Bowl, Green Base
1931 – 1932

MAYDAY dinnerware made in Crystal only

#2440 Bowl 10½" 35.00
#2375 Candlestick 3" ....pair 45.00
#2400 Comport 6" 32.00
#2400 Cream 18.00
#2440 Cup 10.00
#2440 Finger Bowl 8.00
#2440 Plate
    6" 10.00
    7" 12.00
    8" 20.00
    9" 24.00
#2440 Saucer...7.00
#2440 Sugar 22.00

MAYDAY stemware made in Crystal Bowl,
** Green Base**

#6005 Claret 24.00
#6005 Cocktail..20.00
#6005 Cordial 30.00

#6005 Goblet 22.00
#6005 Oyster Cocktail 16.00
#6005 Parfait 22.00
#6005 Sherbet
    High 20.00
    Low 16.00
#6005 Tumbler, Footed
    2½ oz...20.00
    5 oz. 18.00
    9 oz. 15.00
    12 oz. 22.00
#6005 Wine 26.00

⇒ MAYFLOWER Plate Etching #332 ⇐

Crystal
1939 – 1955

With a flower basket and garland design, MAYFLOWER'S complete service made it popular for use in formal entertaining.

#2560 Bon Bon 10.00
#2560 Bon Bon, 3 Toed 14.00
#2430 Bowl 11" 30.00
#2545 Bowl, Oval 12½" 30.00
#2496 Bowl, Handled 40.00
#2560 Bowl, Crimped 11½" 40.00
#2560 Bowl, Flared 12" 35.00
#2560 Bowl, Handled 30.00
#2560 Cake Plate 24.00
#2545 Candelabra, "Flame", 2 Light, 2"
    Prisms ....pair 100.00
#2430 Candlestick 2" ....pair 14.00
#2496 Candlestick, Duo ....pair 80.00
#2545 Candlestick, "Flame" 4½"...... pair 125.00
#2545 Candlestick, "Flame" Duo ....pair 60.00
#2560 Candlestick 4½" ....pair 25.00
#2560 Candlestick, Duo ....pair 24.00
#2560½ Candlestick 4" ....pair 36.00
#2430 Candy Jar, Covered 25.00
#2560 Celery 11" 16.00
#2560 Cereal 6" 10.00
#6020 Champagne, Saucer........................14.00
#2560 Cheese & Cracker 35.00
#6020 Claret 4½ oz. 30.00
#6020 Cocktail 3½ oz. 20.00
#2560 Comport 6" 28.00
#6020 Cordial 1 oz. 26.00
#2560 Cream, Footed 7 oz. 15.00
#2560 Cream, Individual, Footed 4 oz. 12.00

#2560 Cup 13.00
#869 Finger Bowl 8.00
#2560 Fruit 5" 10.00
#2560 Fruit Bowl 13" 50.00
#2560 Goblet 9 oz. 25.00
#2560 Ice Bucket, Chrome Handled,
    Tongs 60.00
#4140 Jug 60 oz. 150.00
#2560 Lemon Dish 15.00
#2545 Lustre, 8 Prisms ....pair 80.00
#2560 Mayonnaise
    Bowl..25.00
    Plate 12.00
    Ladle 20.00
#2560 Mayonnaise, 2 part 20.00
#2560 Mayonnaise, 2 part, 2 Ladles 40.00
#2430 Mint Dish 4½" 14.00
#2560 Muffin Tray 22.00
#2560 Nut Bowl, 3 Toed, Cupped 16.00
#2560 Oil, Footed, Stoppered 50.00
#2560 Olive Dish 6¾"...............................12.00
#6020 Oyster Cocktail 4 oz. 10.00
#6020 Parfait 5½ oz..................................18.00
#2560 Pickle Dish 8¾" 15.00
#2560 Plate
    6" 8.00
    7" 14.00
    8" 20.00
    9" 25.00
#2560 Relish
    2 part 18.00
    3 part 22.00
    4 part 30.00
    5 part 40.00
#2560 Salad Bowl 10" 35.00
#2560 Saucer...8.00

MAYFLOWER Plate Etching #332 cont.

#2560 Serving Dish 20.00
#2560 Shakers ....pair 75.00
#6020 Sherbet, Low 6 oz. 16.00
#2560 Sugar, Footed 3½" 15.00
#2560 Sugar, Individual 3" 12.00
#2560 Sweetmeat.............................14.00
#2586 Syrup, Sani-Cut Top 35.00
#2560 Tid Bit, 3 Toed, Flat................20.00
#2580 Torte Plate 14" 40.00
#2560 Tray for Cream & Sugar 7½" 22.00
#6020 Tumbler, Footed
    5 oz. 16.00

9 oz. 14.00
12 oz. 18.00
#2276 Vanity Set 50.00
#2430 Vase
    3¾" 30.00
    8" 50.00
#2545 Vase, "Flame" 10" 80.00
#2560 Vase, Handled 6" 60.00
#5100 Vase, Footed 10" 90.00
#2560 Whip Cream 50.00
#6020 Wine 3½ oz. 30.00

MAYTIME Cutting #845

Crystal
1956 – 1958

#6064 Champagne 8 oz. 5¾" 20.00
#6064 Claret 5¾ oz. 5¾" 25.00
#6064 Cocktail 4 oz. 4½" 16.00
#6064 Cordial 1 oz. 3⅝" 30.00
#6064 Goblet 9¾ oz. 7"............................23.00
#6064 Ice Tea, Footed 13½ oz. 6½"...........22.00
#6064 Juice, Footed 5½ oz. 4⅞" 15.00
#6064 Oyster Cocktail 7¾ oz. 3⅝" 18.00
Plate
    7" 10.00

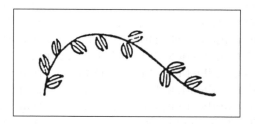

8" 10.00
#6064 Sherbet, Low 7 oz. 4⅝".....................16.00
#6064 Wine 3¼ oz. 5⅛" 25.00

MEADOW ROSE Plate Etching #328

Crystal 1982
Azure Bowl with Crystal Base 1936 – 1944
1936 – 1975

The climbing rose of garden hedges with an elegant stem that enhances the delicacy of the etching. MEADOW ROSE, NAVARRE and CHINTZ were Fostoria's three most popular etchings.

MEADOW ROSE included in Patterns of the Past and Nostalgia Programs

#2496/137 Bon Bon, 3 Toed 30.00
#2545 Bowl, "Flame," Oval 12½"...............60.00
#2496/249 Bowl, Flared 12".....................55.00
#2496 Bowl, Handled 10½".....................45.00

#2496/306 Cake Plate, 2-handled 10" 40.00
#2510 Candelabra, 2 Light (Crystal
    only) ....pair 80.00
#2545 Candelabra, 2 Light, "Flame,"
    8 Prisms ....pair 125.00
#2496/315 Candlestick 4"....................pair 50.00
#2496 Candlestick 5½" ....pair 60.00
#2496 Candlestick, Duo ....pair 70.00
#2496 Candlestick, Trindle ....pair 100.00
#2545 Candlestick, "Flame," Duo,
    6¾" ....pair 80.00
#2545 Candlestick, "Flame," 2 Light,
    8 Prisms ....pair 140.00
#2496 Candy Box, Covered, 3 part 6¼"......60.00
#2496 Celery 11" 22.00
#6016/8 Champagne/High Sherbet 6 oz. ..24.00
#2496 Cheese & Cracker 50.00

#6016/25 Claret 4½ oz. 35.00

#6016/21 Cocktail 3½ oz. 20.00

#2496 Comport 5½" 35.00

#6016/29 Cordial ¾ oz. 50.00

#2496/681 Cream, Footed 20.00

#2496/688 Cream, Individual, Footed 18.00

#2496/396 Cup, Footed 15.00

#869 Finger Bowl 15.00

#2496 Floating Garden 10".......................85.00

#6016/2 Goblet 10 oz. 25.00

#2496 Ice Bucket, Chrome Handled 4⅜"..110.00

#2496 Jelly, Covered 7½" 155.00

#5000 Jug 7, Footed 3 Pints.....................75.00

#6016/88 Juice, Footed 5 oz. 20.00

#6016/60 Luncheon Goblet/Ice Tea 13 oz.
5⅞"...24.00

#2375 Mayonnaise
Bowl 24.00
Plate 20.00
Ladle 20.00

#2496 Mayonnaise
Bowl 24.00
Plate 20.00
Ladle 20.00

#2496 Mayonnaise, 2 part 6½" 48.00

#2496/500 Nappy, Handled, Flared 18.00

#2496/501 Nappy, Handled, 3 Cornered ..20.00

#2496/33 Oyster Cocktail 4 oz. 20.00

#2496 Pickle Dish 8" 20.00

#2666/454 Pitcher, quart 100.00

#2337/549 Plate 7" (Crystal only).............12.00

#2364 Plate 16" 40.00

#2496 Plate
6" 10.00
7" (Crystal only) 14.00
8" 18.00
9" 30.00

#2419 Relish, 5 part (Crystal only) 55.00

#2440 Relish, 3 part (Crystal only) 35.00

#2496/620 Relish, 2 part 25.00

#2496/622 Relish, 3 part 30.00

#2083 Salad Dressing Bottle, Stoppered (Crystal
only) 75.00

#2496 Sauce Dish, Oblong 6½" 35.00

#2496/397 Saucer 10.00

#2495 Serving Dish, Deep, 3 Handles 8½" 35.00

#2364/655 Shaker, Chrome Top ....pair 60.00

#2375 Shaker, Footed ....pair 80.00

#6016/11 Sherbet, Low 6 oz. 20.00

#2496/679 Sugar, Footed........................22.00

#2496/687 Sugar, Individual, Footed 18.00

#2496 Sweetmeat, Square 6" 20.00

#2496/707 Tid Bit, 3 Toed, Flat 25.00

#2496/567 Torte Plate 14" 50.00

#2364/573 Torte Plate 16" 70.00

#2496½/697 Tray for Cream & Sugar
6½" 30.00

#2375/723 Tray, Lunch, Handled 11" 55.00

#2496 Tray, Oblong 8" 40.00

#2470 Vase 10" 115.00

#4128 Vase 5" 70.00

#6016/72 Water, Footed 10 oz. 5⅜" 18.00

#6016/26 Wine 3¼ oz. 30.00

MEADOW ROSE items included in Patterns of the Past and Nostalgia Programs

#008 Champagne/High Dessert 6 oz. 7⅝"..24.00

#001 Champagne/Low Dessert 6 oz. 4⅜" ..20.00

#025 Claret 4½ oz. 6" 35.00

#002 Goblet 10 oz. 7⅝"............................25.00

#060 Goblet, Luncheon/Ice Tea 13 oz.
5⅞"..24.00

#988 Juice, Footed 5 oz. 20.00

MELBA Cutting #761

Optic Pattern
Rock Crystal
Crystal
1936 – 1944

#2470½ Bowl 10½" 25.00
#2472 Candlestick, Duo ....pair 40.00
#6016 Champagne, Saucer 6 oz. 19.00
#6016 Claret 4½ oz. 23.00
#6016 Cocktail 3½ oz. 19.00
#2400 Comport 6" 25.00
#6016 Cordial ¾ oz. 26.00
#869 Finger Bowl 12.00
#6016 Goblet 10 oz. 22.00
#5000 Jug, Footed 100.00
#6016 Oyster Cocktail 4 oz. 15.00
#2337 Plate
   6" 8.00
   7" 10.00
   8" 12.00

#6016 Sherbet, Low 5½ oz.........................15.00
#6016 Tumbler, Footed
   5 oz. 14.00
   10 oz. 12.00
   13 oz. 19.00
#6016 Wine 3¼ oz. 23.00

MELROSE Deep Plate Etching #268

Crystal
1924 – 1929

#1697 Bedroom Set (Carafe, Tumbler) 30.00
#1697 Carafe 18.00
#661 Champagne, Saucer 6 oz. 10.00
#661 Claret 5½ oz. 12.00
#661 Cocktail 3 oz.....................................10.00
#803 Comport
   5" 5.00
   6" 5.00
#661 Cordial ¾ oz. 15.00
#1480 Cream 12.00
#300 Decanter, Cut Neck quart 30.00
#1769 Finger Bowl 5.00
#661 Fruit, Footed 6 oz. 10.00
#661 Goblet 9 oz. 10.00
#945½ Grapefruit 15.00
#945½ Grapefruit Liner 12.00
#825 Jelly 16.00
#825 Jelly, Covered 20.00
#303 Jug 7..10.00
#1852 Jug 6..18.00
#4095 Jug, Footed
   4..40.00

7..50.00
#2287 Lunch Tray, Fleur-de-Lis 26.00
#4087 Marmalade, Covered 22.00
#2138 Mayonnaise
   Bowl..18.00
   Plate...14.00
   Ladle 20.00
#803 Nappy, Footed
   5" 5.00
   6" 5.00
   7" 8.00
#1465 Oil, Cut Neck 5 oz. 16.00
#837 Oyster Cocktail 8.00
#5039 Oyster Cocktail 8.00
#5039 Oyster Cocktail Liner 5.00
#661 Parfait 5½ oz. 10.00
#2283 Plate
   6" 8.00
   7" 10.00
   8" 14.00
   11" 20.00
   11" Cut Star 24.00
#2235 Shaker, Glass Top...................pair 45.00
#2235 Shaker, Pearl Top ....pair 65.00
#4082 Sugar, 2-handled 18.00

MELROSE Deep Plate Etching #268 cont.

#4085 Tumbler, Table 8.00
#4023 Tumbler 6 oz. 7.00
#4085 Tumbler
    2½ oz...6.00
    6 oz...6.00
    13 oz..10.00
#4085 Tumbler, Handled 13 oz. 15.00

#4095 Tumbler, Footed
    2½ oz...8.00
    5 oz...8.00
    10 oz..10.00
    13 oz..12.00
#661 Wine 2 oz. 12.00

MELODY Cutting #881

Crystal
1960 – 1966

#6093/21 Cocktail 4 oz. 18.00
#6093/29 Cordial 1¼ oz. 20.00
#6093/2 Goblet 10 oz. 18.00
#6093/88 Juice, Footed 5 oz. 18.00
#6093/63 Luncheon Goblet/Ice Tea 12 oz...20.00
#2337 Plate
    7" 10.00
    8" 10.00
#6093/11 Sherbet 7 oz. 14.00
#6093/26 Wine 4½ oz. 15.00

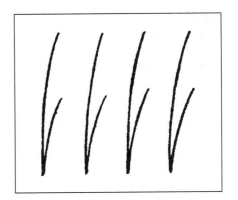

MEMORIES Cutting #750

Rock Crystal
Crystal
1935 – 1936

#2424 Bowl 8" 35.00
#2481 Candlestick 5" ....pair 55.00
#6000 Cocktail 3½ oz. 14.00
#869 Finger Bowl, Optic 10.00
#6000 Goblet 10 oz. 15.00
#5000 Jug, Footed 100.00
#6000 Oyster Cocktail 4 oz. 12.00
#2337 Plate
    6" 6.00
    7" 8.00
    8" 10.00
#2337 Service Plate 11" 15.00
#6000 Sherbet
    High 6 oz. 13.00
    Low 6 oz. 10.00

#6000 Tumbler, Footed
    5 oz...11.00
    13 oz...14.00
#701 Tumbler, Sham or Plain 10 oz. 10.00
#6000 Wine 3 oz. 18.00

METEOR Cutting #726

Crystal
1933 – 1939

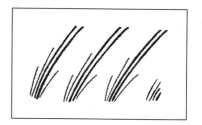

#4024 Bowl, Footed 10" 40.00
#4024 Candlestick 6" ....pair 30.00
#4024 Champagne, Saucer 6½ oz. 20.00
#4024 Cocktail 4 oz....................................15.00
#4115 Cocktail, Footed 3 oz.......................15.00
#4024 Comport 5" 15.00
#4024 Cordial 1 oz. 22.00
#6011 Decanter, Footed 70.00
#869 Finger Bowl 8.00
#4024 Goblet 10 oz.....................................20.00
#4024½ Goblet 11 oz. 20.00
#6011 Jug, Footed 50.00
#1184 Old Fashioned Cocktail, Sham or Plain
    7 oz. 6.00
#4024 Oyster Cocktail 4 oz. 12.00
#2337 Plate
    6" 6.00
    7" 8.00
    8" 10.00
    11" 15.00
#4024 Rhine Wine 3½ oz. 22.00
#4024 Sherbet 5½ oz.................................15.00
#4024 Sherry 2 oz......................................18.00
#701 Tumbler, Sham or Plain
    10 oz. 6.00
    12 oz. 6.00

#4024 Tumbler, Footed
    5 oz. 12.00
    8 oz. 12.00
    12 oz. 20.00
#887 Whiskey, Sham or Plain 1¾ oz. 6.00
#4024 Wine 3½ oz. 20.00

MIAMI Cutting #661

Optic
Cut Bowl, Gold Band and Foot
1924 – 1930

Champagne, Saucer 6 oz. 13.00
Claret 5½ oz. 15.00
Cocktail 3 oz. 13.00
Cordial ¾ oz. 20.00
Parfait 5½ oz. 14.00
Sherbet/Low 6 oz. 12.00
Wine 2 oz. 15.00

Crystal
1933 – 1957

#2440 Bon Bon, Handled 5" 16.00
#2470½ Bowl
    7" 30.00
    10½" 45.00
#2481 Bowl, Oblong 11" 50.00
#906 Brandy Inhaler 14.00
#2375 Cake Plate 30.00
#2440 Cake Plate, Oval 10½" 35.00
#2470½ Candlestick 5½" ....pair 44.00
#2472 Candlestick, Duo ....pair 50.00
#2481 Candlestick 5" ....pair 44.00
#2482 Candlestick, Trindle ....pair 60.00
#4099 Candy Jar, Covered 30.00
#2440 Celery 11½" 24.00
#795 Champagne, Hollow Stem 5½ oz. 16.00
#6009 Champagne, Saucer 5½ oz. 16.00
#6009 Claret/Wine 3¾ oz. 26.00
#6009 Cocktail 3¾ oz. 18.00
#6009 Cordial 1 oz. 40.00
#2440 Cream, Footed 20.00
#2440 Cup 12.00
#869 Finger Bowl 10.00
#6009 Goblet 9 oz. 23.00
#2464 Ice Jug 40.00
#2440 Lemon, Handled 5" 16.00
#2440 Mayonnaise, 2 part 6½" 20.00
#1184 Old Fashioned Cocktail, Sham or Plain
    7 oz. 10.00
#2440 Olive Dish 6½" 15.00
#6009 Oyster Cocktail 4¾ oz. 12.00
#2440 Pickle Dish 8½" 18.00
#2440 Plate
    6" 8.00
    7" 12.00
    8" 20.00
    9" 30.00
#2419 Relish
    4 part 35.00
    5 part 40.00
#2440 Relish, Handled
    2 part 24.00
    3 part 30.00
#2462 Relish, Metal Handled 50.00
#2462 Relish, 5 part................................40.00
#2470 Relish, 4 part................................35.00
#2440 Sauce Dish, Oval 6½" 25.00

#2440 Saucer...8.00
#6009 Sherbet
    High 5½ oz...18.00
    Low 5½ oz. 16.00
#846 Sherry 2 oz. 12.00
#2440 Sugar, Footed 18.00
#2440 Sweetmeat, Handled 4½" 16.00
#2440 Torte Plate 13" 45.00
#2440 Tray, Oval 8½" 40.00
#2470 Tray for Cream & Sugar.................30.00
#2464 Tumbler 10 oz. 20.00
#6009 Tumbler, Footed
    5 oz. 12.00
    9 oz. 12.00
    12 oz. 22.00
#2467 Vase 7½" 50.00
#2470 Vase 10" 70.00
#2485 Vase, Crescent
    5" 45.00
    7" 60.00
#2486 Vase, Square
    6" 40.00
    9" 60.00
#4110 Vase 7½" 45.00
#4111 Vase 6½" 50.00
#4112 Vase 8½" 60.00
#887 Whiskey, Sham or Plain 1¾ oz. 12.00

◈ MILADY Cutting #895 ◈

Rock Crystal
Crystal
1963 – 1965

#6102/31 Brandy 4 oz. 22.00
#6102/25 Claret 7½ oz. 22.00
#4185/495 Dessert/Finger Bowl 12.00
#6102/2 Goblet 10 oz. 25.00
#6102/63 Luncheon Goblet/Ice Tea
    14 oz. 23.00
#2337 Plate
    7" 10.00

    8" 10.00
#6102/11 Sherbet 8 oz. 22.00
#6102/26 Tulip Wine 5½ oz. 23.00

◈ MILKWEED Crystal Print #7 ◈

Crystal
1936 – 1960

#2630 Bon Bon 3 Toed 7¼" 35.00
#2630 Bowl, Flared 12" 65.00
#2630 Butter, Covered, Oblong 7½" 75.00
#2630 Cake Plate, Handled 48.00
#2630 Candlestick 4½" ....pair 50.00
#2630 Candlestick, Duo 7" ....pair 100.00
#2630 Cream, Footed 4¼" 15.00
#2630 Cream, Footed, Individual 15.00
#2630 Jug, Ice 3 Pints 7⅛" 300.00
#2630 Lily Pond 9" 70.00
#2630 Mayonnaise
    Bowl 20.00
    Plate 15.00
    Ladle 20.00
#2630 Nappy, Handled 4½" 18.00
#2630 Pickle Dish, Oval 8¾" 35.00
#2630 Relish
    2 part 7⅜"....................................25.00
    3 part 11⅛"..................................45.00
#2630 Salad Bowl 10½" 55.00
#2630 Shaker, Chrome Top...............pair 75.00
#2630 Sugar, Footed 4" 15.00
#2630 Sugar, Footed, Individual...............15.00
#2630 Torte Plate 14" 55.00
#2630 Tray for Cream & Sugar.................15.00
#2630 Tray, Handled, Lunch 11¼" 45.00
#2630 Tricorne Bowl, 3 Toed 7⅛" 40.00

⚞ MILLEFLEUR Cutting #195 ⚟

1929 – 1940
Crystal 1929 – 1940; Crystal Bowl with
  Ebony Base 1929 – 1935

*Crystal Bowl with Ebony Base

#4020 Champagne, Saucer/High Sherbet
  7 oz. 24.00
#4020 Claret 4 oz. 26.00
#4020 Cocktail 3½ oz. 18.00
#4020½ Cocktail 4 oz. 18.00
#4120 Cocktail 3½ oz.*.........................18.00
#4020 Cream, Footed 12.00
#2350 Cream Soup...................................15.00
#2350½ Cup, Footed 12.00
#2350 Cup, After Dinner 12.00
#4021 Finger Bowl 8.00
#4121 Finger Bowl 8.00
#4020 Goblet 11 oz. 24.00
#4121 Goblet* 24.00
#4020 Jug, Footed 60.00
#2350 Plate
  6" 8.00
  7" 10.00
  9" 15.00
#2419 Plate
  6" 8.00
  7" 10.0
  8" 15.00
#2350 Saucer...6.00
#2419 Saucer...6.00
#2350 Saucer, After Dinner 6.00
#2419 Saucer, After Dinner 6.00
#4020 Sherbet
  High 7 oz. 24.00
  Low 5 oz. 18.00
  Low 7 oz. 18.00
#4120 Sherbet *
  High 24.00
  Low 5 oz. 18.00
  Low 7 oz. 18.00
#4020 Tumbler, Footed
  5 oz. 18.00
  10 oz. 18.00

  13 oz. 24.00
  16 oz. 24.00
#4120 Tumbler, Footed *
  5 oz. 18.00
  10 oz. 18.00
  13 oz. 24.00
  16 oz. 24.00
#4020 Whiskey 2 oz. 18.00
#4120 Whiskey 2 oz.*..............................18.00
#4020 Wine 3 oz. 25.00

✎ MINUET Plate Etching #285 ✎

Green, Topaz
1930 – 1934
Topaz Bowl with Crystal Base; Crystal Bowl with Green Base
Do not confuse with MINUET Design Cutting #826.

MINUET dinnerware made in Green and Topaz

#2419 Baker 10" 22.00
#2419 Bon Bon, 2-handled.......................18.00
#2394 Bowl
    7½" 20.00
    12" 35.00
#2430 Bowl 11" 32.00
#2441 Bowl 12" 36.00
#2433 Bowl
    7½" 30.00
    12" 40.00
#2419 Cake Plate, Handled 28.00
#2430 Candy Dish, Covered ½ lb..............22.00
#2375 Candlestick 3" ....pair 40.00
#2394 Candlestick 2" ....pair 36.00
#2430 Candlestick 9½" ....pair 60.00
#2433 Candlestick 3" ....pair 40.00
#2419 Celery 11" 18.00
#2419 Cereal 6" 14.00
#2400 Comport 6" 18.00
#2433 Comport
    Tall...20.00
    Low 16.00
#2419 Cream 14.00
#2419 Cream, Tea 12.00
#2419 Cream Soup................................20.00
#2419 Cup..10.00
#2419 Cup, After Dinner 14.00
#2439 Decanter 40.00
#2419 Fruit 5" 8.00
#2375 Ice Bucket 60.00
#2451 Ice Dish....................................40.00
#2419 Jelly, 2-handled..........................24.00
#2430 Jelly 7" 22.00
#2419 Lemon Dish, 2-handled 26.00
#2419 Mayonnaise, 2-handled 24.00
#2430 Mint Dish 5½" 18.00
#2375 Oil, Footed.................................60.00
#2419 Pickle Dish 8½" 18.00
#2419 Plate
    6" 8.00
    7" 10.00
    8" 14.00

    9" 20.00
#2419 Platter
    12" 45.00
    15" 60.00
#2419 Relish Dish 8½" 30.00
#2483 Salad Dressing Bottle 85.00
#2419 Sauce Bowl and Stand...........each 45.00
#2419 Saucer......................................8.00
#2419 Saucer, After Dinner 10.00
#2419 Soup 7" 22.00
#2419 Sugar 20.00
#2419 Sugar, Tea 18.00
#2430 Vase 8" 60.00

MINUET stemware made with Crystal Bowl, Green Base

#4020 Cocktail 3½ oz. 26.00
#4020½ Cocktail 4 oz. 26.00
#4120 Cocktail 3½ oz. 30.00
#4020 Cream, Footed 18.00
#4120 Cream 18.00
#4020 Decanter, Footed 70.00
#4021 Finger Bowl 10.00
#4121 Finger Bowl 8.00
#4020 Goblet 32.00
#4121 Goblet 35.00
#4020 Jug, Footed 60.00
#4120 Jug, Footed 65.00
#4020 Shaker, Footed ....set 70.00
#4020 Sherbet
    High 30.00

⋑ MINUET Plate Etching #285 cont. ⋐

Low 7 oz.	26.00
Low 5 oz.	26.00

#4120 Sherbet
High	32.00
Low 7 oz.	18.00
Low 5 oz.	28.00

#4020 Sugar, Footed 20.00

#4020 Tumbler, Footed
5 oz.	24.00
10 oz.	28.00
13 oz.	30.00
16 oz.	30.00

#4120 Tumbler, Footed
5 oz.	27.00
10 oz.	30.00
13 oz.	45.00
16 oz.	35.00

#4020 Whiskey 2 oz. 24.00
#4120 Whiskey 2 oz. 27.00

MINUET stemware made with Topaz Bowl, Crystal Base

#6002 Claret	22.00
#6002 Cordial	24.00
#4020 Cream, Footed	20.00
#4020 Decanter, Footed	70.00
#6002 Finger Bowl	8.00
#6002 Goblet	18.00
#5000 Jug 7, Footed	65.00
#6002 Oyster Cocktail	10.00
#4020 Shaker, Footed	pair 70.00

#6002 Sherbet
High	16.00
Low	14.00

#4020 Sugar, Footed 20.00

#6002 Tumbler, Footed
2 oz.	20.00
5 oz.	20.00
10 oz.	18.00
13 oz.	14.00

#6002 Wine 22.00

⋑ MINUET Cutting #826 ⋐

Combination Rock Crystal and Gray Cutting
Rock Crystal
Crystal
1950 – 1960
   Do not confuse with MINUET Design Etching #285.

#2574 Bowl, Flared 12"	25.00
#2574 Cake Plate, Handled 10"	26.00
#2574 Candlestick, Duo	pair 50.00
#6025 Claret/Wine 4 oz. 4"	24.00
#6025 Cocktail 3½ oz. 3½"	17.00
#6025 Cordial 1 oz. 2⅞"	26.00
#2574 Cream, Footed 4"	14.00
#2574 Cup	8.00
#6025 Goblet 10 oz. 5½"	21.00
#6025 Ice Tea, Footed 12 oz. 5⅝"	19.00
#6025 Juice, Footed 5 oz. 4¼"	13.00

#2574 Mayonnaise
Bowl	12.00
Plate	10.00
Ladle	20.00

#6025 Oyster Cocktail 4 oz. 3½" 13.00

#2574 Plate
7"	10.00
8"	12.00
#2574 Relish, 3 part 10"	25.00
#2574 Saucer	6.00
#2574 Shaker 3¼"	pair 30.00
#6025 Sherbet 6 oz. ¾"	17.00
#2574 Sugar, Footed 3¾"	18.00
#2574 Torte Plate 14"	40.00

Crystal
1913 – 1929

Cutting #116 was also used on BILLOW. See additional items listed there.

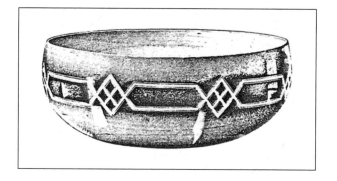

#863 Almond 10.00	
#880 Bon Bon 4½" 10.00	
#858 Champagne, Saucer 5½ oz. 8.00	
#863 Champagne, Hollow Stem, Cut Flute	
5½ oz....................................10.00	
#863 Champagne, Saucer 5½ oz. 8.00	
#863 Champagne, Tall 5½ oz....................12.00	
#863 Claret 4½ oz....................................8.00	
#863 Cocktail 3½ oz. 8.00	
#803 Comport	
5" 10.00	
6" 10.00	
#863 Cordial 10.00	
#863 Creme de Menthe 2½ oz. 10.00	
#1478 Cream 12.00	
#1480 Cream 12.00	
#1759 Cream 12.00	
#1851 Cream 12.00	
#481 Custard..7.00	
#300 Decanter, Cut Neck quart 35.00	
#858 Finger Bowl 7.00	
#858 Finger Bowl Plate.............................4.00	
#1769 Finger Bowl 7.00	
#1769 Finger Bowl Plate...........................4.00	
#48 Flower Set, 3 Pieces 45.00	
#858 Fruit 10.00	
#863 Fruit 10.00	
#736 Fruit Plate 6" 4.00	
#840 Fruit Plate 5" 4.00	
#858 Goblet 9 oz. 8.00	
#863 Goblet	
9 oz. 8.00	
10 oz. 8.00	
#945½ Grapefruit 12.00	
#945½ Grapefruit Liner 7.00	
#1132 Horseradish..................................22.00	
#4061 Ice Tea, Footed, Handled 22.00	
#300 Jug 7 with 2 Bands 40.00	
#303 Jug 7 with 1 Band 40.00	
#303 Jug 7 with 2 Bands 40.00	
#724 Jug 2 with 2 Bands 40.00	
#1851 Jug 8 with 2 Bands 40.00	
#1733 Marmalade, Covered 20.00	
#1831 Mustard, Covered 20.00	
#803 Nappy, Footed	
5" 12.00	

   6" 15.00
   7" 18.00
#1227 Nappy
   4½" 6.00
   8" 15.00
#300½ Oil, Small 40.00
#822 Parfait 8.00
#1848 Plate, Sandwich 9" 12.00
#863 Pousse-Cafe......................................8.00
#862 Rhine Wine 4½ oz. 8.00
#1165 Shaker, Silver-Plated Top...............12.00
#1165½ Shaker, Pearl Top 12.00
#2022 Shaker, Glass Top 10.00
#862 Sherry 2 oz. 8.00
#1478 Sugar 12.00
#1480 Sugar 12.00
#1759 Sugar 12.00
#1851 Sugar 12.00
#2194 Syrup, Nickel Top
   8 oz. 45.00
   12 oz. 55.00
#858 Sweetmeat......................................10.00
#724 Tankard 7, 2 Bands.........................55.00
#922 Toothpick, Cut #19 ....20.00
#820 Tumbler, Table 10.00
#701 Tumbler
   8 oz. 6.00
   12 oz. 8.00
   14 oz. 10.00
#701 Tumbler Plate 7.00
#820 Tumbler, Sham, Punty.....................8.00
#833 Tumbler, Sham, Punty 8 oz.............8.00
#858 Tumbler, Table 10.00
#858 Tumbler, Table, Sham, Cut #19
   8 oz. 8.00
   12 oz. 10.00
   14 oz. 12.00
#858 Tumbler
   5 oz. 6.00

8 oz. 8.00	#889 Tumbler 5 oz. 6.00
12 oz. 10.00	#4028 Tumbler 9 oz. 8.00
14 oz. 12.00	#1558 Water Bottle, Cut Neck...............35.00
#887 Tumbler 3 oz. 6.00	#863 Wine 3 oz. 8.00

⤙ MODERN VINTAGE Plate Etching #225 ⤚

Crystal
1920 – 1929

#880 Bon Bon 4½" 8.00	7 oz. 26.00
#869 Bowl, Footed, Covered 20.00	#837 Oyster Cocktail 4½ oz. 6.00
#2219 Candy Jar, Covered	#766½ Parfait 6 oz...............7.00
¼ lb. 18.00	#1897 Plate, Optic 7" 6.00
½ lb. 24.00	#1848 Plate, Sandwich 9"...............10.00
1 lb. 30.00	#2083 Salad Dressing Bottle 35.00
#697 Carafe 12.00	#2022 Shaker, Glass Top...............pair 40.00
#697 Carafe Tumbler 8.00	#1478 Sugar 14.00
#766 Champagne, Saucer 5 oz. 7.00	#2214 Sugar, Covered 18.00
#766 Cocktail 3 oz...............7.00	#2194 Syrup, Nickel Top
#803 Comport	8 oz. 20.00
5" 10.00	12 oz. 30.00
6" 12.00	#858 Sweetmeat 10.00
#766 Cordial ¾ oz. 9.00	#820 Tumbler, Table 6.00
#1478 Cream 10.00	#4011½ Tumbler, Table 8.00
#2214 Cream, Covered 14.00	#701 Tumbler 14 oz. 10.00
#766 Finger Bowl 5.00	#4011 Tumbler
#766 Finger Bowl Plate 6"...............6.00	5 oz. 6.00
#766 Fruit, Footed 4½ oz. 6.00	8 oz. 8.00
#766 Goblet 9 oz. 7.00	12 oz. 8.00
#945½ Grapefruit 14.00	#4011 Tumbler, Handled 12 oz. 14.00
#945½ Grapefruit Liner 10.00	#701 Tumbler Plate 6.00
#766 Ice Tea, Footed, Handled 10.00	#766 Wine 2¾ oz. 7.00
#300 Jug 7 ....16.00	
#303 Jug 7 ....16.00	
#318 Jug 7 ....16.00	
#317½ Jug, Covered 16.00	
#1968 Marmalade, Covered 20.00	
#2138 Mayonnaise	
Bowl 16.00	
Plate 12.00	
Ladle 20.00	
#1831 Mustard, Covered 22.00	
#803 Nappy, Footed	
5" 6.00	
6" 6.00	
7" 6.00	
#1465 Oil, Cut Neck	
5 oz. 20.00	

MONACO Crystal Print #24

Crystal, Honey Gold
1970 – 1975

#2834/135 Bon Bon................................10.00
#2834/191 Bowl 8" 24.00
#2834/195 Bowl 9" 30.00
#2834/300 Butter, Covered, Oblong..........32.00
#2834/680 Cream 18.00
#2834/540 Pickle Dish............................16.00
#2834/560 Plate, Service 12" 40.0
#2834/567 Plate, Torte 14" 45.00
#2834/620 Relish, 2 part 30.00
#2834/624 Relish, 3 part 35.00
#2834/651 Shaker, Chrome Top ....pair 30.00
#2834/677 Sugar..................................22.00

MONARCH NEEDLE ETCHING #79

Decoration #60 Yellow Gold Trim
1926 – 1928

See BRUNSWICK

EARLY PERSONALLY MONOGRAMMED STEM/ACCESSORY ITEMS

Custom Order
Available as special orders throughout etched production time. The term "Regency" was used to indicate script. "Tempo" described a more stylized monogram. No values can be ascribed to this individually ordered glass.

#415 Brandy Inhaler 20 oz.
#417 Brandy Inhaler, Small 4 oz.
#906 Brandy Inhaler 17 oz.
#4099 Candy Jar (Some colors as well as Crystal)

#52 Champagne, Hollow Stem
#795 Champagne, Hollow Stem 5½ oz.
#863 Champagne, Hollow Stem 5 oz.
#2492 Canapé Plate (Fish Shape) 8½"
    To accompany #6294 but not monogrammed
#3105 Canapé Plate
#3105 Cocktail, Footed
#6294 Cocktail, Footed
#2525 Cocktail Shaker, Metal Top 42 oz. 12½"
#2525½ Cocktail Shaker, Metal Top 30 oz.
#2525 Decanter 28 oz. 10½"

⚡ MONROE Needle Etching #86 ⚡

Crystal
1933 – 1940

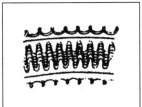

#6000 Champagne, Saucer/High Sherbet
    6 oz. 10.00
#6000 Cocktail 3½ oz. 10.00
#6000 Goblet 10 oz. 12.00
#6000 Oyster Cocktail 4 oz. 6.00
#2283 Plate 7" 8.00
#6000 Sherbet, Low 6 oz. 8.00
#887 Tumbler 2½ oz. 6.00
#889 Tumbler 5 oz. 8.00

#4076 Tumbler 9 oz. 8.00
#6000 Tumbler, Footed 13 oz. 10.00
#6000 Wine 3 oz. 12.00

⚡ MONTE CARLO Cutting #912 ⚡

Rock Crystal
Crystal 1967 – 1970

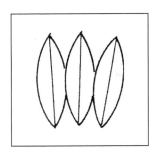

#6104/25 Claret 7 oz. 23.00
#6104/29 Cordial 1½ oz. 28.00
#6104/2 Goblet 11oz.................................25.00
#6104/63 Luncheon Goblet/Ice Tea
    13½ oz..24.00
#2337 Plate
    7" 10.00
    8" 10.00
#6104/11 Sherbet 9 oz. 23.00
#6104/26 Wine 6 oz. 25.00

⚡ MONTICELLO Cutting #886 ⚡

Rock Crystal
Crystal
1961 – 1970

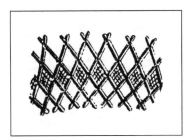

#6097/27 Cocktail/Wine 3½ oz. 21.00
#6097/29 Cordial 1 oz. 23.00
#6097/2 Goblet 10 oz. 21.00
#6097/88 Juice, Footed 5 oz. 16.00
#6097/63 Luncheon Goblet/Ice Tea
    12 oz. 20.00
#2337 Plate
    7" 10.00
    8" 10.00
#6097/11 Sherbet 7 oz. 16.00

⤜⊸ MOONBEAM Cutting #856 ⊶⤛

Rock Crystal
Crystal
1957 – 1965

#6072 Cordial 1 oz. 3⅛" 27.00
#2574 Cream, Footed 7 oz. 4"...................18.00
#6072 Goblet 10 oz. 6⅜"...........................25.00
#6072 Juice 5¼ oz. 4⅞" 16.00
#6072 Luncheon Goblet/Ice Tea
    13 oz. 6⅜"..22.00
#2337 Plate
    7" 10.00
    8" 10.00
#2574 Relish, 3 part 10" 22.00
#6072 Sherbet 7¼ oz. 5" 18.00
#2574 Sugar, Footed 3¾" 20.00
#2337 Torte Plate 14".............................30.00

⤜⊸ MOONGLOW Decoration #649 ⊶⤛

Platinum Band
Gray Cutting
Crystal
1960 – 1968

#6085/27 Cocktail/Wine 4 oz. 5" 24.00
#6085/29 Cordial 1¼ oz. 3½" 28.00
#6085/2 Goblet 8¾ oz. 6½" 25.00
#6085/88 Juice, footed 5½ oz. 4⁹⁄₁₆" 16.00
#6085/63 Luncheon Goblet/Ice Tea 11¾ oz.
    6³⁄₁₆" 22.00
#2337 Plate
    7" 10.00
    8" 10.00
#6085/11 Sherbet 6 oz. 5³⁄₁₆" 18.00

⤝ MORNING GLORY Plate Etching #313 ⤞

Crystal
Crystal Bowl with Amber Base 1931 – 1935
1931 – 1944
  Do not confuse with MORNING GLORY
  Carving #12.

PRICING REFLECTS CRYSTAL AS WELL AS
CRYSTAL WITH AMBER BASE.

MORNING GLORY items made in Solid Crystal, Crystal Bowl with Amber Base

#2470 Bowl 12" 50.00
#2470 Candlestick 5½" ....pair 65.00
#6007 Champagne, Saucer/High Sherbet
    5½ oz...22.00
#6007 Claret 4 oz. 30.00
#6007 Cocktail 3½ oz. 20.00
#2470 Comport, Low 6" 32.00
#6007 Cordial 1 oz. 52.00
#6007 Goblet 10 oz. 25.00
#6007 Oyster Cocktail 4½ oz. 14.00
#6007 Sherbet, Low 5½ oz.........................15.00
#6007 Tumbler, Footed
    2 oz. 28.00
    5 oz. 12.00
    9 oz. 14.00
    12 oz. 20.00
#6007 Wine 3 oz. 30.00

MORNING GLORY items made in Crystal Only

#2440 Baker 10" 40.00
#2470½ Bowl 10½".....................................40.00
#2470 Bon Bon 24.00
#2470 Cake Plate 10" 35.00
#2470½ Candlestick 5½" ....pair 65.00
#2440 Celery 11½" 26.00
#2440 Cereal 6" 24.00
#2440 Cream, Footed 20.00
#2440 Cream Soup....................................26.00

#2440 Cup...12.00
#2440 Cup, After Dinner 24.00
#2440 Fruit 5" 16.00
#869 Finger Bowl 10.00
#2451 Ice Dish..30.00
#2451 Ice Dish Plate...............................14.00
#2270 Jug 75.00
#2470 Lemon Dish 32.00
#2440 Olive Dish 6½".............................20.00
#2440 Pickle Dish 8½" 28.00
#2440 Plate
    6" 12.00
    7" 15.00
    8" 20.00
    9" 25.00
    10" 30.00
#2440 Platter 12" 45.00
#2419 Relish, 4 part................................40.00
#2470 Relish, 3 part................................36.00
#2440 Saucer...10.00
#2440 Saucer, After Dinner 18.00
#2440 Sugar, Footed 22.00
#2470 Sweetmeat 26.00
#2440 Torte Plate 13"..............................50.00
#2470 Tray/Sugar, Cream 55.00
#2440 Vase 7" 80.00
#2467 Vase 7½" 85.00

MORNING GLORY Carving #12

Crystal
1939 – 1944
Do not confuse with MORNING GLORY Etching #313.

Selected items reissued in Crystal and Light Blue in 1982

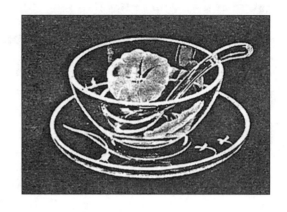

#2427 Ash Tray, Oblong 3½" 10.00
#2516 Ash Tray 10.00
#2618 Ash Tray, Square 4" 15.00
#315 Bowl
    7" 25.00
    9" 30.00
#2364 Bowl, Flared 12" 40.00
#2596 Bowl, Oblong, Shallow 11" 50.00
#6023 Bowl, Footed 9¼" 50.00
#2419 Cake Plate, 2-handled 9½" 35.00
#2324 Candlestick 6" ....pair 50.00
#2596 Candlestick 5" ....pair 90.00
#6023 Candlestick, Duo ....pair 150.00
#2364 Cheese & Cracker 50.00
#2427 Cigarette Box, Divided, Covered 7"..30.00
#2364 Cracker Plate 11" 40.00
#2364 Fruit Bowl 13" 40.00
#4132 Ice Bowl 4¾" 50.00
#2364 Lily Pond 12" 60.00
#2364 Mayonnaise
    Bowl 20.00
    Plate 15.00
    Ladle 20.00
#2337 Plate
    7" 30.00
    8" 40.00
#2364 Salad Bowl
    9" 40.00
    10½" 50.00
#2364 Sandwich Plate 11" 40.00
#2364 Torte Plate

    14" 50.00
    16" 70.00
#2364 Tray, Lunch, Handled 50.00
#2577 Vase, Wide 5½" 40.00
#2577 Vase
    6" 60.00
    8½" 70.00
#2591 Vase 15" 100.00
#4128½ Vase 5" 70.00
#4132½ Vase 8" 80.00
#5100 Vase 10" 80.00
#4126½ Vase, Footed 11" 100.00
#4143½ Vase, Footed
    6" 60.00
    7½" 80.00

MORNING GLORY items reissued in 1982 Crystal, Light Blue

MO/249 Bowl 12"....................................50.00
MO/314 Candlestick 3".....................pair 30.00
MO/319 Candlestick 6".....................pair 50.00
MO/567 Torte Plate 14" 50.00
MO/789 Vase, Blue 8" 40.00

⇜ MOUNT VERNON Cutting #817 ⇝

Gray Cutting
Crystal
1942 – 1957

#6023 Candlestick, Duo ....pair 50.00
#6030 Champagne/High Sherbet 6 oz.
    5⅝"...18.00
#6031 Champagne, Saucer 6 oz. 18.00
#6031 Claret/Wine 3½ oz. 6" 22.00
#6031 Cocktail 3½ oz. 5¼" 16.00
#6031 Cordial 1 oz. 3¾" 30.00
#1769 Finger Bowl 12.00
#2364 Fruit Bowl 13" 35.00
#6031 Goblet, High 10 oz. 8⅛" 24.00
#6031 Goblet, Low 10 oz. 6¼".................22.00
#6031 Ice Tea, Footed 12 oz. 5⅞" 20.00
#6011 Jug, Footed 90.00
#6031 Juice, Footed 5 oz. 4½" 16.00
#6031 Oyster Cocktail 4 oz. 3⅝" 15.00
#2337 Plate
    6" 8.00
    7" 10.00
    8" 12.00
#6031 Sherbet, Low 6 oz. 15.00

⇜ MULBERRY Cutting #799 ⇝

Rock Crystal
Crystal
1940 – 1960

MULBERRY included in Patterns of the Past
   and Nostalgia Programs

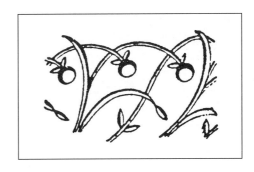

#2545 Bowl, Oval 12½" 30.00
#6023 Bowl, Footed 25.00
#2545 Candlestick 4½" ....pair 40.00
#6023 Candlestick, Duo ....pair 50.00
#6026 Champagne/High Sherbet/Dessert
    6 oz. 5½"...16.00
#6026 Champagne, Saucer 6 oz. 16.00
#6026 Claret/Wine 4½ oz. 5⅜" 22.00
#6026 Cocktail 4 oz. 5"............................16.00
#6026 Cordial 1 oz. 3⅞" 28.00
#869 Finger Bowl 8.00
#6026 Goblet 9 oz. 7⅝"............................20.00
#6026 Goblet, Low 9 oz. 6⅛"....................16.00
#6026 Ice Tea, Footed 13 oz. 6" 18.00
#5000 Jug, Footed 60.00

#6026 Juice, Footed 5 oz. 3¾" 12.00
#6026 Oyster Cocktail 4 oz. 3⅝" 12.00
#2337 Plate
    6" 8.00
    7" 8.00
    8" 10.00
#6026 Sherbet, Low 6 oz. 12.00

◁═ **MULBERRY Cutting #799 cont.** ═▷

MULBERRY items included in Patterns of the Past and Nostalgia Programs

MU01/008 Champagne/High Dessert 6 oz.
  5½"...16.00
MU01/011 Champagne/Low Dessert 6 oz.
  4⅜"..14.00
MU01/027 Claret/Wine 4½ oz. 5⅜" 22.00
MU01/002 Goblet 9 oz. 7⅝" 20.00
MU01/003 Goblet/Low 9 oz. 6⅛" 16.00
MU01/060 Luncheon Goblet/Ice Tea 13 oz.
  6" 12.00

◁═ **MYSTIC Deep Plate Etching #270** ═▷

Crystal
1924 – 1929

***Produced also as MYSTIC #207½ Green, Spiral Optic**

#660 Champagne, Saucer...........................10.00
#660 Claret 10.00
#660 Cocktail..10.00
#5082 Cocktail* 14.00
#660 Cordial 10.00
#4095 Finger Bowl 4½"* 6.00
#4095 Finger Bowl 4½".............................4.00
#660 Fruit 10.00
#660 Goblet 10.00
#5082 Goblet* 15.00
#4095 Jug 7, Footed* 86.00
#4095 Jug 4, Footed..................................50.00
#835 Oyster Cocktail 10.00
#4095 Oyster Cocktail*.............................12.00
#660 Parfait 10.00
#6082 Parfait* 14.00
#2283 Plate*
  7" 8.00
  8" 10.00
  13" 20.00
#5082 Sherbet *
  Low 14.00
  High 15.00
#4095 Tumbler, Footed
  2½ oz..10.00
  5 oz. 10.00
  10 oz. 10.00
  13 oz. 12.00

#4095 Tumbler, Footed *
  2½ oz...12.00
  5 oz. 10.00
  10 oz. 12.00
  13 oz. 15.00
#4095 Vase, Rolled Edge 8½" 45.00
#660 Wine 10.00
#5082 Wine*...15.00

❧ NAIRN Cutting #708 ❧

Rock Crystal
Crystal
1933 – 1944

#2470½ Bowl 10½" 30.00
#2470½ Candlestick 5½" ....pair 45.00
#6004 Champagne, Saucer/High Sherbet
    5½ oz. 16.00
#6004 Claret 4 oz. 22.00
#6004 Cocktail 3 oz. 16.00
#869 Finger Bowl 8.00
#2283 Finger Bowl Plate 6.00
#6004 Goblet 9 oz. 18.00
#2451 Ice Dish 15.00
#2451 Ice Dish Plate 6.00
#6004 Oyster Cocktail 4½ oz. 12.00
#2283 Plate
    7" 8.00
    8" 12.00
#6004 Sherbet, Low 5½ oz. 12.00
#6004 Tumbler, Footed
    2½ oz. 20.00
    5 oz. 12.00
    9 oz. 12.00
    12 oz. 18.00
#6004 Wine 2½ oz. 22.00

❧ NARCISSUS Carving #17 ❧

Crystal
1940 – 1944

#2577 Vase 6" 80.00
#4142½ Vase 11" 135.00
#4143½ Vase, Footed 6" 100.00
#4125½ Vase, Footed 11" 150.00

⇒ NATIONAL Cutting #727 ⇐

Crystal
1933-1944

#4024 Bowl, Footed 10" 40.00
#4024 Candlestick 6" ....pair 35.00
#4024 Champagne, Saucer 6½ oz. 20.00
#4024 Cocktail 4 oz. 18.00
#4115 Cocktail, Footed 3 oz. 10.00
#4024 Comport 5" 15.00
#4024 Cordial 1 oz. 22.00
6011 Decanter, Footed..........................70.00
#869 Finger Bowl 8.00
#4024 Goblet 10 oz. 20.00
#4024½ Goblet 11 oz. 20.00
#6011 Jug, Footed 50.00
#1184 Old Fashioned Cocktail, Sham or Plain
    7 oz. 6.00
#4024 Oyster Cocktail 4 oz. 15.00
#2337 Plate
    6" 6.00
    7" 7.00
    8" 8.00
    11" 15.00
#4024 Rhine Wine 3½ oz. 20.00
#4024 Sherbet 5½ oz. 18.00
#4024 Sherry 2 oz. 18.00
#701 Tumbler, Sham or Plain
    10 oz. 6.00
    12 oz. 6.00
#4024 Tumbler, Footed
    5 oz. 15.00
    8 oz. 15.00
    12 oz. 20.00
#887 Whiskey, Sham or Plain 1¾ oz. 6.00
#4024 Whiskey, Footed 2 oz. 15.00
#4024 Wine 3½ oz. 20.00
#021 Cocktail/Sherry 8 oz.......................50.00
#029 Cordial ¾ oz. 50.00
#681 Cream, Footed 20.00
#023 Double Old Fashioned Cocktail
    13 oz. 30.00

#002 Goblet 10 oz. 26.00
#063 Goblet, Luncheon/Ice Tea 24.00
#064 Highball 12 oz. 30.00
#448 Jelly 20.00
#088 Juice, Footed 5 oz............................20.00
#035 Magnum/Wine Goblet 16 oz. 46.00
#500 Nappy, Handled...............................22.00
#539 Plate 7 "..15.00
#550 Plate 8" 20.00
#620 Relish, 2 part...................................25.00
#622 Relish 3 part 35.00
#648 Serving Dish, Handled 8½" 30.00
#650 Shaker, Chrome Top.................pair 60.00
#679 Sugar, Footed 22.00
#707 Tid Bit, 3 Toed.................................20.00
#567 Torte Plate 14" 50.00
#573 Torte Plate 16" 70.00

⇒ NAVARRE Plate Etching #327 ⇐

1937 – 1982
   Crystal 1936 – 1982
   Azure Bowl with Crystal Base 1973 – 1982
   Pink Bowl with Crystal Base 1973 – 1978

NAVARRE included in Part of Patterns of the Past Program in Pink, Part of the Nostalgia Program in Crystal or Blue Bowl with Crystal Base.

From first to last, formally designed NAVARRE is, without question, Fostoria's most successful etched pattern. Design by Edgar Bottome, NAVARRE illustrated the detailed hand work involved in producing the same design on different sized items at a time when photographic reduction and enlargement were not yet used. Slightly diverse details of the etching on various sized items illustrate the complexity of plate etching work. Artistry so achieved demonstrates the willingness of the Fostoria Company to extend designs beyond the concerns of cost. It is said to be "a classic example of good design," high praise from Jon Saffel, himself a former design director at Fostoria. In 1977, the Picard China Company and Fostoria advertised a companion dinnerware line. The late Nostalgia program production extended the line to include new items. The line was sold to Lenox in 1982 and they continued to produce the later stems in crystal, pink, and blue.

CRYSTAL

#2496/137 Bon Bon, 3 Toed	75.00
#2470/218½ Bowl, Toed 10½"	20.00
#2496 Bowl, Handed 10½"	60.00
#2496/249 Bowl, Flared, Toed 12"	65.00
#2545 Bowl, Flame, Oval 12½"	75.00
#2440 Cake Plate	60.00
#2496/306 Cake Plate, 2-handled 10"	60.00
#2545 Candelabra, 2 Light "Flame," Prisms	pair 130.00
#2545 Candlestick, Flame, Duo 7½"	pair 100.00
#2572 Candlestick, Duo	pair 80.00
#2482/336 Candlestick, Trindle	pair 100.00
#2496/315 Candlestick	
4"	pair 45.00
5½"	pair 65.00
#2496/332 Candlestick, Duo	pair 15.00
#2496/336 Candlestick, Trindle	pair 100.00
#2496/344 Candy Box, Covered, 3 part	60.00
#2440 Celery 11½"	22.00
#6016/8 Champagne/Dessert/High Sherbet 6 oz.	22.00
#2496 Cheese & Cracker (Cheese 5¼", Plate 11")	50.00
#6016/25 Claret 4½ oz.	35.00
#6016/27 Claret, Large 6½ oz.	40.00
#6016/21 Cocktail 3½ oz.	23.00
#2400 Comport 6"	25.00

#2496 Comport 5½"	25.00
#6016/29 Cordial ¾ oz.	50.00
#2440/681 Cream, Footed	18.00
#2496/688 Cream, Individual	16.00
#2440/396 Cup	10.00
#869 Finger Bowl	12.00
#2496 Floating Garden 10"	30.00
#6016/2 Goblet 10 oz.	28.00
#2375 Ice Bucket	85.00
#2496 Ice Bucket, Metal Handle, Tongs	125.00
#2496/448 Jelly	18.00
#5000 Jug, Footed 9¾"	85.00
#6016/88 Juice, Footed 5 oz.	24.00
#6016/60 Luncheon Goblet/Ice Tea 13 oz. 5⅞"	25.00
#2375 Mayonnaise	
Bowl	20.00
Plate	18.00
Ladle	25.00
#2496 Mayonnaise, 2 part	35.00
#2496½ Mayonnaise	
Bowl	20.00
Plate	18.00
Ladle	25.00
#2496 Nappy, Footed 5"	15.00
#2496 Nappy, Handled 4¾"	15.00
#2496/500 Nappy, Handled, Flared	20.00
#2496/501 Nappy, Handled, 3 Cornered 4⅝"	20.00
#2496 Nappy, Square, Handled 4"	20.00
#2496 Nut Bowl, 3 Toed 6¼"	18.00
#6016/33 Oyster Cocktail 4 oz.	20.00
#2440 Pickle Dish 6½"	20.00
#2496 Pickle Dish 8"	25.00
#2666/454 Pitcher, quart	35.00
#2440 Plate	
6"	10.00
7"	12.00
8"	18.00
9"	25.00

#2364 Plate 16" 50.00
#2419 Relish
    4 part 45.00
    5 part 50.00
#2496 Relish
    2 part 33.00
    3 part 45.00
    4 part 50.00
#2083 Salad Dressing Bottle, Stoppered 75.00
#2496 Sauce Dish, Oblong 6½' 23.00
#2440/397 Saucer 12.00
#2496/648 Serving Dish, Handled 8½"......25.00
#2364/650 Shaker, Chrome Top ....pair 80.00
#2375 Shaker, Footed ....pair 100.00
#6016/11 Sherbet, Low/Dessert 6 oz. 18.00
#2440/679 Sugar, Footed.........................20.00
#2496/687 Sugar, Individual 16.00
#2496 Sweetmeat......................................16.00
#2496/707 Tid Bit, 3 Toed 20.00
#2496/567 Torte Plate 14" 55.00
#2364/573 Torte Plate 16" 65.00
#2496 Tray, Oblong 8½"...........................40.00
#2496/697½ Tray for Sugar & Cream 6½" ..35.00
#6016 Tumbler, Footed
    5 oz. 20.00
    10 oz. 20.00
    13 oz. 22.00
#2470 Vase, Footed 10" 95.00
#4121 Vase 5" 50.00
#4128 Vase 5" 50.00
#2660 Vase, Flip 8" 70.00
#6016/72 Water, Footed 10 oz. 5⅜" 20.00
#6016/26 Wine 3¼ oz. 30.00
#6016/35 Wine Goblet 16 oz. 7¼" 45.00

NAVARRE items included in Nostalgia program, azure bowl with crystal base as well as solid crystal. Pink bowl items were special order only.

Listing includes late production items still being made when Nostalgia program was presented.

*Azure Bowl with Crystal Base
**Items added to existing line when Nostalgia Program was introduced.

Add 20% for Azure Bowl, 40% for Pink Bowl.

#047 Bell 75.00
#137 Bon Bon, 3 Toed 25.00
#031 Brandy Inhaler 15 oz.** 35.00
#306 Cake Plate, Handled 30.00
#344 Candy Box, Covered, 3 part 50.00
#011 Champagne/Low Dessert 6 oz. 18.00
#008 Champagne/Low Dessert 5 oz.* 18.00
#084 Champagne, Continental 5 oz.** 30.00
#025 Claret 4½ oz.* 30.00
#027 Claret, Large 6½ oz.* 35.00

NAVARRE items produced in Patterns of the Past Program

All in Pink Bowl with Crystal Base

NA03/008 Champagne/High Dessert 6 oz.
    5⅝"..27.00
NA03/025 Claret 4½ oz. 6" 50.00
NA03/027 Claret, Large 6½ oz. 6½" 55.00
NA03/002 Goblet 10 oz. 7⅝" 35.00
NA03/063 Luncheon Goblet/Ice Tea 13 oz.
    5⅞"...30.00

☞ NECTAR Plate Etching #322 ☜

Crystal
1936 – 1943

#4024 Bowl, Footed 10" 40.00
#6011 Brandy 1 oz. 20.00
#906 Brandy Inhaler 18.00
#4024 Candlestick 6" ....pair 50.00
#795 Champagne, Hollow Stem 5½ oz. 16.00
#863 Champagne, Hollow Stem 5 oz. 16.00
#6011 Champagne, Saucer 5½ oz. 14.00
#2511 Cheese & Cracker 30.00
#6011 Claret 4½ oz. 15.00
#6011 Cocktail 3 oz. 14.00
#4024 Comport 5" 18.00
#6011 Cordial 1 oz. 28.00
#2350½ Cream, Footed.........................10.00
#6011 Creme de Menthe 2 oz. 14.00
#2350 Cup, After Dinner 12.00
#2350½ Cup, Footed 8.00
#6011 Decanter, Footed 45.00
#2449 Dessert Dish 8.00
#1769 Finger Bowl 8.00
#6011 Goblet 10 oz. 15.00
#6011 Jug, Footed 50.00
#1184 Old Fashioned Cocktail, Sham or Plain
    7 oz. 8.00
#6011 Oyster Cocktail 4 oz. 8.00
#2337 Plate
    6" 8.00
    7" 10.00
    8" 15.00
    11" 20.00
#6011 Rhine Wine 4½ oz. 15.00
#2350 Saucer.................................6.00
#2350 Saucer, After Dinner 6.00
#2235 Shaker, Glass Top.................pair 40.00

#6011 Sherbet, Low 5½ oz.......................8.00
#6011 Sherry 2 oz. 12.00
#2350½ Sugar, Footed 10.00
#2440 Torte Plate 13" 45.00
#701 Tumbler, Sham or Plain
    10 oz. 8.00
    12 oz. 10.00
#6011 Tumbler, Footed
    5 oz. 16.00
    10 oz. 10.00
    13 oz. 12.00
#4122 Whiskey, Sham or Plain 1½ oz. 8.00
#6011 Whiskey, Footed 2 oz. 16.00
#6011 Wine 3 oz. 15.00
#2503 Wine Jug 30.00

☞ NEEDLE ETCHING #37 ☜

Crystal Optic Ware
Crystal
Turn of the Century – 1928

#873 Almond 8.00
#880 Bon Bon 4½" 10.00
#858 Champagne 7.00
#932 Champagne, Saucer 7.00
#5070 Champagne, 4½ oz. 7.00
#5050 Champagne, Saucer 5½ oz. 7.00

NEEDLE ETCHING #37 cont.

#5070 Champagne, Tall, 5½ oz. 8.00
#5070 Champagne, Saucer 5½ oz. 7.00
#5070 Champagne, Hollow Stem 10.00
#5050 Claret
    4½ oz. 7.00
    6½ oz. 7.00
#5070 Claret
    4½ oz. 7.00
    5½ oz. 7.00
    6 oz. 7.00
#5070 Cocktail 3½ oz. 7.00
#5070 Cocktail 3½ oz. 7.00
#5071 Cocktail 7.00
#5050 Cordial 1 oz. 10.00
#5070 Cordial 1 oz. 10.00
#5089 Cordial 10.00
#5070 Cordial ¾ oz. 10.00
#5050 Cocktail 3½ oz. 7.00
#5068 Cocktail 7.00
#803 Comport
    5" 8.00
    6" 10.00
#5050 Creme de Menthe 2½ oz. 7.00
#5070 Creme de Menthe 2½ oz. 7.00
#1478 Cream 8.00
#480 Custard 6.00
#858 Custard 6.00
#5050 Egg 8.00
#1769 Finger Bowl 6.00
#1769 Finger Bowl Plate 4.00
#823 Fruit
    4½" 6.00
    5" 6.00
#5050 Goblet
    9 oz. 7.00
    10 oz. 7.00
    11 oz. 7.00
#5070 Goblet
    8 oz. 7.00
    9 oz. 7.00
    10 oz. 7.00
#880 Grapefruit 8.00

#880½ Grapefruit 8.00
#5070 Hot Whiskey 4 oz. 8.00
#701 Ice Tea 14 oz. 10.00
#303 Jug 7 ....40.00
#803 Nappy, Shallow
    4½" 6.00
    6" 7.00
    7" 7.00
    8" 8.00
#803 Nappy, Deep
    4½" 6.00
    5" 6.00
    6" 7.00
    7" 7.00
#303½ Oil, Cut Stopper 35.00
#822 Parfait 7.00
#5050 Pousse-Cafe 8.00
#5070 Pousse-Cafe
    ¾ oz. 8.00
    1 oz. 8.00
#882 Rhine Wine 4½ oz. 7.00
#5070 Rhine Wine 4½ oz. 7.00
#1478 Sugar 8.00
#840 Sherbet 7.00
#5050 Sherbet 7.00
#5070 Sherbet 7.00
#5050 Sherry 2 oz. 7.00
#5070 Sherry 2 oz. 7.00
#300 Tankard 7 ....40.00
#318 Tankard 7 ....40.00
#1236 Tankard 6 ....38.00
#933 Toothpick 20.00
#820 Tumbler 7.00
#833 Tumbler
    4 oz. 7.00
    6 oz. 7.00
#4015 Tumbler, 14 oz. 10.00
#5050 Wine 3½ oz. 7.00
#5070 Wine
    2 oz. 7.00
    3 oz. 7.00
#160½ Water Bottle 30.00

Narrow Optic
Crystal
1898 – 1928

Produced also as GREEK DESIGN, Colored
  Bowls with Crystal Bases 1930 – 1933

*Rose, Green, Amber Bowl with Crystal Base.
#880 Ale, Tall 6½ oz. 8.00
#863 Almond 8.00
#880 Bon Bon 4½" 10.00
#801 Brandy ¾ oz. 10.00
#825 Champagne, Saucer 7.00
#858 Champagne 7.00
#863 Champagne 7.00
#880 Champagne
    4½ oz. 7.00
    5 oz. tall 8.00
#880 Champagne, Saucer
    5 oz. Saucer 7.00
    7 oz. Saucer 7.00
#932 Champagne, Saucer 6 oz. 7.00
#932 Champagne, Saucer, Optic 5½ oz. 10.00
#5025 Champagne
    5½ oz. 7.00
    6½ oz. 7.00
#5050 Champagne, Tall, Optic 5½ oz........10.00
#5050 Champagne, Saucer 6 oz. 7.00
#801 Claret
    4 oz. 7.00
    5 oz. 7.00
#880 Claret
    5½ oz. 7.00
#5025 Claret
    4¾ oz. 7.00
    5 oz. 7.00
#5050 Claret, Optic
    4½ oz. 7.00
    6½ oz. 7.00
#5097 Claret* 10.00
#5297 Claret 7.00
#880 Cocktail...7.00
#5025 Cocktail
    5½ oz...7.00
    6½ oz...7.00
#5050 Cocktail, Optic 3½ oz. 7.00
#5097 Cocktail* 10.00
#5297 Cocktail* 10.00
#952 Cocktail..7.00
#953 Cocktail..7.00
#803 Compote
    5" 8.00

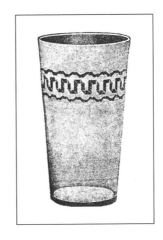

    6" 8.00
#801 Cordial 1 oz. 10.00
#5025 Cordial 1 oz. 10.00
#5050 Cordial 1 oz. 10.00
#5097 Cordial* 10.00
#5297 Cordial 10.00
#1478 Cream 8.00
#880 Creme de Menthe 7.00
#5050 Creme de Menthe, Optic 2½ oz. 7.00
#480 Custard...6.00
#480 Custard Plate 4.00
#481 Custard...6.00
#481 Custard Plate 4.00
#858 Custard...7.00
#858 Custard Plate 4.00
#1755 Custard...6.00
#300 Decanter, Cut Neck, pint 35.00
#300 Decanter, Cut Neck, quart 40.00
#1491 Decanter, Optic, Cut Neck 45.00
#1464 Decanter, Cut Neck, 18 oz.............45.00
#5050 Egg, Optic 8.00
#315 Finger Bowl 6.00
#858 Finger Bowl 4.00
#858 Finger Bowl Plate...............................4.00
#869 Finger Bowl* 8.00
#1499 Finger Bowl 6.00
#1499 Finger Bowl Plate.............................4.00
#1769 Finger Bowl 6.00
#1769 Finger Bowl Plate.............................4.00
#823 Fruit
    4½" 6.00
    5" 6.00
#863 Fruit 6.00
#880 Goblet
    8 oz. 7.00
    9 oz. 7.00

10 oz. 7.00

11 oz. 7.00

#801 Goblet 11 oz. 7.00

#5025 Goblet

    8 oz. 7.00

    9 oz. 7.00

    10 oz. 7.00

#5050 Goblet

    9 oz. 7.00

    10 oz. 7.00

    11 oz. 7.00

#5097 Goblet* 12.00

#5297 Goblet 7.00

#880 Grapefruit 8.00

#880 Grapefruit Liner.........................6.00

#880½ Grapefruit 8.00

#880½ Grapefruit Liner 6.00

#945 Grapefruit 8.00

#945½ Grapefruit Liner 6.00

#5297½ Grapefruit* 8.00

#945½ Grapefruit Liner* 6.00

#303 Jug 7 ....40.00

#318 Jug 7, Optic 45.00

#1111 Jug 6, Optic..............................45.00

#1111 Jug 7, Optic..............................45.00

#1227 Jug 7 ....40.00

#1232 Jug Optic..................................45.00

#1236 Jug

    3..35.00

    6..40.00

    7..45.00

#5000 Jug 7, Footed* 55.00

#315 Nappy

    4" 5.00

    5" 5.00

    6" 6.00

    7" 6.00

    8" 8.00

    9" 8.00

    10" 10.00

#803 Nappy, Footed, Deep

    4½" 6.00

    5" 6.00

    6" 6.00

    7" 7.00

#803 Nappy, Footed, Shallow

    4½" 5.00

    5" 6.00

    6" 7.00

    7" 7.00

    8" 8.00

#1227 Nappy

    4½" 5.00

    8" 8.00

#300½ Oil, Small 6½ oz. 30.00

#300½ Oil, Large Oil, Cut Stopper 45.00

#312 Oil...35.00

#1465 Oil, Cut Neck 7 oz. 40.00

#5000 Oyster Cocktail*.......................10.00

#5200 Oyster Cocktail 7.00

#5097 Parfait* 10.00

#5297 Parfait* 10.00

#2283 Plate, Optic 6"* 8.00

#2283 Plate

    7"* 8.00

    8"* 10.00

#880 Pousse-Cafe ¾ oz. 8.00

#880 Pousse-Cafe 1 oz. 8.00

#5025 Pousse-Cafe ¾ oz. 8.00

#5050 Pousse-Cafe, Optic 1 oz. 8.00

#1227 Punch Bowl with Stand 85.00

#880 Rhine Wine 4 oz. 7.00

#840 Sherbet 5½ oz. 7.00

#840 Sherbet Plate 4.00

#880 Sherbet 7.00

#5008 Sherbet 7.00

#5050 Sherbet, Optic 7.00

#5097 Sherbet, Low* 10.00

#5097 Sherbet, High* 10.00

#5297 Sherbet, Low* 10.00

#5297 Sherbet, High* 12.00

#840 Sherry 7.00

#846 Sherry 7.00

#880 Sherry 7.00

#5050 Sherry, Optic 2 oz. 7.00

#1478 Sugar 8.00

#858 Sweetmeat..................................10.00

#300½ Tankard 7 ....40.00

#724 Tankard 7 ....40.00

#300 Tankard, Claret

    1..30.00

    2..30.00

    3..35.00

    3½ 35.00

    4..35.00

    5..40.00

    6..40.00

    7..45.00

    8..50.00

#858 Tumbler, Table

    3½ oz...7.00

    5 oz. 7.00

6½ oz.	7.00
8 oz.	7.00
9 oz.	7.00
10 oz.	7.00
12 oz.	7.00
14 oz.	8.00

#858 Tumbler Plate 4.00

#701 Tumbler
8 oz.	7.00
10 oz.	7.00
12 oz.	7.00

#820 Tumbler 9 oz. 7.00
#820½ Tumbler, Sham 7.00
#833 Tumbler 8 oz. 7.00
#833 Tumbler, Sham, 8 oz. 7.00

#887 Tumbler
2½"	7.00
3"	7.00
5"	7.00

#889 Tumbler
5 oz.	7.00
14 oz.	8.00

#5000 Tumbler, Footed
2½ oz.*	10.00
5 oz.*	10.00
9 oz.*	10.00
12 oz.*	10.00

#5200 Tumbler, Footed
2½ oz.*	10.00
5 oz.*	10.00
9 oz.*	10.00
12 oz.*	12.00

#160½ Water Bottle, Cut Neck 8¼" 35.00
#1558 Water Bottle, Cut Neck...................35.00
#5050 Hot Whiskey, Optic 4 oz. 8.00

#880 Wine
2½ oz.	7.00
3½ oz.	7.00

#5050 Wine, Optic 3½ oz. 7.00

#5025 Wine
2 oz.	7.00
2¾ oz.	7.00

#5097 Wine*...10.00
#5297 Wine*...10.00

⋙ NEW ADAM Deep Plate Etching #252 ⋘

**Crystal
1918 – 1928**

Also offered with Decoration #34, Encrusted Gold Trim

#863 Almond	7.00
#880 Bon Bon 4½"	8.00
#896 Bowl and Cover	18.00
#1697 Carafe	20.00
#1697 Carafe, Tumbler	8.00
#1691 Carafe, Whiskey	8.00
#858 Champagne, Saucer 5½ oz.	8.00
#858 Claret 4½ oz.	8.00
#858 Cocktail 3½ oz.	8.00

#803 Comport
5"	10.00
6"	10.00

#858 Cordial 1 oz.	10.00
#2133 Cream	8.00
#858 Custard	7.00
#300 Decanter, Cut Neck quart	35.00
#858 Finger Bowl	7.00
#858 Finger Bowl Plate 6"	5.00

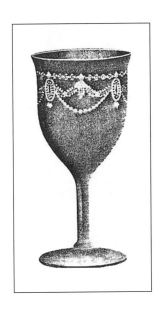

#858 Fruit, Footed 5½ oz.	8.00
#858 Goblet 9 oz.	8.00
#945½ Grapefruit	8.00
#945½ Grapefruit Liner	7.00

⇜ NEW ADAM Deep Plate Etching #252 cont. ⇝

#979 Horseradish......................18.00
#766 Ice Tea, Footed, Handled 10.00
#4061 Ice Tea, Footed, Handled 10.00
#300 Jug 7............................32.00
#300½ Jug 5 ....30.00
#303 Jug 7............................32.00
#318 Jug 7............................32.00
#724 Jug 7............................32.00
#1236 Jug 6...........................30.00
#2104 Jug and Tumbler Set 40.00
#1968 Marmalade, Covered 18.00
#2138 Mayonnaise
    Bowl, Footed 4⅛" 10.00
    Plate............................4.00
    Ladle 20.00
#1831 Mustard, Covered 15.00
#803 Nappy, Footed
    5".............................10.00
    6".............................12.00
    7".............................12.00
#1227 Nappy
    4½ oz. 6.00
    8 oz. 10.00
#1465 Oil, Cut Neck
    5 oz. 30.00
    7 oz. 35.00
#837 Oyster Cocktail 8.00
#822 Parfait..........................8.00
#1898 Plate, Salad 7" 6.00

#1719 Plate, Sandwich 10½" 12.00
#1848 Plate, Sandwich 9"................10.00
#840 Plate, Sherbet 5"..................4.00
#1736 Plate, Sherbet 6"..................4.00
#2083 Salad Dressing Bottle 30.00
#2022 Shaker, Glass Top 10.00
#858 Sherry 2 oz. 10.00
#2133 Sugar, 2-handled 10.00
#2015 Spoon Tray 6½" 12.00
#2194 Syrup, Nickel Top
    8 oz. 35.00
    12 oz. 40.00
#922 Toothpick 20.00
#820 Tumbler, Table 6.00
#858 Tumbler, Table 6.00
#710 Tumbler
    8 oz. 6.00
    14 oz. 8.00
#701 Tumbler, Handled 14 oz. 10.00
#701 Tumbler Plate 5"...................4.00
#833 Tumbler 8 oz. 6.00
#858 Tumbler
    5 oz. 6.00
    8 oz. 6.00
    10 oz. 7.00
    12 oz. 8.00
    14 oz. 10.00
#160½ Water Bottle, Cut Neck 25.00
#858 Wine 2¾ oz. 8.00

⇜ NEW GARLAND DESIGN Plate Etching #284 ⇝

Amber, Rose, Topaz
1929 – 1935
Amber, Rose or Topaz Bowl with Amber Base; Rose with Crystal Base 1931 – 1934; Crystal Bowl with Amber Base (#4120) 1930 – 1931

New Garland Dinnerware made in Amber, Rose, Topaz; Add 25% for Rose

#4020 Almond, Individual 9.00
#2419 Baker, 10" 35.00
#2419 Bon Bon, 2-handled...........15.00
#2394 Bowl
    7½".............................35.00
    12" 45.00
#2433 Bowl

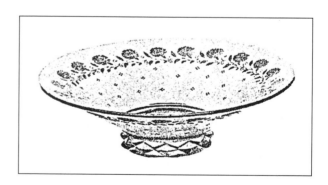

    7½"..............................45.00
    12" 45.00
#2441 Bowl 12" 45.00
#2430 Bowl, Footed 11" 45.00
#2430 Candy Jar, Covered ½ lb. 45.00

#2375 Candlestick 3" ....pair 20.00
#2394 Candlestick 2" ....pair 15.00
#2430 Candlestick 9½" ....pair 35.00
#2433 Candlestick 3" ....pair 15.00
#2419 Celery 11" 18.00
#2419 Cereal 6" 12.00
#2400 Comport 6" 20.00
#2433 Comport
    High 25.00
    Low 18.00
#4020 Cream, Footed 15.00
#2419 Cream 12.00
#2419 Cream, Tea 15.00
#2419½ Cream, Footed........................15.00
#2419 Cake Plate, Handled 10" 22.00
#2419 Cream Soup..............................15.00
#2419 Cup, After Dinner 12.00
#1429 Cup, Footed 10.00
#2439 Decanter 45.00
#4020 Decanter, Footed 65.00
#2419 Fruit 5" 8.00
#2375 Ice Bucket 40.00
#2451 Ice Dish 25.00
#2419 Jelly, 2-handled..........................15.00
#2430 Jelly 7" 17.00
#2419 Lemon Dish, 2-handled 15.00
#2419 Mayonnaise, 2-handled 15.00
#2375 Oil, Footed................................55.00
#2419 Pickle Dish 8½" 15.00
#2419 Plate
    6" 4.00
    7" 6.00
    8" 10.00
    9" 15.00
#2419 Platter
    12" 30.00
    15" 35.00
#2419 Relish, 4 part.............................22.00
#2419 Relish, 8½" 15.00
#2375 Salad Dressing Bottle 45.00
#2419 Sauce Boat with Stand 45.00
#2419 Saucer.......................................5.00
#2419 Saucer, After Dinner 6.00

#2419 Shaker ....pair 36.00
#4020 Shaker, Footed ....pair 65.00
#2419 Sugar 15.00
#2419 Sugar, Tea 12.00
#2419½ Sugar, Footed 15.00
#4010 Sugar, Footed 15.00
#2430 Vase 8" 30.00

New Garland Stemware made in Amber, Crystal, Rose or Topaz Bowl with Crystal Base. Add 25% for Rose.

#4120 Cocktail 3½ oz. 22.00
#4120 Goblet 25.00
#4120 Jug, Footed 150.00
#4120 Sherbet, High 20.00
#4120 Sherbet, Low 7 oz. 15.00
#4120 Sherbet, Low 5 oz. 15.00
#4120 Tumbler, Footed 5 oz. 10.00
#4120 Tumbler, Footed 10 oz. 10.00
#4120 Tumbler, Footed 13 oz. 14.00
#4120 Tumbler, Footed 16 o.z 18.00

New Garland Stemware made in Rose Bowl, Crystal Optic Base.

#6002 Claret 20.00
#6002 Cordial 30.00
#6002 Cream 15.00
#6002 Finger Bowl 8.00
#6002 Goblet 26.00
#5000 Jug 7, Footed............................175.00
#6002 Oyster Cocktail 18.00
#6002 Sherbet
    High 18.00
    Low 16.00
#4220 Sugar 15.00
#6002 Tumbler, Footed
    2 oz. 15.00
    5 oz. 10.00
    10 oz. 15.00
    13 oz. 20.00
#6002 Wine 20.00

Crystal
1913 – 1928

#858 Ale, Bass 7 oz. 12.00
#860 Ale, Tall 6½ oz. 12.00
#863 Almond, Individual 7.00
#825 Champagne, Saucer 8.00
#880 Bon Bon 4½" 8.00
#858 Brandy 1 oz. 10.00
#2219 Candy Jar and Cover
    ¼ lb. 18.00
    ½ lb. 20.00
    1 lb. 22.00
#2228 Candy Jar and Cover ½ lb..............20.00
#794 Champagne, Hollow Stem 10.00
#858 Champagne, Hollow Stem 10.00
#858 Champagne, Long Stem 10.00
#858 Champagne, Saucer
    5½ oz. 8.00
    7 oz. 8.00
#858 Champagne, Tall 12.00
#863 Champagne, Hollow Stem 10.00
#863 Champagne, Saucer 5½ oz. 8.00
#863 Champagne, Tall 5½ oz....................12.00
#864 Champagne, Peach 8.00
#880 Champagne, Saucer
    5 oz. 4.00
    7 oz. 5.00
#880 Champagne, Hollow Stem, Cut Foot
    4½ oz..10.00
#880 Champagne, Tall 5 oz. 12.00
#932 Champagne, Saucer 8.00
#858 Claret
    4½ oz..8.00
    6½ oz..8.00
#863 Claret 4½ oz. 8.00
#880 Claret
    4½ oz..8.00
    6½ oz..8.00
#858 Cocktail 3½ oz. 8.00
#863 Cocktail
    3 oz. 8.00
    3½ oz. 8.00
#880 Cocktail
    3 oz. 8.00
    3½ oz. 8.00
#803 Comport
    5" 10.00
    6" 10.00
#858 Cordial 1 oz. 10.00
#863 Cordial
    ¾ oz...10.00

    1 oz. 10.00
#880 Cordial
    ¾ oz...10.00
    1 oz. 10.00
#1061 Cracker Jar and Cover....................45.00
#858 Creme de Menthe 2½ oz. 10.00
#863 Creme de Menthe 2½ oz. 10.00
#880 Creme de Menthe 2½ oz. 10.00
#1478 Cream 7.00
#1480 Cream 7.00
#1759 Cream 7.00
#480 Custard 7.00
#480 Custard Plate 4.00
#481 Custard 7.00
#858 Custard 7.00
#858 Custard Plate 4.00
#1491 Decanter, Cut Neck 40.00
#858 Finger Bowl 7.00
#858 Finger Bowl Plate.............................4.00
#863 Fruit 7.00
#858 Fruit Salad 10.00
#858 Goblet
    8 oz. 8.00
    9 oz. 8.00
    10 oz. 10.00
    11 oz. 10.00
#863 Goblet
    5½ oz..6.00
    7 oz. 6.00
    9 oz. 10.00
    10½ oz..10.00
#863 Goblet, Long Stem 7½ oz. 12.00
#863½ Goblet, Short Stem 10.00
#880 Grapefruit 9.00
#880 Grapefruit Liner...............................7.00
#880½ Grapefruit 9.00

#880½ Grapefruit Liner 4.00

#945½ Grapefruit 8.00

#945½ Grapefruit Liner 7.00

#1132 Horseradish.............................18.00

#858 Ice Cream 4½" 6.00

#303 Jug 7.......................................30.00

#1111 Jug 6.....................................28.00

#803 Nappy, Footed, Deep

    4½".....................................5.00

    5"......................................5.00

    6"......................................8.00

    7".....................................10.00

    8".....................................10.00

#803 Nappy Footed, Shallow

    4½".....................................5.00

    5"......................................5.00

    6"......................................8.00

    7".....................................10.00

    8".....................................10.00

#1227 Nappy

    4½".....................................5.00

    5"......................................5.00

    6"......................................8.00

    7".....................................10.00

    8".....................................10.00

    9".....................................12.00

#312 Oil...30.00

#1465 Oil, Cut Neck, Cut Stopper 35.00

#858 Oyster Cocktail 8.00

#5036 Parfait 8.00

#5054 Parfait 8.00

#1897 Plate 7" 6.00

#2238 Plate, Salad

    8¼".....................................8.00

    11"....................................15.00

#1847 Plate, Sandwich 9"....................10.00

#1719 Plate, Sandwich 10½" 12.00

#863 Pousse-Cafe 1½ oz. 10.00

#863½ Pousse-Cafe ¾ oz. 10.00

#880 Pousse-Cafe

    ¾ oz....................................10.00

    1 oz....................................10.00

#1227 Punch Bowl and Foot....................85.00

#863 Rhine Wine 4½ oz. 8.00

#880 Rhine Wine 4 oz. 8.00

#863 Roemer

    4½ oz....................................8.00

    5½ oz....................................8.00

#1165 Shaker....................................10.00

#840 Sherbet....................................8.00

#840 Sherbet Plate 4.00

#880 Sherbet.....................................8.00

#858 Sherbet 8.00

#846 Sherry 8.00

#858 Sherry 2 oz.................................10.00

#863 Sherry 2 oz.................................10.00

#880 Sherry 2 oz.................................10.00

#858 Short Cake Comport 10.00

#1478 Sugar, 2-handled 10.00

#1480 Sugar 8.00

#1759 Sugar 8.00

#803 Sweetmeat..................................10.00

#300 Tankard

    6.......................................30.00

    7.......................................35.00

#724 Tankard 7 ....35.00

#858 Tumbler, Table

    10 oz....................................5.00

    12 oz....................................5.00

    14 oz....................................6.00

    16 oz....................................6.00

#858 Tumbler, Table Cut #19.....................8.00

#701 Tumbler 6.00

#701 Tumbler Plate 4.00

#820 Tumbler 6.00

#820 Tumbler, Sham 6.00

#833 Tumbler, Sham

    6 oz.....................................5.00

    7 oz.....................................5.00

    8 oz.....................................5.00

    10 oz....................................5.00

#858 Tumbler

    3½ oz....................................5.00

    5 oz.....................................5.00

    6½ oz....................................5.00

    8 oz.....................................5.00

#858 Tumbler, Cut #19

    3½ oz....................................6.00

    5 oz.....................................6.00

    6½ oz....................................6.00

    8 oz.....................................7.00

    10 oz....................................7.00

    12 oz....................................8.00

    14 oz....................................8.00

    16 oz...................................10.00

#858 Tumbler Plate 4.00

#885 Tumbler 2½ oz. 10.00

#887 Tumbler 3 oz. 6.00

#889 Tumbler 5 oz. 6.00

#1462 Tumbler....................................6.00

#160½ Water Bottle, Cut Neck 32.00

#1558 Water Bottle, Cut Neck.................32.00

#858 Wine

    2¾ oz....................................8.00

NEW VINTAGE Deep Etching #227 cont.

3½ oz..8.00
#863 Wine 3 oz. 8.00
#880 Wine
   3½ oz..8.00

3¾ oz..8.00
#858 Whiskey, Hot 10.00
#880 Whiskey, Hot 4½ oz. 10.00

NEW YORKER Cutting #703

Crystal
1930 – 1944
Crystal Bowl with Green Base 1930 – 1932;
Crystal Bowl with Ebony Base 1934

#4020 Champagne, Saucer/High Sherbet
   7 oz. 20.00
#4020 Claret 4 oz. 20.00
#4020½ Cocktail 4 oz. 18.00
#4020 Cream, Footed 12.00
#4020 Decanter 50.00
#4021 Finger Bowl 8.00
#4020 Goblet 11 oz. 20.00
#4020 Jug, Footed 50.00
#2419 Plate (Crystal only)
   6" 8.00
   7" 10.00
   8" 12.00
#4020 Sherbet, Low 7 oz. 18.00
#4020 Sugar, Footed 15.00
#4020 Tumbler, Footed
   5 oz. 18.00

10 oz. 18.00
13 oz. 20.00
16 oz. 20.00
#4020 Whiskey, Footed 2 oz. 16.00
#4020 Wine 3 oz. 20.00

NEWPORT Decoration #9

Engraved Band on Bowl with Gold Bands on
   each side
Crystal
1924 – 1930

Champagne, Saucer 6 oz. 15.00
Claret 5½ oz. 17.00
Cocktail 3 oz. 15.00
Cordial ¾ oz. 22.00
Parfait 5½ oz. 15.00
Sherbet/Low 6 oz. 13.00
Wine 2 oz. 20.00

⮎ NIGHTMARE Carving #39 ⮌

Decoration #621 (#39 Carving with 5 Enamel Colors)
Crystal
1940 – 1944

Various threatening animals in different poses.

#2306 Ash Tray, Nesting
    2¾"..10.00
    3"..12.00
    3½"..15.00
    4"..15.00
#4146 Cocktail 4 oz. 2½" 15.00
#4146 Cordial 1½" 1 oz. 15.00
#4146 Scotch & Soda 3⅛" 9 oz. 10.00

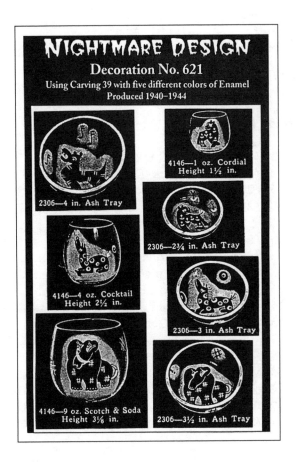

⮎ 19TH HOLE Carving #15 ⮌

Crystal
1940 – 1944

#2419 Ash Tray, Square (Approaching)
    4" 20.00
#2427 Ash Tray, Oblong (Putting) 3½" 20.00
#2391 Cigarette Box, Covered (Driving)
    4¾"..80.00
#4132 Decanter & Stopper (Driving) 9¾"..100.00
#4132 Ice Bowl (Putting) 4¾" 40.00
#4132 Old Fashioned Cocktail (Putting)
    7½ oz..15.00
#4132½ Scotch & Soda, Sham (Exploding)
    9 oz..15.00
#4132 Tumbler, Sham (Exploding) 5 oz. 15.00

#4132 Tumbler, Sham (Driving) 12 oz. 15.00
#4132 Whiskey, Sham (Approaching)
    1½ oz..15.00

Rock Crystal
Crystal
1953 – 1972

NOSEGAY included in Patterns of the Past and Nostalgia Programs.

Stems listed as 6051½ by 1968

#2666/189 Bowl, Oval 8¼" 35.00
#2666/311 Candlestick (Flora Candle) 6" ..30.00
#6051/27 Claret/Wine 4 oz. 4½" 23.00
#6051/20 Cocktail 3¼ oz. 3⅞" 17.00
#6051/29 Cordial 1¼ oz. 3⅛" 28.00
#2666/680 Cream 3½" 14.00
#2666/688 Cream, Individual 12.00
#4185/495 Dessert/Finger Bowl 10.00
#6051/2 Goblet 10½ oz. 6³⁄₁₆" 21.00
#6051/88 Juice, Footed 5 oz. 4" 13.00
#6051/63 Luncheon Goblet/Ice Tea 12¼ oz.
    6⅛" 20.00
#2364/477 Mayonnaise
    Bowl 12.00
    Plate 10.00
    Ladle 10.00
#6051/33 Oyster Cocktail 4¼ oz. 3¾" 13.00
#2337 Plate
    7" 8.00
    8" 10.00
#2666/620 Relish, 2 part 7⅜" 16.00
#2666/622 Relish, 3 part 10¾" 20.00
#2364/654 Shaker, Chrome Top,
    Large ....pair 30.00
#6051/7 Sherbet 6½ oz. 4⅜" 19.00
#2666/729 Snack Plate 10" 12.00
#2666/677 Sugar 2⅝" 16.00
#2666/687 Sugar, Individual 12.00
#6051/567 Torte Plate 14" 30.00

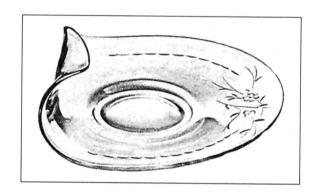

NOSEGAY items included in Patterns of the Past and Nostalgia Programs.

N001/007 Champagne/Dessert 7 oz.
    5⁷⁄₁₆" 19.00
N001/025 Claret 7 oz. 6⅛" 23.00
N001/002 Goblet 10½ oz.
    6¼" 21.00
N001/060 Luncheon Goblet/Ice Tea 14 oz.
    6¹¹⁄₁₆" 20.00

⊶≕ NOTTINGHAM Cutting #720 ≕⊷

Rock Crystal
Regular Optic
Crystal
1933 – 1935

#2470½ Bowl 10½" 30.00
#2470½ Candlestick 5½" ....pair 45.00
#6009 Claret/Wine 3¾ oz. 5⅞" 25.00
#6009 Cocktail 3¾ oz. 4¾" 18.00
#2400 Comport 6" 22.00
#6009 Cordial 1 oz. 3¾" 30.00
#869 Finger Bowl 8.00
#6009 Goblet 9 oz. 7⅝" 22.00
#6009 Oyster Cocktail 4¾ oz. 3¾" 12.00
#2337 Plate
    6" 6.00
    7" 8.00
    8" 10.00
#6009 Sherbet
    High 5½ oz. 5⅝" 18.00
    Low 5½ oz. 4⅜" 16.00
#6009 Tumbler, Footed

    5 oz. 4⅜" 12.00
    9 oz. 5¼" 12.00
    12 oz. 5⅞" 18.00
#4112 Vase 8½" 50.00

⊶≕ NOUVEAU Plate Etching #42 ≕⊷

Crystal
Gray Bowl with Crystal Base
1980 – 1982

#011 Dessert/Cocktail 7 oz. 6⅛"...............24.00
#002 Goblet 10 oz. 7⅞"............................24.00
#063 Luncheon Goblet/Ice Tea 14 oz.
    6⁵⁄₁₆" 20.00
#025 Wine 7½ oz. 7⁷⁄₁₆" 24.00

⊶≕ NOVA DESIGN #934 ≕⊷

Gray Cutting
1976 – 1978

NOVA items included in Patterns of the Past
  Program. Not included in Nostalgia Pro-
  gram.

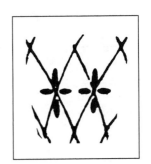

#6128/25 Claret 7 oz. 6⅛" 22.00
#6128/11 Dessert/Champagne 7 oz.
    5⁷⁄₁₆" 22.00
#6128/2 Goblet 10 oz. 6¾"........................22.00
#6128/63 Luncheon Goblet/Ice Tea 14 oz.
    6¹¹⁄₁₆"...22.00

NUMBER 200 Engraving #111 or Etching #32

Crystal Ware
Early Turn of the Century Line

#200 Butter and Cover 20.00
#200 Bowl, Open, High Foot
    6" 8.00
    7" 12.00
    8" 16.00
#200 Bowl, Open, Low Foot
    6" 6.00
    7" 10.00
    8" 12.00
#200 Can Individual 20.00
#200 Celery 20.00
#200 Cream 14.00
#200 Custard 10.00
#200 Custard Plate 6.00
#200 Finger Bowl 8.00
#200 Jelly 10.00
#200 Jug 25.00
#200 Molasses Can 30.00
#225 Nappy
    4½" 8.00
    4¾" 8.00
#200 Oil, Cut Stopper.............................18.00
#200 Spoon 20.00
#200 Sugar 22.00

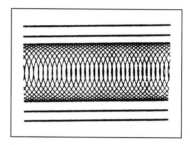

#200 Sugar, Covered 28.00
#200 Sugar Shaker 30.00
#200 Tankard 16.00
#127 Tumbler...10.00

NUMBER 226 WARE Etching #32

Crystal
Turn of the Century

Butter and Cover 20.00
Butter, Cut Star 22.00
Can #225 ....20.00
Cream 14.00
Custard 14.00
Mustard 25.00
Nappy
    4½"...8.00
    4¾"...8.00
    7" 10.00
    8" 15.00
    9" 15.00

Ovals/Plates
    7" 10.00
    8" 12.00
    9" 18.00
Plate 6¾" 10.00
Rose Bowl
    3" 12.00
    4" 14.00
    5" 15.00
    7" 20.00
Shaker Nickel..22.00
Shaker Silver-Plated...............................25.00
Spoon..20.00
Sugar, Covered 25.00

⚜ NUMBER 1229 Cutting #83 ⚜

Crystal
1904 – 1913

Butter, Covered	25.00
Cream	15.00
Cracker Jar, Covered	45.00
Ice Pitcher ½ Gal.	50.00
Oil, Cut Stopper	30.00
Shaker, Silver-Plated Top	pair 30.00

Spoon	40.00
Sugar, Covered	30.00
Syrup, Straight, Silver Top	30.00
Syrup, Welled, Silver Top	30.00
Tankard, ½ Gal.	40.00
Toothpick	20.00
Tumbler, Belled	14.00
Tumbler, Restaurant	10.00
Tumbler, Ice Tea	10.00

⚜ NUPTIAL Crystal Print #21 ⚜

Crystal
1969 – 1974

#6103/31 Brandy 3½ oz.	20.00
#6103/25 Claret 7½ oz.	20.00
#6103/2 Goblet 12 oz.	22.00
#6103/63 Luncheon Goblet/Ice Tea 14 oz.	20.00
#2337 Plate	
7"	10.00
8"	10.00
#6103/11 Sherbet/Dessert/Champagne	
8 oz.	18.00
#6103/26 Tulip Wine 7 oz.	22.00

⚜ OAK LEAF Brocade Plate Etching #290 ⚜

Optic
Crystal, Ebony, Green, Rose (Dawn)
Crystal 1928 – 1931; Rose, Green 1928 – 1931; Selected items in Ebony 1929 – 1931; 1928 – 1931

OAK LEAF, as well as its sister OAKWOOD, is a prized design, very formal and costly when found.

*Items made in Ebony in addition to regular colors
**Items not made in Crystal
***Items made in Crystal and Green Only

#2375 Bon Bon	35.00
#2308 Bowl, Footed 11"	80.00
#2395 Bowl 10"*	70.00
#2342 Bowl 12"	100.00

#2394 Bowl 12"	100.00
#2398 Bowl 11"	90.00
#2415 Bowl, Combination**	100.00

⌐═⇒ OAK LEAF Brocade Plate Etching #290 cont. ⇐═⌐

#2375 Cake Plate 10" 40.00
#2375 Candlestick 3" ....pair 60.00
#2375½ Candlestick ....pair 75.00
#2394 Candlestick 2" ....pair 60.00
#2395 Candlestick* ....pair 50.00
#2331 Candy Box, Covered 100.00
#2375 Centerpiece 12" 80.00
#2375½ Centerpiece, Oval 70.00
#2368 Cheese, Footed 30.00
#2368 Cheese & Cracker 50.00
#2368 Cheese Plate 35.00
#2391 Cigarette Box, Covered
　　Small* 45.00
　　Large* 65.00
#877 Claret*** 34.00
#877 Cocktail*** 22.00
#2350 Comport 8" 50.00
#2400 Comport 8" 50.00
#2380 Confection, Covered** 45.00
#2395 Confection, Covered,
　　Oval** 75.00
#877 Cordial*** 42.00
#2375 Dessert, Large 60.00
#869 Finger Bowl*** 20.00
#877 Goblet, Optic 10 oz.*** 25.00
#877 Grapefruit*** 30.00
#877 Grapefruit Liner*** 10.00
#2378 Ice Bucket, Nickel Plate
　　Handle 80.00
#5000 Jug 7, Footed, Optic*** 390.00
#2375 Lemon Dish 55.00
#2315 Lettuce Plate 13" 65.00
#2315 Mayonnaise 28.00
#2332 Mayonnaise Plate 7" 18.00
#2394 Mint Dish 4½" 30.00

#877 Oyster Cocktail, Optic 4½ oz.*** 19.00
#877 Parfait*** 24.00
#2383 Plate
　　6"*** 18.00
　　7" 25.00
　　8" 35.00
#2315 Salver 12" 50.00
#877 Sherbet, Optic
　　High, 6 oz.*** 24.00
　　Low, 6 oz.*** 18.00
#2378 Sugar Pail 80.00
#2375 Sweetmeat 20.00
#2342 Tray, Handled, Lunch 40.00
#877 Tumbler, Optic, Footed
　　2½ oz.*** 24.00
　　5 oz.*** 18.00
　　9 oz.*** 18.00
　　12 oz.*** 26.00
#2413 Urn, Covered** 150.00
#877 Wine*** 34.00
#2369 Vase, Optic
　　7" 100.00
　　9" 120.00
#2292 Vase 8" 90.00
#2385 Vase, Fan, Footed* 160.00
#2387 Vase 8" 90.00
#4103 Vase, Optic 3" 50.00
#4105 Vase, Optic
　　6" 80.00
　　8" 100.00
#2375 Whip Cream 35.00
#2373 Window Vase, With Flower Frog
　　Small 50.00
　　Large* 95.00

⌐═⇒ OAKWOOD Brocade Etching #290 ⇐═⌐

Decoration #72 Iridescent with Gold Band on
　Foot and Bowl
Azure, Orchid
1928 – 1931

**OAKWOOD is an example of the most sought-
after designs Fostoria made, combining an
intricate etching with seldom seen colors,
beautifully iridized. OAK LEAF, using the
same etching, was offered in a variety of
colors, but none so elegant as OAKWOOD.**

#2342 Bowl 12" 75.00
#2394 Bowl 12" 75.00
#2398 Bowl 11" 70.00
#2375 Bon Bon, Handled 35.00
#2375 Candlestick 3" ....pair 40.00
#2375½ Candlestick ....pair 110.00
#2394 Candlestick 2" ....pair 100.00
#2331 Candy Box, Covered 100.00
#2375 Centerpiece 11" 60.00
#2375½ Centerpiece, Oval 70.00

OAKWOOD Brocade Etching #290 cont.

#2391 Cigarette Box, Covered
    Large 80.00
    Small 60.00
#877 Claret 65.00
#877 Cocktail 40.00
#2400 Comport 8" 65.00
#2380 Confection, Covered 80.00
#877 Cordial 85.00
#869 Finger Bowl 18.00
#877 Goblet 50.00
#877 Grapefruit 60.00
#877 Grapefruit Liner.....................20.00
#2378 Ice Bucket 120.00
#5000 Jug 7, Footed.....................420.00
#2375 Lemon Dish, 2 handles 55.00
#2315 Mayonnaise 24.00
#2332 Mayonnaise Plate 7".................18.00
#877 Oyster Cocktail 35.00
#877 Parfait 46.00
#2315 Plate 13" 48.00
#2383 Plate
    7" 25.00

    8" 35.00
#2331 Salver 100.00
#877 Sherbet
    High 45.00
    Low 35.00
#2378 Sugar Pail 90.00
#2375 Sweetmeat 20.00
#2342 Tray, Handled, Lunch 40.00
#877 Tumbler, Footed
    2½ oz.....................................50.00
    5 oz. 35.00
    9 oz. 35.00
    12 oz. 40.00
#2385 Vase, Footed, Fan 8½" 140.00
#4105 Vase
    6" 70.00
    8" 100.00
#2373 Vase, Window, Covered
    Large 85.00
    Small 50.00
#2378 Whip Cream Pail 95.00

OLYMPIC PLATINUM Decoration #679

Platinum Band with Gray Cutting
Crystal
1968 – 1970

Produced also as OLYMPIC GOLD, crystal
with gold band.

#6111/25 Claret 7½ oz. 26.00
#6111/29 Cordial 2 oz. 26.00
#4185/495 Dessert/Finger Bowl 18.00
#6111/2 Goblet 12 oz. 26.00
#6111/63 Luncheon Goblet/Ice Tea
    15 oz. 24.00

#2337 Plate
    7" 12.00
    8" 12.00
#6111/11 Sherbet 9 oz. 18.00
#6111/26 Wine 7 oz. 24.00

OLYMPIC GOLD Decoration #680

Gold Band with Gray Cutting
Crystal
1968 – 1970

SEE OLYMPIC PLATINUM

⊰⊷ ORANGE BLOSSOM Cutting #911 ⊷⊱

Rock Crystal
Crystal
1966 – 1967

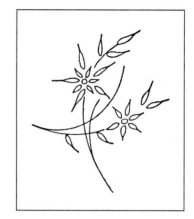

#6107/25 Claret 7½ oz. 25.00
#6107/2 Goblet 11 oz. 25.00
#6107/29 Liqueur 2 oz. 30.00
#6107/63 Luncheon Goblet/Ice Tea
    14 oz. 23.00
#2337 Plate
    7" 10.00
    8" 10.00
#6107/11 Sherbet 9 oz. 23.00
#6107/26 Tulip Wine 6½ oz. 25.00

⊰⊷ ORBIT Cutting #742 ⊷⊱

Rock Crystal
Crystal
1934 – 1938

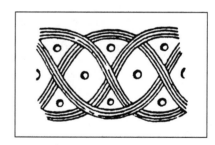

#319 Bar Bottle 40.00
#2470½ Bowl 10½" 35.00
#6012 Brandy 1 oz. 28.00
#2470 Candlestick, Duo ....pair 50.00
#863 Champagne. Hollow Stem 20.00
#6012 Champagne, Saucer 5½ oz. 21.00
#6012 Claret 4½ oz. 26.00
#6012 Cocktail 3 oz. 21.00
#2525 Cocktail Shaker 42 oz. 40.00
#2525½ Cocktail Shaker 30 oz. 45.00
#2400 Comport 6" 20.00
#6012 Cordial 1 oz. 32.00
#2550½ Cream, Footed...........................16.00
#6012 Creme de Menthe 2 oz. 21.00
#2525 Decanter 55.00
#6011 Decanter, Footed 65.00
#1769 Finger Bowl 13.00
#6012 Goblet 10 oz. 24.00
#6011 Jug, Footed 100.00
#1185 Old Fashioned Cocktail, Sham........12.00
#6012 Oyster Cocktail, Footed 4 oz. 13.00
#2337 Plate
    6" 8.00
    7" 10.00
    8" 12.00
#6012 Rhine Wine 4½ oz. 26.00
#6012 Sherbet, Low 5½ oz.......................17.00
#6012 Sherry 2 oz. 21.00
#2550½ Sugar, Footed 16.00
#2440 Torte Plate 13" 35.00
#701 Tumbler, Sham
    10 oz. 10.00
    13 oz. 10.00
#6012 Tumbler, Footed
    5 oz. 8.00
    10 oz. 10.00
    13 oz. 12.00
#4122 Whiskey, Sham 1½ oz. 14.00
#6012 Wine 3 oz. 26.00

✦ ORCHID Carving #48 ✦

Crystal
1941 – 1943

#892 Champagne, Saucer 7 oz. 23.00
#892 Claret 4 oz. 28.00
#893 Cocktail 4 oz....................................20.00
#892 Goblet 11 oz. 25.00
#892 Oyster Cocktail 4¼ oz. 16.00
#2337 Plate
    7" 10.00
    8" 10.00
#892 Sherbet, Low 6½ oz.........................23.00

#892 Tumbler, Footed 5 oz. 18.00
#892 Tumbler 12 oz. 25.00
#892 Wine 3 oz. 25.00

✦ ORIENT Deep Plate Etching #265 ✦

Optic Pattern
Crystal
1922 – 1929

#880 Bon Bon 14.00
#1697 Carafe 26.00
#4023 Carafe Tumbler 12.00
#661 Champagne, Saucer 6 oz. 7.00
#661 Claret 8.00
#661 Cocktail..7.00
#803 Comport
    5" 5.00
    6" 5.00
#2133 Cream 12.00
#300 Decanter, Cut Neck, quart 30.00
#1759 Finger Bowl 5.00
#661 Fruit, Footed 6 oz. 6.00
#661 Goblet 9 oz. 7.00
#945½ Grapefruit 15.00
#945½ Grapefruit Liner 12.00
#825 Jelly 14.00
#825 Jelly, Covered 18.00
#317 Jug, Cut Neck 20.00
#318 Jug 7...20.00
#317½ Jug, Covered 24.00
#4087 Marmalade, Covered 21.00
#803 Nappy
    5" 5.00
    6" 5.00
    7" 8.00
#803 Nappy, Covered 5" 12.00
#1465 Oil, Cut Neck
    5 oz. 15.00

    7 oz. 18.00
#897 Oyster Cocktail 6.00
#661 Parfait 5½ oz. 7.00
#840 Plate 5" 6.00
#1736 Plate 6" 7.00
#2238 Plate
    8½" 12.00
    11" 15.00
#2083 Salad Dressing Bottle 70.00
#2022 Shaker, Glass Top.................pair 40.00
#2022 Shaker, Pearl Top ....pair 60.00
#2133 Sugar 18.00
#1852 Tankard 6" 16.00
#4085 Tumbler, Table 8.00
#889 Tumbler 5 oz. 6.00
#4085 Tumbler 13 oz. 12.00
#4085 Tumbler, Handled 13 oz. 16.00
#661 Wine 2 oz. 9.00

⊸⊸ ORIENTAL Deep Plate Etching #250 ⇌

Blown Ware
Crystal
1918 – 1928

#766 Almond 4.00
#880 Bon Bon 4½" 8.00
#766 Brandy ¾ oz. 12.00
#1697 Carafe 20.00
#1691 Carafe, Tumbler 6 oz. 25.00
#1691 Carafe, Whiskey 2½ oz. 30.00
#766 Champagne, Saucer 5 oz. 10.00
#766 Claret 4½ oz. 10.00
#766 Cocktail 3 oz. 10.00
#803 Comport
    5" 5.00
    6" 5.00
#766 Cordial ¾ oz. 15.00
#1851 Cream 14.00
#2133 Cream 12.00
#766 Custard 6.00
#300 Decanter, quart 30.00
#766 Finger Bowl 5.00
#766 Finger Bowl Plate 6" 5.00
#766 Fruit 3¼" 8.00
#766 Goblet 9 oz. 15.00
#945½ Grapefruit 12.00
#945½ Grapefruit Liner 8.00
#979 Horseradish 22.00
#701 Ice Tea, Handled 14 oz. 12.00
#766 Ice Tea, Footed, Handled 12.00
#4061 Ice Tea, Footed, Handled 14.00
#300 Jug 7 ....20.00
#303 Jug 7 ....20.00
#724 Jug 7 ....20.00
#317½ Jug, Covered 30.00
#1761 Jug, Claret 30.00
#2104 Jug and Tumbler, Punty 24.00
#1968 Marmalade, Covered 18.00
#2138 Mayonnaise
    Bowl 18.00
    Plate 14.00
    Ladle 20.00
#1831 Mustard, Covered 22.00
#803 Nappy, Footed
    5" 5.00
    6" 5.00
    7" 8.00
#1227 Nappy
    4½" 5.00
    8" 10.00
#1465 Oil, Cut Neck
    5 oz. 18.00

    7 oz. 25.00
#837 Oyster Cocktail 3⅝" 6.00
#766 Parfait 5½ oz. 10.00
#766½ Parfait 10.00
#1897 Plate, Salad 7" 8.00
#1719 Plate, Sandwich 10½" 12.00
#1848 Plate, Sandwich 9" 12.00
#1227 Punch Bowl and Foot ....set 50.00
#2083 Salad Dressing Bottle 50.00
#2169 Salad Dressing Bottle 50.00
#2022 Shaker, Glass Top ....pair 40.00
#766 Sherbet 2⅝" 8.00
#840 Sherbet Plate 5" 6.00
#766 Sherry 2 oz. 10.00
#1851 Sugar 14.00
#2133 Sugar, 2-handled 16.00
#858 Sweetmeat 10.00
#820 Tumbler, Table 8.00
#937 Tumbler, Table 9 oz. 8.00
#4011½ Tumbler, Table 8.00
#701 Tumbler
    5 oz. 6.00
    8 oz. 6.00
    14 oz. 10.00
#887 Tumbler 3 oz. 6.00
#899 Tumbler 5 oz. 6.00
#4011 Tumbler
    3 oz. 8.00
    5 oz. 5.00
    8 oz. 5.00
    12 oz. 10.00
    15 oz. 12.00
#701 Tumbler, Handled 10.00
#701 Tumbler Plate 5" 8.00
#766 Wine 2¾ oz. 10.00

⇨ ORLEANS Cutting #204 ⇦

Azure, Topaz
1929 – 1930

#2375 Bon Bon 32.00
#2375 Bowl 12" 60.00
#2394 Bowl 12" 60.00
#2395 Bowl 10" 50.00
#2375 Cake Plate 10" 40.00
#2394 Candy Jar, Covered 70.00
#2375 Candlestick 3" ....pair 45.00
#2394 Candlestick 2" ....pair 40.00
#2395½ Candlestick 5" ....pair 50.00
#2368 Cheese, Footed 20.00
#2368 Cracker Plate...............................24.00
#2400 Comport 6" 30.00
#2395 Confection, Oval, Covered 70.00
#2375 Dessert, Large 40.00
#2375 Ice Bucket, Nickel Handle 60.00

#2375 Lemon Dish 45.00
#2375 Sweetmeat.....................................18.00
#2375 Tray, Lunch, Handled 45.00
#2417 Vase, Optic 8" 60.00
#4105 Vase, Optic 8" 50.00

⇨ OVERTURE Cutting #867 ⇦

Rock Crystal
Crystal
1959 – 1961

#6068/29 Cordial 1¼ oz. 3" 20.00
#6068/2 Goblet 10 oz. 5¾".......................16.00
#6068/63 Ice Tea, Footed 13 oz. 5⅞" 15.00
#6068/88 Juice, Footed 5 oz. 4½" 12.00
#2337 Plate
    7" 10.00
    8" 10.00
#6068/11 Sherbet 6½ oz. 4⅝" 14.00
#6068/27 Wine/Cocktail 4¼ oz. 4½" 16.00

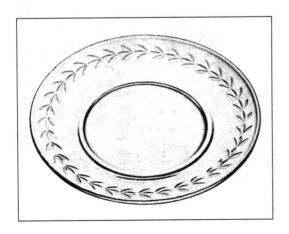

OXFORD Cutting #714

Rock Crystal
Crystal
1933 – 1944

#2470 Bon Bon 18.00
#2470½ Bowl 10½" 30.00
#2481 Bowl, Oblong 11" 35.00
#2470 Cake Plate 35.00
#2440 Candy Dish, Covered ½ lb. 20.00
#2470½ Candlestick 5½" ....pair 45.00
#2472 Candlestick, Duo pair 40.00
#2482 Candlestick, Trindle ....pair 75.00
#6007 Champagne, Saucer/High Sherbet
    5½ oz. 16.00
#6007 Claret 4 oz. 23.00
#6007 Cocktail 3½ oz. 16.00
#2400 Comport 6" 22.00
#6007 Cordial 1 oz. 27.00
#2440 Cream, Footed 16.00
#869 Finger Bowl 8.00
#2283 Finger Bowl Plate.........................6.00
#6007 Goblet 10 oz. 18.00
#2451 Ice Dish 15.00
#2451 Ice Dish Plate............................10.00
#2470 Lemon Dish 16.00

#6007 Oyster Cocktail 4½ oz. 12.00
#2283 Plate
    7" 8.00
    8" 10.00
#2419 Relish, 5 part.............................40.00
#6007 Sherbet, Low 5½ oz.........................10.00
#2440 Sugar, Footed 15.00
#2470 Sweetmeat 12.00
#2440 Torte Plate 13"...........................40.00
#6007 Tumbler, Footed
    2 oz. 18.00
    5 oz. 10.00
    9 oz. 10.00
    12 oz. 16.00
#6007 Wine 3 oz. 23.00

PAGODA Needle Etching #90

Optic
Crystal
1935 – 1944

#660 Champagne, Saucer/High Sherbet
    5 oz. 8.00
#660 Claret 4 oz. 8.00
#660 Cocktail 3 oz...............................8.00
#660 Cordial ¾ oz. 10.00
#869 Finger Bowl 6.00
#660 Goblet 9 oz. 8.00
#4095 Oyster Cocktail 8.00
#2237 Plate
    6" 6.00
    7" 7.00
    8" 10.00
#660 Sherbet, Low 5 oz. 8.00
#4095 Tumbler, Footed
    5 oz. 8.00
    10 oz. 8.00

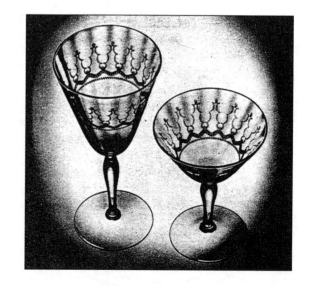

    13 oz. 10.00
#660 Wine 2¾ oz. 8.00

⊷⊶ PALMETTO Cutting #755 ⊶⊷

Optic
Rock Crystal
Crystal
1935 – 1939

#2470½ Bowl 10½" 50.00
#2533 Bowl, Handled 9" 50.00
#2472 Candlestick, Duo ....pair 60.00
#2533 Candlestick, Duo ....pair 60.00
#6014 Champagne, Saucer 5½ oz. 21.00
#6014 Claret 4 oz. 25.00
#6014 Cocktail 3½ oz. 20.00
#6014 Cordial 1 oz. 30.00
#869 Finger Bowl 13.00
#6014 Goblet 9 oz. 22.00
#5000 Jug, Footed 125.00
#6014 Oyster Cocktail 4 oz. 16.00
#2337 Plate
   6" 6.00

   7" 8.00
   8" 10.00
#6014 Sherbet, Low 5½ oz. 16.00
#6014 Tumbler, Footed
   5 oz. 16.00
   9 oz. 16.00
   12 oz. 18.00
#6014 Wine 3 oz. 25.00

⊷⊶ PAPYRUS Cutting #795 ⊶⊷

Combination Rock Crystal and Gray Cutting
Crystal
1939 – 1944

#6023 Bowl, Footed 20.00
#2324 Candlestick 6" ....pair 40.00
#892 Champagne, Saucer 7 oz. 10.00
#892 Claret 4 oz. 12.00
#892 Cocktail 4 oz......................................8.00
#892 Cordial 1 oz. 15.00
#1759 Finger Bowl 8.00
#892 Goblet 11 oz. 12.00
#6011 Jug, Footed 50.00
#892 Oyster Cocktail 4½ oz. 8.00
#2337 Plate
   6" 8.00
   7" 8.00
   8" 10.00
#892 Sherbet, Low 6 oz. 8.00
#892 Tumbler, Footed
   5 oz. 6.00
   12 oz. 8.00
#892 Wine 3 oz. 10.00

⊷≈ **PARADISE Plate Etching #289** ⇐⊷

Green, Orchid
1927 – 1930

See also VICTORIA, Decoration #71.
PARADISE, not a full dinnerware line,
assumes importance in Fostoria's etchings
because of the intricacy of the design and
the colors which harmonized with plain,
pressed lines, presenting an opportunity for
a lovely table, less expensively assembled.

#2297 Bowl

    Shallow..50.00

    Deep..60.00

#2315 Bowl, Footed 55.00

#2342 Bowl 12" 70.00

#2362 Bowl 12" 70.00

#2331 Candy Box, Covered.................100.00

#2324 Candlestick 4" ....pair 60.00

#2362 Candlestick 3" ....pair 50.00

#2372 Candle Block 2" ....pair 40.00

#2329 Centerpiece 11" 60.00

#2371 Centerpiece 13" 65.00

#2327 Comport 7" 70.00

#2350 Comport 8" 60.00

#2362 Comport 11" 80.00

#2380 Confection, Covered......................70.00

#2378 Ice Bucket, Nickel Plate Handle 80.00

#2378 Ice Bucket, Nickel Plate Handle 80.00

    Drainer, Tongs Add.............................50.00

#2378 Ice Bucket, Nickel Plate Handle 80.00

Silver Drainer, Tongs Add 50.00

#2342 Tray, Lunch....................................40.00

#2369 Vase, Optic

    7" 80.00

    9" 100.00

#4100 Vase, Optic

    6" 70.00

    8" 100.00

#4103 Vase, Optic

    3" 50.00

    5" 70.00

⊷≈ **PARISIAN Needle Etching #53** ⇐⊷

Optic Pattern
Crystal
1904 – 1927

#863 Almond 6.00

#880 Bon Bon 4½" 10.00

#867 Champagne, Saucer 6 oz. 8.00

#867 Claret 5 oz. 8.00

#867 Cocktail...6.00

#803 Comport

    5" 12.00

    6" 15.00

#867 Cordial 10.00

#303 Cream 6.00

#858 Custard..6.00

#858 Finger Bowl 10.00

#858 Finger Bowl Plate............................8.00

#867 Fruit Salad, Footed 5½ oz. 8.00

#867 Goblet 10 oz. 9.00

#766 Ice Tea, Footed, Handled 12.00

#300 Jug 7..40.00

#303 Jug 7..50.00

#318 Jug 7..60.00
#1237 Jug 6......................................70.00
#858 Mineral Water 2¾" 15.00
#803 Nappy, Footed
    5" 6.00
    6" 7.00
    7" 8.00
#300½ Oil, Small 10.00
#300½ Oil, Large 15.00
#822 Parfait 8.00
#867 Sherbet 6 oz. 8.00
#840 Sherbet Plate 5".......................5.00
#867 Sherry 2 oz. 6.00
#303 Sugar 3⅞" 10.00
#858 Sweetmeat................................10.00
#820 Tumbler, Table 6.00
#858 Tumbler, Table 3½ oz. 6.00
#4011½ Tumbler, Table 6.00

#701 Tumbler
    8 oz. 8.00
    14 oz. 10.00
#701 Tumbler Plate 5" 6.00
#833 Tumbler 8 oz. 8.00
#833 Tumbler, Sham 8 oz. 8.00
#858 Tumbler
    5 oz. 8.00
    8 oz. 8.00
    12 oz. 10.00
    14 oz. 10.00
#887 Tumbler 2½ oz. 6.00
#889 Tumbler 5 oz. 7.00
#4011 Tumbler
    5 oz. 6.00
    8 oz. 6.00
    12 oz. 8.00
#867 Wine 2¾ oz..............................8.00

⊶ PERSIAN Deep Plate Etching #253 ⊷

Crystal
1920 – 1928

#880 Bon Bon 4½" 15.00
#2219 Candy Jar, Covered
    ¼ lb. 15.00
    ½ lb. 20.00
    1 lb. 25.00
#863 Champagne, Saucer 5½ oz. 8.00
#863 Cocktail 3½ oz. 7.00
#2241 Cologne with Stopper.....................60.00
#2242 Cologne with Stopper.....................60.00
#2243 Cologne with Stopper.....................60.00
#803 Comport
    5" 18.00
    6" 20.00
#863 Cordial 1 oz. 10.00
#2214 Cream, Covered 15.00
#1769 Finger Bowl 10.00
#1769 Finger Bowl Plate............................8.00
#863 Fruit, Footed 5 oz. 8.00
#863 Goblet
    7 oz. 10.00
    9 oz. 10.00
#945½ Grapefruit 25.00
#945½ Grapefruit Liner 25.00
#4061 Ice Tea, Footed, Handled 18.00
#303 Jug 7...100.00

#803 Nappy, Footed
    5" 10.00
    6" 12.00
    7" 15.00
#1465 Oil, Cut Neck, Cut Stopper 5 oz. 30.00
#899 Parfait 10.00
#2238 Plate, Salad 8¼"............................8.00
#2214 Sugar, Covered 20.00

☞ PERSIAN Deep Plate Etching #253 cont. ☜

#820 Tumbler, Table 6.00
#701 Tumbler
    8 oz. 6.00
    14 oz. 10.00

#889 Tumbler 5 oz. 6.00
#701 Tumbler Plate 10.00
#863 Wine 3 oz. 10.00

☞ PERSIAN SCROLL Deep Plate Etching #203 ☜

Blown Ware
Crystal
1904 – 1910

#1163 Catsup, Cut Stopper 30.00
#932 Champagne, Saucer 8.00
#226 Cheese, Covered, with Plate 35.00
#444 Cheese, Covered 8" 30.00
#1061 Cracker Jar, Covered, Optic 40.00
#1227 Cream 12.00
#480 Custard 5.00
#481 Custard 5.00
#1227 Custard 5.00
#1241 Custard 5.00
#200 Custard Plate 6" 5.00
#315 Finger Bowl 5.00
#315 Finger Bowl Plate 5.00
#701 Ice Tea 16 oz. 15.00
#200 Liner/Ice Tea 18.00
#300 Jug
    1 ....18.00
    2 ....18.00
    3 ....18.00
    3½ 18.00
    4 ....18.00
    5 ....18.00
    6 ....18.00
    7 ....18.00
#303 Jug
    6 ....18.00
    7 Cut Star Bottom 20.00
#318 Jug 7 ....20.00
#724 Jug
    6 ....20.00
    7 ....20.00
#1227 Jug 7, Cut Neck, Cut Star 20.00
#1227 Nappy
    4½" 5.00
    8" 10.00
#300½ Oil, Cut Stopper
    Small 18.00
    Large 26.00
#312 Oil, Cut Stopper 24.00

#1164 Oil, Cut Stopper 30.00
#801 Stems
    ¾ oz. 8.00
    1 oz. 8.00
    2 oz. 8.00
    3 oz. 8.00
    4 oz. 8.00
    5 oz. 8.00
    9 oz. 8.00
    10 oz. 8.00
    11 oz. 8.00
#902 Stems
    3 oz. 8.00
    4 oz. 8.00
    5 oz. 8.00
#931 Stemware 5 oz. 8.00
#952 Stemware 3 oz. 8.00
#1227 Sugar, Covered 14.00
#701 Tumbler
    14 oz. 10.00
    16 oz. 10.00
#820 Tumbler 8.00
#820½ Tumbler, Sham 8.00
#833 Tumbler, Sham
    7 oz. 8.00
    10 oz. 10.00
#887 Tumbler 3 oz. 8.00
#889 Tumbler 5 oz. 6.00
#160½ Water Bottle, Cut Neck 20.00

↭ PETITE FLEUR Cutting #922 ↭

Gray Cutting
1971 – 1972

#6123/2 Goblet 8½ oz. 20.00
#6123/63 Luncheon Goblet/Ice Tea
    11½ oz. 18.00
#2337/549 Plate 7" 10.00
#6123/11 Sherbet 7½ oz. 16.00
#6123/26 Wine 5½ oz. 18.00

↭ PIERETTE Cutting #764 ↭

Rock Crystal
Crystal
1937 – 1940

#6012 Champagne, Saucer 5½ oz. 20.00
#6012 Claret 4½ oz. 27.00
#6012 Cocktail 3 oz. 20.00
#6012 Cordial 1 oz. 32.00
#1769 Finger Bowl 10.00
#6012 Goblet 10 oz. 25.00
#6011 Jug, Footed 100.00
#6012 Oyster Cocktail 4 oz. 14.00
#2337 Plate
    6" 10.00
    7" 10.00

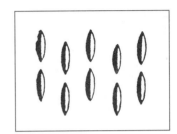

    8" 10.00
#6012 Sherbet, Low 5½ oz. 15.00
#6012 Tumbler, Footed 10 oz. 15.00
#6012 Tumbler, Footed 5 oz. 15.00
#6012 Wine 3 oz. 25.00

↭ PILGRIM Cutting #787 ↭

Rock Crystal
Crystal
1939 – 1952

PILGRIM was in perfect harmony with 18th Century Colonial or Early American settings; its promotional slogan was "extravagant beauty, modest cost."

#2574 Bon Bon 16.00
#2574 Bowl, Flared 12" 30.00
#2574 Bowl, Handled 9½" 40.00
#6023 Bowl, Footed 20.00
#2574 Cake Plate 10" 24.00
#2324 Candlestick 4" ....pair 35.00

PILGRIM Cutting #787 cont.

#2574 Candlestick 6" ....pair 50.00
#2574 Celery 10½" 24.00
#6023 Champagne, Saucer 6 oz. 16.00
#6023 Claret/Wine 4 oz.........................20.00
#6023 Cocktail 3¾ oz. 14.00
#2574 Comport 5" 24.00
#6023 Comport 5" 15.00
#6023 Cordial 1 oz. 26.00
#2574 Cream, Footed 16.00
#2574 Cream, Individual 20.00
#2574 Cup, Footed 8.00
#766 Finger Bowl 7.00
#2574 Fruit Bowl 13" 35.00
#6023 Goblet 9 oz. 19.00
#2574 Ice Tub 45.00
#6011 Jug, Footed 140.00
#2574 Lemon Dish 24.00
#2574 Mayonnaise
    Bowl......................................22.00
    Plate......................................18.00
    Ladle 20.00
#2575 Oil, Ground Stopper 4½ oz. 35.00
#2564 Olive Dish 6" 22.00
#6023 Oyster Cocktail 4 oz. 10.00

#2574 Pickle Dish 8" 28.00
#2574 Plate
    6" 8.00
    7" 12.00
    8" 20.00
    9" 25.00
#2574 Relish, 3 part...............................30.00
#2574 Saucer..7.00
#6023 Sherbet, Low 6 oz. 12.00
#2574 Serving Dish 8½" 35.00
#2574 Sugar, Footed 20.00
#2574 Sugar, Individual 26.00
#2574 Sweetmeat...................................22.00
#2586 Syrup, Sani-Top 45.00
#2574 Torte Plate 14" 40.00
#6023 Tumbler, Footed
    5 oz. 12.00
    9 oz. 12.00
    12 oz. 18.00
#2567 Vase, Footed
    6" 40.00
    7½" 60.00
    8½" 85.00
#2574 Whip Cream 40.00

PINE DESIGN Cutting #835

Gray Cutting
1953 – 1972

Stem numbers were listed under #6052½ by 1968.

#2666/136 Bon Bon, Curved Handle 6⅞"..16.00
#2666/189 Bowl, Oval 8¼".......................25.00
#2666/300 Butter, Covered, Oblong.........30.00
#2666/311 Candlestick (Flora Candle) 6"..30.00
#6052/27 Claret/Wine 4¼ oz. 4⅜" 25.00
#6052/20 Cocktail 3¾ oz. 3⅞" 16.00
#6052/29 Cordial 1¼ oz. 3⅛" 22.00
#2666/680 Cream 3½" 16.00
#2666/688 Cream, Individual 12.00
#2666/396 Cup 8.00
#4185/495 Dessert/Finger Bowl 10.00
#6052/2 Goblet 9¾ oz. 5⅞" 20.00
#6052/63 Luncheon Goblet/Ice Tea 13 oz.
    9⅛"...................................19.00
#6052/88 Juice, Footed 5½ oz. 4⅞" 13.00

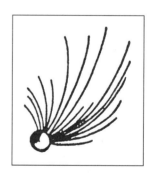

⇢⇛ PINE DESIGN Cutting #835 cont. ⇚⇠

#2666/477 Mayonnaise
    Bowl 12.00
    Plate 10.00
    Ladle 20.00
#6052/33 Oyster Cocktail 4½ oz. 3⅞"........13.00
#2666/454 Pitcher, quart......................60.00
#2337 Plate
    7" 8.00
    8" 10.00
#2666/620 Relish, 2 part 7⅜" 16.00
#2666/622 Relish, 3 part 10¾" 30.00
#2666/238 Salad Bowl 10½" 25.00

#2685/630 Salver, footed 12¼"................55.00
#2666/397 Saucer 6.00
#2666/568 Serving Plate 14" 15.00
#2364/654 Shaker, Chrome Top,
    Large ....pair 30.00
#6052/7 Sherbet 6½ oz. 4⅜" 16.00
#2666/729 Snack Plate, Curved Handle
    10" 15.00
#2666/677 Sugar 2⅝" 20.00
#2666/687 Sugar, Individual 14.00
#2666/686 Tray, Sugar and Cream ....set 40.00

⇢⇛ PINNACLE Cutting #753 ⇚⇠

Optic Pattern
Rock Crystal
Crystal
1935 – 1938

#660 Champagne, Saucer 5 oz. 7.00
#660 Claret 4 oz. 7.00
#660 Cocktail 3 oz. 7.00
#660 Cordial ¾ oz. 10.00
#869 Finger Bowl 4.00
#660 Goblet 9 oz. 10.00
#2337 Plate
    6" 6.00
    7" 7.00
    8" 10.00
#660 Sherbet
    Low 5 oz. 10.00

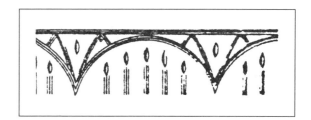

    High 5 oz. 10.00
#5095 Tumbler
    5 oz. 8.00
    10 oz. 10.00
    13 oz. 12.00
#660 Wine 2¾ oz. 10.00

⇢⇛ PLAIN 'N FANCY Crystal Print #11 ⇚⇠

Yellow
1958 – 1962

Tumblers produced to accompany similarly
decorated melamine dinnerware.

Juice Tumbler 7 oz. 10.00
Water Tumbler 12 oz. 10.00

PLANET Cutting #735

Crystal
1934 – 1936

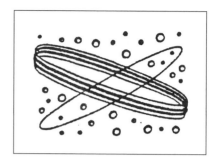

#4024 Bowl, Footed 10" 40.00
#6011 Brandy 1 oz. 20.00
#906 Brandy Inhaler 15.00
#4024 Candlestick 6" ....pair 30.00
#795 Champagne, Hollow Stem 5½ oz. 12.00
#863 Champagne, Hollow Stem, Cut Flute
    5 oz. 15.00
#6011 Champagne, Saucer 5½ oz. 14.00
#6011 Claret 4½ oz. 14.00
#6011 Cocktail 3 oz. 14.00
#6011 Cordial 1 oz. 22.00
#6011 Creme de Menthe 2 oz. 16.00
#6011 Decanter, Footed 70.00
#1769 Finger Bowl 8.00
#6011 Goblet 10 oz. 16.00
#6011 Jug, Footed 50.00
#1184 Old Fashioned Cocktail 7 oz. 6.00
#6011 Oyster Cocktail 4 oz. 10.00
#2337 Plate
    6" 6.00
    7" 7.00
    8" 8.00
#6011 Rhine Wine 4½ oz. 18.00

#6011 Sherbet, Low 5½ oz..........................12.00
#6011 Sherry 2 oz. 16.00
#701 Tumbler, Sham or Plain
    10 oz. 6.00
    12 oz. 6.00
#6011 Tumbler, Footed
    5 oz. 10.00
    10 oz. 8.00
    13 oz. 14.00
#887 Whiskey, Sham or Plain 1¾ oz. 6.00
#4122 Whiskey, Sham or Plain 1½ oz. 6.00
#6011 Whiskey, Footed 2 oz. 18.00
#6011 Wine 3 oz. 18.00

PLATINA ROSE Decoration #633

Crystal Print with Platinum on Bowl
Crystal
1964 – 1974

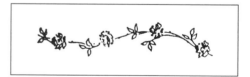

PLATINA ROSE included in Patterns of the
Past Program, not included in Nostalgia
Program

#6102/31 Brandy 4 oz. 28.00
#610/25 Claret 7½ oz. 25.00
#4185/495 Dessert/Finger Bowl 12.00
##6102/2 Goblet 10 oz. 28.00
#6102/63 Luncheon Goblet/Ice Tea
    14 oz. 26.00
#2337 Plate
    7" 10.00
    8" 10.00
#6102/11 Sherbet/Dessert/Champagne
    8 oz. 26.00

#6102/26 Tulip Wine 5½ oz. 26.00

PLATINA ROSE items included in Patterns of
the Past

PL04/011 Champagne/Dessert 8 oz. 5⅛" ..26.00
PL04/025 Claret 7½ oz. 5¾" 22.00
PL04/002 Goblet 10 oz. 7" 28.00
PL04/063 Luncheon Goblet/Ice Tea 14 oz.
    6⅝"..26.00
PL04/026 Tulip Wine 5½ oz. 5⅞" 26.00

⇌ PLUME Cutting #141 ⇌

Crystal
1919 – 1925
Do not confuse with PLUME Cutting #839.

#880 Bon Bon 4½" 8.00
#2219 Candy Jar, Covered
    ¼ lb. 15.00
    ½ lb. 20.00
    1 lb. 25.00
#1697 Carafe 12.00
#1697 Carafe Tumbler 6 oz. 8.00
#802½ Champagne, Saucer 7.00
#802 Cocktail...7.00
#2218 Cologne 50.00
#803 Comport
    5" 10.00
    6" 12.00
#1480 Cream 10.00
#1712½ Cream 10.00
#2214 Cream, Covered 14.00
#802½ Fruit, Footed 3½" 8.00
#1769 Finger Bowl 6.00
#1769 Finger Bowl Plate 6.00
#1736 Fruit Plate 6" 6.00
#802 Goblet 10 oz. 9.00
#300 Jug 7..10.00
#1236 Jug 6..10.00
#2040 Jug 3..10.00
#1968 Marmalade, Covered 24.00
#2138 Mayonnaise
    Bowl...20.00
    Plate...14.00
    Ladle 20.00
#1831 Mustard, Covered 24.00
#803 Nappy, Footed
    5" 6.00
    6" 6.00
    7" 8.00

#300½ Oil, Small 14.00
#899 Parfait 6 oz. 8.00
#2022 Shaker, Glass Top.............pair 40.00
#1712 Sugar 12.00
#2214 Sugar, Covered 16.00
#2194 Syrup, Nickel Top
    8 oz. 20.00
    12 oz. 30.00
#820 Tumbler, Table 6.00
#4011½ Tumbler, Table 8.00
#701 Tumbler 14 oz. 10.00
#833 Tumbler 8 oz. 6.00
#833 Tumbler, Sham, Punty....................6.00
#4011 Tumbler 12 oz. 10.00
#4011½ Tumbler 10 oz. 8.00
#4011 Tumbler, Handled 12 oz. 16.00
#701 Tumbler Plate 5" 8.00
#4069 Vase 9" 30.00

⇌ PLUME Cutting #839 ⇌

Conbination Gray and Rock Crystal Cutting
Crystal
1954 – 1960
   Do not confuse with PLUME Cutting #141.

#2666 Bowl, Oval 8¼" 30.00
#2666 Canapé Plate 7⅜"...........................15.00
#2666 Candlestick (Flora Candle) 6" 18.00

~ PLUME Cutting #839 cont. ~

#6051 Claret/ Wine 4 oz. 4½"....................20.00
#6051 Cocktail 3¾ oz. 3⅞" 16.00
#6051 Cordial 1¼ oz. 3⅛".........................25.00
#2666 Cream 3½"....................................15.00
#2666 Cream, Individual 12.00
#2666 Serving Plate 14" 40.00
#6051 Goblet 10½ oz. 6³⁄₁₆".....................18.00
#6051 Ice Tea, Footed 12¼ oz. 6⅛" 18.00
#6051 Juice, 5 oz. 4" 10.00
#2666 Mayonnaise
    Bowl..15.00
    Plate...12.00
    Ladle 20.00
#6051 Oyster Cocktail 4¼ oz. 3¾" 10.00
#2666 Relish
    2 part 7⅜"..30.00
    3 part 10¾"..35.00
#2364 Shaker, Chrome Top................set 20.00
#2666 Snack Plate 10" 30.00

#2666 Sugar 2⅝" 15.00
#2666 Sugar, Individual 12.00
#2666 Tray for Cream & Sugar.................18.00
#2337 Plate
    7" 10.00
    8" 12.00
#6051 Sherbet 6½ oz. 4 ⅜" 14.00

~ PLYMOUTH Plate Etching #336 ~

**Crystal
1939 – 1945**

This charming old coach design is perfect in Colonial or Early American settings.

#2574 Bon Bon, 2-handled 5"...................20.00
#2574 Bowl, Flared 12" 40.00
#6023 Bowl, footed...................................35.00
#2574 Bowl, Handled 30.00
#2574 Cake Plate 10" 30.00
#2574 Candlestick
    4"..18.00
    6" 24.00
#2574 Celery Dish 10½" 14.00
#6025 Claret/Wine 4 oz...........................18.00
#6025 Cocktail 3½ oz. 14.00
#6025 Cordial 1 oz. 26.00
#2574 Comport 5" 12.00
#6023 Comport, Blown 5".........................18.00
#2574 Cream, Footed 4"...........................12.00
#2574 Cream, Individual 3½" 14.00
#2574 Cup, Footed....................................10.00
#2574 Fruit Bowl 13" 40.00
#6025 Goblet 10 oz...................................18.00
#2574 Ice Tub 50.00

#6011 Jug, Footed 8⅞"..............................55.00
#2574 Lemon Dish, 2-handled 6½"...........15.00
#2574 Mayonnaise
    Bowl..20.00
    Plate...15.00
    Ladle 20.00
#2574 Oil, Ground Stopper 4½ oz. 5⅝"......30.00
#2574 Olive Dish 6" 15.00
#6025 Oyster Cocktail 4 oz. 10.00
#2574 Pickle Dish 8" 18.00
#2574 Plate
    6" 8.00
    7" 10.00
    8" 15.00
    9" 20.00
#2574 Relish, 3 part 10".............................26.00

⚞ PLYMOUTH Plate Etching #336 cont. ⚟

#2574 Saucer..8.00
#2574 Serving Dish, Deep, 2-handled 8½" 20.00
#2574 Shaker ....set 40.00
#6025 Sherbet 6 oz. 14.00
#2574 Sugar, Footed 3¾" 16.00
#2574 Sugar, Individual 2⅞" 12.00
#2574 Sweetmeat Bowl, 2-handled 5¼" 15.00

#2574 Torte Plate 14"..............................40.00
#2574 Tray, Muffin, Handled 35.00
#6025 Tumbler, Footed
    5 oz. 10.00
    12 oz. 16.00
#2574 Whip Cream Bowl, 2-handled 5" 40.00

⚞ POETRY Crystal Print #32 ⚟

1972 – 1982

Note: SOME COMPANY LISTINGS INCLUDE THE PREFIX "PO" BEFORE THE SHAPE NUMBER GIVEN HERE.

#6123 Goblet 8½ oz. 6½" 20.00
#6123/63 Luncheon Goblet/Ice Tea 11½ oz.
    6" 20.00
#6123/11 Sherbet/Dessert/Champagne

    7½ oz. 5¼" 19.00
#6123/26 Wine 5½ oz. 5¾"........................20.00

⚞ POUPEE Etching #231 ⚟

Crystal
1913 – 1928

#863 Almond 5.00
#803 Comport
    5" 6.00
    6" 8.00
#481 Custard, Optic...................................6.00
#5070 Champagne, Saucer, Optic 5½ oz. 8.00
#5070 Champagne, Tall, Optic 5½ oz. 7.00
#5070 Champagne, Hollow Stem, Optic
    4½ oz. 8.00
#5070 Claret, Optic
    4½ oz..8.00
    6 oz. 8.00
#5070 Cocktail, Optic
    3 oz. 6.00
    3½ oz. 6.00
#5070 Cordial, Optic
    ¾ oz..10.00
    1 oz. 10.00
#5070 Creme de Menthe, Optic 2½ oz. 8.00

#1478 Cream 12.00
#480 Custard, Optic...................................6.00
#300 Decanter, Handled, quart..................30.00
#300 Decanter, Handled, Cut Neck, quart..40.00

POUPEE Etching #231 cont.

#1195 Decanter, Cut Neck, Large	40.00	#945½ Grapefruit	10.00
#1491 Decanter, Cut Neck, Optic	40.00	#303 Jug 7	15.00
#1499 Finger Bowl	6.00	#803 Nappy, Deep, Optic	
#1499 Finger Bowl Plate	5.00	5"	5.00
#1769 Finger Bowl	6.00	6"	5.00
#1769 Finger Bowl Plate	5.00	7"	5.00
#5070 Goblet, Optic		#300½ Oil	20.00
8 oz.	8.00	#1465 Oil, Cut Neck	18.00
9 oz.	8.00	#822 Parfait	7.00
10 oz.	8.00	#840 Plate	5.00
#945 Grapefruit	12.00	#932 Plate 6"	7.00

PRESIDENT'S HOUSE Morgantown Etched Decoration #7780

Custom Order
Crystal
1961 – 1982

Jacqueline Kennedy chose PRESIDENT'S HOUSE, a Morgantown glassware pattern as the official glassware for the White House in 1961. The Fostoria purchase of Morgantown in 1965 gave them the right to use the molds and prestige accrued to the company because of the association with America's most admired hostess. Original production, which incorporated the Presidential Seal, included 21 items but the line was enlarged to the listing shown here. In 1981 it was made with the etched seal of the Senate or House of Representatives and shortly after that it was available for use with personalization for corporate seal or logo. PRESIDENT'S HOUSE has a place in political collections as well as advertising collections with added value to those who specialize in those areas.

Ash Tray, Round 5"	10.00	Champagne, Tulip 11 oz.	15.00
Ash Tray, Round 7½"	10.00	Cigarette Box	25.00
Ash Tray, Square 9"	10.00	Claret	20.00
Ash Tray, Square 7"	10.00	Claret, Large	20.00
Ash Tray, Square 5"	10.00	Cocktail 5 oz.	15.00
Bell	30.00	Cordial 1½ oz.	25.00
Bowl, 10½"	25.00	Double Old Fashioned Cocktail	10.00
Bowl, Flared 12"	25.00	Finger Bowl	15.00
Brandy 2½ oz.	25.00	Goblet	16.00
Brandy Inhaler 9 oz.	20.00	Luncheon Goblet/Ice Tea, Footed 12 oz.	16.00
Candy Dish	25.00	Nappy	10.00
Champagne, Saucer	15.00	Parfait	15.00
		Pitcher	40.00
		Plate 7½"	10.00
		Sherbet	12.00

⊶ PRESIDENT'S HOUSE cont. ⊷

Sherry 20.00
Tumblers
    Highball 12.00
    Juice 10.00
Torte Plate 14" 30.00
Vase, Footed......................................40.00

Wine
    3 oz. 20.00
    5 oz. 20.00
    8 oz. 20.00
Wine, Burgundy 9½ oz. 20.00
Wine, Rhine 20.00

⊶ PRINCESS Needle Etching #74 ⊷

Coin Gold Band #43
Optic
Crystal
1925 – 1928

See RICHMOND

⊶ PRINCESS Cutting #824 ⊷

Rock Crystal
Crystal
1950 – 1951

#6027 Cocktail....................................16.00
#6027 Cordial 18.00
#6027 Goblet 16.00
#6027 Ice Tea, Footed 16.00
#6027 Juice, Footed............................12.00
#6027 Oyster Cocktail 16.00
#6027 Sherbet, Low 14.00

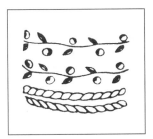

⊶ PRINCESS ANN Cutting #893 ⊷

Rock Crystal
Crystal
1962 – 1968

#6100/31 Brandy 1½ oz. 25.00
#6100/25 Claret 7½ oz. 25.00
#4185/495 Dessert/Finger Bowl 10.00
#6100/2 Goblet 11 oz. 26.00

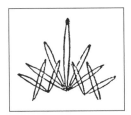

#6100/63 Luncheon Goblet/Ice Tea
  14½ oz.......................................25.00
#2337 Plate
  7"...10.00

  8"...10.00
#6100/11 Sherbet 7½ oz........................24.00
#6100/26 Tulip Wine 5½ oz. 24.00

⌁ PRISCILLA Cutting #130 ⌁

Narrow Optic Pattern
Crystal
1918 – 1928

#766 Almond 6.00
#766 Bon Bon 12.00
#766 Burgundy 2 oz. 12.00
#766 Champagne, Hollow Stem 12.00
#766 Champagne, Saucer 5 oz. 10.00
#766 Claret 4½ oz. 10.00
#766 Cocktail 3 oz..........................6.00
#766 Comport, Footed
  5"...12.00
  6"...16.00
#766 Cordial ¾ oz. 11.00
#2084 Cream 13.00
#766 Creme de Menthe 2½ oz. 9.00
#766 Custard 4 oz. 6.00
#766 Custard Plate 4.00
#766 Finger Bowl 8.00
#766 Finger Bowl Plate.......................6.00
#766 Fruit, Footed 4½ oz. 8.00
#766 Goblet 9 oz............................10.00
#766 Grapefruit 12.00
#766 Grapefruit Liner........................6.00
#766 Ice Tea, Footed, Handled 12 oz. 15.00
#303 Jug 7..................................35.00
#1236 Jug 6.................................50.00
#766 Nappy, Footed
  4½"...6.00
  5"..8.00
  6"..8.00
  7"..8.00
#300½ Oil, Small 20.00
#766 Parfait 7⅛".............................11.00
#2238 Plate, Salad 8¼".......................8.00
#766 Pousse-Cafe ¾ oz. 12.00
#766 Rhine Wine 4 oz. 10.00

#722 Shaker, Glass Top ....pair 30.00
#1165 Shaker, Silver-Plated Top ....pair 24.00
#766 Sherbet 2" 7.00
#766 Sherry 2 oz...........................10.00
#2084 Sugar 18.00
#300 Tankard 7 ....12.00
#922 Toothpick 15.00
#820 Tumbler, Table 8.00
#833 Tumbler 8 oz. 8.00
#833 Tumbler, Sham 8 oz. 8.00
#4011 Tumbler
  3 oz.....................................10.00
  5½ oz. 8.00
  8 oz......................................8.00
  12 oz....................................12.00
  15 oz....................................12.00
#300½ Water Bottle, Cut Neck 30.00
#4011 Whiskey 3½ oz. 8.00
#766 Wine 2¾ oz. 10.00

PUSSY WILLOW Cutting #769

Rock Crystal
Crystal
1937 – 1944

#4132 Decanter, Stopper 50.00
#4132 Ice Bowl..30.00
#4132 Old Fashioned Cocktail, Sham
    7½ oz...8.00

#2337 Plate 7" 8.00
#4132 Tumbler, Sham
    5 oz...8.00
    9 oz...8.00
    12 oz...10.00
    14 oz...10.00
#4132 Whiskey, Sham 7½ oz......................8.00

QUEEN ANN Plate Etching #306

Solid Crystal, Crystal Bowl with Amber Base
1929 – 1934
  Do not confuse with QUEEN ANNE Cutting
  #905.

ADD 10% FOR AMBER BASE

#4020 Cocktail 3 oz...................................18.00
#4020½ Cocktail 4 oz. 18.00
#4120 Cocktail 3½ oz. 18.00
#4020 Cream, Footed 15.00
#4121 Cream 12.00
#2350 Cream Soup....................................16.00
#2350½ Cup, Footed 8.00
#2350 Cup, After Dinner 12.00
#4021 Finger Bowl 10.00
#4121 Finger Bowl 10.00
#4020 Goblet 22.00
#4120 Goblet 22.00
#4020 Jug, Footed 120.00
#4021 Jug, Footed 130.00
#2350 Plate
    6" 8.00
    7" 12.00
    8" 20.00
#2419 Plate, Square
    6" 10.00
    7" 12.00
    8" 20.00
#2350 Saucer..8.00
#2350 Saucer, After Dinner 8.00
#2419 Saucer..8.00
#2419 Saucer, After Dinner 8.00
#4020 Sherbet
    High 22.00

    Low 5 oz. 18.00
    Low 7 oz. 18.00
#4120 Sherbet
    High 22.00
    Low 5 oz. 18.00
    Low 7 oz. 18.00
#4020 Sugar, Footed 18.00
#4020 Shaker, Footed ....pair 60.00
#4020 Tumbler, Footed
    5 oz...18.00
    10 oz...18.00
    13 oz...20.00
    16 oz...22.00
#4120 Tumbler, Footed
    5 oz...18.00
    10 oz...18.00
    13 oz...20.00
    16 oz...22.00
#4020 Whiskey 2 oz. 20.00
#4121 Sugar 20.00

⊰≋ QUEEN ANNE Cutting #905 ≋⊱

Rock Crystal
Crystal
1965 – 1970

#6104/25 Claret 7 oz. 25.00
#6104/29 Cordial 1½ oz. 30.00
#6104/2 Goblet 11 oz. 25.00
#6104/63 Luncheon Goblet/Ice Tea
    13½ oz..25.00
#2337 Plate
    7" 10.00
    8" 10.00

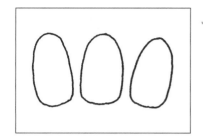

#6104/11 Sherbet 9 oz. 22.00
#6104/26 Wine 6 oz. 23.00

⊰≋ QUINFOIL Cutting #737 ≋⊱

Crystal
1934 – 1938

#319 Bar Bottle 15.00
#4024 Bowl, Footed 10" 40.00
#6011 Brandy 1 oz. 21.00
#906 Brandy Inhaler 15.00
#4024 Candlestick 5½" ....pair 30.00
#795 Champagne, Hollow Stem 12.00
#6011 Champagne, Saucer 5½ oz. 14.00
#6011 Claret 4½ oz. 18.00
#6011 Cocktail 3 oz. 14.00
#2518 Cocktail Shaker 38 oz. 40.00
#2518 Cocktail Shaker 28 oz. 40.00
#2400 Comport 6" 20.00
#6011 Cordial 1 oz. 22.00
#2350½ Cream, Footed.............................15.00
#6011 Creme de Menthe 2 oz. 16.00
#2518 Decanter 30.00
#6011 Decanter, Footed 70.00
#1769 Finger Bowl 8.00
#6011 Goblet 10 oz. 16.00
#6011 Jug, Footed 60.00
#1185 Old Fashioned Cocktail, Sham..........6.00
#6011 Oyster Cocktail 4 oz. 10.00
#2337 Plate
    6" 6.00
    7" 7.00
    8" 8.00
#6011 Rhine Wine 4½ oz. 18.00
#6011 Sherbet, Low 5½ oz........................12.00

#6011 Sherry 2 oz. 16.00
#2350½ Sugar, Footed 15.00
#701 Tumbler, Sham
    10 oz. 6.00
    12 oz. 6.00
#6011 Tumbler, Footed
    5 oz..8.00
    10 oz. 10.00
    13 oz. 14.00
#2518 Whiskey...10.00
#4122 Whiskey, Sham 6.00
#6011 Whiskey, Footed 2 oz. 18.00
#2518 Wine 5 oz. 12.00
#6011 Wine 3 oz. 18.00

⤙ **RAMBLER** Plate Etching #323 ⤚

Crystal
1935 – 1958

#2440 Bon Bon, Handled 5" 12.00
#2470½ Bowl 10½" 30.00
#2484 Bowl, Handled 10" 35.00
#6012 Brandy 1 oz. 28.00
#2470½ Candlestick 5½" ....pair 40.00
#2472 Candlestick, Duo ....pair 50.00
#2482 Candlestick, Trindle ....pair 70.00
#2496 Candlestick, Trindle ....pair 70.00
#4117 Candy Jar, Bubble, Covered...........20.00
#795 Champagne, Hollow Stem 15.00
#6012 Champagne, Saucer/High Sherbet
    5½ oz...20.00
#6012 Claret 4½ oz. 25.00
#6012 Cocktail 3 oz..................................20.00
#2524 Cocktail Mixer 30.00
#2525 Cocktail Shaker, Gold Top 42 oz. 40.00
#2525½ Cocktail Shaker, Gold Top 30.00
#6012 Cordial 1 oz. 30.00
#2350½ Cream, Footed.............................16.00
#6012 Creme de Menthe 2 oz. 20.00
#2350½ Cup, Footed 12.00
#2525 Decanter 35.00
#6011 Decanter, Footed 50.00
#1769 Finger Bowl 8.00
#6012 Goblet 10 oz...................................22.00
#6011 Jug, Footed 50.00
#2440 Lemon, Handled 5" 14.00
#2440 Mayonnaise, Oval 2 part 18.00
#1184 Old Fashioned Cocktail, Sham.........8.00
#6012 Oyster Cocktail, Footed 4 oz. 14.00
#2337 Plate
    6" 10.00
    7" 12.00
    8" 15.00
#2419 Relish
    4 part 30.00
    5 part 35.00
#2440 Relish, Handled
    2 part 22.00
    3 part 30.00
#2514 Relish, Square, 5 part 50.00
#6012 Rhine Wine 4½ oz. 25.00

#2440 Sauce Dish 6½" 20.00
#2350 Saucer...8.00
#2235 Shaker, Glass Top..................pair 60.00
#6012 Sherbet, Low 5½ oz.......................16.00
#6012 Sherry 2 oz. 20.00
#2350½ Sugar, Footed 14.00
#2440 Sweetmeat, Handled 4½" 12.00
#2440 Torte Plate 13" 40.00
#2440 Tray, Oval 8½" 35.00
#701 Tumbler, Sham
    10 oz. 10.00
    12 oz. 12.00
#6012 Tumbler, Footed
    5 oz. 14.00
    10 oz. 10.00
    13 oz. 20.00
#2470 Vase 11½" 45.00
#4122 Whiskey, Sham 1½ oz.....................12.00
#6012 Wine 3 oz. 25.00

269

⊸⊸ RAYNEL Cutting #777 ⊷⊷

Rock Crystal
Crystal
1938 – 1940

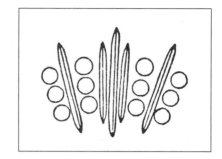

#6017 Champagne, Saucer 5 oz. 18.00
#6017 Claret 4 oz. 24.00
#6017 Cocktail 3½ oz. 16.00
#6017 Cordial ¾ oz. 26.00
#4132 Decanter 60.00
#766 Finger Bowl 8.00
#6017 Goblet 9 oz. 20.00
#4132 Ice Bowl..25.00
#6011 Jug, Footed 70.00
#4132 Old Fashioned Cocktail, Sham
    7½ oz. 6.00
#6017 Oyster Cocktail 4 oz. 16.00
#6017 Sherbet, Low 6 oz. 13.00
#4132 Tumbler, Sham
    5 oz. 6.00
    9 oz. 6.00
    12 oz. 8.00

#6017 Tumbler, Footed
    5 oz. 10.00
    9 oz. 12.00
    12 oz. 17.00
#2337 Plate
    6" 8.00
    7" 8.00
    8" 10.00
#4132 Whiskey, Sham 5 oz. 6.00
#6017 Wine 3 oz. 22.00

⊸⊸ REGAL Cutting #782 ⊷⊷

Optic
Rock Crystal
Crystal
1938– 1943
   Do not confuse with REGAL Cutting #842.

#6024 Claret 4½ oz. 30.00
#6024 Cocktail 3½ oz. 20.00
#6024 Cordial 1 oz. 35.00
#869 Finger Bowl, Optic 12.00
#6024 Goblet 10 oz. 25.00
#5000 Jug, Footed (Optic) 80.00
#6024 Oyster Cocktail 4 oz. 14.00
#2337 Plate (Optic)
    6" 8.00
    7" 8.00

    8" 10.00
#6024 Sherbet, Low 6 oz. 16.00
#6024 Tumbler, Footed
    5 oz. 14.00
    9 oz. 12.00
    12 oz. 18.00
#6024 Wine 3½ oz. 30.00

⇌ REGAL Cutting #842 ⇌

Gray Cutting
Crystal
1955 – 1958

Do not confuse with REGAL Cutting #782.

#6061 Cocktail/Wine/Seafood 4 oz. 3⅞".....20.00
#6061 Cordial 1 oz. 2½" 20.00
#6061 Goblet 11 oz. 5⅛" 20.00
#6061 Ice Tea, Footed 6 oz. 4¾" 16.00
#6061 Juice, Footed 6 oz. 4¾" 16.00
#2337 Plate
    7" 8.00
    8" 10.00

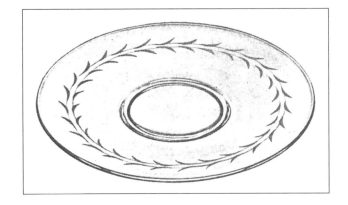

#6061 Sherbet 7½ oz. 4" 17.00

⇌ REGENCY Cutting #744 ⇌

Crystal
1935 – 1944

#319 Bar Bottle 40.00
#2470½ Bowl 10½" 35.00
#6012 Brandy 1 oz. 30.00
#2472 Candlestick, Duo ....pair 50.00
#863 Champagne, Hollow Stem 20.00
#6012 Champagne, Saucer 5½ oz. 22.00
#6012 Claret 4½ oz. 26.00
#6012 Cocktail 3 oz.................................20.00
#2525 Cocktail Shaker 42 oz. 40.00
#2525½ Cocktail Shaker 30 oz.................45.00
#2400 Comport 6" 20.00
#6012 Cordial 1 oz. 30.00
#2550½ Cream, Footed...........................16.00
#6012 Creme de Menthe 2 oz. 20.00
#2525 Decanter 55.00
#6011 Decanter, Footed 65.00
#1769 Finger Bowl 13.00
#6012 Goblet 10 oz. 23.00
#6011 Jug, Footed 100.00
#1185 Old Fashioned Cocktail, Plain 7 oz. 12.00
#6012 Oyster Cocktail, Footed 4 oz. 13.00
#2337 Plate
    6" 8.00

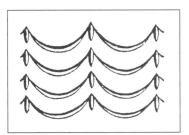

    7" 10.00
    8" 12.00
#6012 Rhine Wine 4½ oz. 26.00
#6012 Sherbet, Low 5½ oz...............................17.00
#6012 Sherry 2 oz. 21.00
#2550 ½ Sugar, Footed..................................16.00
#2440 Torte Plate 13" 35.00
#701 Tumbler, Sham or Plain
    10 oz. 10.00
    12 oz. 10.00
#6012 Tumbler, Footed
    5 oz. 8.00
    10 oz. 10.00
    13 oz. 12.00
#6012 Wine 3 oz. 26.00

❦ RENAISSANCE GOLD Decoration and Crystal Print #678 ❦

Crystal Print with Gold Band
1968 – 1982

SEE RENAISSANCE PLATINUM

❦ RENAISSANCE PLATINUM Decoration #682 ❦

Crystal Print with Platinum Band
1969 – 1982

Produced also as RENAISSANCE GOLD, Crystal Print with Gold Band.

#6111/25 Claret 7½ oz. 6" 35.00
#6111/29 Cordial 2 oz. 60.00
#6111/2 Goblet 12 oz. 7⅛".......................40.00
#6111/63 Luncheon Goblet/Ice Tea 15 oz.
    6⅝"..35.00
#2337 Plate
    7" 20.00
    8" 20.00

#6111/11 Sherbet/Dessert/Champagne
    9 oz. 5⅛"..35.00
#6111/26 Wine 7 oz. 6⅛" 35.00

❦ REVERE Cutting #825 ❦

Rock Crystal
Crystal
1950 – 1960

#6023 Champagne/High Sherbet 6 oz.
    4⅞"..17.00
#6023 Claret/Wine 4 oz. 4¾" 21.00
#6023 Cocktail 3¾ oz. 4⅜" 15.00
#6023 Cordial 1 oz. 3⅜" 26.00
#6023 Goblet 9 oz. 6⅜"..............................20.00
#6023 Ice Tea, Footed 12 oz. 5¾" 18.00
#6023 Juice, Footed 5 oz. 4½" 13.00
#6023 Oyster Cocktail 4 oz. 3⅝"...............11.00
#2337 Plate
    7" 8.00
    8" 10.00
#6023 Sherbet, Low 6 oz. 4⅛".....................13.00

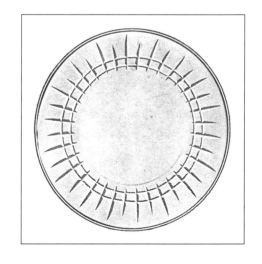

⚜ RHEIMS Cutting #803 ⚜

Regular Optic
Rock Crystal
Crystal
1940 – 1944

#2545 Bowl, Oval 12½" 30.00
#6023 Bowl, Footed 25.00
#2545 Candlestick 4½" ....pair 40.00
#6023 Candlestick, Duo pair 50.00
#6026 Champagne, Saucer 6 oz. 17.00
#6026 Claret/Wine 4½ oz. 20.00
#6026 Cocktail 4 oz...............................15.00
#6026 Cordial 1 oz. 26.00
#869 Finger Bowl 8.00
#6026 Goblet 9 oz. 18.00
#5000 Jug, Footed 60.00
#2337 Plate, Optic
    7" 6.00
    8" 8.00

#6026 Sherbet, Low 6 oz. 10.00
#6026 Tumbler, Footed
    5 oz. 12.00
    13 oz. 18.00

⚜ RHYTHM Cutting #773 ⚜

Rock Crystal
Crystal
1938 – 1943

#4020 Champagne, Saucer 7 oz. 16.00
#4020 Claret 4 oz. 21.00
#4020 Cocktail 3 oz................................16.00
#4020½ Cocktail 4 oz. 16.00
#4021 Finger Bowl 8.00
#4020 Goblet 11 oz. 20.00
#4020 Jug, Footed 70.00
#2419 Plate
    7" 8.00
    8" 10.00
#4020 Sherbet, Low
    5 oz. 15.00
    7 oz. 15.00
#4020 Tumbler, Footed
    5 oz. 13.00

    10 oz. 15.00
    13 oz. 18.00
#4020 Whiskey 2 oz. 14.00
#4020 Wine 3 oz. 20.00

⊶ RICHELIEU Decoration #515 ⊷

Etched and Gold Filled Bowl
Crystal
1938 – 1940

#2560 Bon Bon 12.00
#2560 Bon Bon 3 Toed............................15.00
#2439 Bowl 11" 30.00
#2560 Bowl, Flared 12" 35.00
#2560 Bowl, Crimped 11½" 30.00
#2560 Bowl, Fruit 13" 30.00
#2560 Cake Plate 25.00
#2560 Candlestick 4" ....pair 30.00
#2560 Candlestick 4½" ....pair 50.00
#2560 Candlestick, Duo ....pair 50.00
#6016 Champagne, Saucer 6 oz. 5⅝" 20.00
#6016 Claret 4½ oz. 6" 26.00
#6016 Cocktail 3½ oz. 5¼" 16.00
#6016 Cordial ¾ oz. 3⅞"...........................35.00
#2560 Cream, Footed 10.00
#2560 Cream, Individual 10.00
#6016 Goblet 10 oz. 7⅝" 25.00
#6016 Juice, Footed 5 oz. 4⅝" 15.00
#6016 Ice Tea, Footed 13 oz. 5⅞" 23.00
#2560 Lemon Dish 12.00
#2560 Mayonnaise
    Bowl...18.00
    Plate...10.00

    Ladle 20.00
#6016 Oyster Cocktail 4 oz. 15.00
#2337 Plate
    6" 8.00
    7" 8.00
    8" 10.00
#2560 Relish
    2 part 22.00
    3 part 30.00
#6016 Sherbet 6 oz. 4⅜"..........................15.00
#2560 Sugar, Footed 10.00
#2650 Sugar, Individual 10.00
#2560 Sweetmeat....................................15.00
#2560 Torte Plate 14"..............................38.00
#2560 Whip Cream 15.00
#6016 Wine 3¾ oz. 30.00
#6016 Water, Footed 10 oz. 18.00

⊶ RICHMOND Needle Etching #74 ⊷

Regular Optic
Crystal
1924 – 1942

Also produced as PRINCESS with gold band
on foot and bowl.

#5082 Champagne, Saucer/High Sherbet
    5 oz. 13.00
#5082 Claret 4½ oz. 15.00
#5082 Cocktail 2½ oz. 11.00
#5078 Comport 5" 25.00
#5082 Cordial ¾ oz. 20.00
#5078 Grapefruit 25.00
#5078 Grapefruit Liner...........................25.00
#1769 Finger Bowl 13.00
#5082 Fruit, Footed 5 oz. 20.00
#5082 Goblet 9 oz. 15.00
#303 Jug 7...100.00

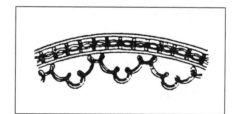

#318 Jug 7...100.00
#2270 Jug 7...100.00
#2270 Jug and Cover 150.00
#5078 Nappy, Footed
    5" 15.00
    6" 15.00
#837 Oyster Cocktail 13.00
#4095 Oyster Cocktail 4 oz. 15.00
#5082 Parfait 6 oz. 12.00

✐ RICHMOND Needle Etching #74 cont. ✐

#5082 Sherbet, Low 5 oz. 8.00
#858 Sweetmeat......................................12.00
#701 Plate 8.00
#2283 Plate
    6" 8.00
    7" 8.00
#701 Tumbler
    8 oz. 10.00
    13 oz. 10.00
#820 Tumbler, Table 10.00
#869 Tumbler, Handled 12 oz. 20.00

#887 Tumbler 2½ oz. 10.00
#889 Tumbler 5 oz. 10.00
#837 Tumbler, Footed 12 oz. 15.00
#4095 Tumbler, Footed
    2½ oz. 10.00
    5 oz. 10.00
    10 oz. 10.00
    12 oz. 15.00
    13 oz. 15.00
#5082 Wine 2¾ oz. 15.00

✐ RINGLET Crystal Tracing #95 ✐

Crystal
1940 – 1944

#892 Champagne, Saucer 7 oz. 8.00
#892 Claret 4 oz. 8.00
#892 Cocktail 4 oz....................................7.00
#1769 Finger Bowl 6.00
#892 Goblet 11 oz. 8.00
#892 Oyster Cocktail 4½ oz. 6.00
#2237 Plate 7" 8.00
#892 Sherbet, Low 6½ oz...........................7.00
#892 Tumbler, Footed
    5 oz. 6.00
    12 oz. 8.00

✐ RING O' ROSES Crystal #9 ✐

Fawn
1958 – 1962

Tumblers produced to accompany similarly decorated melamine dinnerware.

Juice Tumbler 7 oz. 10.00
Water Tumbler 12 oz. 10.00

RIPPLES Cutting #766

Crystal
1937 – 1944

#2545 Bowl, "Flame," Oval 12½".................70.00
#2545 Candelabra, "Flame," 2 Light ..pair 60.00
#2545 Candlestick, "Flame," Duo ......pair 50.00
#6017 Champagne, Saucer 6 oz. 18.00
#6017 Claret 4 oz. 22.00
#6017 Cocktail 3½ oz. 16.00
#6017 Cordial ¾ oz. 26.00
#766 Finger Bowl 9.00
#6017 Goblet 9 oz. 20.00
#6011 Jug, Footed 100.00
#4132 Old Fashioned Cocktail, Sham
    7½ oz...10.00
#6017 Oyster Cocktail 4 oz. 15.00
#2337 Plate
    6" 8.00
    7" 10.00
    8" 12.00
#6017 Sherbet, Low 6 oz. 13.00
#4132 Tumbler, Sham
    4 oz. 10.00
    5 oz. 10.00
    7 oz. 10.00
    9 oz. 10.00

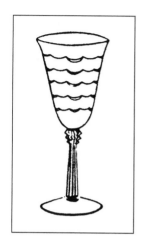

    12 oz. 10.00
    14 oz. 10.00
#6017 Tumbler, Footed
    5 oz. 14.00
    9 oz. 14.00
    12 oz. 18.00
    14 oz. 18.00
#4132 Whiskey, Sham 1½ oz. 10.00
#6017 Wine 3 oz. 22.00

ROCK CRYSTAL #4

Optic Pattern
Crystal
1903 – 1914

#803 Almond 15.00
#5061 Champagne, Saucer.......................20.00
#5061 Cocktail 15.00
#1478 Cream, Cut Star Bottom 15.00
#858 Custard, Cut Star Bottom 10.00
#5061 Goblet 9 oz. 18.00
#303 Jug 7 (not Optic) 150.00
#803 Nappy, Deep 5" 22.00
#5061 Sherbet 13.00
#1478 Sugar, 2-handled, Cut Star Bottom 15.00
#858 Tumbler, Table, Cut #19 ....12.00

⇝ ROCK GARDEN Cutting #739 ⇜

Rock Crystal
1934 – 1944

#319 Bar Bottle 15.00
#4024 Bowl, Footed 10" 40.00
#6012 Brandy 1 oz. 26.00
#4024 Candlestick 6" ....pair 30.00
#4117 Candy Jar, Covered, Bubble Style ..20.00
#863 Champagne, Hollow Stem 15.00
#6012 Champagne, Saucer 5½ oz. 20.00
#6012 Claret 4½ oz. 25.00
#6012 Cocktail 3 oz. 20.00
#2525 Cocktail Shaker 42 oz. 40.00
#2525½ Cocktail Shaker 30 oz....................40.00
#2400 Comport 6" 20.00
#6012 Cordial 1 oz. 30.00
#2350½ Cream, Footed...........................15.00
#6012 Creme de Menthe 2 oz. 20.00
#2525 Decanter 30.00
#6011 Decanter, Footed 70.00
#1769 Finger Bowl 8.00
#6012 Goblet 10 oz. 22.00
#6011 Jug, Footed 50.00
#1185 Old Fashioned Cocktail, Sham..........6.00
#6012 Oyster Cocktail 4 oz. 12.00
#2337 Plate
    6" 6.00
    7" 7.00
    8" 8.00
#2364 Plate 16" 40.00
#2440 Plate 13" 35.00

#6012 Rhine Wine 4½ oz. 25.00
#6012 Sherbet, Low 5½ oz........................16.00
#6012 Sherry 2 oz. 20.00
#2350½ Sugar, Footed 15.00
#701 Tumbler, Sham
    10 oz. 6.00
    12 oz. 6.00
#6012 Tumbler, Footed
    5 oz. 12.00
    10 oz. 11.00
    13 oz. 20.00
#2470 Vase 10" 60.00
#4122 Whiskey, Sham 1½ oz......................6.00
#6012 Wine 3 oz. 25.00

⇝ ROCKET Cutting #729 ⇜

Crystal
1934 – 1943

#4024 Bowl, Footed 10" 40.00
#6011 Brandy 1 oz. 22.00
#906 Brandy Inhaler 15.00
#4024 Candlestick 6" ....pair 30.00
#795 Champagne, Hollow Stem 5½ oz. 12.00
#863 Champagne, Hollow Stem, Cut Flute
    5 oz. 15.00
#6011 Champagne, Saucer 5½ oz. 14.00
#6011 Claret 4½ oz. 18.00
#6011 Cocktail 3 oz. 14.00
#6011 Cordial 1 oz. 22.00
#6011 Creme de Menthe 2 oz. 16.00

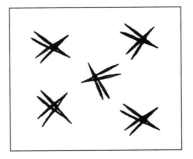

#6011 Decanter, Footed 70.00
#869 Finger Bowl 8.00
#1769 Finger Bowl 8.00

ROCKET Cutting #729 cont.

#6011 Goblet 10 oz. 18.00
#6011 Jug, Footed 50.00
#1184 Old Fashioned Cocktail, Sham or Plain
   7 oz. 8.00
#6011 Oyster Cocktail 4 oz. 10.00
#2337 Plate
   6" 6.00
   7" 8.00
   8" 10.00
#6011 Rhine Wine 4½ oz. 18.00
#6011 Sherbet, Low 5½ oz. 12.00
#6011 Sherry 2 oz. 16.00

#701 Tumbler, Sham or Plain
   10 oz. 6.00
   12 oz. 6.00
#6011 Tumbler, Footed
   5 oz. 10.00
   10 oz. 8.00
   13 oz. 14.00
#887 Whiskey 1¾ oz. 6.00
#4122 Whiskey, Sham or Plain 1½ oz. 6.00
#6011 Whiskey, Footed 2 oz. 18.00
#6011 Wine 3 oz. 18.00

ROGENE Deep Plate Etching #269

Crystal
1924 – 1929

#4095 Almond, Footed 6.00
#1697 Bedroom Set (Carafe, Tumbler) 40.00
#1697 Carafe 28.00
#5082 Champagne, Saucer......................15.00
#5082 Claret 18.00
#5082 Cocktail 12.00
#5078 Comport
   5" 6.00
   6" 8.00
#5082 Cordial 22.00
#1851 Cream 15.00
#300 Decanter, Cut Neck, quart 30.00
#766 Finger Bowl 6.00
#5082 Fruit 12.00
#5082 Goblet 18.00
#945½ Grapefruit 18.00
#945½ Grapefruit Liner 12.00
#825 Jelly 15.00
#825 Jelly, Covered 20.00
#318 Jug 7 ....22.00
#1852 Jug 6 ....22.00
#2270 Jug 7 ....22.00
#2270 Jug 7, Covered..........................30.00
#4095 Jug, Footed
   4...40.00
   7...50.00
#1968 Marmalade, Covered 30.00
#2138 Mayonnaise
   Bowl 18.00
   Plate 14.00
   Ladle 20.00
#766 Mayonnaise
   Bowl 16.00

   Plate 12.00
   Ladle 20.00
#5078 Nappy, Footed
   5" 5.00
   6" 5.00
   7" 8.00
#1465 Oil, Cut Neck 5 oz. 20.00
#837 Oyster Cocktail 10.00
#5082 Parfait 15.00
#4076 Tumbler, Table 10.00
#701 Plate, Tumbler............................8.00
#2283 Plate
   5" 7.00
   6" 8.00
   7" 10.00
   8" 14.00
   11" 16.00
   11" (Cut Star) 18.00
#2235 Shaker, Glass Top..............pair 50.00
#2235 Shaker, Pearl Top ....pair 160.00
#1851 Sugar, 2-handled 20.00
#887 Tumbler 2½ oz. 10.00
#889 Tumbler
   5 oz. 10.00
   8 oz. 8.00
   13 oz. 12.00
#4023 Tumbler 6 oz. 8.00
#869 Tumbler, Handled 12 oz. 18.00
#4095 Tumbler, Footed.........................15.00
   2½ oz. 10.00
   5 oz. 8.00
   10 oz. 12.00
   13 oz. 15.00
#4095 Vase, Rolled Edge 8½" 50.00
#5082 Wine 18.00

❧ ROMANCE Plate Etching #341 ❧

Crystal
1942 – 1972

Those who study details will not confuse ROMANCE with JUNE in spite of similarities. There is no single long extension of ribbon in Romance and the linear treatment at the top of JUNE is absent in the ROMANCE etching.

ROMANCE included in Patterns of the Past and Nostalgia Programs

#2364 Ash Tray, Individual 2⅝"	12.00
#2364 Bowl, Baked Apple 6"	16.00
#2364/249 Bowl, Flared 12"	38.00
#2364 Bowl 13"	35.00
#2594 Bowl, Handled 10"	45.00
#2364 Bowl, Ornamental 8"	35.00
#2364 Bowl, Ornamental 10½"	40.00
#2596 Bowl, Oblong, Shallow 11"	35.00
#2364 Bowl, Soup, Rim	20.00
#6023 Bowl, Footed, Blown 9¼"	pair 35.00
#2324/315 Candlestick 4"	pair 58.00
#2594 Candlestick 5½"	pair 55.00
#2596 Candlestick 5"	pair 44.00
#6023/332 Candlestick, Duo	pair 62.00
#2594 Candlestick, Trindle	75.00
#2364 Candy Box, Covered	40.00
#2364 Celery 11"	22.00
#6017/8 Champagne/High Sherbet 6 oz.	22.00
#2364 Cheese, Footed	18.00
#2364/369 Cheese & Cracker	35.00
#2364 Cigarette Holder, Blown 2"	36.00
#6017/25 Claret 4 oz.	30.00
#6017/21 Cocktail 3½ oz.	23.00
#6030 Comport 5"	20.00
#2364 Comport 8"	30.00
#6017/29 Cordial ¾ oz.	50.00
#2364 Cracker Plate 11"	35.00
#2350/681½ Cream, Footed	20.00
#2350/396½ Cup, Footed	16.00
#766 Finger Bowl	12.00
#2364/259 Fruit Bowl 13"	40.00
#6017/2 Goblet 9 oz.	25.00
#4132 Ice Bowl	50.00
#6011 Jug, Footed	60.00
#6017/88 Juice, Footed 5 oz.	17.00
#2364/251 Lily Pond 12"	55.00
#6017/63 Luncheon Goblet/Ice Tea 12 oz.	
6"	24.00
#2364/477 Mayonnaise	

Bowl	37.00
Plate	14.00
Ladle	20.00
#6017/33 Oyster Cocktail 4 oz.	16.00
#2364 Pickle Dish 8"	27.00
#2366/454 Pitcher, 1 quart	250.00
#2337 Plate	
6"	10.00
7"	14.00
8"	15.00
9"	32.00
#2364 Relish 2 part	25.00
#2364/622 Relish 3 part	35.00
#2364/195 Salad Bowl 9"	35.00
#2364/221 Salad Bowl 10½"	40.00
#2364/579 Salad Plate, Crescent	22.00
#2364/557 Sandwich Plate 11"	30.00
#2350/397 Saucer	10.00
#2364/655 Shaker, Chrome Top	pair 50.00
#6017/11 Sherbet, Low 6 oz.	15.00
#2350/679½ Sugar, Footed	15.00
#2364/567 Torte Plate 14"	60.00
#2364/723 Tray, Lunch, Handled	38.00
#2614 Vase 10"	65.00
#2470 Vase 10"	70.00
#2470 Vase, Footed 10"	80.00
#2619½ Vase, Ground Bottom	
5"	50.00
7½"	70.00
9½"	90.00
#2660 Vase, Flip 8"	80.00
#4121 Vase 5"	60.00
#4143 Vase, Footed	
6"	50.00
7½"	70.00
#6021 Vase, Bud, Footed	50.00
#6017/72 Water, Footed 9 oz. 5½"	12.00
#6017/26 Wine 3 oz.	28.00

ROMANCE Plate Etching #341 cont.

ROMANCE items included in Patterns of the Past and Nostalgia Programs

R002/008 Champagne/High Dessert 6 oz.
5½" 22.00
R002/011 Champagne/Low Dessert 6 oz.

4½" 15.00
R002/025 Claret 4 oz. 5⅞" 30.00
R002/002 Goblet 9 oz. 7⅜" 25.00
R002/063 Luncheon Goblet/Ice Tea 12 oz.
6" 24.00
R002/026 Wine 3 oz. 5½" 28.00

RONDEAU Cutting #740

Rock Crystal
Crystal
1934 – 1936
Do not confuse with RONDO Cutting #830.

#2470½ Bowl 10½" 30.00
#4024 Bowl, Footed 10" 40.00
#6012 Brandy 1 oz. 28.00
#4024 Candlestick 6" ....pair 30.00
#2472 Candlestick, Duo ....pair 40.00
#2496 Candlestick, Trindle ....pair 80.00
#4117 Candy Jar, Covered, Bubble Style ..20.00
#863 Champagne, Hollow Stem, Cut Flute
5 oz. 15.00
#6012 Champagne, Saucer 5½ oz. 20.00
#6012 Claret 4½ oz. 25.00
#6012 Cocktail 3 oz. 20.00
#2524 Cocktail Mixer 30.00
#2525 Cocktail Shaker 42 oz. 40.00
#2525½ Cocktail Shaker 30 oz. 35.00
#2400 Comport 6" 20.00
#6012 Cordial 1 oz. 30.00
#2350½ Cream, Footed..............................12.00
#6012 Creme de Menthe 2 oz. 20.00
#2525 Decanter 30.00
#6011 Decanter, Footed 70.00
#1769 Finger Bowl 8.00
#6012 Goblet 10 oz. 22.00
#6011 Jug, Footed 50.00
#2440 Mayonnaise, 2 part 20.00
#1185 Old Fashioned Cocktail, Sham..........6.00
#6012 Oyster Cocktail 4 oz. 13.00
#2337 Plate
6" 6.00

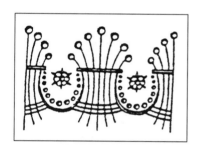

7" 7.00
8" 8.00
#2364 Plate 16" 30.00
#2440 Relish
2 part 22.00
3 part 26.00
#6012 Rhine Wine 4½ oz. 25.00
#6012 Sherbet, Low 5½ oz. 16.00
#6012 Sherry 2 oz. 20.00
#2350½ Sugar, Footed 8.00
#2440 Sweetmeat, Handled 4½" 18.00
#2440 Torte Plate 13" 40.00
#2440 Tray, Oval 8½" 30.00
#701 Tumbler, Sham
10 oz. 6.00
12 oz. 6.00
#6012 Tumbler, Footed
5 oz. 10.00
10 oz. 12.00
13 oz. 15.00
#2470 Vase 10" 50.00
#4122 Whiskey, Sham 1½ oz. 6.00
#6012 Wine 3 oz. 25.00

⌐⌐⌐ RONDO Cutting #830 ⌐⌐⌐

Rock Crystal
Crystal
1952 – 1954
Do not confuse with RONDEAU Cutting #740.

#6045 Claret/Wine 4¾ oz. 4" 21.00
#6045 Cocktail 4¾ oz. 3" 19.00
#6045 Cordial 1½ oz. 2⅝".........................23.00
#6045 Goblet 15¾ oz.. 5⅞" 21.00
#6045 Ice Tea, Footed 16 oz. 6⅛" 21.00
#6045 Juice, Footed 7¼ oz. 4⅝" 19.00
#2337 Plate 8" 8.00
#6045 Sherbet 9 oz. 3¾".............................19.00

⌐⌐⌐ ROSALIE Crystal Print #19 ⌐⌐⌐

Crystal
1963 – 1975

#6102/31 Brandy 3 oz. 22.00
#6102/25 Claret 7½ oz. 22.00
#4185/495 Dessert/Finger Bowl 12.00
#6102/2 Goblet 10 oz. 22.00
#6102/63 Luncheon Goblet/Ice Tea
    14 oz. 20.00
#2336 Plate
    7" 10.00
    8" 10.00

#6102/11 Sherbet/Dessert/Champagne
    8 oz. 20.00
#6102/26 Tulip Wine 5½ oz. 20.00

⌐⌐⌐ ROSE Cutting #827 ⌐⌐⌐

Combination Gray and Polished Cutting
1951 – 1973

ROSE included in Patterns of the Past and
Nostalgia Programs

#2666/360 Celery Dish 9" 30.00
#6036/8 Champagne/High Sherbet 6 oz.
    4¾"..21.00
#6036/27 Claret/Wine 3¼ oz. 4¾" 25.00
#6036/21 Cocktail 3½ oz. 4⅛" 25.00
#6036/29 Cordial 1 oz. 3¼" 36.00
#2666/680 Cream 3½"..............................15.00
#2666/688 Cream, Individual 12.00

#2666/396 Cup 10.00
#4185/495 Dessert/Finger Bowl 12.00

⚬═ ROSE Cutting #827 cont. ═⚬

#2666/508 Dessert/Individual Salad Bowl
    2¼" High..15.00
#6036/2 Goblet 9½ oz. 6⅞" 24.00
#6011 Jug, Footed 8⅞"............................70.00
#6036/88 Juice, Footed 5 oz. 4⅝" 14.00
#6036/63 Luncheon Goblet/Ice Tea 12 oz.
    6⅛"...17.00
#2666/477 Mayonnaise
    Bowl...15.00
    Plate...12.00
    Ladle 20.00
#6036/33 Oyster Cocktail 4 oz. 3¾" 14.00
#6036/18 Parfait 5½ oz. 5⅞" 26.00
#2666/540 Pickle Dish 7¼" 25.00
#2666/454 Pitcher, quart........................40.00
#2337 Plate
    7" 7.00
    8" 8.00
#2666/620 Relish 2 part 7 ⅜" 30.00
#2666/622 Relish 3 part 10¾" 35.00
#2666/238 Salad Bowl 11".......................50.00

#2666/397 Saucer 8.00
#2666/568 Serving Plate 14" 40.00
#2364/655 Shaker, Chrome Top ....pair 25.00
#6036/11 Sherbet, Low 6 oz.
    4⅛"...15.00
#2666/677 Sugar 2⅝" 15.00
#2666/687 Sugar, Individual 12.00
#2666/686 Tray, Cream & Sugar 10.00

ROSE items included in Patterns of the Past and Nostalgia Programs

R004/008 Champagne/High Dessert 6 oz.
    4¾"..21.00
R004/011 Champagne/Low Dessert 6 oz.
    4⅛"...15.00
R004/027 Claret/Wine 3¾ oz. 4¾" 25.00
R004/002 Goblet 9½ oz. 6⅞" 24.00
R004/063 Luncheon Goblet/Ice Tea 12 oz.
    6⅛"...17.00

⚬═ ROSEDALE Engraving #25 ═⚬

Crystal
1924 – 1928

#2219 Candy Jar, Covered ½ lb. 20.00
#802½ Champagne, Saucer 8.00
#802½ Fruit 8.00
#802 Goblet 8.00
#4085 Ice Tea 13 oz. 8.00
#4085 Ice Tea, Handled 13 oz. 16.00
#1852 Jug 6...40.00
#803 Nappy, Deep 7" 25.00
#661 Parfait 8.00
#4085 Tumbler..6.00

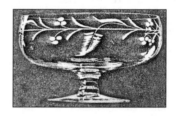

#2276 Vanity Set 75.00
#4069 Vase 9" 60.00
#802 Wine 2½ oz. 8.00

⚬═ ROSETTE Crystal Intaglio #2501 ═⚬

1937 – 1944
Do not confuse with ROSETTE INTAGLIO Carving #57 or ROSETTE Crystal Print #3.

#2496 Ash Tray, Oblong 3¾" 15.00
#2501 Ash Tray, Large 5" 16.00

#2501 Ash Tray, Individual 4" 12.00
#2510 Ash Tray, Square 3"........................12.00
#2510½ Ash Tray, Individual 2½" 12.00
#2501 Cake Plate, Oval, Handled 10½"......20.00
#2501 Cigarette Box, Covered 4¾" x 3½" ..20.00
#2496 Plate 7" 8.00

ROSETTE Crystal Intaglio #2501 cont.

#2501 Plate
    7" 8.00
    8" 8.00
#2501 Torte Plate 13" 35.00
#2496 Torte Plate 14" 40.00
#2510 Tray, Sugar and Cream 6½" 25.00

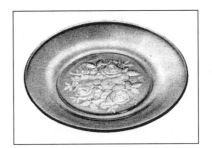

ROSETTE Crystal Print #3

Crystal
1956 – 1961
    Do not confuse with ROSETTE CRYSTAL INTAGLIO #2501 or ROSETTE Intaglio Carving #57.

#6064 Champagne 22.00
#6064 Claret 24.00
#6064 Cocktail...20.00
#6064 Cordial 30.00
#6064 Ice Tea, Footed 22.00
#6064 Juice, Footed 16.00
#664 Oyster Cocktail 18.00
#2337 Plate
    7" 8.00

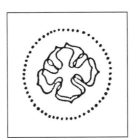

    8" 8.00
#6064 Sherbet, Low 14.00
#6064 Wine 25.00

ROSETTE INTAGLIO Carving #57

1969
    Do not confuse with ROSETTE CRYSTAL INTAGLIO Carving #2501 or with ROSETTE Crystal Print #3.

#2364/114 Ash Tray, Round 7½" 15.00
#2364/259 Fruit Bowl 13" 40.00
#2364/197 Lily Pond 9" 45.00
#2364/195 Salad Bowl 9"..........................35.00
#2364/557 Sandwich Plate 11" 35.00
#2364/567 Torte Plate 14" 50.00

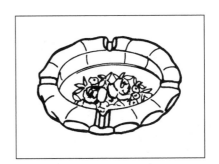

☞ ROSILYN Deep Plate Etching #249 ☜

Blown Ware
Crystal
1918 – 1928

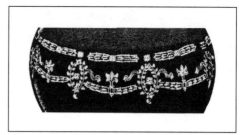

#5051 Almond, Small 4.00
#5051 Almond, Large 6.00
#880 Bon Bon 4½" 8.00
#1697 Carafe 25.00
#880 Champagne, Saucer 5 oz. 10.00
#802 Champagne, Saucer 5½ oz. 8.00
#802 Claret 4½ oz. 10.00
#880 Claret 4½ oz. 10.00
#802 Cocktail 3½ oz. 8.00
#880 Cocktail 3½ oz. 8.00
#803 Comport
    5" 5.00
    6" 5.00
#802 Cordial ¾ oz. 12.00
#880 Cordial 1 oz. 12.00
#481 Custard 5.00
#1480 Cream 10.00
#1759 Finger Bowl 5.00
#1759 Finger Bowl Plate 6" 5.00
#802 Goblet 10 oz. 10.00
#880 Goblet 9 oz. 10.00
#945½ Grapefruit 12.00
#945½ Grapefruit Liner 8.00
#4061 Ice Tea, Footed, Handled 14.00
#300 Jug 7 ....20.00
#303 Jug 7 ....20.00
#318 Jug 7 ....20.00
#724 Jug 7 ....20.00
#1733 Marmalade, Covered 18.00
#803 Nappy
    5" 5.00
    6" 5.00
    7" 6.00
#1465 Oil, Cut Neck 7 oz. 18.00
#802 Oyster Cocktail 60.00

#837 Oyster Cocktail 6.00
#822 Parfait 8.00
#1848 Plate, Sandwich 9" 14.00
#801 Rhine Wine 10.00
#2083 Salad Dressing Bottle 40.00
#802 Sherbet 6.00
#880 Sherbet 8.00
#840 Sherbet Plate 5" 5.00
#880 Sherry 2 oz. 8.00
#1480 Sugar 10.00
#820 Tumbler, Table 8.00
#4110½ Tumbler, Table 8.00
#701 Tumbler
    8 oz. 6.00
    14 oz. 10.00
#701 Tumbler, Handled 14 oz. 18.00
#833 Tumbler 8 oz. 8.00
#889 Tumbler 5 oz. 8.00
#4011 Tumbler
    8 oz. 8.00
    12 oz. 10.00
#1697 Tumbler, Carafe 6 oz. ....set 20.00
#1697 Tumbler, Whiskey 2½ oz. 8.00
#701 Tumbler Plate 5" 6.00
#1806 Water Bottle, Cut Neck Cut
    #112 ....20.00
#802 Wine 3½ oz. 10.00
#880 Wine 2¾ oz. 10.00

☞ ROSEMARY Etching #339 ☜

Crystal
1939 – 1944

#2364 Bowl, Flared 12" 30.00
#6023 Bowl, Footed 9" 30.00
#6023 Candlestick, Duo 5½" Spread
    6" ....pair 60.00

#892 Champagne, Saucer 7 oz. 5⅛" 12.00
#892 Claret 4 oz. 4⅞" 15.00
#892 Cocktail 4 oz. 4½" 10.00
#892 Cordial 1 oz. 3⅜" 15.00
#1769 Finger Bowl 6.00
#2364 Fruit Bowl 13" 40.00
#892 Goblet 11 oz. 6½" 12.00

⇒ ROSEMARY Etching #339 cont. ⇐

#6011 Jug, Footed 8⅞" 70.00
#892 Oyster Cocktail 4½ oz. 2⅞" 10.00
#2337 Plate
    6" 8.00
    7" 10.00
    8" 14.00
#2364 Salad Bowl 10½" 30.00
#892 Sherbet, Low 6½ oz. 4".....................10.00

#2364 Torte Plate 14".............................40.00
#892 Tumbler, Footed
    5 oz. 3⅞"...10.00
    12 oz. 5½"...12.00
#4143 Vase, Footed
    6"...30.00
    7½"...45.00
#892 Wine 3 oz. 4⅜" 15.00

⇒ ROYAL Plate Etching #273 ⇐

Crystal, Amber, Blue, Green
1925 – 1938
Blue 1925 – 1928; Crystal 1925 – 1938;
  Amber, Green 1925 – 1934; Selected Items
  in Ebony 1925 – 1926

Produced also as CORONADO, Decoration
  #49, Blue with white or yellow gold trim

* Ebony Items
** CORONADO items

ADD 30% FOR AMBER, GREEN; DOUBLE
VALUES FOR BLUE

#2350 Ash Tray, Small 20.00
#2350 Baker, Oval
    9" 30.00
    10½" 35.00
#2350 Bouillon..18.00
#2350½ Bouillon, Footed 21.00
#2267 Bowl, Footed, Low 7"* 26.00
#2297 Bowl, Deep 12"** 40.00
#2297 Bowl, Shallow 10¼"**.....................35.00
#2315 Bowl, Footed 10½"** 40.00
#2324 Bowl, Footed
    10"**..35.00
    13"...45.00
#2350 Butter, Covered 60.00
#2324 Candlestick
    2"** ....pair 30.00
    4"* ** ....pair 50.00
    9"** ....pair 100.00
    12" ....pair 150.00
#2231 Candy Box, Covered* 100.00
#2250 Candy Jar, Covered ½ lb.** 120.00
#2329 Centerpiece
    11"* ** 60.00

    13" 70.00
#2371 Centerpiece, Oval 13".....................60.00
#2350 Celery 24.00
#2350 Cereal 5" 20.00
#869 Champagne, Saucer.......................10.00
#2276 Cheese Plate, Covered (Amber, Green
    only) 100.00
#869 Cocktail...10.00
#2322 Cologne, Tall** 100.00
#2323 Cologne, Short** 80.00
#2327 Comport 7"* ** 50.00
#2350 Comport 8" 50.00
#869 Cordial 40.00
#2315½ Cream** 20.00
#2350½ Cream.......................................20.00
#2350 Cream Soup.................................22.00
#2350½ Cream Soup, Footed 28.00
#2350 Cream Soup Plate 7" 12.00
#2350 Cup...12.00
#2350½ Cup, Footed 14.00
#2350 Cup, After Dinner 20.00
#2350 Egg Cup (Crystal, Amber, Green
    only) 40.00
#869 Finger Bowl 5.00
#869 Fruit 8.00
#2350 Fruit 5" 8.00
#869 Goblet 10.00

☞ ROYAL Plate Etching #273 cont. ☜

#945½ Grapefruit 18.00
#945½ Grapefruit Liner 10.00
#2315 Grapefruit/Mayonnaise **20.00
#2378 Ice Bucket, Nickel Plate Handle 100.00
    Drainer, Tongs 50.00
#1861½ Jelly 30.00
#1236 Jug 6..75.00
#5000 Jug 7, Footed.............................350.00
#5100 Jug 7, Footed.............................320.00
#2350 Nappy
    8" 20.00
    9" 25.00
#869 Oyster Cocktail 8.00
#869 Parfait 10.00
#2350 Pickle Dish 20.00
#2283 Plate (CORONADO only)
    8" 20.00
    10" 25.00
    13" 40.00
#2290 Plate 13" 35.00
#2316 Plate, Soup** 40.00
#2321 Plate 8" 20.00
#2350 Plate
    6" 12.00
    7" 16.00
    8" 20.00
    9" 25.00
    10" 30.00
#2383 Plate
    7" 16.00
    8" 22.00
    9" 28.00
    10" 30.00
#2350 Plate, Chop
    13" 35.00
    15" 50.00
#2390 Plate
    7" 15.00
    8" 24.00

#2350 Platter, Oval
    10½" 30.00
    12" 40.00
    15" 50.00
#2328 Puff Box, Covered (CORONADO
    only)** 75.00
#2350 Salad Bowl 35.00
#2350 Sauce Boat 60.00
#2350 Sauce Boat Plate 30.00
#2350 Saucer...12.00
#2350 Saucer, After Dinner 15.00
#5100 Shaker, Glass Top.................pair 100.00
#869 Sherbet
    Low 8.00
    High 10.00
#2350 Soup 14.00
#2315 Sugar** 20.00
#2350½ Sugar 24.00
#2350½ Sugar, Covered.......................... 50.00
#2287 Tray, Handled, Lunch 11"** 35.00
#869 Tumbler, Table 10.00
#869 Tumbler
    2 oz. 10.00
    5 oz. 8.00
    8 oz. 10.00
    12 oz. 12.00
#5000 Tumbler, Footed
    2½ oz. 12.00
    5 oz. 8.00
    9 oz. 10.00
    12 oz. 12.00
#5100 Tumbler, Footed
    2½ oz. 12.00
    5 oz. 8.00
    9 oz. 10.00
    12 oz. 12.00
#869 Tumbler, Handled 12 oz. 16.00
#2324 Urn, Small.....................................40.00
#2276 Vanity Set * ** 100.00

☞ ROYAL GARDEN Cutting #704 ☜

Crystal, Topaz
1931 – 1933

#2394 Bowl 12" 55.00
#2430 Bowl 11" 50.00
#2433 Bowl 12" 60.00

ROYAL GARDEN Cutting #704 cont.

#2375 Cake Plate 10" 35.00
#2430 Candy Jar, Covered ½ lb. 70.00
#2394 Candlestick 2" ....pair 38.00
#2430 Candlestick 9½" ....pair 120.00
#2433 Candlestick 3" ....pair 50.00
#2477 Candlestick, Duo ....pair 70.00

#2433 Comport, Tall 6" 60.00
#2443 Ice Tub 6" 65.00
#2430 Vase 8" 90.00
#4107 Vase 12" 120.00
#4108 Vase 6" 70.00

RYE Plate Etching #321

Crystal
1933 – 1944

#319 Bar Bottle, Stoppered 29 oz. 25.00
#322 Bar Bottle, Stoppered 26 oz. 35.00
#1918 Bar Decanter, Stoppered 24 oz. 30.00
#1918 Bar Decanter, Stoppered, Handled
    24 oz. 45.00
#1928 Pinch Decanter, Stoppered 24 oz.....35.00
#2052 Pinch Decanter, Stoppered 29 oz.....45.00

SALON Cutting #804

Crystal
1940 – 1944

#6023 Candlestick, Duo ....pair 50.00
#6027 Champagne, Saucer 5½ oz. 16.00
#6027 Cocktail 3½ oz. 14.00
#6027 Cordial 1 oz. 25.00
#4021 Finger Bowl 12.00
#6027 Goblet 10 oz. 18.00
#6011 Jug, Footed 100.00
#2364 Lily Pond 12" 80.00
#6027 Oyster Cocktail 4 oz. 10.00
#2337 Plate, Plain
    7" 10.00
    8" 12.00
#6027 Sherbet, Low 5½ oz.......................12.00
#6027 Tumbler, Footed

    5 oz. 8.00
    12 oz. 10.00
#6027 Wine 4 oz. 20.00

SAMPLER Plate Etching #337

Crystal
1939 – 1944

A cross-stitch on crystal, said to be just right for an Early American home.

#2574 Bon Bon	15.00
#2574 Bowl, Flared 12"	40.00
#2574 Bowl, 2-handled 9 ½"	35.00
#6023 Bowl, Footed 9¼"	30.00
#2574 Cake Plate 10"	25.00

#2574 Candlestick
4"	each 18.00
6"	each 24.00

#2574 Celery Dish 10½"	18.00
#6025 Claret/Wine 4 oz.	18.00
#6025 Cocktail 3½ oz.	14.00
#2574 Comport 5"	12.00
#6023 Comport 5"	14.00
#6025 Cordial 1 oz.	20.00
#2574 Cream, Footed 4"	12.00
#2574 Cream, Individual 3½"	8.00
#2574 Cup, Footed	8.00
#2574 Fruit Bowl	6.00
#6025 Goblet 10 oz.	16.00
#2574 Ice Tub	40.00
#6011 Jug, Footed 8⅞"	50.00
#2574 Lemon Dish	18.00

#2574 Mayonnaise
Bowl	20.00
Plate	16.00
Ladle	20.00

#2574 Oil, Ground Stopper 4¼ oz. 5⅝"	30.00
#2574 Olive Dish 6"	15.00
#6025 Oyster Cocktail 4 oz.	15.00
#2584 Pickle Dish 8"	20.00

#2574 Plate
6"	8.00
7"	12.00
8"	15.00
9"	20.00

#2574 Relish, 3 part	25.00
#2574 Saucer	5.00
#2574 Serving Dish 8½"	20.00
#2574 Shaker	pair 30.00
#6025 Sherbet 6 oz.	12.00
#2574 Sugar, Individual 2⅞"	18.00
#2574 Sweetmeat	14.00
#2574 Torte Plate 14"	40.00
#2574 Tray, Muffin, Handled	30.00

#6025 Tumbler, Footed
5 oz.	10.00
12 oz.	14.00

#2574 Whip Cream Bowl	50.00

SAVANNAH Cutting #902

Rock Crystal
Crystal
1964 – 1969

#6104/25 Claret 7 oz.	23.00
#6104/29 Cordial 1½ oz.	30.00
#6104/2 Goblet 11 oz.	25.00

#6104/63 Luncheon Goblet/Ice Tea
13½ oz.	23.00

#2337
7"	10.00
8"	10.00
#6104/11 Sherbet 9 oz.	22.00

#6104/26 Wine 6 oz.	23.00

⊷ SAYBROOKE Cutting #813 ⊷

Rock Crystal
Full Cut and Polished Stem
Crystal
1941 – 1944

#6029 Champagne, Saucer 6½ oz. 18.00
#6029 Claret 4 oz. 20.00
#6029 Cocktail 3½ oz. 15.00
#6029 Cordial 1 oz. 25.00
#766 Finger Bowl 15.00
#6029 Goblet 9 oz. 20.00
#6011 Jug, Footed 85.00
#2337 Plate
    6" 8.00
    7" 10.00
    8" 12.00
#6029 Wine 3 oz. 20.00

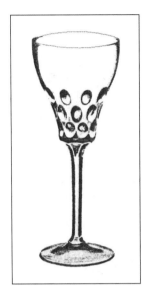

⊷ SCOTCH PLAID Needle Etching #38 ⊷

Crystal
Turn of the Century – 1915

#882 Ale 4½ oz. 8.00
#863 Almond 6.00
#882 Bon Bon Etched #38 Footed, Cut Stem
    4½" 10.00
#882 Champagne
    4½ oz. 8.00
    5 oz. 8.00
#882 Champagne, Saucer
    5 oz. 9.00
    7 oz. 10.00
#882 Claret
    4½ oz. 8.00
    6½ oz. 9.00
#883 Comport Etched #38 5" 12.00
#882 Cocktail
    3 oz. 7.00
    3½ oz. 8.00
#882 Cordial
    1 oz. 10.00
    ¾ oz. 9.00
#882 Creme de Menthe 2½ oz. 8.00
#1478 Cream 12.00
#810 Custard, Cut Flute 8.00
#1867 Finger Bowl 10.00
#1867 Finger Bowl Plate...........................8.00

#882 Goblet
    8 oz. 7.00
    9 oz. 8.00
    10 oz. 9.00
    11 oz. 10.00
#882 Grapefruit, Footed, Cut Stem, Etched
    #38...12.00
#882 Grapefruit Liner.............................12.00
#882½ Grapefruit 10.00
#882½ Grapefruit Liner 12.00
#803 Nappy, Footed, Deep 6" 10.00
#1127 Nappy
    4½ oz...6.00

⊰⊱ SCOTCH PLAID Needle Etching #38 cont. ⊰⊱

8 oz. 8.00
#1465 Oil, Nickel or Cut Stopper 20.00
#882 Pousse-Cafe
    1 oz. 10.00
    ¾ oz. 10.00
#882 Rhine Wine 4 oz. 9.00
#882 Sherbet 8.00
#882 Sherry 2 oz. 9.00
#1478 Sugar 12.00
#300 Tankard 7 Cut Flute 10.00
#922 Toothpick, Sham, Cut Flute, Punty ..20.00
#858 Tumbler, Table Cut Flute #19
    3½ oz. 5.00
    5 oz. 6.00
    6½ oz. 6.00
    8 oz. 8.00
    10 oz. 10.00

12 oz. 10.00
14 oz. 10.00
16 oz. 10.00
#701 Tumbler Cut B Punty
    8 oz. 8.00
    10 oz. 9.00
    14 oz. 10.00
#820 Tumbler, Cut B Punty 8.00
#820½ Tumbler, Cut #19 Punty 8.00
#833 Tumbler, Sham Cut #19 Punty 8 oz. ..8.00
#887 Tumbler, Cut Flute 3 oz. 6.00
#889 Tumbler, Cut Flute 5 oz. 6.00
#1558 Water Bottle, Cut Neck................40.00
#882 Hot Whiskey 4½ oz. 7.00
#882 Wine
    2¾ oz. 6.00
    3½ oz. 8.00

⊰⊱ SELMA Cutting #800 ⊰⊱

Rock Crystal
Crystal
1940 – 1944

#2545 Bowl, Oval 12½" 30.00
#6023 Bowl, Footed 25.00
#2545 Candlestick 4½" ....pair 40.00
#6023 Candlestick, Duo ....pair 50.00
#6026 Champagne, Saucer 6 oz. 16.00
#6026 Claret/Wine 4½ oz. 20.00
#6026 Cocktail 4 oz. 15.00
#6026 Cordial 1 oz. 25.00
#869 Finger Bowl 7.00
#6026 Goblet 9 oz. 20.00
#5000 Jug, Footed 60.00
#2337 Plate, Optic
    7" 6.00
    8" 8.00
#6026 Sherbet, Low 6 oz. 12.00

#6026 Tumbler, Footed
    5 oz. 12.00
    13 oz. 16.00

SEAWEED Cutting #732

Crystal
1934 – 1936

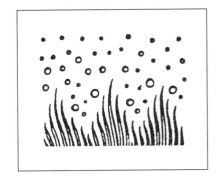

#4024 Bowl, Footed 10" 40.00
#906 Brandy Inhaler 15.00
#4024 Candlestick 6" ....pair 30.00
#795 Champagne, Hollow Stem
    5½ oz. 12.00
#863 Champagne, Hollow Stem
    5 oz. 15.00
#4024 Champagne, Saucer 6 oz. 20.00
#4024 Claret 3½ oz. 20.00
#4024 Cocktail 4 oz. 18.00
#4024 Comport, Footed 5" 15.00
#4024 Cordial 1 oz. 22.00
#6011 Decanter, Footed 70.00
#869 Finger Bowl 8.00
#4024 Goblet 10 oz. 20.00
#4024½ Goblet 11 oz. 20.00
#6011 Jug, Footed 50.00
#1184 Old Fashioned Cocktail, Sham or Plain
    7 oz. 6.00
#4024 Oyster Cocktail 4 oz. 15.00
#2337 Plate
    6" 6.00
    7" 7.00
    8" 8.00

#4024 Rhine Wine 3½ oz. 20.00
#4024 Sherbet 5½ oz. 18.00
#4024 Sherry 2 oz. 18.00
#701 Tumbler, Sham or Plain
    10 oz. 6.00
    12 oz. 6.00
#4024 Tumbler, Footed
    5 oz. 15.00
    8 oz. 15.00
    12 oz. 20.00
#887 Whiskey, Sham or Plain
    1½ oz. 6.00
#4024 Whiskey, Footed 2 oz. 15.00

SENTIMENTAL Crystal Print #25

Crystal
1971 – 1975

#6097/25 Claret 7 oz. 23.00
#6097/2 Goblet 10 oz. 23.00
#6097/63 Luncheon Goblet/Ice Tea
    12 oz. 20.00
#2337/549 Plate 7" 10.00
#6097/11 Sherbet/Dessert/Champagne
    7 oz. 20.00

⇜ SERENADE Cutting #780 ⇝

Crystal
1938-1944
   Do not confuse with SERENADE Cutting #864.

#4132 Decanter (Guitar) 50.00
#4132 Ice Bowl (Accordion) 27.00
#4132 Old Fashioned Cocktail (Accordion) .7.00

#4132½ Scotch & Soda 9 oz. (Trumpet) . . .6.00
#4132 Tumbler
   5 oz. (Violin) .5.00
   9 oz. (Trumpet) 8.00
   12 oz. (Guitar) 8.00
   14 oz. (Guitar) 8.00
#4132 Whiskey 1½ oz. (Bass Drum) 6.00

⇜ SERENADE Cutting #864 ⇝

Crystal
1959 – 1965

Do not confuse with SERENADE Cutting #780.

#6086/27 Cocktail/Wine 5½ oz. 4⁷⁄₁₆" 22.00
#6086/29 Cordial 1¼ oz. 3 ³⁄₁₆" 24.00
#4185/495 Dessert/Finger Bowl 12.00
#6086/2 Goblet 11¾ oz. 6⅜" 24.00
#6086/63 Luncheon Goblet/Ice Tea 13 oz.
   6³⁄₁₆" 22.00
#6086/88 Juice, Footed 5½ oz. 4½" 18.00
#2337 Plate
   7" 10.00
   8" 10.00

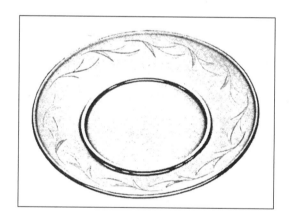

#6086/11 Sherbet 7½ oz. 4⅞" 18.00

⇜ SERENITY Plate Etching #35 ⇝

Crystal
1975 – 1982
Yellow Bowl with Crystal Foot 1975-1980;
Blue Bowl with Crystal Foot 1976-1982

SERENITY included in Patterns of the Past Program. Not included in Nostalgia Program.

Bell 6" 40.00
#6127/11 Champagne/High Dessert 9 oz.
   5¾" 22.00

#6127/25 Claret 7 oz. 6¼" 22.00
#6127/2 Goblet 12 oz. 7⅜" 22.00
#6127/63 Luncheon Goblet/Ice Tea 15 oz.
   7" 22.00

SERENITY items included in Programs of the Past, Yellow Bowl with Crystal Base.

#011 Champagne/High Dessert 9 oz. 5¾"..22.00
#025 Claret 7 oz. 6¼" 22.00
#002 Goblet 12 oz. 7⅜" 22.00
#063 Luncheon Goblet/Ice Tea 15 oz. 7" ..22.00

⇜ SERENITY Cutting #868 ⇝

Rock Crystal
Crystal
1958 – 1965
  Do not confuse with SERENITY Etching #35.

#6072/27 Cocktail/Wine 4½ oz. 20.00
#6072/29 Cordial 1 oz. 25.00
#6072/2 Goblet 10 oz. 22.00
#6072/63 Luncheon Goblet/Ice Tea,
    13 oz. 20.00
#6072/88 Juice, Footed 5¼ oz. 14.00

#2337 Plate
    7" 10.00
    8" 10.00
#6072/11 Sherbet 7¼ oz. 17.00

⇜ SEVILLE Plate Etching #274 ⇝

Crystal, Blue, Amber, Green
1926 – 1934
Blue 1926 – 1928; Amber, Green 1926 –
  1934; 1926 – 1934

Also Produced as AMHERST, Decoration #58
  Green, White Gold Trim

*AMHERST

#2350 Ash Tray 20.00
#2350 Baker, Oval
    9" 30.00
    10½" 35.00
#2267 Bowl, Low Foot 7" 50.00
#2297 Bowl, Shallow 10"
    (AMHERST only)* 70.00
#2297 Bowl, Bowl, Deep, Flared 12"* 60.00
#2315 Bowl, Deep 10½" (AMHERST only) ..60.00
#2315 Bowl, Footed, Flared 10½" 60.00
#2324 Bowl, Footed 10"* 50.00
#2350 Butter, Covered 85.00
#2350 Bouillon, 2-handled 24.00
#2350½ Bouillon, Footed 20.00
#2234 Candlesticks
    2"* ....pair 40.00
    4"* ....pair 50.00
    9" ....pair 100.00
#2331 Candy Box, Covered* 80.00
#2250 Candy Jar, Covered* 110.00
#2350 Celery Dish 26.00
#2329 Centerpiece
    11"* 55.00
    13" 70.00

#2371 Centerpiece, Oval 13".....................50.00
#2350 Cereal Bowl 6" 22.00
#870 Champagne/Saucer/High Sherbet....11.00
#2368 Cheese...30.00
#2368 Cheese & Cracker 40.00
#870 Cocktail...10.00
#2327 Comport 7"* 30.00
#2350 Comport 8" 35.00
#870 Cordial 22.00
#2315½ Cream* 20.00
#2350½ Cream.......................................22.00
#2350 Cream Soup.................................30.00
#2350 Cream Soup Plate 12.00
#2350½ Cream Soup, Footed 35.00
#2350 Cup 18.00
#2350 Cup, After Dinner 30.00
#2350½ Cup, Footed 24.00

293

#2350 Egg Cup 60.00
#869 Finger Bowl 8.00
#870 Fruit/Low Sherbet, Footed...............10.00
#2350 Fruit 5" 15.00
#870 Goblet 12.00
#945½ Grapefruit 20.00
#945½ Grapefruit Liner 14.00
#2315 Grapefruit (Mayonnaise), Footed....*60.00
#2378 Ice Bucket, Nickel Plate Handle 70.00
#2378 Ice Bucket, Nickel Plate Handle 70.00
    Drainer and Tongs 50.00
#5084 Jug 7, Footed....................................200.00
#2350 Nappy
    8" 30.00
    9" 40.00
    10" 50.00
#870 Oyster Cocktail 10.00
#870 Parfait 12.00
#2350 Pickle Dish 20.00
#2283 Plate
    6" 15.00
    7"* 20.00
    8"* 24.00
    10"* 30.00
    13"* 40.00
#2350 Plate
    6" 12.00
    7" 18.00

    8" 24.00
    9" 30.00
    10" 35.00
    13" 50.00
    15" 60.00
#2368 Plate, Cracker 22.00
#2350 Platter, Oval
    12" 50.00
    15" 70.00
#2350 Sauce Boat 75.00
#2350 Sauce Boat Plate 30.00
#2350 Saucer 12.00
#2350 Saucer, After Dinner 16.00
#5100 Shaker, Footed ....pair 100.00
#2350 Soup 7" 26.00
#2315 Sugar* 35.00
#2350½ Sugar* 35.00
#2350½ Sugar, Covered 70.00
#2287 Tray, Handled, Lunch 11"*............45.00
#5084 Tumbler, Footed
    2 oz. 20.00
    5 oz. 16.00
    9 oz. 18.00
    12 oz. 22.00
#2324 Urn, Small....................................50.00
#2276 Vanity Set (AMHERST only)* 100.00
#2292 Vase 8" 110.00
#870 Wine 12.00

⤳ SHERATON Plate Etching #317 ⤳

Regular Optic
Crystal
1933 – 1938

#6010 Claret/Wine 4¼ oz. 26.00
#6010 Cocktail 4 oz.................................18.00
#6010 Cordial 1 oz. 35.00
#869 Finger Bowl 10.00
#6010 Goblet 9 oz. 22.00
#6010 Oyster Cocktail 5½ oz. 12.00
#2283 Plate 5" 8.00
#2237 Plate
    7" 10.00
    8" 12.00
#6010 Sherbet
    High 5½ oz..................................18.00
    Low 5½ oz. 15.00

#6010 Tumbler, Footed
    5 oz. 12.00
    9 oz. 12.00
    12 oz. 22.00

⊶⧉ SHERMAN Needle Etching #77 ⧉⊷

Crystal
1925 – 1931

Also produced as ALASKA, Decoration #54
 with White Gold Trim
*Not produced as ALASKA

#869 Champagne, Saucer.........................10.00
#869 Cocktail...8.00
#5078 Comport 5" 15.00
#766 Finger Bowl 10.00
#869 Fruit 8.00
#869 Goblet 10.00
#945½ Grapefruit 15.00
#945½ Grapefruit Liner 15.00
#2270 Jug 7..80.00
#2270 Jug 7 and Cover 110.00
#4095 Jug 7..90.00
#4095 Nappy*
    5"* 10.00
    6"* 10.00
    7"* 12.00

#4095 Oyster Cocktail 10.00
#869 Parfait 10.00
#2283 Plate
    7" 8.00
    8" 8.00
#869 Tumbler, Table 8.00
#869 Tumbler
    5 oz. 8.00
    8 oz. 10.00
    12 oz. 12.00
#4095 Tumbler, Footed
    2½ oz. 8.00
    5 oz. 8.00
    10 oz. 10.00
    13 oz. 12.00
#5100 Tumbler, Footed*
    2½ oz.* 8.00
    5 oz.* 8.00
    9 oz.* 8.00
    12 oz.* 10.00
#869 Tumbler, Handled 12 oz. 15.00
#869 Wine 10.00

⊶⧉ SHIRLEY Plate Etching #331 ⧉⊷

Crystal
1938 – 1957

A large and popular floral design created in
 honor of Shirley Temple.

#2496 Bon Bon, 3 Toed 20.00
#2496 Bowl, Flared 12" 35.00
#2496 Bowl, Handled 10½"......................30.00
#2496 Bowl, Vegetable 9½"......................30.00
#2545 Bowl, Flame, Oval 12½" 40.00
#2496 Cake Plate, 2-handled 10" 26.00
#2545 Candelabra, "Flame", 2 Light ..pair 40.00
#2496 Candlestick
    4" ....pair 48.00
    5½" ....pair 60.00
#2496 Candlestick, Duo ....pair 60.00
#2545 Candlestick, "Flame" 4½" ....pair 40.00
#2545 Candlestick, "Flame", Duo ......pair 50.00
#2496 Candy Box, Covered, 3 part 30.00
#2496 Celery 11" 17.00
#6017 Champagne, Saucer 6 oz. 17.00-20.00
#2496 Cheese & Cracker 35.00
#6017 Claret 4 oz. 28.00

#6017 Cocktail 3½ oz. 20.00
#2496 Comport 5½" 20.00
#6017 Cordial ¾ oz. 33.00
#2496 Cream, Footed 7½ oz. 18.00
#2496 Cream, Individual, Footed 4 oz. 14.00
#2496 Cream Soup, 2-handled 22.00
#2350½ Cup, Footed 20.00
#766 Finger Bowl 10.00
#2496 Fruit 5½" 10.00
#6017 Goblet 9 oz. 25.00
#2496 Ice Bucket, Chrome Handled 45.00
#6011 Jug, Footed 8⅞"............................85.00
#2545 Lustre, "Flame"....................pair 100.00

#2496½ Mayonnaise

    Bowl 20.00

    Plate 18.00

    Ladle 20.00

#2496½ Mayonnaise, 2 part 23.00

#2496 Nappy, Handled

    Regular..16.00

    Flared..16.00

    Square 16.00

    3 Cornered.....................................16.00

#2496 Nut Bowl, Cupped 18.00

#6017 Oyster Cocktail 4 oz. 12.00

#2496 Pickle Dish 8" 20.00

#2337 Plate

    6" 10.00

    7" 12.00

    8" 20.00

    9" 25.00

#2496 Platter, Oval 12"............................35.00

#2496 Relish

    2 part 24.00

    3 part 30.00

#2350 Saucer......................................10.00

#2496 Sauce Dish, Oblong 6½" 16.00

#2496 Shaker, Glass Top..................pair 40.00

#6017 Sherbet, Low 6 oz. 16.00

#2496 Sugar, Footed 3½" 18.00

#2496 Sugar, Individual 2⅞" 14.00

#2496 Sweetmeat 13.00

#2496 Tid Bit, 3 Toed, Flat......................16.00

#2496 Torte Plate 14" 40.00

#6017 Tumbler, Footed

    5 oz. 12.00

    9 oz. 14.00

    12 oz. 18.00

    14 oz. 25.00

#2545 Vase 10" 45.00

#6017 Wine 3 oz. 27.00

⚒ SHOOTING STARS Cutting #375 ⚒

Crystal
1934 – 1944

#4024 Bowl, Footed 10" 40.00

#6011 Brandy 1 oz. 22.00

#906 Brandy Inhaler 15.00

#4024 Candlestick 6" ....pair 30.00

#795 Champagne, Hollow Stem 5½ oz. 12.00

#863 Champagne, Hollow Stem, Cut Flute

    5 oz. 15.00

#6011 Champagne, Saucer 5½ oz. 14.00

#6011 Claret 4½ oz. 18.00

#6011 Cocktail 3 oz..................................14.00

#6011 Cordial 1 oz. 22.00

#6011 Creme de Menthe 2 oz. 16.00

#6011 Decanter, Footed 70.00

#1769 Finger Bowl 8.00

#6011 Goblet 10 oz. 16.00

#6011 Jug, Footed 50.00

#1184 Old Fashioned Cocktail, Sham or Plain

    7 oz. 6.00

#6011 Oyster Cocktail 4 oz. 10.00

#2337 Plate

    6" 6.00

    7" 7.00

    8" 8.00

#6011 Rhine Wine 4½ oz. 18.00

#6011 Sherbet, Low 5½ oz......................12.00

#6011 Sherry 2 oz. 16.00

#701 Tumbler, Sham or Plain

    10 oz. 6.00

    12 oz. 6.00

#6011 Tumbler, Footed

    5 oz. 10.00

    10 oz. 8.00

    13 oz. 14.00

#887 Whiskey, Sham or Plain 1¾ oz. 6.00

#4122 Whiskey, Sham or Plain 1½ oz. 6.00

#6011 Whiskey, Footed 2 oz. 18.00

#6011 Wine 3 oz. 18.00

⇌ SKI Carving #2 ⇌

Crystal, Sham Bottom
1938 – 1944

Figures on skis, snowy trees

#2550 Ash Tray, Round 3¼" 12.00
#2391 Cigarette Box & Cover 4¾" 30.00
#4132 Decanter 9¾" 85.00
#4132 Ice Bowl 4¾" 40.00

#4139 Old Fashioned Cocktail 2¾" 15.00
2337 Plate 7"..20.00
#4139 Tumbler
    5 oz. 15.00
    10 oz. 15.00
    12 oz. 15.00
    14 oz. 15.00
    16 oz. 15.00
#4139 Water Tumbler 9 oz.........................15.00

⇌ SKYFLOWER Crystal Print #2 ⇌

Crystal
1955 – 1959

#2666 Bon Bon, Rolled Edge, Footed 6⅞" ..15.00
#2666 Bowl, Oval 8¼" 20.00
#2666 Butter, Covered Oblong 7" 30.00
#2666 Canape Plate 7⅜".............................15.00
#2666 Candlestick (Flora Candle) 6" 15.00
#2666 Celery 9" 20.00
#6061 Cocktail/Wine/Seafood 4 oz. 3⅞"....20.00
#6061 Cordial 1 oz. 2½" 12.00
#2666 Cream 3½" 15.00
#2666 Cream, Individual 12.00
#2666 Cup 10.00
#6061 Goblet 11 oz. 5⅛"...........................20.00
#6061 Ice Tea, Footed 12 oz. 6" 20.00
#6061 Juice, Footed 6 oz. 4¾" 18.00
#2666 Mayonnaise
    Bowl 15.00
    Plate 12.00
    Ladle 20.00
#2666 Plate
    7" 12.00

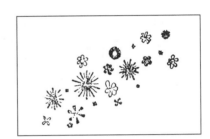

    10" 20.00
#2685 Preserve, Handled 6½" 30.00
#2666 Relish
    2 part 7⅜"...30.00
    3 part 10¾".......................................35.00
#2685 Salver, Footed 12⅓" 60.00
#2666 Saucer...8.00
#2666 Serving Plate, Rolled Edge 14" 50.00
#2364 Shaker, Chrome Top 3½" ....pair 40.00
#6061 Sherbet 7½ oz. 4" 18.00
#2666 Snack Plate, Rolled Edge 10" 40.00
#2666 Sugar 2⅝" 15.00
#2666 Sugar, Individual 12.00

⇌ SKYLARK Cutting #846 ⇌

1956 – 1959

#6064 Champagne/High Sherbet 8 oz.
    5¾"...20.00
#6064 Claret 5¾ oz. 5¾" 24.00
#6064 Cocktail 4 oz. 4½" 16.00
#6064 Cordial 1 oz. 3⅝".............................28.00
#6064 Goblet 9¾ oz. 7"..............................24.00

#6064 Ice Tea, Footed 13½ oz. 6⁷⁄₁₆" 22.00
#6064 Juice, Footed 5½ oz. 4⅞" 20.00
#2337 Plate
    7" 8.00
    8" 8.00
#6064 Seafood Cocktail 7¾ oz. 3⅝"...........18.00
#6064 Sherbet, Low 7 oz. 4⅝"....................18.00
#6064 Wine 3¼ oz. 5⅛" 25.00

Crystal
Turn of the Century – 1927

#863 Almond, Individual 8.00
#880 Bon Bon 4½" 8.00
#810 Brandy 1 oz. 10.00
#810 Champagne, Tall 6 oz. 8.00
#810 Champagne, Saucer
    5½ oz. 7.00
    7 oz. 7.00
#863 Champagne, Saucer 5½ oz. 7.00
#863 Champagne, Tall 5½ oz. 8.00
#863 Champagne, Hollow Stem 8.00
#932 Champagne Plate 6" 4.00
#810 Claret
    3½ oz. 7.00
    4 oz. 7.00
    5½ oz. 7.00
#862 Claret 4½ oz. 7.00
#810 Cocktail 2½ oz. 7.00
#863 Cocktail
    3 oz. 7.00
    3½ oz. 4.00
#803 Comport
    5" 8.00
    6" 8.00
#803 Comport, Footed
    5" 10.00
    6" 10.00
#810 Cordial 1 oz. 10.00
#863 Cordial 1¼ oz. 10.00
#863½ Cordial ¾ oz. 10.00
#810 Creme de Menthe 2½ oz. 10.00
#863 Creme de Menthe 2½ oz. 10.00
#810 Custard..7.00
#810 Finger Bowl 7.00
#810 Finger Bowl Plate 6"......................4.00
#863 Fruit 6.00
#1736 Fruit Plate 6".............................4.00
#840 Fruit Plate 5" 4.00
#810 Goblet 9 oz. 7.00
#863 Goblet
    5½ oz. 7.00
    7 oz. 7.00
    9 oz. 7.00
    10 oz. 8.00

    10½ oz. 8.00
#863½ Goblet
    7 oz. 7.00
    9 oz. 7.00
#803 Nappy, Shallow
    4½" 5.00
    5" 5.00
    6" 6.00
    7" 8.00
    8" 10.00
#803 Nappy, Deep
    4½" 5.00
    5" 5.00
    6" 6.00
    7" 8.00
#803 Nappy, Footed
    5" 6.00
    6" 7.00
    7" 8.00
#863 Pousse-Cafe 1½ oz. 10.00
#863½ Pousse-Cafe ¾ oz. 10.00
#863 Rhine Wine 4½ oz. 7.00
#810 Sherbet 7.00
#842 Sherbet 7.00
#843 Sherbet 7.00
#810 Sherry 2 oz. 7.00
#862 Sherry 2 oz. 7.00
#858 Sweetmeat...................................8.00
#820 Tumbler, Table 7.00
#701 Tumbler 14 oz. 8.00
#701 Tumbler Plate 4.00
#810 Tumbler 9" 7.00
#810 Tumbler, Tall
    5 oz. 7.00
    8 oz. 7.00
    10 oz. 7.00
#810 Wine 3 oz. 7.00
#863 Wine 3 oz. 7.00

⇜ SMALL SUNBURST STAR Cutting #11 ⇝

Blown Ware
Crystal
1898 – 1913

#319 Bar Bottle 16.00
#319 Bar Bottle, Cut Neck 22.00
#825 Champagne, Saucer 8.00
#858 Champagne, 7 oz. 7.00
#858 Champagne, Hollow Stem 7.00
#932 Champagne, Saucer 8.00
#300 Claret 6.00
#952 Cocktail..6.00
#1480 Cream 8.00
#481 Custard 10.00
#300 Decanter, Cut Neck, quart 22.00
#1195 Decanter, Cut Neck, Large 30.00
#315 Finger Bowl 5.00
#200 Finger Bowl Plate 5".........................4.00
#315 Finger Bowl Plate..............................4.00
#801 Goblet
    9 oz. 8.00
    10 oz. 8.00
#810 Goblet
    9 oz. 8.00
    10 oz. 8.00
#826 Goblet 8.00
#1132 Horseradish....................................15.00
#303 Jug 7 Cut Star Bottom.....................20.00
#315 Nappy
    4" 5.00
    4½"...5.00
    5" 5.00
    6" 5.00
    7" 8.00
    8" 10.00
    9" 10.00
    10" 10.00
#1227 Nappy
    4½"...5.00
    8" 10.00
#300½ Oil, Cut Stopper, Cut Star Bottom
    Small 20.00

    Large 30.00
#1465 Oil, Cut, Cut Stopper.....................25.00
#1165 Shaker, Silver-Plated Top ....pair 40.00
#810 Sherbet 6.00
#840 Sherbet 6.00
#841 Sherbet 6.00
#1480 Sugar 10.00
#300 Tankard, Cut Star Bottom
    1..20.00
    2..20.00
    3..20.00
    3½ 20.00
    4..20.00
    5..20.00
    6..20.00
    7..20.00
#820 Tumbler 6.00
#820½ Tumbler, Sham 6.00
#833 Tumbler, Sham, Bell 8 oz. 8.00
#889 Tumbler 8 oz. 6.00
#981 Tumbler, Sham, Bell 2½ oz. 8.00
#160½ Water Bottle, Cut Neck, Cut Star
    Bottom 20.00
#1332 Water Bottle, Cut Neck..................20.00
#845 Whiskey, Hot 8.00
#801 Wine 3 oz. 8.00
#837 Wine 2 oz. 8.00

SOCIETY Cutting #757

Rock Crystal
Optic
Crystal
1935 – 1938

#2527 Bowl, Footed 9" 60.00
#2527 Candelabra, 2 Light 70.00
#6013 Champagne, Saucer 6 oz. 18.00
#6013 Claret 4 oz. 25.00
#6013 Cocktail 3½ oz. 18.00
#6013 Comport 5" 25.00
#6013 Cordial 1 oz. 32.00
#766 Finger Bowl 15.00
#6013 Goblet 10 oz. 23.00
#5000 Jug, Footed 130.00
#6013 Oyster Cocktail 4 oz. 16.00

#2337 Plate
    6" 10.00
    7" 10.00
    8" 12.00
#6013 Sherbet, Low 5 oz. 16.00
#6013 Tumbler, Footed
    5 oz. 16.00
    13 oz. 18.00
#6013 Wine 3 oz. 25.00

SOUTH SEAS Cutting #779

Crystal
1938 – 1944

Native dancers in various poses on each item

#4132 Cocktail, (Running) 10.00
#4132 Decanter (Hands Out) 50.00
#4132 Ice Bowl (Running)........................30.00

#4132 Scotch & Soda 9 oz. (Knee Lifted)......6.00
#4132 Tumbler
    5 oz. (Hands Out) 5.00
    9 oz. (Knee Lifted) 8.00
    12 oz. (Hands in Air) 8.00
    14 oz. (Hands in Air) 8.00
#4132 Whiskey 1½ oz. (Hands on Hips) 6.00

SPARTAN Needle Etching #80

Regular Optic
1927 – 1944
Crystal 1927 – 1944; Orchid Bowl/Crystal
   Foot 1927 – 1929; Amber, Green Bowl with
   Crystal Foot 1927 – 1940

#5097 Champagne, Saucer/High
    Sherbet 5½ oz. 16.00
#5097 Claret 4 oz. 20.00
#5097 Cocktail 3 oz..................................15.00
#5097 Cordial ¾ oz. 22.00
#869 Finger Bowl 12.00
#315 Finger Bowl Plate
    (Not made in colors) 8.00
#5097 Goblet 9 oz. 18.00
#5297½ Grapefruit 25.00

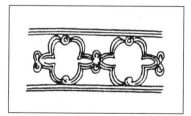

#945½ Grapefruit Liner 25.00
#5000 Jug 7, Footed...............................85.00
#5000 Oyster Cocktail 4½ oz. 12.00
#5097 Parfait 5½ oz..................................18.00
#2283 Plate (Not made in colors)
    7" 8.00

⚒ SPARTAN Needle Etching #80 cont. ⚒

8" 8.00
#5097 Sherbet, Low 5½ oz......................12.00
#869 Tumbler, Table 8.00
#869 Tumbler

    2 oz. 8.00
    5 oz. 8.00
    12 oz. 10.00

#5000 Tumbler, Footed

    2½ oz......................................6.00
    5 oz. 8.00
    9 oz. 8.00
    12 oz. 10.00
#5097 Wine 2½ oz. 20.00

⚒ SPENCERIAN Tracing #94 ⚒

Crystal
1940 – 1944

#6023 Claret/Wine 4 oz.............................14.00
#6023 Champagne, Saucer 6 oz. 12.00
#6023 Cocktail 3¾ oz. 8.00
#6023 Cordial 1 oz. 18.00
#766 Finger Bowl 6.00
#6023 Goblet 9 oz. 14.00
#6023 Oyster Cocktail 4 oz. 6.00
#2337 Plate 7" 8.00
#6023 Sherbet, Low 6 oz. 8.00
#6023 Tumbler, Footed

    5 oz. 8.00
    9 oz. 8.00
    12 oz. 12.00

⚒ SPINET Cutting #821 ⚒

Rock Crystal
Crystal
1950 – 1960

#6033 Champagne/High Sherbet 6 oz.
    4¾"......................................18.00
#6033 Claret/Wine 4 oz. 4¾" 22.00
#6033 Cocktail 4 oz. 4¼" 18.00
#6033 Cordial 1 oz. 3⅝" 30.00
#6033 Goblet 10 oz. 6¼" 22.00
#6033 Ice Tea, Footed 13 oz. 5⅞" 18.00
#6033 Juice, Footed 5 oz. 4½" 12.00
#6033 Oyster Cocktail 4 oz. 3¾" 14.00

#6033 Parfait 6 oz. 5⅝" 20.00
#2337 Plate
    7" 8.00
    8" 10.00
#6033 Sherbet, Low 6 oz. 4" 14.00

⟨⟩ SPIRE Cutting #793 ⟨⟩

Rock Crystal
Crystal
1939 – 1944

#6023 Bowl, Footed 20.00
#2324 Candlestick 6" ....pair 40.00
#6023 Champagne, Saucer 6 oz. 16.00
#6023 Claret/Wine 4 oz............................20.00
#6023 Cocktail 3¾ oz. 14.00
#6023 Comport 5" 12.00
#6023 Cordial 1 oz. 25.00
#766 Finger Bowl 8.00

#6023 Goblet 9 oz. 20.00
#6011 Jug, Footed 50.00
#6023 Oyster Cocktail 4 oz. 10.00
#2337 Plate
    6" 6.00
    7" 8.00
    8" 10.00
#6023 Sherbet, Low 6 oz. 12.00
#6023 Tumbler, Footed
    5 oz. 18.00
    9 oz. 12.00
    12 oz. 12.00

⟨⟩ SPRAY Cutting #841 ⟨⟩

Combination Rock Crystal and Gray Cutting
Crystal
1954 – 1973

SPRAY included in Nostalgia Program, not a part of Patterns of the Past Program.

Late listings show stem items to be numbered 6055½.

#2666/189 Bowl, Oval 8¼".......................20.00
#2666/300 Butter, Covered, Oblong 7"......30.00
#2666/309 Canape Plate 7⅜" 15.00
#2666/311 Candlestick (Flora Candle) 6" ..18.00
#6055/27 Claret/Wine 4¼ oz. 4⅝" 25.00
#6055/20 Cocktail 3½ oz. 3⅞"................. 20.00
#6055/29 Cordial 1¼ oz. 3⁵⁄₁₆" 30.00
#2666/396 Cup 10.00
#2666/680 Cream 3½".............................15.00
#2666/688 Cream, Individual 12.00
#4185/495 Dessert/Finger Bowl 10.00
#6055/2 Goblet 10 oz. 6⅛".......................22.00
#6055/88 Juice, Footed 5½ oz. 4⅞" 12.00
#6055/60 Luncheon Goblet/Ice Tea 12¼ oz.
    6⅛" 22.00
#2666/477 Mayonnaise
    Bowl 15.00
    Plate 12.00
    Ladle 20.00
#6055/33 Oyster Cocktail 4¾ oz. 4" 12.00
#2666/454 Pitcher, quart 40.00
#2337 Plate
    7" 7.00
    8" 8.00
#2666/620 Relish 2 part 7⅜" 30.00

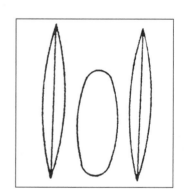

#2666/622 Relish 3 part 10¾" 35.00
#2666/238 Salad Bowl 10½" 60.00
#2685/630 Salver, Footed 12¼" 70.00
#2666/397 Saucer 8.00
#2666/568 Serving Plate 14" 40.00
#2666/654 Shaker, Chrome Top,
    Large ....pair 20.00
#6055/7 Sherbet 6 oz. 4½".......................18.00
#2666/729 Snack Plate, Curved Handle
    10" 40.00
#2666/677 Sugar 2⅝" 15.00
#2666/687 Sugar, Individual 12.00
#2666/567 Torte Plate 14" 50.00
#2666 Tray, Cream & Sugar 10.00

SPRAY items included in Nostalgia Program

SP03/007 Champagne/Dessert 6 oz. 4½"..18.00
SP03/027 Claret/Wine 4¼ oz. 4⅝" 25.00
SP03/002 Goblet 10 oz. 6⅛".....................22.00
SP03/060 Luncheon Goblet/Ice Tea 12¼ oz.
    6⅛" 22.00

⇜⇝ SPRING Cutting #844 ⇜⇝

Gray Cutting
Crystal
1955 – 1959

#6060 Cocktail/Wine/Seafood 5 oz. 4½"....20.00
#6060 Cordial 1 oz. 2⅞" 20.00
#6060 Goblet 10½ oz. 5⅞" 18.00
#6060 Ice Tea, Footed 14 oz. 6¼" 18.00
#6060 Juice, Footed 5½ oz. 4½" 16.00
#2337 Plate
    7" 8.00
    8" 10.00
#6060 Sherbet 6½ oz. 4½" 16.00

⇜⇝ SPRINGTIME Plate Etching #318 ⇜⇝

Crystal, Topaz
Topaz 1933 – 1936
1933 – 1944

Add 25% to items made in Topaz.

SPRINGTIME items made in Crystal.

#2440 Bon Bon, Handled 5" 10.00
#2470½ Bowl
    7" 20.00
    10½" 35.00
#2481 Bowl, Oblong 11" 40.00
#6012 Brandy 1 oz. 28.00
#2470 Cake Plate 30.00
#2470½ Candlestick 5½" ....pair 45.00
#2481 Candlestick 5" ....pair 50.00
#2482 Candlestick, Trindle ....pair 60.00
#2440 Celery Dish 11½" 22.00
#2440 Cereal 6" 14.00
#6012 Champagne, Saucer/High Sherbet
    5½ oz...20.00
#6012 Claret 4½ oz. 25.00
#6012 Cocktail 3 oz..................................20.00
#2400 Comport 6" 20.00
#6012 Cordial 1 oz. 30.00
#2440 Cream, Footed 14.00
#2440 Cream Soup....................................22.00
#6012 Creme de Menthe 2 oz. 20.00
#2440 Cup 10.00
#2440 Fruit 5" 8.00
#6012 Goblet 10 oz. 22.00
#6011 Jug, Footed 50.00

#2470 Lemon Dish 14.00
#2440 Lemon Dish, Handled 5" 18.00
#2440 Mayonnaise, 2 part 6½" 30.00
#2440 Olive Dish 6½" 14.00
#6012 Oyster Dish 6½".............................14.00
#2440 Pickle Dish 8½" 16.00
#2440 Plate
    6" 8.00
    7" 10.00
    8" 18.00
    9" 25.00
#2419 Relish
    4 part 30.00
    5 part 35.00
#2440 Relish, Handled 2 part 22.00
#2440 Relish, Handled 3 part 30.00
#2470 Relish, Oval 4 part 30.00
#6012 Rhine Wine 4½ oz. 24.00
#2440 Sauce Dish 6½" 22.00
#2440 Saucer...8.00
#6012 Sherbet, Low 5½ oz.......................16.00
#6012 Sherry 2 oz.....................................20.00

⇜ **SPRINGTIME Plate Etching #318 cont.** ⇝

#2440 Sugar, Footed 16.00
#2470 Sweetmeat 10.00
#2440 Sweetmeat, Handled 4½" 12.00
#2440 Torte Plate 13" 35.00
#2440 Tray, Oval 8½" 25.00
#6012 Tumbler, Footed
     5 oz. 12.00
     10 oz. 10.00
     13 oz. 20.00
#2470 Vase 10" 60.00
#4111 Vase 6½" 30.00
#4112 Vase 8½" 35.00
#6012 Wine 3 oz. 25.00

SPRINGTIME items made in Crystal, Topaz

#2470½ Bowl 7" 25.00
#2470½ Bowl 10½" 35.00
#2481 Bowl, Oblong 11" 35.00
#2470½ Candlestick 5½" 30.00
#2481 Candlestick 5" 28.00
#2482 Candlestick, Trindle...............40.00
#2470 Cake Plate 26.00
#2440 Celery 11½" 24.00
#2440 Cereal 6" 16.00
#891 Claret/Wine 4 oz......................18.00
#891 Cocktail 4 oz..........................15.00
#2400 Comport 6" 20.00
#891 Cordial 1 oz. 25.00
#2440 Cream, Footed 12.00

#2440 Cream Soup...........................16.00
#2440 Cup 12.00
#869 Finger Bowl 10.00
#2440 Fruit 5" 15.00
#891 Goblet 9 oz. 25.00
#2470 Lemon Dish 12.00
#2440 Olive Dish 6½" 15.00
#891 Oyster Cocktail 5 oz. 14.00
#2440 Pickle Dish 8½" 22.00
#2440 Plate
     6" 8.00
     7" 10.00
     8" 10.00
     9" 25.00
#2419 Relish, 4 part........................25.00
#2419 Relish, 5 part........................27.00
#2470 Relish, Oval, 4 part 30.00
#2440 Saucer..................................5.00
#891 Sherbet, High 6½ oz. 18.00
#891 Sherbet, Low 6½ oz..................15.00
#2440 Sugar, Footed 12.00
#2470 Sweetmeat 18.00
#2440 Torte Plate 13" 35.00
#891 Tumbler, Footed
     5 oz. 8.00
     9 oz. 10.00
     12 oz. 12.00
#4111 Vase 6½" 16.00
#4112 Vase 8½" 25.00

⇜ **SPRING SONG Cutting #884** ⇝

Crystal
1961 – 1962

#6092/29 Cordial 1½ oz. 22.00
#6092/2 Goblet 10½" 20.00
#6093/88 Juice, Footed 5½ oz. 14.00
#6092/63 Luncheon Goblet/Ice Tea
     14 oz. 20.00
#2337 Plate
     7" 10.00
     8" 10.00

#6092/11 Sherbet 7 oz. 16.00
#6092/27 Wine/Cocktail 4 oz. 18.00

⇒ SPRITE Cutting #823 ⇐

Combination Gray and Polished Cutting
Crystal
1950 – 1968

SPRITE included in Nostalgia Program, not included in Patterns of the Past Program.

#2630/137 Bon Bon, 3 Toed 7¼" 20.00
#2630/224 Bowl, Footed, Flared 10¾" 35.00
#2630/306 Cake Plate, Handled................28.00
#2630/332 Candlestick Duo ....pair 60.00
#2630/336 Candlestick Trindle.........pair 70.00
#6033/8 Champagne/High Sherbet 6 oz.
    4¾" 19.00
#6033/27 Claret/Wine 4 oz. 4¾" 25.00
#6033/21 Cocktail 4 oz. 4¼" 18.00
#2630/388 Comport 4⅜" 20.00
#6033/29 Cordial 1 oz. 3⅝" 30.00
#2630/681 Cream, Footed 16.00
#2630/396 Cup, Footed 8.00
#6033/2 Goblet 10 oz. 6¼" 21.00
#6011 Jug, Footed 8⅞"............................105.00
#6033/88 Juice, Footed 5 oz. 4½" 13.00
#6033/6 Luncheon Goblet/Ice Tea 13 oz.
    5⅞" 19.00
#2630/477 Mayonnaise
    Bowl 12.00
    Plate 10.00
    Ladle 10.00
#6033/33 Oyster Cocktail 4 oz. 3¾" 13.00
#6033/18 Parfait 6 oz. 3¾".......................19.00
#2666/454 Pitcher, quart.........................80.00
#2337 Plate
    7" 10.00

8" 12.00
#2630/620 Relish, 2 part 7⅜" 16.00
#2630/397 Saucer 6.00
#2630/654 Shaker, Chrome Top ....pair 30.00
#6033/11 Sherbet, Low 6 oz. 4" 15.00
#2630/679 Sugar, Footed 4".....................20.00
#2630/567 Torte Plate 14" 40.00

SPRITE Items included in Nostalgia Program

SP02/008 Champagne/High Dessert 6 oz.
    4¾"..19.00
SP02/011 Champagne/Low Dessert 6 oz.
    4" 15.00
SP02/027 Claret/Wine 4 oz. 4¾" 25.00
SP02/002 Goblet 10 oz. 6⅛"....................21.00
SP02/060 Luncheon Goblet/Ice Tea 13 oz.
    5⅞"...19.00

⇒ STARS AND BARS Cutting #47 ⇐

Crystal
1941 – 1944

#2596 Ash Tray, Square 4".......................20.00

#2596 Bowl, Oblong, Shallow 11" 60.00
#2596 Bowl, Square 7½" 50.00
#2596 Bowl, Oblong, Shallow 11" 40.00
#2596 Cigarette Box, Covered 4" 50.00

ST. REGIS Cutting #873

Rock Crystal
Crystal
1959 – 1960

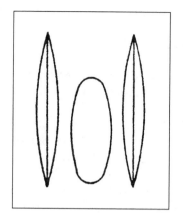

#6083/29 Cordial 1¼ oz. 3⁵⁄₁₆" 26.00
#6083/2 Goblet 11¼ oz. 6¼" 22.00
#6083/63 Ice Tea, Footed 14 oz. 6¼" 22.00
#6083/88 Juice, Footed 5½ oz. 4¾" 18.00
#2337 Plate
   7" 10.00
   8" 10.00
#6083/11 Sherbet 7¾ oz. 4¾" 18.00
#6083/27 Wine/Cocktail 3¾ oz. 4⁹⁄₁₆" 22.00

STAR SONG Cutting #871

Rock Crystal
Crystal
1959 – 1965

#6086/27 Cocktail/Wine 5½ oz. 4⁷⁄₁₆" 22.00
#6086/29 Cordial 1¼ oz. 3³⁄₁₆" 24.00
#6086/2 Goblet 11¾ oz. 6⅜" 22.00
#6086/88 Juice, Footed 5½ oz. 4½" 18.00
#6086/63 Luncheon Goblet/Ice Tea 12 oz.
   6³⁄₁₆" 20.00
#2337 Plate
   7" 10.00

   8" 10.00
#6086/11 Sherbet 7½ oz. 4⅞" 18.00

STARDUST Cutting #851

Rock Crystal
Crystal
1957 – 1970

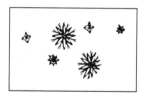

#2666/136 Bon Bon 6⅞" 18.00
#6068 Cocktail/Wine/Seafood 4¼ oz.
   4½" 16.00
#6068 Cordial 1¼ oz. 3" 18.00
#2666/681 Cream 3½" 18.00
#6068 Goblet 10 oz. 5¾" 16.00
#6068 Ice Tea, Footed 13 oz. 5⅞" 16.00
#6068 Juice, Footed 5 oz. 4½" 12.00
#2337 Plate
   7" 8.00

   8" 10.00
#2364/620 Relish, 2 part 8¼" 15.00
#2364/622 Relish, 3 part 10" 20.00
#6068 Sherbet 6½ oz. 4⅝" 14.00
#6068/679 Sugar 2⅝" 20.00
#2364/567 Torte Plate 14" 30.00

<del>⚍</del> **STARFLOWER** Etching #345 <del>⚍</del>

Crystal
1952 – 1958

#2630 Basket, Reed Handle 10¼" 25.00
#2630 Bowl, Flared
  8" 22.00
  10" 26.00
#2630 Bowl, Footed, Flared 10¾" 26.00
#2630 Bowl, Footed, Rolled Edge 11" 32.00
#2630 Bon Bon, 3 Toed 7¼" 16.00
#2630 Butter, Covered, Oblong 7½" 22.00
#2630 Cake Plate, Handled 18.00
#2630 Candlestick
  4½" ....pair 20.00
  Duo ....pair 25.00
  Trindle.......................................pair 35.00
#2630 Candy Jar, Footed, Covered 7" 40.00
#2630 Cereal 6" 12.00
#2630 Cheese & Cracker
  Bowl, Footed................................25.00
  Plate 20.00
#6049 Claret 5 oz. 5⅝" 22.00
#6049 Cocktail 4 oz. 4⅞" 16.00
#2630 Comport 4⅜" 15.00
#6049 Cordial 1¼ oz. 3½" 26.00
#2630 Cream, Footed 4¼" 10.00
#2630 Cream, Individual 10.00
#2630 Cruet, Stoppered 5 oz. 30.00
#2630 Cup, Footed...................................8.00
#2630 Fruit 5" 8.00
#6049 Goblet 11¼ oz. 7" 20.00
#2630 Ice Bucket, Chrome Handle/Tongs
  7⅜" 40.00
#6049 Ice Tea, Footed 15¼ oz. 6¼" 18.00
#2630 Jug, Ice 3 Pint 7⅛" 60.00
#6049 Juice, Footed 5¾ oz. 4⅞" 12.00
#2630 Lily Pond
  9" 60.00
  11¼"..65.00
#2630 Mayonnaise
  Bowl 15.00
  Plate 12.00
  Ladle 20.00
#2630 Muffin Tray, Handled, Curved Sides
  9½"..20.00
#2630 Mustard, Covered, Spoon 4"...........30.00
#2630 Nappy, Handled 4½" 13.00
#6049 Oyster Cocktail 4½ oz. 4" 12.00
#6049 Parfait 6¾ oz. 6" 18.00
#2630 party Plate, Cup Indentation 8" 20.00
#2630 Pickle Dish, Oval 8¾".....................15.00
#2630 Pitcher, Cereal, Pint 6⅛" 30.00

#2630 Plate
  6" 8.00
  7" 10.00
  8" 15.00
  9" 20.00
  10½" 25.00
#2630 Platter, Oval 12"............................25.00
#2630 Preserve, Covered 6" 25.00
#2630 Relish
  2 part 7⅜".....................................20.00
  3 part 11⅛"....................................26.00
#2630 Salad Bowl
  8½" 22.00
  10½" 26.00
#2630 Salad, Crescent 7½"........................40.00
#2630 Salver, Footed 12¼" 60.00
#2630 Saucer...6.00
#2630 Serving Dish, Handled, Oval 2½"
  high 16.00
#2630 Shaker, Chrome Top ....pair 25.00
#6049 Sherbet/Champagne 7¼ oz. 5¼" 18.00
#6049 Sherbet, Low 7¼ oz. 4⅜" 16.00
#2630 Snack Bowl 3½"..............................10.00
#2630 Snack Tray 10½" 20.00
#2630 Sugar, Individual 12.00
#2630 Tid Bit, 3 Toed 8⅛" 16.00
#2630 Tid Bit, 2 Tiered, Metal Handle 35.00
#2630 Torte Plate
  14" 40.00
  16" 50.00
#2630 Tray for Cream & Sugar/Cruets
  7⅛" ....set 100.00
#2630 Tray, Handled, Lunch 11¼" 28.00
#2630 Tray, Utility, Handled 9⅛" 30.00
#2630 Tricorne, 3 Toed 7⅛" 20.00
#2630 Utility Bowl, Oval, Handled 2⅞"
  high 18.00

STARFLOWER Etching #345 cont.

#2470 Vase, Footed 10" 28.00
#2657 Vase, Footed 10½" 30.00
#4143 Vase, Footed 6" 20.00
#2630 Vase, Bud 6" 18.00
#6021 Vase, Bud, Footed 6" 18.00
#5092 Vase, Bud, Footed 8" 20.00

#2630 Vase, Oval 8½" 32.00
#2630 Vase, Handled 7½" 30.00
#2660 Vase, Flip 8" 36.00
#2630 Vegetable Dish, Oval 9½" 20.00
#6049 Wine 4 oz. 5⅛" 22.00

STOCKHOLM Cutting #879

Polished, Cut Stem
Crystal
1960 – 1968

#6093/21 Cocktail 4 oz. 4⅜" 20.00
#6093/29 Cordial 1¼ oz. 3⅝" 25.00
#4185/495 Dessert/Finger Bowl 12.00
#6093/2 Goblet 10¼ oz. 7³⁄₁₆" 20.00
#833½/64 Highball 14 oz. 5¾" 12.00
#6093/88 Juice, Footed 5 oz. 5¹⁄₁₆" 10.00
#6093/63 Luncheon Goblet/Ice Tea 12 oz.
    6⅞" 18.00
#833½/23 Double Old Fashioned Cocktail
    13 oz. 3¾" 12.00
#2337 Plate
    7" (not cut) 8.00
    8" (not cut) 8.00
#6093/11 Sherbet 7 oz. 5½" 14.00
#6093/26 Wine 4½ oz. 5⁵⁄₁₆" 16.00

STRATFORD Cutting #914

Rock Crystal
Crystal
1967 – 1968

#6105/25 Claret 7 oz. 22.00
#6105/29 Cordial 1½ oz. 29.00
#6105/2 Goblet 11 oz. 25.00
#6105/63 Luncheon Goblet/Ice Tea
    13½ oz..25.00
#2337
    7 oz. 10.00
    8 oz. 10.00
#6105/11 Sherbet 9 oz. 25.00
#6105/26 Wine 6 oz. 25.00

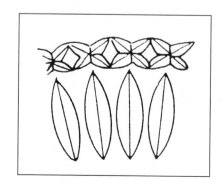

STAUNTON Cutting #707

Rock Crystal
Optic
Crystal
1933 – 1944

#2470½ Bowl 10½" 30.00
#2470½ Candlestick 5½" ....pair
#6004 Champagne, Saucer/High Sherbet
    5½ oz. 16.00
#6004 Claret 4 oz. 22.00
#6004 Cocktail 3 oz. 16.00
#869 Finger Bowl 8.00
#2283 Finger Bowl Plate 6" 6.00
#6004 Goblet 9 oz. 18.00
#2451 Ice Dish 15.00
#2451 Ice Dish Bowl................................6.00
#6004 Oyster Cocktail 4½ oz. 12.00
#2283 Plate
    7" 8.00

    8" 12.00
#6004 Sherbet, Low 5½ oz. 12.00
#2440 Torte Plate 13" 40.00
#6004 Tumbler, Footed
    2 oz. 18.00
    5 oz. 12.00
    9 oz. 12.00
    12 oz. 16.00
#6004 Wine 2½ oz. 22.00

SUFFOLK Cutting #789

Rock Crystal
1939 – 1960

#6023 Bowl, Footed 30.00
#6025 Claret/Wine 4 oz. 4" 20.00
#6025 Cocktail 3½ oz. 3½" 15.00
#6025 Cordial 1 oz. 2⅞" 25.00
#1769 Finger Bowl 10.00
#6025 Goblet 10 oz. 5½" 18.00
#6011 Jug, Footed 80.00
#6025 Oyster Cocktail 4 oz. 3½" 10.00
#2337 Plate
    6" 8.00
    7" 8.00
    8" 11.00
#6025 Sherbet 6 oz. 3¾" 14.00
#6025 Tumbler, Footed
    5 oz. 10.00

    9 oz. 12.00
    12 oz. 16.00

✦═○ SUNGLOW Cutting #650 ○═✦

Gold Band with Gray Cutting
Crystal
1960 – 1967

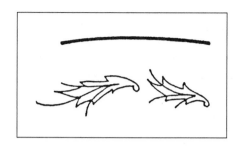

#6085/27 Cocktail/Wine 4 oz. 5" 24.00
#6085/29 Cordial 1¼ oz. 3½" 26.00
#4185/495 Dessert/Finger Bowl 12.00
#6085/2 Goblet 8¾ oz. 6½" 24.00
#6085/88 Juice, Footed 5½ oz. 4⁹⁄₁₆"..........22.00
#6085/63 Luncheon Goblet/Ice Tea
    11¾ oz. 6³⁄₁₆" 22.00
#2337 Plate
    7" 10.00

8" 10.00
#6085/11 Sherbet 6 oz. 5³⁄₁₆" 18.00

✦═○ SUN VALLEY Crystal Print #15 ○═✦

Yellow
1958 – 1962

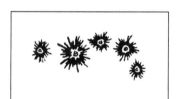

Tumblers produced to accompany similarly
decorated melamine dinnerware.

Juice Tumbler 7 oz. 10.00
Water Tumbler 12 oz. 10.00

✦═○ SWEETBRIAR Cutting #857 ○═✦

Rock Crystal
Crystal
1958 – 1959

#6074 Cocktail/Wine/Seafood 4 oz. 5" 25.00
#6064/29 Cordial 1 oz. 3¼" 45.00
#6074/2 Goblet 9½ oz. 6¼" 22.00
#6074/63 Ice Tea, Footed 13 oz. 6⅜" 24.00
#6074/88 Juice, Footed 5 oz. 4¾" 20.00
#2337 Plate
    7" 8.00
    8" 10.00
#6074/11 Sherbet 6 oz. 4¾" 20.00

⤖ SWEETHEART ROSE Cutting #877 ⤖

**Combination Rock Crystal and Gray Cutting
Crystal
1960 – 1974**

**SWEETHEART ROSE included in Patterns of
the Past Program, Not in Nostalgia Program.**

#6092/25 Claret 7 oz. 20.00
#6092/27 Cocktail/Wine 4 oz. 3¼".............22.00
#6092/29 Cordial 1½ oz. 3½" 26.00
#2666/680 Cream 15.00
#4185/495 Dessert/Finger Bowl 12.00
#6092/2 Goblet 10½ oz. 7¹⁄₁₆" 22.00
#6092/88 Juice, Footed 5½ oz. 4¾" 14.00
#6092/63 Luncheon Goblet/Ice Tea 14 oz.
    6⅜"..22.00
#2337 Plate
    7" 10.00
    8" 10.00
#2666/620 Relish 2 part 15.00
#2666/622 Relish 3 part 18.00
#2364/654 Shaker, Large, Chrome
    Top ....pair 25.00
#6092/11 Sherbet/Dessert/Champagne 7 oz.
    5⁷⁄₁₆"..20.00

#2666/677 Sugar......................................18.00
#2364/567 Torte Plate 14" 30.00

SWEETHEART ROSE items included in Patterns of the Past Program

SW01/011 Champagne/Dessert 6½ oz.
    4⅜"..20.00
SW01/027 Wine/Cocktail 4 oz. 4½" 22.00
SW01/002 Goblet 10½ oz. 7⅛" 22.00
SW01/063 Luncheon Goblet/Ice Tea 12¼ oz.
    6⅛"..22.00

⤖ SWIRL Cutting #848 ⤖

**Polished Cutting
Crystal
1956 – 1967**

#6065/21 Cocktail/Wine 4 oz. 26.00
#6065/29 Cordial 1 oz. 30.00
#6065/2 Goblet 11 oz. 26.00
#6065/88 Juice, Footed 6 oz. 20.00
#6065/63 Luncheon Goblet/Ice Tea
    12 oz. 24.00
#2337 Plate
    7" 10.00
    8" 10.00
#6065/7 Sherbet 7½ oz. 20.00

⮜═ **SYLVAN Crystal Print #1** ═⮞

**Crystal
1955 – 1965**

#2666/136 Bon Bon, Footed 6⅞" 15.00
#2666/189 Bowl, Oval 8¼".......................20.00
#1666/300 Butter, Covered, Oblong 7"......20.00
#2666/309 Canape Plate 7⅜" 15.00
#2666/311 Candlestick (Flora Candle) 6" ..20.00
#2666/360 Celery 9" 25.00
#6060/21 Cocktail/Wine/Seafood 5 oz.
    4½"...20.00
#6060/29 Cordial 1 oz. 2⅞" 20.00
#2666/680 Cream 3½"............................15.00
#2666/688 Cream, Individual 12.00
#2666/396 Cup 10.00
#6060/2 Goblet 10½ oz. 5⅞" 18.00
#6060/88 Juice, Footed 5½ oz. 4½" 16.00
#6060/63 Luncheon Goblet/Ice Tea 14 oz.
    6¼"...18.00
#2666/477 Mayonnaise
    Bowl..15.00
    Plate..12.00
    Ladle 20.00
#2666 Plate
    7" 12.00
    10" 20.00
#2685/500 Preserve, Handled 6½" 28.00

#2666/620 Relish 2 part 7⅜" 30.00
#2666/622 Relish 3 part 10¾" 35.00
#2685/630 Salver, Footed 12¼" 45.00
#2666/397 Saucer 8.00
#2666/568 Serving Plate, Rolled Edge
    14" 40.00
#2364/654 Shaker, Chrome Top,
    Large ....Pair 20.00
#6060/11 Sherbet 6½ oz. 4½" 16.00
#2666/729 Snack Plate, Rolled Edge 10" ..30.00
#2666/677 Sugar 2⅝" 15.00
#2666/687 Sugar, Individual 12.00

⮜═ **TAPESTRY Cutting #701** ═⮞

**Crystal
1930 – 1931**

#4020 Cocktail 3½ oz. 18.00
#2350 Cup, After Dinner 10.00
#2350½ Cup, Footed 8.00
#4021 Finger Bowl 8.00
#4020 Goblet 23.00
#2419 Plate, Square
    6" 8.00
    7" 10.00
    8" 12.00
#2419 Saucer..8.00
#2419 Saucer, After Dinner 6.00
#2420 Sherbet, High 23.00
#4020 Sherbet, Low
    4 oz. 18.00
    5 oz. 18.00
#4020 Tumbler, Footed

    5 oz. 18.00
    10 oz. 18.00
    13 oz. 23.00
    16 oz. 23.00
#4120 Whiskey 2 oz. 18.00

 TARA Plate Etching #34

Crystal
1974 – 1982

#6126/2 Goblet 12 oz. 7" 24.00
#6126/63 Luncheon Goblet/Ice Tea 13 oz.
   6" 22.00
#6126/11 Sherbet/Dessert/Champagne 9 oz.
   5⅝" 22.00
#6126/26 Wine 7 oz. 5¾" 24.00

THELMA Cutting #186

Amber, Green, Rose, Orchid
1928 – 1929

#2297 Bowl, Deep 12" 50.00
#2342 Bowl, Deep 12½" 50.00
#2362 Bowl 12½" 50.00
#2324 Candlestick 4" ....pair 40.00
#2362 Candlestick 3" ....pair 35.00
#2331 Candy Box, Covered.......................60.00
#2329 Centerpiece
   11" 50.00
   13" 60.00
#2368 Cheese...20.00
#2368 Cheese and Cracker Plate 11½" 28.00
#2327 Comport 7" 25.00
#2378 Ice Bucket, Nickel Plate Handle 65.00
#2378 Sugar Pail, Nickel Plate Handle 55.00
#2287 Tray, Lunch, Handled 11" 24.00
#2342 Tray, Lunch, Handled 12" 30.00
#2369 Vase, Optic
   7" 60.00
   9" 80.00

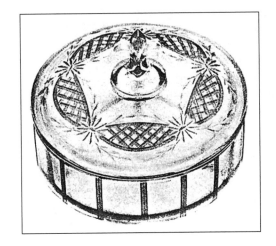

#4100 Vase, Optic
   6" 60.00
   8" 80.00
#4103 Vase, Optic
   3" 40.00
   4" 45.00
   5" 50.00

THISTLE Etching #346

Crystal
1953 – 1970

#2666 Bon Bon, Footed 6⅞" 15.00
#2666 Bowl, Oval 8¼" 20.00
#2666 Butter Pat 3½" 10.00
#2666 Canapé Plate 7⅜" 15.00
#2666 Candlestick (Flora Candle) 6" 20.00

#2666 Celery 9" 25.00
#6052 Claret 4¼ oz. 4⅜" 20.00
#6052 Cocktail 3¾ oz. 3⅞" 16.00
#6052 Cordial 1¼ oz. 3⅛" 25.00
#2666 Cream 3½".......................................15.00
#2666 Cream, Individual 12.00
#2666 Cup 10.00
#6052 Goblet 9¾ oz. 5⅞" 20.00

THISTLE Etching #346 cont.

#6052 Ice Tea, Footed 13 oz. 9⅛" 18.00
#6052 Juice, Footed 5½ oz. 4⅞" 12.00
#2666 Mayonnaise
    Bowl...15.00
    Plate...12.00
    Ladle 20.00
#6052 Oyster Cocktail 4½ oz. 3⅞" 12.00
#2666 Pickle Dish 7¼" 20.00
#2666 Pitcher, 3 Pint 8¾" 50.00
#2666 Pitcher, Pint 5¼" 30.00
#2666 Pitcher, Quart 6⅞" 40.00
#2666 Plate
    7" 12.00
    10"...20.00
#2666 Relish
    2 part 7⅜"...30.00
    3 part 10¾".......................................35.00
#2666 Salad Bowl
    9" 50.00
    11" 60.00
#2666 Salad/Dessert Bowl, Individual 2¼"..15.00
#2666 Saucer...8.00
#2666 Serving Plate 14" 40.00

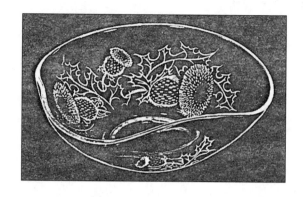

#2364 Shaker, Chrome Top................pair 40.00
#6052 Sherbet 6½ oz. 4⅜" 16.00
#2666 Snack Plate, Rolled Edge 10" 40.00
#2666 Sugar 2⅝" 15.00
#2666 Sugar, Individual 12.00
#2666 Tray, Cream & Sugar.....................10.00
#2660 Vase, Flip 8" 50.00
#2470 Vase, Footed 10" 70.00
#6021 Vase, Bud, Footed 6" 40.00

THISTLE WITH BAND Etching #202

Blown Ware
Crystal
1904 – 1910

#300 Jug 7...60.00
#1227 Jug 7...60.00
#820 Tumbler 8.00
#820½ Tumbler, Sham 8.00

THISTLE WITHOUT BAND Etching #202½

Blown Ware
Crystal
1904 – 1910
    Do not confuse with THISTLE WITH BAND Etching #202 or THISTLE Etching #346.

#481 Custard 10.00
#1227 Custard 8.00

Custard Plate 6.00
#315 Finger Bowl 10.00
#300 Jug 7..60.00
#303 Jug 7..60.00
#1227 Jug 7, Cut Neck, Cut Star Bottom ..70.00
#1227 Pitcher 7, Cut Star Bottom.............70.00
#1227 Punch Bowl 100.00
#1227 Punch Bowl and Foot...................150.00

THISTLE WITHOUT BAND Etching #202½ cont.

#300 Tankard 7 ....20.00
#820 Tumbler 8.00
#820½ Tumbler, Sham 8.00

#160½ Water Bottle, Cut Neck, Cut Star
　　Bottom 60.00

TIARA Cutting #903

Rock Crystal
Crystal
1964 – 1970

#6104/25 Claret 7 oz. 24.00
#6104/29 Cordial 1½ oz. 30.00
#6104/2 Goblet 11 oz. 25.00
#6104/63 Luncheon Goblet/Ice Tea
　　13½ oz...25.00
#2337 Plate
　　7" 10.00
　　8" 10.00
#6104/11 Sherbet 9 oz. 23.00
#6104/26 Wine 6 oz. 25.00

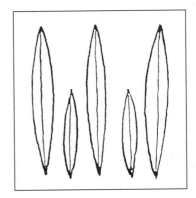

TIGER LILY Carving #18

Crystal
1940 – 1944

#2557 Vase, Wide 5½" 125.00
#2577 Vase 6" 100.00
#4132 Vase, (Ice Bowl) 5" 80.00

TOY Carving #33

Crystal
Decoration #620 (5 Enamel Colors)
1940 – 1944

Various children's toys each on different items.

#2306 Ash Tray, Nesting
　　2¾"...10.00
　　3"..12.00
　　3½"...15.00
#4146 Cocktail 4 oz................................15.00
#4146 Cordial 1 oz. 15.00
#4146 Scotch & Soda 9 oz. 10.00

⤜ **TRELLIS Cutting #169** ⤛

Crystal
1924 – 1928
Do not confuse with TRELLIS Design, Cutting #822.

#2250 Candy Jar, Covered
    ¼ lb. 50.00
    ½ lb. 60.00
    1 lb. 80.00
#1697 Carafe 22.00
#4023 Carafe Tumbler 6 oz. 10.00
#1697 Carafe Set (Carafe & Tumbler) 35.00
#660 Champagne, Saucer 5 oz. 8.00
#660 Cocktail 3 oz............................9.00
#5078 Comport
    5" 15.00
    6" 18.00
#5078 Comport, Covered 5" 26.00
#660 Cordial ¾ oz. 14.00
#1851 Cream 16.00
#30 Decanter, Cut Neck, quart 35.00
#766 Finger Bowl 6.00
#810 Finger Bowl 6.00
#660 Fruit, Footed 5 oz. 8.00
#660 Goblet 9 oz. 10.00
#945½ Grapefruit 40.00
#945½ Grapefruit Liner 18.00
#825 Jelly 20.00
#825 Jelly, Covered 30.00
#303 Jug 7...30.00
#724 Jug 7...30.00
#1787 Jug 3..30.00
#2270 Jug 30.00
#2270 Jug, Plain Covered.......................45.00
#1968 Marmalade, Covered 28.00
#766 Mayonnaise Set
    Bowl...20.00
    Plate...15.00
    Ladle 20.00
#1831 Mustard, Covered 26.00
#5078 Nappy
    5" 10.00
    6" 10.00
    7" 12.00
    8" 20.00

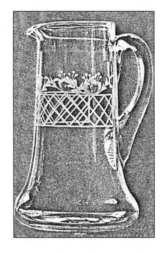

#1465 Oil, Cut Neck, Polished Stopper
    5 oz. 40.00
#837 Oyster Cocktail 6.00
#660 Parfait 5 oz. 10.00
#1848 Plate, Cut Star 9" 18.00
#2237 Plate
    7" 12.00
    8" 18.00
#2283 Plate
    5" 10.00
    6" 13.00
#2235 Shaker, Glass Top....................pair 70.00
#2235 Shaker, Pearl Top ....pair 80.00
#1851 Sugar, 2-handled 20.00
#766 Sweetmeat....................................19.00
#2194 Syrup 8 oz. 35.00
#887 Tumbler 2½ oz. 12.00
#889 Tumbler
    5 oz. 8.00
    8 oz 8.00
    13 oz. 10.00
#4076 Tumbler 9 oz. 10.00
#4095 Tumbler, Footed
    5 oz. 10.00
    10 oz. 10.00
    13 oz. 12.00
#4011 Tumbler, Handled 12 oz. 18.00
#2276 Vanity Set 120.00
#660 Wine 2½ oz. 10.00

☜ TRELLIS Cutting #822 ☞

Combination Rock Crystal and Gray Cutting Crystal
1950 – 1955
  Do not confuse with TRELLIS Pattern, Cutting #169.

#6030 Champagne/High Sherbet 6 oz.
    5⅝"...18.00
#6030 Claret/Wine 3½ oz. 6" 24.00
#6030 Cocktail 3½ oz. 5¼" 15.00
#6030 Cordial 1 oz. 3⅞" 30.00
#6030 Goblet 10 oz. 7⅞".............................22.00
#6030 Goblet, Low 10 oz. 6⅜"....................20.00
#6030 Ice Tea, Footed 12 oz. 6" 18.00
#6030 Juice, Footed 5 oz. 4⅝" 12.00
#6030 Oyster Cocktail 4 oz. 3¾" 10.00
#2337 Plate
    7" 8.00

8" 10.00
#6030 Sherbet, Low 6 oz. 4⅜"....................13.00

☜ TROJAN Plate Etching #280 ☞

Rose, Gold Tint, Topaz with Crystal Bases
1929 – 1944
Gold Tint 1938 – 1944; Rose 1929 – 1935;
  Topaz 1929 – 1938; Colors with Crystal
  Bases 1931 – 1944

#2350 Ash Tray
    Small 22.00
    Large 35.00
#2375 Baker 9" 40.00
#2375 Bon Bon 20.00
#2375 Bouillon, Footed 22.00
#2375 Bowl 12" 45.00
#2394 Bowl
    6" 30.00
    12" 50.00
#2395 Bowl 10" 60.00
#2415 Bowl, Combination 70.00
#2375 Cake Plate 10" 37.00
#2375 Canape Plate 22.00
#2375 Candlestick 3" ....pair 40.00
#2375½ Candlestick ....pair 40.00
#2394 Candlestick 2" ....pair 50.00
#2395½ Candlestick 5" ....pair 50.00
#2394 Candy Jar, Covered ½ lb. 145.00
#2375 Celery 11½" 40.00
#2375 Centerpiece 12" 45.00
#2375 Cereal 6" 30.00

#5099 Champagne, Saucer/High Sherbet
    6 oz. 26.00
#2368 Cheese, Footed 27.00
#2375 Cheese, Footed 27.00
#2368 Cheese and Cracker Plate 23.00
#2375 Cheese and Cracker Plate 23.00
#2375 Chop Plate 13".............................55.00
#5099 Claret 50.00
#5299 Claret 50.00
#5099 Cocktail 3 oz................................30.00
#5299 Cocktail.......................................30.00

#2400 Comport 6" 40.00
#5099 Comport 6" 40.00
#5299 Comport 6" 40.00
#5099 Cordial ¾ oz. 75.00
#5299 Cordial 75.00
#2375½ Cream, Footed............................30.00
#2375½ Cream, Tea 60.00
#2375 Cream Soup, Footed 25.00
#2375 Cream Soup Plate 14.00
#2375½ Cup, Footed 20.00
#2375 Cup, After Dinner 32.00
#2375 Dessert, Large 50.00
#869 Finger Bowl 28.00
#2375 Fruit 5" 18.00
#5099 Goblet 9 oz. 32.00
#5299 Goblet 32.00
#5082½ Grapefruit 90.00
#5282½ Grapefruit 100.00
#945½ Grapefruit Liner 45.00
#2375 Grill Plate 10" 40.00
#2375 Ice Bucket 90.00
#2451 Ice Dish 45.00
#2451 Ice Dish Plate................................15.00
#5000 Jug 7, Footed...............................350.00
#2375 Lemon Dish 28.00
#2375 Mayonnaise 26.00
#2375 Mayonnaise Plate 14.00
#2394 Mint Dish 35.00
#2375 Nappy, Round 7" 45.00
#2375 Oil, Footed...................................300.00
#5099 Oyster Cocktail 5½ oz. 25.00
#5299 Oyster Cocktail 25.00
#5099 Parfait 5½ oz................................43.00
#5299 Parfait 43.00
#2375 Plate
    6" 10.00
    7" 14.00
    8" 20.00
    9" 35.00

    10" 60.00
#2283 Plate Optic 6".................................10.00
#2375 Platter
    12" 70.00
    15" 130.00
#2350 Relish, 3 Compartment, Round 40.00
#2375 Relish 8½" 30.00
#2375 Sauce Boat 120.00
#2375 Sauce Boat Plate 50.00
#2375 Saucer..10.00
#2375 Saucer, After Dinner 15.00
#2375 Shaker, Footed ....pair 110.00
#5099 Sherbet, Low 6 oz. 23.00
#5299 Sherbet, Low 6 oz. 23.00
#2375 Soup 7" 32.00
#2375½ Sugar, Footed 30.00
#2375½ Sugar, Footed, Covered 90.00
#2375½ Sugar, Tea..................................52.00
#2378 Sugar Pail 110.00
#2375 Sweetmeat....................................25.00
#2375 Tray, Lunch, Handled 50.00
#2429 Tray, Service 100.00
#2429 Tray, Service/Lemon 100.00
#5099 Tumbler, Footed
    2½ oz...38.00
    5 oz. 26.00
    9 oz. 22.00
    12 oz. 30.00
#5299 Tumbler, Footed
    2½ oz...38.00
    5 oz. 26.00
    9 oz. 22.00
    12 oz. 30.00
#2417 Vase, Optic 8" 110.00
#4105 Vase, Optic 8" 150.00
#2375 Whip Cream 26.00
#2378 Whip Cream Pail 140.00
#5299 Wine 52.00

⊷⇨ TRUE LOVE Cutting #862 ⇦⊷

Gray Cutting
Crystal
1958 – 1968

#6080/27 Claret/Wine 4 oz. 5⅛" 20.00
#6080/20 Cocktail 4 oz. 4⅜" 16.00
#6080/29 Cordial 1 oz. 3½" 23.00

⤳ TRUE LOVE Cutting #862 cont. ⤳

#4185/495 Dessert/Finger Bowl 10.00
#6080/2 Goblet 10 oz. 6¾" 20.00
#6080/88 Juice, Footed 5 oz. 4¼" 16.00
#6080/63 Luncheon Goblet/Ice Tea
     13½ oz. 5½" 20.00

#2337 Plate
    7" 8.00
    8" 8.00
#6080/11 Sherbet 7 oz. 4¾" 14.00

⤳ TULIP Cutting #772 ⤳

Rock Crystal
Crystal
1937 – 1944

#2430 Bowl 11" 30.00
#2496 Bowl, Handled 10½".......................30.00
#2430 Candlestick 2" ....pair 30.00
#2496 Candlestick 5½" ....pair 50.00
#6019 Cocktail 3½ oz. 14.00
#4132 Decanter, Stopper 60.00
#766 Finger Bowl 8.00
#6019 Goblet 10 oz. 18.00
#4132 Ice Bowl..25.00
#2430 Jelly 7" 16.00
#2430 Mint Dish 5½" 15.00
#4132 Old Fashioned, Sham 7½ oz. 6.00
#6019 Oyster Cocktail 4¾ oz. 6.00
#6019 Parfait 6 oz. 14.00
#2337 Plate
    6" 8.00
    7" 8.00
    8" 10.00

#6019 Sherbet 6½ oz..............................12.00
#4132 Tumbler, Sham
    5 oz. 6.00
    9 oz. 8.00
    12 oz. 8.00
    14 oz. 10.00
#6019 Tumbler, Footed
    5 oz. 8.00
    12 oz. 14.00
#4132 Whiskey, Sham 1½ oz......................6.00
#6019 Wine 3 oz. 20.00

⤳ TWILIGHT Cutting #883 ⤳

Rock Crystal
Crystal
1961 – 1962

#6092/27 Cocktail/Wine 4 oz. 20.00
#6092/29 Cordial 1½ oz. 25.00
#6092/2 Goblet 10½ oz. 20.00
#6092/88 Juice, Footed 5½ oz. 14.00
#6092/63 Luncheon Goblet/Ice Tea
    14 oz. 18.00
#2337 Plate
    7" 10.00
    8" 10.00
#6092/11 Sherbet 7 oz. 18.00

⚛ VALE Cutting #925 ⚛

Crystal
1974 – 1975

VALE included in Centennial II Collection

Double Old Fashioned Tumbler 11 oz. 12.00
Highball Tumbler 13 oz. 12.00

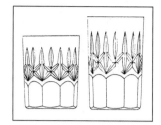

⚛ VENISE Decoration #688 ⚛

Crystal Print with Platinum Bands on Bowl
1970 – 1974

#6120/25 Claret 9 oz. 35.00
#6120/2 Goblet 14 oz. 35.00
#6120/29 Liqueur 2 oz. 50.00

#6120/63 Luncheon Goblet/Ice Tea
    15 oz. 35.00
#2337/549 Plate 7" 15.00
#6120/11 Sherbet/Dessert/Champagne
    10 oz. 35.00

⚛ VENUS Cutting #896 ⚛

Rock Crystal
Crystal
1963 – 1974

#6102/31 Brandy 3 oz. 23.00
#6102/25 Claret 7½ oz. 23.00
#4185/495 Dessert/Finger Bowl 10.00
#6102/2 Goblet 10 oz. 25.00
#6102/63 Luncheon Goblet/Ice Tea
    14 oz. 25.00
#2336 Plate
    7" (not cut) 6.00

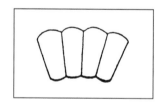

    8" (not cut) 6.00
#6102/11 Sherbet/Dessert/Champagne
    8 oz. 22.00
#6102/26 Tulip Wine 5½ oz. 25.00

⚛ VERNON Plate Etching #277 ⚛

Optic Pattern
Crystal, Amber, Azure, Green, Orchid
1927 – 1934
Amber, Green 1927 – 1934; Azure 1928 –
    1934; Orchid 1927 – 1928

Add 20% for Azure, 30% for Orchid

#2350 Ash Tray, Small 22.00
#2375 Baker 9" 40.00

#2375 Bon Bon 30.00
#2375 Bouillon, Footed 20.00
#2375 Bowl 12" 45.00
#2394 Bowl 12" 50.00
#2415 Bowl, Combination 60.00
#2375 Candleholder 3" ....pair 45.00
#2375½ Candleholder ....pair 40.00
#2294 Candleholder 2" ....pair 32.00
#2331 Candy Box, Covered....................110.00
#2375 Celery Dish 11½" 22.00
#2375½ Centerpiece, Oval 13" 60.00
#2375 Cereal Bowl 6" 18.00
#2368 Cheese, Footed 22.00
#2368 Cracker Plate................................28.00
#2358 Cheese and Cracker Set................45.00
#2375½ Centerpiece, Oval 13" 60.00
#877 Claret 4 oz. 25.00
#877 Cocktail 3½ oz. 18.00
#2375 Comport 7"................................. 45.00
#877 Cordial ¾ oz. 30.00
#2375½ Cream.......................................20.00
#2375 Cream Soup.................................28.00
#2375 Cream Soup Plate 14.00
#2375½ Cup, After Dinner 30.00
#2375½ Cup, Footed 20.00
#869 Finger Bowl 12.00
#2383 Finger Bowl Plate 6".......................8.00
#2375 Fruit 5" 18.00
#877 Goblet 10 oz. 22.00
#877 Grapefruit 30.00
#945½ Grapefruit Liner 10.00
#2378 Ice Bucket, Nickel Plated
    Handle 75.00
#2378 Ice Bucket, Nickel Plated
    Handle 75.00
    Drainer, Tongs 50.00

#5100 Jug 7, Footed.............................300.00
#2375 Lemon Dish 28.00
#2375 Mayonnaise 20.00
#2375 Mayonnaise Plate 16.00
#2375 Oil, Footed.................................160.00
#877 Oyster Cocktail 15.00
#877 Parfait 5½ oz. 22.00
#2375 Plate
    6" 9.00
    7" 12.00
    8" 17.00
    9" 20.00
    10" 50.00
    13" 60.00
#2375 Platter
    12" 70.00
    15" 80.00
#2375 Relish 8½" 28.00
#2375 Sauce Boat 60.00
#2375 Sauce Boat Plate 38.00
#5100 Shaker, Glass Top.................pair 110.00
#877 Sherbet
    Low 6 oz. 18.00
    High 6 oz. 20.00
#2375 Soup 7" 32.00
#2375½ Sugar, Footed 24.00
#2375½ Sugar, Footed, Covered 60.00
#2375 Sweetmeat....................................15.00
#2375 Tray, Handled, Lunch 45.00
#877 Tumbler, Footed
    2½ oz....................................... ....14.00
    5 oz. 14.00
    9 oz. 14.00
    12 oz. 18.00
#2375 Whip Cream Pail 85.00
#877 Wine 2¾ oz. 25.00

☞ VERONA Plate Etching #281 ☜

Crystal, Green, Rose
1929 – 1932
Do not confuse with VERONA #200 Ware.

**Also produced as FIRENZE Decoration #502
in Topaz with Gold Edge Trim.**

#2394 Bowl 12"	.50.00
#2394 Candlestick 2"	pair 40.00
#890 Claret	.16.00
#890 Cocktail	.12.00
#2400 Comport 8"	35.00
#890 Cordial	.20.00
#2375½ Cream, Footed	.12.00
#2375½ Cup, Footed	.10.00
#890 Finger Bowl	.12.00
#890 Goblet	.16.00
#877 Grapefruit	.30.00
#945½ Grapefruit Liner	.18.00
#890 Jug 7, Footed	120.00
#890 Oyster Cocktail	.10.00
#890 Parfait	.16.00
#2283 Plate, Optic 6"	.14.00
#2375 Plate	
6"	.14.00
7"	.20.00
8"	.25.00
13"	.50.00
#2375 Saucer	.10.00

#890 Sherbet	
High	.14.00
Low	.10.00
#2375½ Sugar	.30.00
#2375½ Sugar, Covered	.45.00
#890 Tumbler, Footed	
2½ oz.	.12.00
5 oz.	.10.00
9 oz.	.8.00
12 oz.	.14.00
#890 Wine	.16.00

☞ VERSAILLES Plate Etching #278 ☜

**Azure, Green, Rose, Topaz and Gold Tint with
Crystal Base**
1928 – 1944
**Azure Bowl 1928 – 1944; Gold Tint Bowl
1937 – 1944; Green Bowl 1928 – 1936;
Rose Bowl 1928 – 1940; Topaz 1929 –
1936; Colors with Crystal Bases**

Fostoria advertised that VERSAILLES reflected the glamour and charm of 18th Century
France, inspired by the gardens at Versailles. Sophisticated and elegant, VER-
SAILLES was given a light and delicate
treatment, beautifully accented by its soft
colors. From the first, it has been a favorite
with glass collectors.

VERSAILLES items made in Azure, Green, Rose, Topaz and Gold Tint

ADD 25% TO VALUES FOR TOPAZ AND GOLD TINT, 50% FOR AZURE

#2375 Ash Tray, Small 25.00
#2375 Baker 9" 30.00
#2375 Bouillon, Footed (not made in Rose, Azure)..20.00
#2375 Bon Bon (not made in Azure, Green) 18.00
#2375 Bowl 12" (not made in Green)..........35.00
#2394 Bowl (not made in Green)
    6" 30.00
    12" 50.00
#2395 Bowl 10" (not made in Green)..........45.00
#2375 Cake Plate 10" (not made in Rose, Azure, Green) 32.00
#2375 Candlestick 3" ....pair 75.00
#2375½ Candlestick 5" (not made in Green) ....pair 70.00
    2" ....pair 45.00
#2375½ Candlestick 5" (not made in Green) ....pair 70.00
#2394 Candlestick (not made in Green)
    2" ....pair 45.00
    3" ....pair 50.00
#2395 Candlestick 3" (not made in Topaz) ....pair 50.00
#2395½ Candlestick 5" ....pair 50.00
#2331 Candy Box, Covered.......................95.00
#2375 Celery Dish 11½" (not made in Rose, Azure, Green) 32.00
#2375 Centerpiece 12" (not made in Rose, Azure)...40.00
#2375½ Centerpiece, Oval 13" (not made in Topaz) 50.00
#2395 Centerpiece 11" (not made in Topaz) 45.00
#2375 Cereal Bowl 6" 24.00
#2368 Cheese, Footed 18.00
#2368 Cracker Plate................................20.00
#2375 Cheese & Cracker 30.00
#2375 Chop Plate 13"..............................40.00
#2375 Comport 7" 37.00
#2400 Comport
    6" 30.00
    8" (not made in Topaz) 42.00
#2375½ Cream, Footed 18.00
#2375½ Cream, Tea 28.00
#2375 Cream Soup, Footed 20.00

#2375 Cream Soup Plate 10.00
#2375 Cup, After Dinner, Footed (not made in Rose, Azure, Green) 30.00
#2375½ Cup, Footed 20.00
#2375 Dessert, Large 40.00
#2375 Fruit 5" 18.00
#2375 Grill Plate 10" 22.00
#2451 Ice Dish 30.00
#2351 Ice Dish Plate................................15.00
#2375 Ice Bucket (not made in Rose, Azure, Green) 90.00
#2378 Ice Bucket, Nickel Plated Handle (not made in Topaz) 95.00
#2375 Lemon Dish (not made in Rose, Azure, Green) 18.00
#2375 Mayonnaise, Footed 40.00
#2375 Mayonnaise Plate..........................12.00
#2394 Mint Dish 22.00
#2375 Oil, Footed 350.00
#2375 Plate
    6" 8.00
    7" 10.00
    8" 14.00
    9" 18.00
    10" 40.00
    13" 50.00
#2375 Platter
    12" 45.00
    15" 95.00
#2375 Relish, Divided 8½" (not made in Green) 22.00
#2375 Salad Dressing Bottle....................345.00
#2375 Sauce Boat (not made in Green)......80.00
#2375 Sauce Boat Plate (not made in Green) 35.00
#2375 Saucer...10.00
#2375 Saucer, After Dinner (not made in Rose, Azure, Green) 10.00
#2375 Shaker, Footed ....pair 200.00
#2375 Soup 7" 35.00
#2375½ Sugar, Covered, Footed 95.00
#2375½ Sugar, Tea..................................32.00
#2378 Sugar Pail, Nickel Plate Handle 90.00
#2375 Sweetmeat (not made in Green) 22.00
#2375 Tray, Lunch, Handled (not made in Rose, Azure, Green) 40.00
#2429 Tray, Service 70.00
#2429 Tray, Lemon 60.00
#2378 Vase, Optic 8" 80.00
#2385 Vase, Fan, Footed (not made in Topaz)...130.00
#2375 Whip Cream, Handled (not made in Rose,

☞ VERSAILLES Plate Etching #278 cont. ☜

Azure)...20.00

#2378 Whip Cream Pail, Nickel Plate

Handle 95.00

VERSAILLES items made in Azure, Green and Rose

#2350 Ash Tray, Small 25.00
#2375 Canape Plate 32.00
#2331 Candy Box, Covered.......................90.00
#5298 Claret 50.00
#5299 Cocktail.......................................30.00
#2375 Comport 7" 35.00
#2400 Comport

6" 37.00

8" 40.00

#5298 Comport 5" 40.00
#5298 Cordial 75.00
#5298 Goblet 35.00
#5282½ Grapefruit 75.00
#5298 Nappy, Footed 6" 30.00
#5298 Oyster Cocktail 22.00
#5298 Parfait 35.00
#2375 Shaker, Footed ....pair 110.00
#5298 Sherbet

High 32.00

Low 23.00

#5298 Tumbler, Footed

2½ oz. 35.00

5 oz. 24.00

9 oz. 24.00

12 oz. 35.00

#5298 Wine...52.00

VERSAILLES items made in Topaz

#2350 Ash Tray, Large 35.00
#2394 Candy Jar, Covered ½ lb. 70.00
#5299 Claret 50.00
#5299 Cocktail.......................................35.00
#5299 Comport 6" 30.00
#5200 Cordial 80.00
#5299 Goblet 35.00
#5299 Oyster Cocktail 25.00
#5299 Parfait 50.00
#5299 Sherbet

High 30.00

Low 24.00

#5299 Tumbler, Footed

2½ oz. 40.00

5 oz. 26.00

9 oz. 26.00

12 oz. 35.00

VERSAILLES stemware made in Azure, Green, Rose with Crystal Base; ADD 30% FOR AZURE

#5098 Champagne, Saucer/High Sherbet

6 oz. 32.00

#5098 Claret 4 oz. 50.00
#5098 Cocktail 3 oz. 30.00
#5098 Comport 5" 20.00
#5098 Cordial ¾ oz. 80.00
#869 Finger Bowl 20.00
#2283 Finger Bowl Plate, Optic 6".............14.00
#5098 Goblet 9 oz. 35.00
#5082½ Grapefruit 75.00
#945½ Grapefruit Liner 45.00
#5000 Jug 7, Footed.............................400.00
#5098 Oyster Cocktail 5 oz. 24.00
#5098 Parfait 6 oz. (not made in Rose,

Azure)....................................35.00

#5098 Sherbet, Low 6 oz. 23.00
#5098 Tumbler, Footed

2½ oz. 35.00

5 oz. 24.00

9 oz. 24.00

12 oz. 35.00

#5098 Wine 2½ oz. 52.00

VERSAILLES stemware made in Gold Tint, Topaz with Crystal Base

#5099 Champagne, Saucer/High Sherbet

6 oz. 32.00

#5099 Claret 4 oz. 55.00
#5099 Cocktail 3 oz................................32.00
#5099 Cordial ¾ oz. 70.00
#5099 Comport 6" 35.00
#869 Finger Bowl 20.00
#2283 Finger Bowl Plate 6".......................14.00
#5099 Goblet 9 oz. 35.00
#5082½ Grapefruit 45.00
#5000 Jug, Footed................................360.00
#5099 Oyster Cocktail 4½ oz. 25.00
#5099 Parfait 5½ oz. 35.00
#5099 Sherbet, Low 6 oz. 30.00
#5099 Tumbler, Footed

2½ oz.....................................45.00

5 oz. 24.00

9 oz. 22.00

12 oz. 30.00

#5099 Wine 2½ oz. 52.00

⇒ VESPER Plate Etching #275 ⇐

Optic Pattern
Amber, Blue, Green
1926 – 1934
  Blue 1926 – 1928; Amber, Green 1926 – 1934

A lace-like tracery with a rose medallion cascading from an etched band.

ADD 30% TO VALUES FOR AMBER AND GREEN, 40% FOR BLUE.

*Items not made in Blue

#2350 Ash Tray, Small 20.00
#2350 Baker, Oval
    9" 35.00
    10½" 45.00
#2350 Bouillon.................................15.00
#2267 Bowl, Low Foot 7" 35.00
#2297 Bowl, Deep, Flared 12" 37.00
#2315 Bowl, Footed, Flared 10½" 27.00
#2324 Bowl, Footed 10" 24.00
#2350 Butter, Covered 170.00
#2350½ Bouillon, Footed*................18.00
#2324 Candlestick
    2" ....pair 30.00
    4" ....pair 40.00
    9" ....pair 100.00
#2250 Candy Jar, Covered ½ lb. 90.00
#2331 Candy Box, Covered................105.00
#2350 Celery 23.00
#2329 Centerpiece
    11" 30.00
    13" 45.00
#2371 Centerpiece, Oval..................40.00
#2350 Cereal 6" 20.00
#2368 Cheese.................................20.00
#2368 Cheese and Cracker Plate 21.00
#5093 Cocktail...............................16.00
#2327 Comport 7" 38.00
#2350 Comport 8" 42.00
#5093 Cordial 65.00
#2315½ Cream 18.00
#2350½ Cream 20.00
#2350 Cream Soup............................18.00
#2350½ Cream Soup*.........................18.00
#2350 Cream Soup Plate 10.00
#2350 Cup, After Dinner 26.00
#2350 Cup, Coffee 18.00
#2350½ Cup, Tea 18.00
#2350 Egg Cup*...............................24.00

#869 Finger Bowl 18.00
#2350 Fruit 5" 13.00
#5093 Goblet 22.00
#2315 Grapefruit (Mayonnaise) 55.00
#5082½ Grapefruit 70.00
#945½ Grapefruit Liner 40.00
#2378 Ice Bucket, Nickel Plate Handle 80.00
#2378 Ice Bucket, Nickel Plate Handle, Drainer,
    Tongs ....set 120.00
#5000 Jug 7, Footed* 300.00
#5100 Jug 7, Footed..........................340.00
#2350 Nappy
    8" 24.00
    9" 24.00
#5000 Oyster Cocktail*......................18.00
#5100 Oyster Cocktail 18.00
#5093 Parfait 22.00
#2350 Pickle Dish 20.00
#2321 Plate 8" 15.00
#2383 Plate 6" 12.00
#2350 Plate
    6" Bread & Butter 12.00
    7" Salad 15.00
    8" Salad 18.00
    9" Dinner 30.00
    10" Dinner 55.00
    13" Chop 32.00
    15" Round 60.00
#2350 Platter, Oval
    10½" 35.00
    12" 50.00
    15" 72.00
#2350 Salad Bowl 30.00
#2350 Sauce Boat 82.00
#2350 Sauce Boat Plate 30.00
#2350 Saucer..................................10.00
#2350 Saucer, After Dinner 14.00
#5100 Shaker, Footed........................85.00
#5093 Sherbet
    Low 18.00

☞ VESPER Plate Etching #275 cont. ☜

High 22.00
#2350 Soup 7" 21.00
#2315 Sugar 24.00
#2350½ Sugar 18.00
#2350½ Sugar, Covered 70.00
#2287 Tray, Handled, Lunch 11" 65.00
#5100 Tumbler, Footed*
  2½ oz.* 24.00
  5 oz.* 18.00
  9 oz.* 20.00

12 oz.* 24.00
#5100 Tumbler, Footed
  2 oz. 24.00
  5 oz. 18.00
  9 oz. 19.00
  12 oz. 24.00
#2324 Urn, Small............................90.00
#2296 Vanity Set 130.00
#2292 Vase 8" 80.00
#5093 Wine 28.00

☞ VICTORIA Plate Etching #289 ☜

Decoration #71
Mother of Pearl
1927 – 1930

SEE PARADISE
ADD 10% FOR VICTORIA ITEMS

☞ VICTORY Deep Plate Etching #257 ☜

Optic Pattern
Crystal
1922 – 1929

#766 Almond 5.00
#880 Bon Bon 4½" 6.00
#2219 Candy Jar, Covered
  ¼ lb. 16.00
  ½ lb. 22.00
#2250 Candy Jar, Covered
  ¼ lb. 18.00
  ½ lb. 24.00
  1 lb. 30.00
#1697 Carafe 16.00
#1697 Carafe Tumbler 6 oz. 10.00
#766 Champagne, Saucer 5 oz. 8.00
#852 Champagne, Saucer 8.00
#766 Claret 4½ oz. 8.00
#766 Cocktail 3 oz.........................8.00
#803 Comport
  5 oz. 6.00
  6 oz. 6.00
#803 Comport, Covered 12.00
#1480 Cream 10.00
#766 Finger Bowl 8.00
#766 Finger Bowl Plate 6"..............6.00
#766 Fruit, Footed 4½ oz.................7.00

#766 Goblet
  7 oz. 8.00
  9 oz. 8.00
#766 Grapefruit 12.00
#945½ Grapefruit 10.00
#766 Grapefruit Liner....................6.00
#4057 Grapefruit Liner..................10.00
#566 Ice Tea, Footed, Handled 14.00
#825 Jelly, Covered 14.00
#300 Jug 7....................................16.00
#303 Jug 7....................................16.00
#318 Jug 7....................................16.00

⇒ VICTORY Deep Plate Etching #257 cont. ⇐

#2100 Jug 7..16.00
#1968 Marmalade, Covered 22.00
#2138 Mayonnaise
    Bowl...18.00
    Plate..14.00
    Ladle 20.00
#1838 Mustard, Covered 24.00
#803 Nappy, Footed
    5"..5.00
    6"..5.00
    7"..5.00
#803 Nappy, Footed, Covered 5"...12.00
#1465 Oil, Cut Neck
    5 oz. 15.00
    7 oz. 22.00
#837 Oyster Cocktail 4½ oz..........7.00
#766½ Parfait 6 oz............................7.00
#2238 Plate
    8¼"..8.00
    11"..14.00

#1848 Plate, Sandwich 9"..................12.00
#2083 Salad Dressing Bottle 40.00
#766 Sherbet 7.00
#1480 Sugar 12.00
#858 Sweetmeat...10.00
#2194 Syrup, Nickel Top
    8 oz. 20.00
    12 oz. 32.00
#2100 Tankard #7 ....30.00
#820 Tumbler, Table 6.00
#4011½ Tumbler, Table 8.00
#701 Tumbler 14 oz. 12.00
#4011 Tumbler
    5 oz. 8.00
    8 oz. 8.00
    12 oz. 10.00
#4011 Tumbler, Handled 12 oz. 15.00
#701 Tumbler Plate 5" 6.00
#766 Wine 2¾ oz 8.00

⇒ VINTAGE (Vine and Grapes) Deep Etching #204 ⇐

Blown Ware
Crystal
1904 – 1928

#863 Almond 8.00
#863 Almond, Individual 6.00
#837 Brandy 1 oz. 10.00
#858 Brandy 1 oz. 10.00
#863 Brandy 1 oz. 10.00
#1163 Catsup, Cut Stopper 35.00
#822 Cafe Parfait 8.00
#791 Champagne, Hollow Stem, Cut
    Flute..10.00
#792 Champagne, Hollow Stem 10.00
#793 Champagne, Hollow Stem 10.00
#837 Champagne, Tall 5½ oz....................10.00
#837 Champagne, Saucer 7oz. 8.00
#858 Champagne, Long Stem.....................10.00
#858 Champagne, Long Stem C.R. 10.00
#858 Champagne, Hollow Stem, Cut Flute ..10.00
#858 Champagne, Saucer
    5½ oz..8.00
    7 oz..8.00
#863 Champagne, Saucer 5½ oz. 8.00
#863 Champagne, Tall 5½ oz.....................10.00
#863 Champagne, Cut Flute.....................10.00

#932 Champagne 10.00
#837 Claret
    4½ oz...8.00
    6½ oz...8.00
#858 Claret
    4½ oz...8.00
    6½ oz...8.00
#863 Claret, 4½ oz. 8.00
#837 Cocktail 4 oz..................................8.00
#858 Cocktail 3½ oz. 8.00

#863 Cocktail 3½ oz. 8.00
#952 Cocktail...8.00
#803 Comport, Footed
     5" 10.00
     6" 10.00
#858 Cordial, 1 oz. 10.00
#863 Cordial, 1 oz. 10.00
#1061 Cracker Jar, Covered, Optic 45.00
#1227 Cream 8.00
#1478 Cream 8.00
#1480 Cream 8.00
#1480 Cream, Cut Beaded Top 10.00
#1720 Cream 8.00
#1759 Cream 8.00
#1931 Cream, Covered 12.00
#837 Creme de Menthe 2½ oz. 9.00
#858 Creme de Menthe 2½ oz. 9.00
#863 Creme de Menthe 2½ oz. 9.00
#480 Custard 7.00
#481 Custard 7.00
#482 Custard 7.00
#858 Custard 7.00
#1227 Custard 7.00
#1229 Custard 7.00
#1230 Custard 7.00
#1231 Custard 7.00
#200 Custard Plate 4.00
#858 Custard 7.00
#858 Custard Plate 4.00
#300 Decanter, Cut Neck, Cut Stopper
     Pint 33.00
     Quart 38.00
#1195 Decanter, Cut Neck
     Small 32.00
     Medium 33.00
     Large 35.00
#1464 Decanter, Cut Neck, Cut Flute
     10 oz. 35.00
     18 oz. 35.00
#1464 Decanter, Cut Foot, Cut Neck
     10 oz. 35.00
     18 oz. 35.00
#1491 Decanter, Cut Neck, Cut Stopper, Optic
     25 oz. 38.00
#1483 Decanter, Individual 20.00
#1483 Decanter, Individual, Cut Neck 25.00
#858 Fruit Salad 10.00
#315 Finger Bowl 7.00
#858 Finger Bowl 7.00
#858 Finger Bowl Plate..........................4.00
#1349 Finger Bowl 7.00
#1349 Finger Bowl Plate 4.00

#1499 Finger Bowl 7.00
#1499 Finger Bowl Plate 4.00
#823 Fruit
     4" 7.00
     5" 8.00
#863 Fruit 8.00
#826 Goblet
     7 oz. 8.00
     9 oz. 8.00
#837 Goblet 9 oz. 8.00
#837½ Goblet
     8 oz. 8.00
     10 oz. 10.00
#858 Goblet
     9 oz. 9.00
     10 oz. 10.00
     11 oz. 10.00
#863 Goblet
     7 oz. 8.00
     9 oz. 9.00
     10½ oz. 10.00
#945 Grapefruit 8.00
#945½ Grapefruit 8.00
#945½ Grapefruit Liner 7.00
#1132 Horseradish.................................18.00
#858 Ice Cream 4½" 7.00
#1281 Ice Cream 5" 8.00
#701 Ice Tea 14 oz.................................12.00
#200 Ice Tea Plate 4.00
#303 Jug 7..38.00
#318 Jug 7, Optic...................................40.00
#1236 Jug 6...35.00
#1733 Marmalade, Covered 22.00
#403 Mustard, Covered 20.00
#1831 Mustard, Covered 20.00
#315 Nappy
     4" 6.00
     4½" 6.00
     5" 6.00
     6" 6.00
     7" 7.00
     8" 8.00
     9" 10.00
     10" 15.00
#803 Nappy, Footed, Shallow
     5" 6.00
     6" 6.00
     7" 7.00
     8" 8.00
#803 Nappy, Footed, Deep
     4½" 8.00
     7" 10.00

#1227 Nappy
  4½"..6.00
  8"..8.00
#300½ Oil, Cut Stopper
  Small 30.00
  Large 35.00
#312 Oil, Cut Stopper, Cut Neck...............40.00
#1464 Oil, Cut Stopper.........................35.00
#1465 Oil, Cut Neck, Cut Stopper, Cut Star
  Bottom 40.00
#858 Oyster Cocktail 8.00
#1389 Oyster Cocktail 8.00
#1542 Oyster Cocktail 8.00
#5039 Oyster Cocktail 8.00
#5039 Liner.................................... 7.00
#863 Parfait 8.00
#932 Plate 6"...................................6.00
#897 Plate 7"...................................7.00
#863 Pousse-Cafe ¾ oz. 10.00
#1227 Punch Bowl and Foot.....................85.00
#863 Rhine Wine 4½ oz. 8.00
#863 Roemer
  4 oz. 8.00
  5 oz. 8.00
#1165 Shaker, Silver-Plated Top...............12.00
#837 Sherbet 8.00
#840 Sherbet 8.00
#840 Sherbet, Handled.........................10.00
#840 Sherbet Plate.............................4.00
#842 Sherbet 8.00
#858 Sherbet 8.00
#837 Sherry 2 oz. 10.00
#846 Sherry 2 oz. 10.00
#858 Sherry 2 oz. 10.00
#863 Sherry 2 oz. 10.00
#1227 Sugar, Covered 10.00
#1478 Sugar, 2-handled 10.00
#1480 Sugar, 2-handled 10.00
#1480 Sugar, 2-handled, Cut Beaded
  Top 12.00
#1720 Sugar 8.00
#1759 Sugar 8.00
#1931 Sugar, Covered 10.00
#858 Sweetmeat...............................10.00
#300 Tankard
  1...22.00
  2...22.00
  3...23.00
  3½...23.00
  4...23.00
  5...26.00
  6...26.00

  7...30.00
#300 Tankard, Claret 30.00
#300 Tankard, Cut Flute 35.00
#724 Tankard
  6...26.00
  7...30.00
#1761 Tankard.................................30.00
#922 Toothpick 20.00
#858 Tumbler, Table 6.00
#820 Tumbler 6.00
#833 Tumbler
  7 oz..6.00
  8 oz..6.00
  10 oz...8.00
#837 Tumbler, Optic
  3 oz..5.00
  5 oz..6.00
  9 oz..8.00
#837½ Tumbler, Footed 10.00
#858 Tumbler
  3½ oz..5.00
  5 oz..6.00
  6½ oz..6.00
  8 oz..8.00
  10 oz...8.00
  12 oz..10.00
  14 oz..10.00
  16 oz..10.00
#858 Tumbler, Handled
  8 oz...15.00
  10 oz..18.00
#887 Tumbler 3 oz. 7.00
#889 Tumbler
  5 oz..6.00
  8 oz..8.00
#923 Tumbler, Handled 10.00
#858 Tumbler Plate 4.00
#725 Vase
  6"..15.00
  8"..18.00
  10"..30.00
  12"..32.00
#1558 Water Bottle, Cut Neck.................35.00
#160½ Water Bottle, Cut Neck 35.00
#858 Whiskey, Hot 4 oz.........................10.00
#837 Wine 3½ oz...............................8.00
#847 Wine 8.00
#858 Wine
  2¾ oz..8.00
  3½ oz..8.00
#863 Wine, 3 oz................................8.00

⚔ VIRGINIA Deep Plate Etching #267 ⚔

Blown Ware
Crystal
1923 – 1929

#1697 Bedroom Set (Carafe,
    Tumbler)..30.00
#880 Bon Bon 14.00
#2250 Candy Jar, Covered
    ¼ lb. 15.00
    ½ lb. 22.00
    1 lb. 28.00
#1697 Carafe 16.00
#4023 Carafe Tumbler 8.00
#2275 Candlestick 9½" ....pair 70.00
#661 Champagne, Saucer 6 oz. 10.00
#661 Claret 5½ oz. 12.00
#661 Cocktail 3 oz....................................10.00
#2241 Cologne, Drip Stopper 40.00
#5078 Compote
    5" 5.00
    6" 5.00
#5078 Compote, Covered
    5" 8.00
    6" 12.00
#2267 Console Bowl 9"...........................24.00
#661 Cordial ¾ oz. 15.00
#2133 Cream 12.00
#300 Decanter, Cut Neck, quart 26.00
#1769 Finger Bowl 5.00
#1769 Finger Bowl Plate 6"......................5.00
#661 Fruit, Footed 6 oz. 10.00
#661 Goblet 9 oz. 12.00
#945½ Grapefruit 15.00
#845½ Grapefruit Liner 12.00
#825 Jelly, Footed 12.00
#825 Jelly, Footed, Covered 18.00
#300 Jug 7...18.00
#303 Jug 18.00
    3...18.00
    7...18.00
#318 Jug 7...18.00
#1852 Jug 6 ....18.00
#2270 Jug 18.00
#2270 Jug, Plain Covered........................26.00
#4095 Jug 7, Footed...............................24.00
#4089 Marmalade, Covered 24.00
#2138 Mayonnaise
    Bowl 20.00
    Plate 18.00

Ladle 20.00
#1769 Mayonnaise Set (3 Piece) 40.00
#2138 Mayonnaise Set (3 Piece) 50.00
#1831 Mustard, Covered
#5078 Nappy, Covered
    5" 5.00
    6" 5.00
    7" 8.00
    8" 10.00
#5078 Nappy, Footed
    5" 5.00
    6" 5.00
    7" 8.00
    8" 10.00
#1465 Oil, Cut Neck
    5 oz. 16.00
    7 oz. 20.00
#837 Oyster Cocktail 8.00
#661 Parfait 5½ oz. 10.00
#2283 Plate
    5" 6.00
    6" 8.00
    7" 10.00
    8" 15.00
    11" Star Center..................................18.00
#2283 Plate, Sandwich 9"........................14.00
#2238 Plate, Sherbet 5" 8.00
#2083 Salad Dressing Bottle 80.00
#2235 Shaker, Glass Top....................pair 50.00
#2235 Shaker, Pearl Top ....pair 65.00
#2133 Sugar 16.00
#2194 Syrup 8 oz. 20.00
#880 Sweetmeat.....................................16.00
#4085 Tumbler, Table 8.00
#4085 Tumbler
    2½ oz..8.00
    6 oz. 6.00
    13 oz. 12.00
#869 Tumbler, Handled 12 oz. 16.00
#4085 Tumbler, Handled 13 oz. 18.00
#4095 Tumbler, Footed
    2½ oz..8.00
    5 oz. 6.00
    10 oz. 8.00
    13 oz. 12.00
#4055 Vase D...30.00
#661 Wine 2 oz. 12.00

WAKEFIELD Cutting #820

**Rock Crystal
Crystal
1942 – 1972**

#6023 Candlestick, Duo Cut #807 ....40.00
#6023/8 Champagne/High Sherbet 6 oz.
    4⅞".................16.00
#6023/27 Claret/Wine 4 oz. 4¾" 20.00
#6023/21 Cocktail 3¾ oz. 4⅜" 15.00
#6023/29 Cordial 1 oz. 3⅜" 30.00
#4185/495 Dessert/Finger Bowl 10.00
#766 Finger Bowl 10.00
#6023/2 Goblet 9 oz. 6⅜".......................20.00
#6011 Jug, Footed 90.00
#6023/88 Juice, Footed 5 oz. 4½" 12.00
#2364 Lily Pond Cut #807 12" 25.00
#6023/63 Luncheon Goblet/Ice Tea 12 oz.
    5¾".................18.00
#6023/33 Oyster Cocktail 4 oz. 3⅝" 10.00

#2337 Plate
    6" 8.00
    7" 10.00
    8" 12.00
#6023/11 Sherbet, Low 6 oz. 4⅛".............12.00
#2567 Vase, Cut #807 7½" 55.00

WARWICK Cutting #198

**Regular Optic
Rock Crystal
Crystal
1929 – 1933**

#2394 Bowl 12" 30.00
#2430 Bowl 11" 30.00
#2394 Candlestick 2" ....pair 36.00
#2430 Candy Jar, Covered ½ lb. 20.00
#890 Claret 12.00
#890 Cocktail..8.00
#890 Cordial 20.00
#2350½ Cream, Footed...........................16.00
#2350½ Cream Soup 20.00
#2350 Cream Soup Plate 10.00
#2400 Comport
    6"...20.00
    8"...25.00
#890 Finger Bowl 6.00
#890 Goblet 12.00
#2375 Ice Bucket 35.00
#2430 Jelly 7" 18.00
#2430 Mint Dish 5½" 12.00
#890 Oyster Cocktail 10.00
#2350 Plate 10" 30.00
#2383 Plate
    6" 8.00

    7" 10.00
    8" 12.00
    13" 20.00
#2419 Plate, Square
    6" 8.00
    7" 10.00

8" 15.00	5 oz. 8.00
#890 Sherbet	9 oz. 8.00
High 10.00	12 oz. 10.00
Low 8.00	#2417 Vase 8" 40.00
#2350½ Sugar, Footed 15.00	#2430 Vase 8" 40.00
#2375 Tray, Lunch, Handled 20.00	#4105 Vase 8" 40.00
#890 Tumbler, Footed	#890 Wine 15.00
2½ oz. 8.00	

☞ WASHINGTON Deep Plate Etching #266 ☜

Crystal
1923 – 1929

#1697 Bedroom Set (Tumbler, Carafe) 35.00
#766 Bon Bon, Footed 8.00
#2250 Candy Jar, Covered
   ¼ lb. 22.00
   ½ lb. 25.00
   1 lb. 30.00
#2275 Candlestick 9½" ....pair 50.00
#1697 Carafe 25.00
#4023 Carafe Tumbler 10.00
#660 Champagne, Saucer 7.00
#660 Claret 7.00
#2267 Console Bowl 9" 25.00
#660 Cocktail................................7.00
#5078 Compote
   5" 18.00
   6" 20.00
#5078 Compote, Covered
   5" 25.00
   6" 25.00
#660 Cordial 20.00
#1851 Cream 10.00
#481 Custard................................6.00
#300 Decanter, Cut Neck, quart 45.00
#766 Finger Bowl 6.00
#1736 Finger Bowl Plate.....................4.00
#660 Fruit 10.00
#660 Goblet 7.00
#945½ Grapefruit 15.00
#945½ Grapefruit Liner 8.00
#889 Ice Tea 13 oz. 10.00
#825 Jelly 18.00
#825 Jelly, Covered 20.00
#303 Jug 7................................40.00
#318 Jug 7
   3½ 35.00

7...40.00
#2270 Jug 42.00
#2270 Jug, Covered 45.00
#4089 Marmalade, Covered 22.00
#2138 Mayonnaise
   Bowl................................15.00
   Plate................................5.00
   Ladle 20.00
#766 Mayonnaise
   Bowl................................14.00
   Plate................................6.00
   Ladle 20.00
#832 Mustard, Covered 18.00
#5078 Nappy
   5" 6.00
   6" 6.00
   7" 10.00
   8" 12.00
#5078 Nappy, Covered
   5" 10.00
   6" 12.00
   7" 16.00

☞ WASHINGTON Deep Plate Etching #266 cont. ☜

8" 18.00

#1465 Oil, Cut Neck, Cut Stopper
    5 oz. 45.00
    7 oz. 45.00

#837 Oyster Cocktail 7.00

#660 Parfait 7.00

#2283 Plate
    7" 8.00
    8" 10.00

#2283 Plate, Sherbet 5" 4.00

#2283 Plate
    6" 8.00
    9" 12.00
    11" Cut Star Center 15.00

#2083 Salad Dressing Bottle 35.00

#2235 Shaker, Glass Top..................pair 24.00

#2235 Shaker, Pearl Top ....pair 26.00

#1851 Sugar, 2-handled 12.00

#2194 Syrup, Nickel Top 8 oz. 40.00

#766 Sweetmeat 10.00

#300 Tankard 7 ....45.00

#4076 Tumbler, Table 7.00

#869 Tumbler
    5 oz. 7.00
    12 oz. 7.00

#887 Tumbler, 2½ oz. 7.00

#889 Tumbler
    5 oz. 7.00
    8 oz. 7.00
    13 oz. 8.00

#4095 Tumbler, Footed
    2½ oz. 7.00
    5 oz. 7.00
    10 oz. 7.00
    13 oz. 8.00

#660 Wine 10.00

☞ WATERBURY Cutting #712 ☜

Rock Crystal
Crystal
1933 – 1944

#2424 Bowl 8" 25.00

#6000 Champagne, Saucer/High Sherbet
    6 oz. 10.00

#6000 Cocktail 3½ oz. 8.00

#869 Finger Bowl 8.00

#2283 Finger Bowl Plate............................5.00

#6000 Goblet 10 oz. 12.00

#2451 Ice Dish 10.00

#2451 Ice Dish Plate 5.00

#2453 Lustre 7½" 25.00

#6000 Oyster Cocktail 4 oz. 8.00

#2283 Plate
    7" 8.00
    8" 10.00

#6000 Sherbet, Low 6 oz. 8.00

#6000 Tumbler, Footed
    5 oz. 8.00
    12 oz. 10.00

#6000 Wine 3 oz. 8.00

☞ WATERCRESS Cutting #741 ☜

Rock Crystal
Crystal
1934 – 1944

A modernistic treatment with orbs reflecting
light. A departure from floral cuttings.

#2470½ Bowl 10½" 30.00

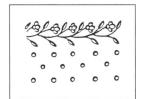

⟿ WATERCRESS Cutting #741 cont. ⟸

#4024 Bowl, Footed 10" 40.00
#6012 Brandy 1 oz. 28.00
#4024 Candlestick 6" ....pair 30.00
#2472 Candlestick, Duo ....pair 40.00
#2496 Candlestick, Trindle ....pair 60.00
#4117 Candy Jar, Covered, Bubble
    Style ....pair 20.00
#863 Champagne, Hollow Stem, Cut Flute
    5 oz. 15.00
#6012 Champagne, Saucer 5½ oz. 20.00
#6012 Claret 4½ oz. 25.00
#6012 Cocktail 3 oz. 20.00
#2524 Cocktail Mixer 30.00
#2525 Cocktail Shaker 42 oz. 35.00
#2525½ Cocktail Shaker 30 oz. 30.00
#2400 Comport 6" 20.00
#6012 Cordial 1 oz. 30.00
#2350½ Cream, Footed............................15.00
#6012 Creme de Menthe 2 oz. 20.00
#2525 Decanter 30.00
#6011 Decanter, Footed 70.00
#1769 Finger Bowl 8.00
#6012 Goblet 10 oz. 22.00
#6011 Jug, Footed 50.00
#2440 Lemon Dish, Handled 5" 15.00
#2440 Mayonnaise, 2 part 18.00
#1185 Old Fashioned Cocktail, Sham..........8.00

#6012 Oyster Cocktail 4 oz. 12.00
#2337 Plate
    6" 6.00
    7" 7.00
    8" 8.00
#2364 Plate 16" 40.00
#2440 Relish
    2 part 20.00
    3 part 25.00
#6012 Rhine Wine 4½ oz. 25.00
#6012 Sherbet, Low 5½ oz.........................16.00
#6012 Sherry 2 oz. 20.00
#2350½ Sugar, Footed 16.00
#2440 Sweetmeat, Handled 4½" 10.00
#2440 Torte Plate 13" 30.00
#2440 Tray, Oval 8½" 30.00
#701 Tumbler, Sham
    10 oz. 6.00
    12 oz. 6.00
#6012 Tumbler, Footed
    5 oz. 8.00
    10 oz. 10.00
    13 oz. 12.00
#2470 Vase 10" 35.00
#4122 Whiskey, Sham 1½ oz. 6.00
#6012 Wine 3 oz. 25.00

⟿ WATERFOWL Carving #1 ⟸

Crystal
1938 – 1944

#2550 Ash Tray, Round (Swan) 12.00
#2391 Cigarette Box, Covered (Swan) 30.00
#4132 Decanter (Gull) 40.00
#4132 Ice Bowl (Goose)............................35.00
#4132 Old Fashioned Cocktail (Goose) 12.00
#2337 Plate (Swan) 7"..............................10.00
#4132½ Scotch & Soda (Duck) 9 oz. 12.00
#4132 Tumbler, (Duck) 5 oz......................12.00
#4132 Tumbler, (Swan) 9 oz. 12.00
#4132 Tumbler, (Crane) 12 oz. 14.00
#4132 Tumbler, (Crane) 14 oz. 16.00
#4132 Whiskey (Gull) 1½ oz. 10.00

☜ WEDDING FLOWER Cutting #920 ☞

Combination Silver Mist and Gray Cutting
Crystal
1969 – 1970

#6102/31 Brandy 3 oz. 27.00
#6102/25 Claret 7½ oz. 27.00
#6102/2 Goblet 11½ oz. 30.00

#6102/63 Luncheon Goblet/Ice Tea
   14 oz. 28.00
#2337 Plate
   7" 10.00
   8" 10.00
#6102/11 Sherbet 8 oz. 25.00
#6102/26 Tulip Wine 5½ oz. 30.00

☜ WELLINGTON Cutting #722 ☞

Regular Optic
Rock Crystal
Crystal
1933 – 1943

Cut Bowl, Cut Stem. See LEICESTER.

#2470½ Bowl 10½" 30.00
#2470½ Candlestick 5½" ....pair 45.00
#6010 Champagne, Saucer/High Sherbet
   5½ oz. 18.00
#6010 Claret/Wine 4¼ oz. 25.00
#6010 Cocktail 4 oz. 18.00
#2400 Comport 6" 20.00
#6010 Cordial 1 oz. 30.00
#869 Finger Bowl 8.00
#6010 Goblet 9 oz. 22.00
#6010 Oyster Cocktail 5½ oz. 12.00
#2337 Plate
   6" 6.00
   7" 8.00
   8" 10.00
#6010 Sherbet, Low 5½ oz......................16.00
#2440 Torte Plate 13" 40.00

#6010 Tumbler, Footed
   5 oz. 12.00
   9 oz. 12.00
   12 oz. 20.00
#2470 Vase 10" 50.00
#4110 Vase 7½" 40.00

☜ WENTWORTH Cutting #802 ☞

Rock Crystal
Crystal
1940 – 1944

#2574 Bowl, Handled 9½" 40.00
#2574 Candlestick, Duo ....pair 60.00
#6023 Champagne, Saucer 6 oz. 16.00
#6023 Claret/Wine 4 oz...........................20.00
#6023 Cocktail 3¾ oz. 16.00

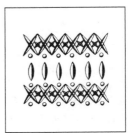

WENTWORTH Cutting #802 cont.

#6023 Comport 5" 20.00
#6023 Cordial 1 oz. 26.00
#766 Finger Bowl 12.00
#6023 Goblet 9 oz. 18.00
#6011 Jug, Footed 100.00

#6023 Oyster Cocktail 4 oz. 10.00
#2337 Plate
   7" 10.00
   8" 12.00
#6023 Sherbet, Low 6 oz. 12.00

WESTMINSTER Cutting #723

Rock Crystal
Crystal
1933 – 1939
   Do not confuse with WESTMINSTER Design
   Cutting #872, Cut Bowl and Stem.

#2470½ Bowl 10½" 30.00
#2470½ Candlestick 5½" ....pair 45.00
#6010 Claret/Wine 4½ oz. 25.00
#6010 Cocktail 4 oz..............................18.00
#2400 Comport 6" 20.00
#6010 Cordial 1 oz. 30.00
#869 Finger Bowl 8.00
#6010 Goblet 9 oz. 22.00
#6010 Oyster Cocktail 5½ oz. 12.00
#2337 Plate
   6" 6.00
   7" 8.00
   8" 10.00

#6010 Sherbet
   High 5½ oz.......................................18.00
   Low 5½ oz. 16.00
#6010 Tumbler, Footed
   5 oz. 20.00
   9 oz. 12.00
   12 oz. 12.00
#2470 Vase 10" 50.00

WESTMINSTER Cutting #872

Rock Crystal
Crystal
1959 – 1972
   Do not confuse with WESTMINSTER Cut-
   ting #723.

#6083/27 Cocktail/Wine 3¾ oz. 4⁹⁄₁₆" 24.00
#6083/29 Cordial 1¼ oz. 3⁵⁄₁₆" 28.00
#4185/495 Dessert/Finger Bowl 12.00
#6083/2 Goblet 11½ oz. 6¼" 24.00
#6083/88 Juice, Footed 5½ oz. 4¾" 16.00
#6083/63 Luncheon Goblet/Ice Tea 14 oz.
   6¼"..24.00

#2337 Plate
   7" 10.00
   8" 10.00
#6083/11 Sherbet 7¾ oz. 4¾" 18.00

☞ WEYLIN Cutting #759 ☜

Optic Pattern
Crystal
1936 – 1939

#2470½ Bowl 10½" 50.00
#2472 Candlestick, Duo ....pair 40.00
#6014 Champagne, Saucer 5½" 20.00
#6014 Claret 4 oz. 26.00
#6014 Cocktail 3½ oz. 20.00
#2400 Comport 6" 20.00
#6014 Cordial 1 oz. 30.00
#869 Finger Bowl 12.00
#6014 Goblet 9 oz. 22.00
#2375 Ice Bucket 30.00
#2451 Ice Dish 25.00
#2451 Ice Dish Plate............................20.00
#5000 Jug, Footed 100.00
#6014 Oyster Cocktail 4 oz. 12.00
#2337 Plate
    6" 8.00
    7" 10.00

    8" 15.00
#6014 Sherbet, Low 5½ oz.........................12.00
#6014 Tumbler, Footed
    5 oz. 10.00
    9 oz. 12.00
    12 oz. 16.00
#2470 Vase 10" 50.00
#4121 Vase 5" 40.00
#4128 Vase 5" 40.00
#6014 Wine 3 oz. 25.00

☞ WHEAT Cutting #760 ☜

Crystal
1936 – 1940
  Do not confuse with FOSTORIA WHEAT
Design, Cutting #837.

#2496 Bon Bon, 2 Toed 18.00
#2496 Bowl, Handled 10½".......................35.00
#2496 Bowl, Flared 12" 45.00
#2545 Bowl, "Flame", Oval 12½"..............50.00
#2440 Cake Plate 10" 30.00
#2496 Cake Plate, 2-handled 10" 25.00
#2496 Candy Box, Covered, 3 part 40.00
#2545 Candelabra, "Flame", 2 Light ..pair 60.00
#2545 Candlestick "Flame", Duo ....pair 70.00
#2496 Candlestick
    4" ....pair 40.00
    5½" ....pair 25.00
    Duo ....pair 70.00
    Trindle..............................pair 90.00
#2440 Celery Dish 11½" 18.00
#2496 Celery Dish 11" 16.00
#2496 Cheese & Cracker 30.00
#2496 Comport 5½" 16.00
#2496 Comport Tall 6½" 20.00
#2440 Cream, Footed 14.00

#2396 Cream, Individual 3⅛" 12.00
#2496 Floating Garden 10"......................40.00
#2375 Ice Bucket 40.00
#2496 Ice Bucket, Gold Handled 4⅜" 65.00
#2496 Jelly, Covered 22.00
#2496 Mayonnaise, 2 part 20.00
#2496½ Mayonnaise & Plate.....................24.00
#2496 Nut Bowl, 3 Toed 16.00
#2440 Pickle Dish 8½" 14.00
#2496 Pickle Dish 8" 12.00
#2419 Relish, 5 part................................35.00

✺ WHEAT Cutting #760 cont. ✺

#2496 Relish
  2 part 22.00
  3 part 30.00
  4 part 30.00
#2496 Sauce Dish, Oblong 22.00
#2496 Serving Dish, 2-handled, Deep
  8½" 25.00

#2440 Sugar, Footed 2⅞" 14.00
#2496 Sugar, Individual 12.00
#2496 Sweetmeat.................................10.00
#2496 Tid Bit, Flat, 3 Toed....................18.00
#2496 Torte Plate 14" 40.00
#2496 Tray, Oblong 40.00
#2470 Vase 10" 35.00

✺ WHIRLPOOL Cutting #730 ✺

Crystal
1934 – 1940

#4024 Bowl, Footed 10" 40.00
#6011 Brandy 1 oz. 22.00
#906 Brandy Inhaler 15.00
#4024 Candlestick 6" ....pair 30.00
#795 Champagne, Hollow Stem 5½ oz. 12.00
#863 Champagne, Hollow Stem, Cut Flute
  5 oz. 15.00
#6011 Champagne, Saucer 5½ oz. 14.00
#6011 Claret 4½ oz. 18.00
#6011 Cocktail 3 oz. 14.00
#2525 Cocktail Shaker, Gold Top 60.00
#6011 Cordial 1 oz. 22.00
#6011 Creme de Menthe 2 oz. 16.00
#6011 Decanter, Footed 70.00
#1769 Finger Bowl 8.00
#6011 Goblet 10 oz. 16.00
#6011 Jug, Footed 50.00
#1184 Old Fashioned Cocktail, Sham or Plain
  7 oz. 6.00
#6011 Oyster Cocktail 4 oz. 10.00
#2337 Plate
  6" 6.00
  7" 8.00

  8" 10.00
#6011 Rhine Wine 4½ oz. 18.00
#6011 Sherbet, Low 5½ oz.......................12.00
#6011 Sherry, 2 oz. 15.00
#701 Tumbler, Sham or Plain
  10 oz. 6.00
  12 oz. 6.00
#6011 Tumbler, Footed
  5 oz. 10.00
  10 oz. 8.00
  13 oz. 14.00
#887 Whiskey, Sham or Plain 1¾ oz. 6.00
#4122 Whiskey, Sham or Plain 1½ oz. 6.00
#6011 Whiskey, Footed 2 oz. 18.00
#6011 Wine 3 oz. 18.00

✺ WHISPER Cutting #875 ✺

Rock Crystal
Crystal
1960 – 1970

#6089/31 Brandy 1½ oz. 4¹⁄₁₆" 20.00
#6089/27 Cocktail/Wine 4½ oz. 5¼" 20.00

⌐ WHISPER Cutting #875 cont. ⌐

#4185/495 Dessert/Finger Bowl 12.00
#6089/2 Goblet 11½ oz. 6³⁄₁₆" 22.00
#6089/88 Juice, Footed 5 oz. 4¾" 18.00
#6089/63 Luncheon Goblet/Ice Tea 13 oz.
    6³⁄₁₆" 22.00

#2337 Plate
    7" 10.00
    8" 10.00
#6089/11 Sherbet 7 oz. 5⁵⁄₁₆" 18.00

⌐ WILDFLOWER Plate Etching #308 ⌐

Amber, Green
1931 – 1933

#2419 Bon Bon 15.00
#2433 Bowl, Oval 10" 40.00
#2433 Bowl 12" 45.00
#2419 Cake Plate 26.00
#2400 Candy Jar, Covered 60.00
#2433 Candlestick
    3" ....pair 35.00
    4" ....pair 45.00
#2447 Candlestick, Duo ....pair 50.00
#2375 Cheese & Cracker 50.00
#2400 Comport 6" 22.00
#2433 Comport
    High 6" 28.00
    Low 6" 18.00
#4020 Cream, Footed 16.00
#4020 Decanter, Footed 95.00

#2433 Ice Tub 6" 70.00
#2419 Jelly 26.00
#2419 Lemon Dish 24.00
#2419 Mayonnaise 22.00
#2364 Plate 16" 50.00
#2419 Relish, 4 part................................40.00
#2419 Syrup 35.00
#2419 Syrup, Plain Cover 30.00
#2419 Syrup Plate 12.00
#4107 Vase
    9" 100.00
    12" 120.00
    15" 150.00
#4108 Vase
    5" 60.00
    6" 70.00
    7" 80.00
#4020 Whiskey 2 oz. 14.00

⌐ WILDWOOD Cutting #854 ⌐

Rock Crystal
1957 – 1958

#6071 Cocktail/Wine/Seafood 4½ oz. 5"....20.00
#6071 Cordial 1 oz. 3¼" 21.00
#6071 Goblet 11½ oz. 20.00
#6071 Ice Tea, Footed 13 oz. 6" 15.00
#6071 Juice, Footed 5¼ oz. 4½" 12.00
#2337 Plate
    7" 10.00
    8" 12.00
#6071 Sherbet 7 oz. 4¾"............................16.00

 WILLIAMSBURG Cutting #874

Crystal
1960 – 1969

#6079/27 Claret/Wine 4 oz. 4⅞" 20.00
#6079/20 Cocktail 3½ oz. 3⅞" 15.00
#6079/29 Cordial 1 oz. 3⅜" 24.00
#6079/2 Goblet 11 oz. 6½" 18.00
#6079/88 Juice, Footed 5½ oz. 4¾" 13.00
#6079/63 Luncheon Goblet/Ice Tea 13½ oz.
   6¼" 18.00
#2337
   7" 10.00
   8" 10.00

#6079/11 Sherbet 6½ oz. 5" 15.00

WILLOW Etching #335

Crystal
1939 – 1945

WILLOW'S etching complemented the old favorite Willow patterned china dinnerware.

#2574 Bon Bon 14.00
#2574 Bowl, Handled 30.00
#2574 Bowl, Flared 12" 40.00
#6023 Bowl, Footed 35.00
#2574 Cake Plate 10" 26.00
#2324 Candlestick 6" ....pair 44.00
#2574 Candlestick 4" ....pair 36.00
#2574 Celery Bowl, 10½" 20.00
#6023 Champagne, Saucer 6 oz. 18.00
#6023 Claret/Wine 4 oz. 18.00
#6023 Cocktail 3¾ oz. 26.00
#2574 Comport 5" 15.00
#6023 Comport, Blown 5" 18.00
#6023 Cordial 1 oz. 26.00
#2574 Cream, Footed 4" 14.00
#2574 Cream, Individual 12.00
#2574 Cup, Footed 10.00
#766 Finger Bowl 8.00
#2574 Fruit Bowl 13" 45.00
#6023 Goblet 9 oz. 22.00
#2574 Ice Tub 40.00
#6011 Jug, Footed 8⅞" 60.00
#2574 Lemon Dish 14.00
#2574 Mayonnaise
   Bowl..16.00
   Plate 12.00
   Ladle 20.00

#2574 Oil, Ground Stopper 4¼ oz. 30.00
#2574 Olive Dish 6" 14.00
#2574 Oyster Cocktail 4 oz. 10.00
#2574 Pickle Dish 8" 18.00
#2574 Plate
   6" 10.00
   7" 14.00
   8" 20.00
   9" 25.00
#2574 Relish, 3 part..................................22.00
#2574 Saucer...8.00
#2574 Serving Dish 8½" 18.00
#2574 Shaker ....pair 35.00
#6023 Sherbet, Low 6 oz. 18.00
#2574 Sugar, Footed 16.00
#2574 Sugar, Individual 2⅞" 14.00
#2574 Sweetmeat......................................13.00
#2574 Torte Plate 14" 40.00
#6023 Tumbler, Footed
   5 oz. 12.00
   9 oz. 12.00
   12 oz. 18.00
#2574 Tray, Muffin, Handled 18.00

WILLOWMERE Plate Etching #333

Crystal
1938 – 1971

WILLOWMERE included in Patterns of the Past Program and Nostalgia Program

#2560 Bon Bon 30.00
#2560 Bon Bon 3 Toed 45.00
#2560 Bowl, Crimped 11½" 75.00
#2560 Bowl, Flared 12" 80.00
#2560/233 Bowl, Handled 11" 85.00
#2560/306 Cake Plate, Handled 11½" 60.00
#2560 Candlestick 4½" ....pair 100.00
#2506/332 Candlestick, Duo 5⅛" ....pair 150.00
#2560½ Candlestick 4" ....pair 80.00
#2560 Celery 11" 25.00
#2560 Cereal 6" 12.00
#6024/8 Champagne, Saucer 6 oz. 5⅝" 30.00
#6024/25 Claret 4 oz. 5¾" 55.00
#6024/21 Cocktail 3½ oz. 4¾" 35.00
#6024/29 Cordial 1 oz. 3¾" 65.00
#2560/681 Cream, Footed 7 oz. 4⅛"..........20.00
#2560 Cream, Individual 4 oz. 3¼" 15.00
#2560/396 Cup, Footed 10.00
#869 Finger Bowl 7.00
#2560 Fruit 5" 12.00
#2560 Fruit Bowl 13" 75.00
#6024/2 Goblet 10 oz. 7⅛".......................28.00
#2560 Ice Bucket. Chrome Handled/Tongs
    4⅞" 110.00
#5000 Jug, Footed, Optic, 3 pints 9¾" 300.00
#2560 Lemon Dish 14.00
#2560 Mayonnaise
    Bowl...16.00
    Plate...12.00
    Ladle 20.00
#2560 Mayonnaise, 2 part, 2 Ladles 60.00
#2560/726 Muffin Tray, Handled 10"........55.00
#2560 Olive Dish 6¾" 25.00
#2560 Oil, Footed, Stoppered 3 oz. 75.00
#6024/33 Oyster Cocktail 4 oz. 3½" 16.00
#2560 Pickle Dish 8¾" 35.00
#2666/454 Pitcher, quart......................300.00
#2560 Plate
    6" 12.00
    7" 15.00
    8" 25.00
    9" 40.00
#2560 Relish
    2 part 40.00
    3 part 75.00
    4 part 85.00

    5 part 85.00
#2560 Saucer...7.00
#2560 Salad Bowl 10" 85.00
#2560 Salad Bowl, 2 part 90.00
#2560 Server, Sani-Cut Top 45.00
#2560 Serving Dish, Handled 8½" 35.00
#2364/655 Shaker, Chrome Top ......pair 125.00
#2560 Shaker, Footed, Glass Top ...pair 140.00
#6024/11 Sherbet, Low 6 oz. 28.00
#2560/679 Sugar, Footed.........................30.00
#2560 Sugar, Individual 25.00
#2560 Sweetmeat.....................................40.00
#2560 Torte Plate 14"...............................90.00
#2560/697 Tray, Cream & Sugar
    7½" ....set 70.00
#2560/723 Tray, Lunch, Handled 11½" 85.00
#6024 Tumbler, Footed
    Juice 5 oz. 4⅝" 25.00
    Water 9 oz. 5¼".............................30.00
    Iced Tea 12 oz. 5¾" 35.00
#2276 Vanity Set 145.00
#2470 Vase 10" 90.00
#2567 Vase 7½" 60.00
#2568 Vase 9" 72.00
#2560 Vase, Handled 6" 45.00
#5100 Vase 10" 60.00
#2560 Whip Cream 50.00
#6024/26 Wine 3½ oz. 5⅜".......................40.00

WILLOWMERE items included in Patterns of the Past and Nostalgia Program

WI05/007 Champagne/High Dessert 6 oz.
    5⅝"...18.00
WI05/008 Champagne/Low Dessert 6 oz.
    4¼"...16.00
WI05/025 Claret 4 oz. 5¾" 30.00
WI05/002 Goblet 10 oz. 25.00
WI05/063 Luncheon Goblet/Ice Tea 12 oz.
    5¾"...32.00
WI05/026 Wine 3½ oz. 5⅜" 35.00

☜ WINDFALL Cutting #870 ☞

Rock Crystal
Crystal
1958 – 1963

#6060/29 Cordial 1 oz. 2⅞" 22.00
#6060/2 Goblet 10½ oz. 5⅞" 20.00
#6060/88 Juice 5½ oz. 4½" 16.00
#6060/63 Luncheon Goblet/Ice Tea 14 oz.
    6¼" 20.00
#6060 Plate
    7" 10.00
    8" 10.00

#6060/11 Sherbet 6½ oz. 4½" 16.00
#6060/27 Wine/Cocktail 5 oz. 4½" 20.00

☜ WOODLAND Plate Etching #264 ☞

Optic Pattern
Crystal
1922 – 1929

**Produced also as GOLDWOOD Plate Etching
#264 with Gold Band on Rim and Foot.**

#2219 Candy Jar, Covered
    ¼ lb. 22.00
    ½ lb. 25.00
    1 lb. 30.00
#1697 Carafe 23 oz. 30.00
#4023 Carafe Tumbler 6 oz. 11.00
#660 Champagne, Saucer.........................11.00
#660 Cocktail...11.00
#660 Cordial 18.00
#803 Comport
    5" 12.00
    6" 15.00
#1851 Cream 8.00
#300 Decanter, Cut Neck, quart 40.00
#766 Finger Bowl 6.00
#660 Fruit 8.00
#945½ Grapefruit 10.00
#945½ Grapefruit Liner 8.00
#1743 Grape Juice Jug, Covered 45.00
#660 Goblet 11.00
#825 Jelly 12.00
#825 Jelly, Covered 15.00
#303 Jug 7..35.00
#1743 Jug, Covered 45.00
#4089 Marmalade, Covered 18.00
#2138 Mayonnaise
    Bowl 10.00

    Plate 8.00
    Ladle 20.00
#1831 Mustard, Covered 15.00
#803 Nappy
    5" 6.00
    6" 6.00
    7" 8.00
#1465 Oil, Cut Neck
    5 oz. 35.00
    7 oz. 40.00
#837 Oyster Cocktail 11.00
#860 Parfait 11.00
#840 Plate, Sherbet 4.00
#1736 Plate 6" 5.00
#1897 Plate, Salad 7" 8.00
#2238 Plate
    8¼"..8.00
    11" 12.00
#2083 Salad Dressing Bottle 30.00
#2022 Shaker, Glass Top 12.00

WOODLAND Plate Etching #264 cont.

#1851 Sugar, 2-handled 10.00	5 oz. 11.00
#766 Sweetmeat...................................12.00	12 oz. 11.00
#2194 Syrup, Nickel Top 8 oz. 35.00	#4011½ Tumbler 11.00
#300 Tankard Cut Neck 65 oz. 40.00	#4011 Tumbler, Handled 12 oz. 11.00
#4095 Toothpick 18.00	#4095 Tumbler, Footed
#4076 Tumbler, Table 10 oz. 11.00	5 oz. 8.00
#889 Tumbler	10 oz. 13.00
5 oz. 11.00	13 oz. 14.00
14 oz. 15.00	#701 Tumbler Plate 4.00
#4011 Tumbler	#660 Wine 11.00
3 oz. 11.00	

YORK Cutting #709

Rock Crystal
Crystal
1933 – 1944

#2470 Bowl 12" 40.00	
#2470½ Bowl 10½"...................................30.00	
#2470 Cake Plate 10" 35.00	
#2470½ Candlestick 5½" ....pair 45.00	
#6007 Champagne, Saucer/High Sherbet	
5½ oz. 16.00	
#6007 Claret 4 oz. 23.00	
#6007 Cocktail 3½ oz. 16.00	
#2470 Comport, Tall 6" 25.00	
#6007 Cordial 1 oz. 27.00	
#869 Finger Bowl 8.00	
#2283 Finger Bowl Plate 6.00	
#6007 Goblet 10 oz. 18.00	
#2451 Ice Dish 15.00	
#2451 Ice Dish Plate..............................10.00	
#6007 Oyster Cocktail 4½ oz. 12.00	
#2283 Plate	
6" 8.00	

7" 10.00
8" 12.00
#6007 Sherbet, Low 5½ oz.......................10.00
#2440 Torte Plate 13" 40.00
#6007 Tumbler, Footed
2 oz. 18.00
5 oz. 10.00
9 oz. 10.00
12 oz. 16.00
#6007 Wine 3 oz. 23.00

Update Information

This section adds to the information presented in Volume I, *An Identification and Value Guide of Pressed, Blown, and Hand Molded Shapes*, published in 1994.

Included in this section are pictures and drawings of several of the important plain shapes listed in Volume I. Readers will find these shape numbers meaningful and helpful in their study as it is upon these plain shapes that the designs and decorations presented in this writing were used.

The design or pattern numbers are shown in each entry's heading. In instances where a number sequence is divided by a slash mark, the first set of numbers corresponds with the shape number found in Volume I. Numbers following the slash indicate the item number. Some early listings present only the shape number of an item, with no slash item number. Some very late lines, typified by the Nouveau listing, show only an item number in the listings.

To clarify: In the Chintz #338 listings on page 88, the first number given in the listings, #2496, indicates the shape (Baroque). The second number is the item number, #137, a bon bon. In the headings you will find the etching number exclusive to that design (#338, Chintz). All numbers

currently available have been included.

The American listings are those shown in Fostoria's 1962 catalog, the most complete listing available which identifies items with numbers. It departs from the alphabetical presentation used in Volume I, but it is believed that the item name, its number, and line drawing will be helpful with visual identification. The absence of item numbers in Volume I was confusing for readers and the writer apologizes for the omission.

Collectors should be aware that the list of American items changed over a long production time making it impossible to account for all rare or unlisted items. It is important, also, to remember that Lancaster Colony has produced items in the Whitehall pattern, an American look-alike, which do not appear in Fostoria lists.

Additional photographs are included which will help in your identification of the blank lines on which the patterned lines in this volume were used. It will be helpful to check the number of the shape, as explained above, and given the item number in the listings here, you will be able to verify the identity of the item you are researching.

AMERICAN PATTERN
No. 2056 Line
STEMWARE

				Retail Price Ea.
2056/2	10	oz.	Goblet (Hex. Foot) _____ Height 6⅞ in.	$2.00
2056/3	9	oz.	Low Goblet _____ Height 5½ in.	2.00
2056/5	4½	oz.	Footed Dessert, (Hex. Foot)____ Height 4¾ in.	2.00
2056/9	4½	oz.	High Sherbet, Flared_____ Height 4⅜ in.	2.00
2056½/10	4½	oz.	High Sherbet, Reg. _____ Height 4½ in.	2.00
2056/12	5	oz.	Low Sherbet, Flared _____ Height 3¼ in.	2.00
2056½/13	5	oz.	Low Sherbet, Reg. _____ Height 3½ in.	2.00
2056/16	6	oz.	Sundae _____ Height 3⅛ in.	2.00
2056/21	3	oz.	Footed Cocktail _____ Height 2⅞ in.	2.00
2056/22	6	oz.	Old Fashioned Cocktail _____ Height 3⅜ in.	1.75
2056/26	2½	oz.	Wine (Hex. Foot)_____ Height 4⅜ in.	2.00
2056/33	4½	oz.	Oyster Cocktail _____ Height 3½ in.	2.00
2056/63	12	oz.	Luncheon Goblet/Ice Tea_____ Height 5¾ in.	2.00
2056½/64	12	oz.	Ice Tea, Reg. _____ Height 5 in.	1.75
2056/65	12	oz.	Ice Tea, Flared _____ Height 5¼ in.	1.75
2056/72	9	oz.	Footed Tumbler _____ Height 4⅜ in.	2.00
2056½/76	8	oz.	Table Tumbler, Reg. _____ Height 3⅞ in.	1.75
2056/77	8	oz.	Table Tumbler, Flared _____ Height 4⅛ in.	1.75
2056/88	5	oz.	Footed Tumbler _____ Height 4¾ in.	2.00
2056½/89	5	oz.	Tumbler, Reg. _____ Height 3⅝ in.	1.65
2056/100	2	oz.	Whiskey _____ Height 2½ in.	1.25

BOWLS, CANDLESTICKS & CANDLE LAMPS

2056/162	6½	in.	Wedding Bowl & Cover _____ Height 8 in.	$9.75
2056/163	6½	in.	Wedding Bowl_____ Height 5¼ in.	6.25
2056/170	7	in.	Bowl, Cupped _____ Height 4½ in.	5.00
2056/188	8½	in.	Handled Bowl _____ Height 3¾ in.	4.75
2056/222	10½	in.	3-Toed Bowl _____ Height 3½ in.	4.75
2056/240	11½	in.	Rolled Edge Bowl_____ Height 2¾ in.	4.75
2056/241	11¾	in.	Oval Bowl _____ Height 2⅞ in. - Width 7½ in.	4.75
2056/250	12	in.	Footed Fruit Bowl _____ Height 7¼ in. - Cap. 1⅛ gal.	12.50
2056/251	12	in.	Lily Pond _____ Height 2¼ in.	4.75
2056/260	13	in.	Shallow Fruit Bowl _____ Height 3 in.	4.75
2056/310			Candle Lamp, complete _____ Height 8½ in. Consisting of: 1 Only 26/460 Candle Lamp Base 1 Only 26/461 Candle Lamp Chimney 1 Only 2056/314 3 in. Candlestick	7.00
2056/314	3	in.	Candlestick _____	3.00
2056/319	6	in.	Candlestick _____	3.75
2056½/331			Twin Candlestick _____ Height 4⅜ in. - With 8½ in.	6.25
2056/363	11	in.	3-Cornered Centerpiece _____ Height 3¾ in.	4.50
2056/416	10	in.	Floating Garden _____ Height 2¼ in.	3.50
2056/602	9½	in.	Centerpiece _____ Height 3⅝ in.	4.75
2056/611	11	in.	Centerpiece _____ Height 4⅜ in.	6.25

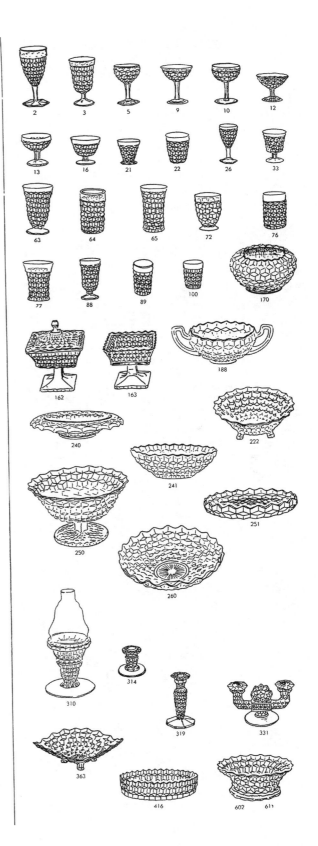

345

AMERICAN PATTERN (Cont.)
No. 2056 Line
DINNERWARE & OTHER ACCESSORIES

				Retail Price Ea.
2056/128	8½ in.	Small Boat		$2.25
2056/129	12 in.	Large Boat		2.75
2056/137		3-Toed Bon Bon		2.50
		Height 2 in. - Diam. 7 in.		
2056/211	10 in.	Salad Bowl		4.75
		Height 4⅜ in.		
2056/259		Shrimp and Dip		10.25
		Height 4¼ in. - Diam. 12¼ in.		
2056/987		Salad Fork and Spoon (Wood)		1.00
2056/286	10 in.	4 Pc. Salad Set		12.00
		Height 5 in.		
		Consisting of:		
		1 Only 2056/211 10 in. Salad Bowl		
		1 Only 2056/567 14 in. Torte Plate		
		1 Only 2056/987 Salad Fork & Spoon (Wood)		
2056/297		Butter & Cover		4.75
2056½/300		Oblong Butter & Cover		3.50
		Height 2⅛ in. - Width 3¼ in. - Length 7½ in.		
2056/306	10 in.	Handled Cake Plate		3.75
2056/307	12 in.	Footed Cake Plate		5.25
		Height 1⅞ in.		
2056/344		3-Part Candy Box & Cover		6.00
		Height 4 in. - Width 6⅛ in.		
2056/347		Footed Candy & Cover		4.25
		Height 7 in.		
2056/360	10 in.	Celery		3.25
		Height 1⅞ in.		
2056/362		Cookie Jar & Cover		7.00
		Height 8⅞ in. - Diam. 5¾ in.		
2056/369		Cheese & Cracker		7.50
		Height 4 in. - Diam. 11½ in.		
2056/370		Footed Cheese		3.00
		Height 3½ in. - Diam. 5¾ in.		
2056/371	11½ in.	Cracker Plate		4.50
2056/380		Coaster		1.10
		Diam. 3¾ in.		
2056/386	5 in.	Comport & Cover		5.00
		Height 9 in.		
2056/388	5 in.	Comport		3.00
		Height 6¼ in.		
2056/396		Footed Cup		1.75
2056/397		Saucer		1.75
2056/424		Ice Bucket, Metal Handle		6.00
		Height 4½ in. - Diam. 6 in.		
2056/971		Ice Tongs (Metal)		1.10
2056½/441		3-Piece Jam Pot Set		7.50
		Height 4½ in.		
2056½/442		Jam Pot & Cover		3.00
		Height 4¼ in.		
2056/447		Jelly & Cover		4.25
		Height 6¾ in. - Diam. 4½ in.		
2056/448		Jelly		2.50
		Height 4¼ in. - Diam. 4¼ in.		
2056/453	1 pt.	Cereal Pitcher		3.25
		Height 5⅜ in.		
2056/454	1 qt.	Jug		4.50
		Height 7¼ in.		
2056/455	3 pt.	Jug		5.00
		Height 8 in.		
2056/456	3 pt.	Ice Jug		5.00
		Height 6½ in.		
2056/457	½ gal.	Jug		6.75
		Height 8 in.		
2056½/458	½ gal.	Ice Jug, Lipped		6.75
		Height 8¼ in.		
2056/462		Lemon & Cover		3.75
		Height 3½ in. - Diam. 5½ in.		
2056/475		Ftd. Mayonnaise & Ladle		4.50
		Height 4⅝ in.		
2056/476		Footed Mayonnaise		3.00
		Height 4⅝ in.		
2056/477		Mayo. & Plate & Ladle		5.75
		Height 3¾ in.		
2056/478		Mayonnaise		2.00
		Height 3⅜ in. - Diam. 5¼ in.		
2056/479	7 in.	Mayonnaise Plate		2.25
2056/480		2-Part Mayo. & 2 Ladles		6.50
		Height 3¾ in. - Diam. 6¼ in.		
2056/481		2-Part Mayonnaise		3.50
		Height 3¾ in. - Diam. 6¼ in.		
2056/482		Mayonnaise Ladle		1.50
		Stainless Steel		

AMERICAN PATTERN (Cont.)
No. 2056 Line
DINNERWARE & OTHER ACCESSORIES (Cont.)

				Retail Price Ea.
2056/528	5	oz.	Oil and Stopper	$4.00
			Height 6½ in.	
2056/531	7	oz.	Oil and Stopper	4.25
			Height 6¾ in.	
2056/536	6	in.	Olive	2.00
			Height 1⅜ in.	
2056/540	8	in.	Pickle	2.50
			Height 1½ in.	
2056/548	6	in.	Bread & Butter Plate	2.00
2056/549	7	in.	Salad Plate	2.35
2056/550	8½	in.	Salad Plate	2.75
2056/552	9½	in.	Dinner Plate	3.25
2056/553	9	in.	Sandwich Plate	3.25
2056/554	10½	in.	Sandwich Plate	3.75
2056/555	10½	in.	Oval Platter	3.75
2056/558	11½	in.	Sandwich Plate	4.50
2056/560	12	in.	Oval Platter	4.25
2056/564	13½	in.	Oval Torte Plate	6.25
2056/567	14	in.	Torte Plate	6.25
2056/576	18	in.	Torte Plate	12.25
2056/600	14	in.	Punch Bowl	13.50
			Height 6½ in. - Cap. 2 gal.	
2056/602			Low Foot for 14 in. Punch Bowl	4.75
			Height 3¾ in.	
2056/610	18	in.	Punch Bowl	21.00
			Height 8⅜ in. - Cap. 3¾ gal.	
2056/611			Foot for 18 in. Punch Bowl	6.25
			Height 4⅝ in.	
2056/615			Punch Cup, Reg.	2.00
2056/616			Punch Cup, Flared	2.00
2056/984			Punch Bowl Hooks (Plastic)	.10
2056/979			Punch Bowl Ladle (Plastic)	1.75
2056/620			2-Part Relish	3.25
			Length 12 in. - Width 5½ in.	
2056½/622			3-Part Combination Relish	6.00
			Length 11½ in. - Width 7½ in.	
2056½/624			4-Division Relish	4.50
			Length 9¼ in. - Width 6½ in.	
2056/630			Round Salver	7.75
			Height 7¼ in. - Diam. 10 in.	
2056/631			Square Salver	8.00
			Height 7¼ in. - 10 in. Square	
2056/632			Individual Salt	1.10
			Height 1 in.	
2056/648	9	in.	Handled Serving Dish	4.00
			Height 2⅜ in.	
2056½/653			Shaker & Chrome Top "A"	1.75
			Height 3½ in.	
2056/656			Ind. Shaker & Chrome Top "C"	1.35
			Height 2⅜ in.	
2056/659			Individual Shaker Tray	1.05
			Length 4 in.	
2056/662			3 Pc. Ind. Shaker Set	3.75
			Height 2⅝ in. - Length 4 in. Consisting of: 1 Only 2056/659 Ind. Shaker Tray 2 Only 2056/656 Ind. Shaker & Chrome Top "C"	
2056½/673			Handled Sugar & Cover	4.00
			Height 5¼ in.	
2056½/674			Handled Sugar	2.40
			Height 3¼ in.	
2056/676			Candy Jar & Cover	3.75
			Height 6¼ in.	
2056/676			Sugar & Cover	3.75
			Height 6¼ in.	
2056/680			Cream	2.50
			Height 4¼ in. - Cap. 9½ oz.	
2056/686	3	Pc.	Ind. Sugar & Cream & Tray	5.00
			Height 3¼ in. - Length 8 in. Consisting of: 1 Only 2056/687 Ind. Sugar 1 Only 2056/688 Ind. Cream 1 Only 2056/697 6¾ in. S. & C. Tray	
2056/687			Individual Sugar	1.75
			Height 2⅜ in.	
2056/688			Individual Cream	1.75
			Height 3 in. - Cap. 4 oz.	
2056½/691			Tea Sugar & Cream & Tray	4.50
			Height 3 in. - Length 8 in. Consisting of: 1 Only 2056½/692 Tea Sugar 1 Only 2056½/693 Tea Cream 1 Only 2056/697 6¾ in. S. & C. Tray	
2056½/692			Tea Sugar	1.50
			Height 2½ in.	
2056½/693			Tea Cream	1.50
			Height 2⅝ in. - Cap. 2½ oz.	
2056/697	6¾	in.	Sugar & Cream Tray	1.50

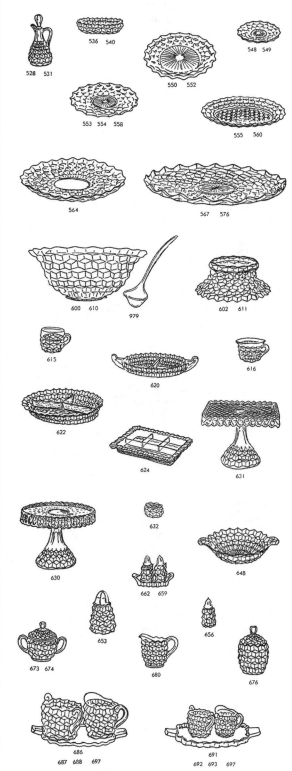

AMERICAN PATTERN (Cont.)
No. 2056 Line
DINNERWARE & OTHER ACCESSORIES (Cont.)

				Retail Price Ea.
2056/707	8	in.	3-Toed Tid Bit	$2.50
			Height 1½ in.	
2056/710			Toothpick	1.25
			Height 2⅜ in.	
2056/723	12	in.	Handled Lunch Tray	6.00
2056/726			Handled Muffin Tray	4.00
			Length 8 in. - Width 10 in.	
2056/732	9	in.	Handled Utility Tray	4.00
2056/836	9	in.	Oval Vegetable Dish	3.50
			Height 2⅛ in. - Width 6¾ in.	
2056½/837	10	in.	2-Part Vegetable Dish	4.00
			Height 2⅛ in. - Width 7 in.	

NAPPIES, HANDLED AND UNHANDLED

2056/211	10	in.	Nappy, Deep	$4.75
			Height 4⅜ in.	
2056/421	4¾	in.	Nappy (Fruit)	2.25
			Height 1½ in.	
2056/495	4½	in.	Nappy	2.00
			Height 1¾ in.	
2056/499	4½	in.	Handled Nappy, Reg.	2.00
			Height 2 in.	
2056/501	5	in.	Handled Nappy, 3-Cor.	2.00
			Height 2¼ in.	
2056/502	4½	in.	Handled Nappy, Square	2.00
			Height 2½ in.	
2056/505	5	in.	Nappy & Cover	4.25
			Height 5 in.	
2056/506	5	in.	Nappy	2.25
			Height 2½ in.	
2056/512	6	in.	Nappy	3.00
			Height 2⅝ in.	
2056/517	7	in.	Nappy	3.75
			Height 3¼ in.	
2056/521	8	in.	Nappy, Reg.	4.25
			Height 3¾ in.	

SMOKING ACCESSORIES

2056/109	3	in.	Square Ash Tray	$1.10
2056/123	5	in.	Ash Tray	2.25

VASES

2056/757	6	in.	Vase	$3.25
2056½/758	6	in.	Vase, Flared	3.50
2056/759	6	in.	Square Urn	4.00
2056/762	6	in.	Footed Bud Vase, Cupped	2.75
2056/763	6	in.	Footed Bud Vase, Flared	2.75
2056/781	7½	in.	Square Urn	5.00
2056/785	8	in.	Vase	3.75
2056½/786	8	in.	Vase, Flared	4.00
2056/798	8½	in.	Footed Bud Vase, Cupped	3.00
2056/799	8½	in.	Footed Bud Vase, Flared	3.00
2056/804	9	in.	Square Footed Vase	6.00
2056½/815	10	in.	Vase, Flared	5.50

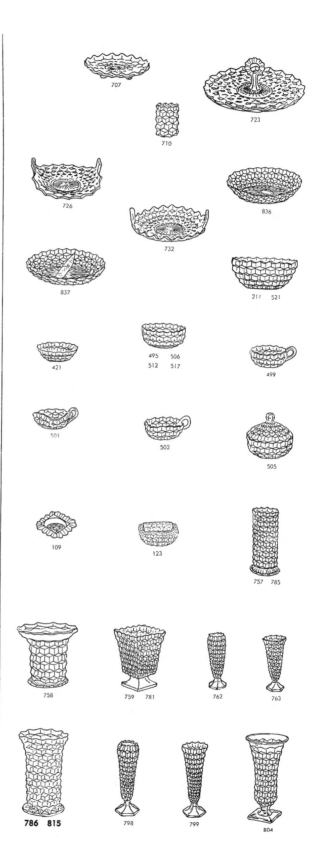

CENTURY PATTERN
No. 2630 Line
STEMWARE

			Retail Price Ea.
2630/2	10½ oz.	Goblet	$2.50
		Height 5¾ in.	
2630/7	5½ oz.	Sherbet	2.50
		Height 4¼ in.	
2630/20	3½ oz.	Cocktail	2.50
		Height 4⅛ in.	
2630/26	3½ oz.	Wine	2.50
		Height 4½ in.	
2630/33	4½ oz.	Oyster Cocktail	2.50
		Height 3¾ in.	
2630/63	12 oz.	Luncheon Goblet/Ice Tea	2.50
		Height 5⅞ in.	
2630/88	5 oz.	Footed Tumbler	2.50
		Height 4¾ in.	

BOWLS AND CANDLESTICKS

2630/179	8 in.	Bowl, Flared	4.25
		Height 3⅝ in.	
2630/197	9 in.	Lily Pond	4.50
		Height 1⅝ in.	
2630/224	10¾ in.	Footed Bowl, Flared	9.75
		Height 4½ in.	
2630/237	11¼ in.	Lily Pond	6.50
		Height 2¼ in.	
2630/316	4½ in.	Candlestick	4.00
2630/332		Duo Candlestick	6.75
		Height 7 in. - Width 6⅝ in.	
2630/336		Trindle Candlestick	8.00
		Height 7¾ in. - Width 7½ in.	

DINNERWARE & OTHER ACCESSORIES

2630/109		Individual Ash Tray	$1.25
		Length 2¾ in.	
2630/137		3-Toed Bon Bon	3.50
		Height 2¼ in. - Diam. 7¼ in.	
2630/190	8½ in.	Salad Bowl	4.25
		Height 3¼ in.	
2630/204		Oval Utility Bowl	4.50
		Height 2⅞ in. - Length 10 in.	
2630/221	10½ in.	Salad Bowl	6.50
		Height 4¼ in.	
2630/987		Salad Fork & Spoon (Wood)	1.00
2630/286	10½ in.	4 Pc. Salad Set	14.25
		Height 4¼ in.	
		Consisting of:	
		1 Only 2630/221 10½ in. Salad Bowl	
		1 Only 2630/567 14 in. Torte Plate	
		1 Only 2630/987 Salad Fork & Spoon (Wood)	
2630/300		Oblong Butter & Cover	3.75
		Height 2 in. - Length 7½ in. -	
		Width 3⅜ in.	
2630/306		Handled Cake Plate	4.50
		Diam. 9½ in.	
2630/350		Candy Jar & Cover	6.25
		Height 7 in.	
2630/351		Candy Jar	3.75
		Height 4¾ in.	
2630/369		Cheese & Cracker	7.75
		Height 2¾ in. - Diam. 11 in.	
2630/370		Footed Cheese	3.50
		Height 2½ in. - Diam. 5⅜ in.	
2630/371	11 in.	Cracker Plate	4.25
2630/388		Comport	3.75
		Height 4⅜ in.	
2630/393		Cereal	2.50
		Diam. 6 in.	
2630/396		Footed Cup	2.00
2630/397		Saucer	2.00
2630/421		Fruit	2.25
		Diam. 5 in.	
2630/424		Ice Bucket, Metal Handle	6.50
		Height 4⅞ in. - Diam. 7⅜ in.	
2630/971		Ice Tongs (Metal)	1.10
2630/453	1 pt.	Cereal Pitcher	4.50
		Height 6⅛ in.	
2630/456	3 pt.	Ice Jug	7.00
		Height 7⅛ in.	
2630/477		Mayonnaise & Plate & Ladle	6.25
		Height 3¼ in.	
2630/478		Mayonnaise	2.35
		Height 3⅛ in. - Diam. 5 in.	
2630/479		Mayonnaise Plate	2.40
		Diam. 7 in.	

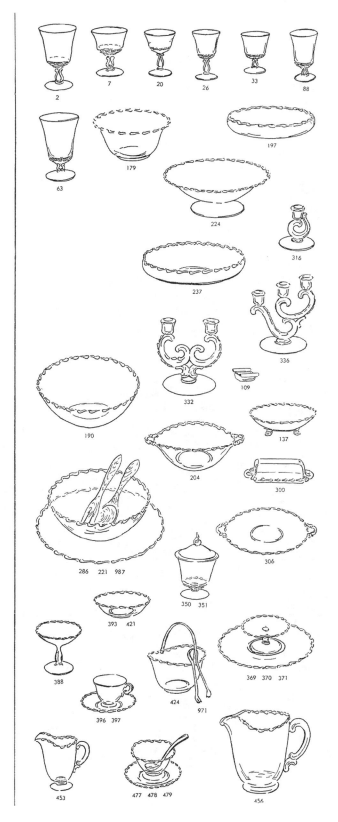

CENTURY PATTERN (Cont.)
No. 2630 Line
DINNERWARE & OTHER ACCESSORIES (Cont.)

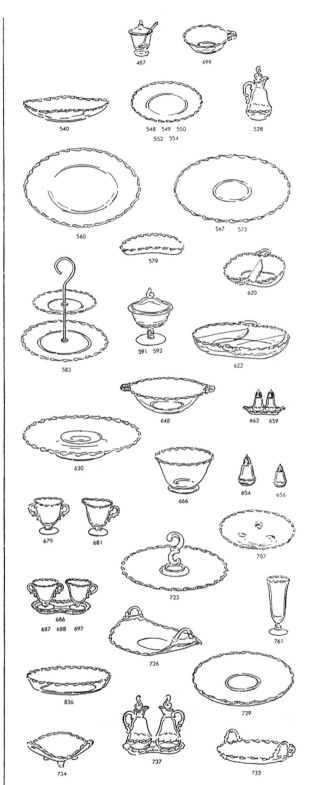

			Retail Price Ea.
2630/482		Mayonnaise Ladle	$1.50
		Stainless Steel	
2630/487		Mustard & Cover & Spoon	4.00
		Height 4 in.	
2630/499	4½ in.	Handled Nappy	2.25
		Height 1½ in.	
2630/528	5 oz.	Oil and Stopper	5.50
		Height 6 in.	
2630/540	8¾ in.	Pickle	2.75
		Height 1⅞ in.	
2630/548	6 in.	Plate	2.25
2630/549	7 in.	Plate	3.00
2630/550	8 in.	Plate	3.25
2630/552	9 in.	Plate	3.50
2630/554	10½ in.	Dinner Plate	4.25
2630/560	12 in.	Oval Platter	5.00
2630/567	14 in.	Torte Plate	6.75
2630/573	16 in.	Torte Plate	12.75
2630/579		Crescent Salad Plate	2.75
		Length 7½ in. - Width 4⅜ in.	
2630/583		3 Pc. Tid Bit Set	10.50
		Height 10¼ in.	
2630/591		Footed Preserve & Cover	6.00
		Height 6 in.	
2630/592		Footed Preserve	3.50
		Height 3⅞ in.	
2630/620		2-Part Relish	3.50
		Length 7⅜ in. - Width 6 in.	
2630/622		3-Part Relish	6.25
		Length 11⅛ in. - Width 8½ in.	
2630/630		Salver	10.50
		Height 2⅛ in. - Diam. 12¼ in.	
2630/648		Handled Serving Dish	4.25
		Height 2½ in.	
2630/654		Shaker & Chrome Top "B"	1.90
		Height 3¼ in.	
2630/656		Ind. Shaker & Chrome Top "C"	1.35
		Height 2⅜ in.	
2630/659		Ind. Shaker Tray	1.30
		Length 4¼ in.	
2630/662		3 Pc. Ind. Shaker Set	4.00
		Height 2½ in. - Length 4¼ in.	
		Consisting of:	
		1 Only 2630/659 Ind. Shaker Tray	
		2 Only 2630/656 Ind. Shaker & Chrome Top "C"	
2630/666		Snack Bowl	3.75
		Height 3½ in.	
2630/679		Footed Sugar	2.75
		Height 4 in.	
2630/681		Footed Cream	2.75
		Height 4¼ in. - Cap. 6 oz.	
2630/686	3 Pc.	Ind. Sugar & Cream & Tray	6.00
		Height 3⅞ in. - Length 7⅛ in.	
		Consisting of:	
		1 Only 2630/687 Ind. Sugar	
		1 Only 2630/688 Ind. Cream	
		1 Only 2630/697 S. & C. Tray	
2630/687		Individual Sugar	2.10
		Height 3⅜ in.	
2630/688		Individual Cream	2.15
		Height 3½ in. - Cap. 3½ oz.	
2630/697	7⅛ in.	Sugar & Cream Tray	1.75
2630/707		3-Toed Tid Bit	3.50
		Height 1¼ in. - Diam. 8½ in.	
2630/723		Handled Lunch Tray	7.00
		Diam. 11¼ in.	
2630/726		Handled Muffin Tray	4.50
		Length 9½ in. - Width 8½ in.	
2630/729		Snack Tray	4.50
		Diam. 10½ in.	
2630/732		Handled Utility Tray	4.50
		Height 1¼ in. - Diam. 9⅛ in.	
2630/734		3-Toed Tricorne	3.50
		Height 2½ in. - Length 7⅛ in.	
2630/737		3 Pc. Condiment Set	12.75
		Height 6½ in. - Length 7⅛ in.	
		Consisting of:	
		2 Only 2630/528 5 oz. Oil, D/S	
		1 Only 2630/697 7⅛ in. Sugar & Cream Tray	
2630/761	6 in.	Bud Vase	3.50
2630/836		Oval Vegetable Dish	3.50
		Height 1¾ in. - Length 9½ in.	
		Width 6½ in.	

COIN GLASS PATTERN
No. 1372 Line
Made in Crystal
Made in Olive Green, Amber and Blue as shown below
*Indicates Gold Decorated Coins

					Retail Price Ea.
1372/64	12	oz.	Ice Tea/Highball	Crystal	$2.50
			Height 5⅛ in.		
1372/73	9	oz.	Water/Scotch & Soda	Crystal	2.50
			Height 4¼ in.		
1372/81	9	oz.	Juice/Old Fashioned	Crystal	2.50
			Height 3⅝ in.		
1372/114	7½	in.	Round Ash Tray	Crystal	4.50
				Olive Green, Amber or Blue	4.75
1372/115			Oblong Ash Tray	Crystal	2.50
				Olive Green, Amber or Blue	2.75
			Width 3 in. - Length 4 in.		
1372/123	5	in.	Ash Tray	Crystal	2.75
				Olive Green, Amber or Blue	3.00
1372/124	10	in.	Ash Tray	Crystal	8.00
				Olive Green, Amber or Blue	8.25
1372/162			Wedding Bowl & Cover	Crystal	8.25
				Olive Green, Amber or Blue	8.50
				Gold Coin	15.00
			Height 8³⁄₁₆ in.		
1372/179	8	in.	Bowl	Crystal	5.00
				Olive Green, Amber or Blue	5.50
1372/189	9	in.	Oval Bowl	Crystal	5.00
				Olive Green, Amber or Blue	5.50
1372/199	8½	in.	Footed Bowl	Crystal	9.50
				Olive Green, Amber or Blue	9.75
1372/316	4½	in.	Candleholder	Crystal	4.00
				Olive Green, Amber or Blue	4.25
1372/347			Candy Jar & Cover	Crystal	5.00
				Olive Green, Amber or Blue	5.50
				Gold Coin	10.50
			Height 6⁵⁄₁₆ in.		
1372/354			Candy Box & Cover	Crystal	6.00
				Olive Green, Amber or Blue	6.50
			Height 4⅛ in. - Diam. 6⅜ in.		
1372/381			Footed Cigarette Urn	Crystal	2.50
				Olive Green, Amber or Blue	2.75
			Height 3⅜ in.		
1372/448			Jelly	Crystal	3.50
				Olive Green, Amber or Blue	3.75
			Height 3¾ in.		
1372/453			Quart Pitcher	Crystal	5.75
				Olive Green, Amber or Blue	6.25
			Height 6¹⁵⁄₁₆ in.		
1372/499			Handled Nappy	Crystal	2.75
				Olive Green, Amber or Blue	3.00
			Diam. 5⅜ in.		
1372/531	7	oz.	Cruet & Stopper	Crystal	6.25
				Olive Green, Amber or Blue	6.50
			Height 6 in.		
1372/600	14	in.	Punch Bowl	Crystal	18.50
			Capacity 1½ gal. Height 6⅜ in.		
1372/602	14	in.	Punch Bowl Ft.	Crystal	6.50
			Height 5½ in.		
1372/615			Punch Cup	Crystal	2.50
			Height 3½ in. - Diam. 3 in.		

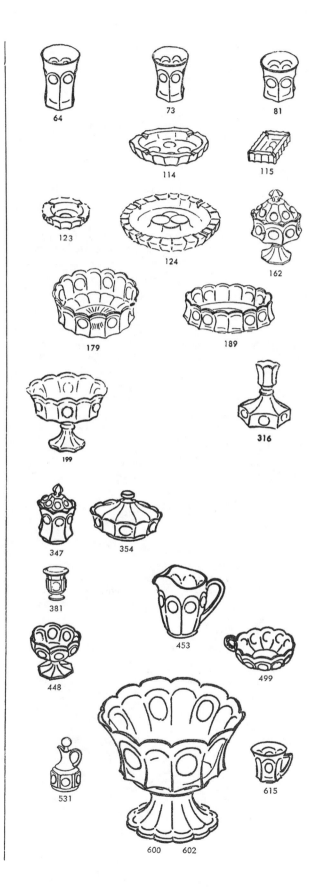

COIN GLASS PATTERN (Cont.)

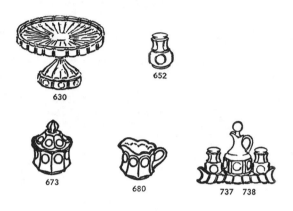

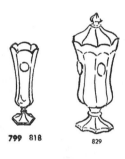

			Retail Price Ea.
1372/630	Salver	Crystal	$11.00
	Olive Green, Amber or Blue		11.50
	Height 6½ in. - Diam. 10 in.		
1372/652	Shaker & Chrome Top "E"		
		Crystal	1.75
	Olive Green, Amber or Blue		1.85
	Height 3¼ in.		
1372/673	Sugar & Cover	Crystal	4.75
	Olive Green, Amber or Blue		5.25
	Height 5⅜ in.		
1372/680	Cream	Crystal	3.00
	Olive Green, Amber or Blue		3.25
	Height 3½ in.		
1372/737	4 pc. Condiment Set	Crystal	13.00
	Olive Green, Amber or Blue		13.75

Consisting of:
1 only 1372/738 9⅝ in. Condiment Tray (Crystal)
1 only 1372/531 7 oz. Cruet & Ground Stopper
2 only 1372/652 Shaker & Chrome Top "E"
Height 7 in. - Width 4⅞ in. - Length 9⅝ in.

1372/738	9⅝ in. Condiment Tray	Crystal	3.25
	Olive Green, Amber or Blue		3.55
1372/799	8 in. Bud Vase	Crystal	3.75
	Olive Green, Amber or Blue		4.00
1372/818	10 in. Footed Vase	Crystal	8.00
1372/829	Footed Urn & Cover	Crystal	11.00
	Olive Green, Amber or Blue		11.75
	Height 12¾ in.		
1372/292	Handled Courting Lamp Chimney		
		Struck Gold or Blue	3.50
	Height 5¾ in. - Diam. Base 2⁹⁄₁₆ in.		
1372/310	Handled Courting Lamp complete (Oil)		
		Amber or Blue	11.25
	Height 9¾ in.		

Consisting of:
1 Only 1372/315 Hld. Courting Lamp Base with Brass Collar
1 Only 1372/910 Oil Burner No. 1
1 Only 1372/292 Hld. Courting Lamp Chimney

1372/311	Handled Courting Lamp complete (Electric)	Amber or Blue	12.75
	Height 10⅛ in.		

Consisting of:
1 Only 1372/315 Hld. Courting Lamp Base with Brass Collar
1 Only 1372/911 Electric Fixture No. 1
1 Only 1372/292 Hld. Courting Lamp Chimney

1372/320	Coach Lamp complete (Oil)	Crystal	11.50
		Amber or Blue	12.00
	Height 13½ in.		

Consisting of:
1 Only 1372/324 Coach Lamp Base with Brass Collar
1 Only 1372/912 Oil Burner No. 2
1 Only 1372/461 Coach Lamp Chimney

1372/321	Coach Lamp complete (Electric)	Crystal	13.00
		Amber or Blue	13.50
	Height 13½ in.		

Consisting of:
1 Only 1372/324 Coach Lamp Base with Brass Collar
1 Only 1372/913 Electric Fixture No. 2
1 Only 1372/461 Coach Lamp Chimney

1372/461	Coach Lamp Chimney	Crystal	4.25
		Struck Gold or Blue	4.50
	Height 8 in. - Diam. Base 3 in.		
1372/459	Patio Lamp complete (Oil)	Crystal	15.00
		Amber or Blue	15.50
	Height 16⅝ in.		

Consisting of:
1 Only 1372/327 Patio Lamp Base with Brass Collar
1 Only 1372/912 Oil Burner No. 2
1 Only 1372/461 Patio Lamp Chimney

1372/466	Patio Lamp complete (Electric)	Crystal	16.50
		Amber or Blue	17.00
	Height 16⅝ in.		

Consisting of:
1 Only 1372/327 Patio Lamp Base with Brass Collar
1 Only 1372/913 Electric Fixture No. 2
1 Only 1372/461 Patio Lamp Chimney

1372/461	Patio Lamp Chimney	Crystal	4.25
		Struck Gold or Blue	4.50
	Height 8 in. - Diam. Base 3 in.		

630   652

673   680   737 738

799 818   829

310 311   320 321   459 466

2496—9 oz. Goblet
Height 6¾ in.

2496
5 oz. Sherbet
Height 3⅝ in.

2496½
14 oz. Ice Tea
Height 5⅞ in.

2496½
5 oz. Tumbler
Height 3⅞ in.

2496—3½ oz.
Footed Cocktail
Height 3 in.

2496½—6½ oz.
Old Fashioned Cocktail
Height 3⅜ in.

2496—6, 7, 8, 9 in. Plate

2496—Footed Cup
2496—Saucer

2496—Footed Sugar
Height 3½ in.

2496—Footed Cream
Height 3¾ in.
Capacity 7½ oz.

2496—Individual Sugar
Height 2⅞ in.

2496—Individual Cream
Height 3⅛ in.
Capacity 4 oz.

2496—8 in. Pickle

2496—11 in. Celery

←≡ FAIRFAX PATTERN #2375 ≡→

2375—6, 7, 8, 9, 10, 13-in. Plate

2375—10 in. Grill Plate

2375—Cup
2375—Saucer

2375½—Footed Cup
2375 —Saucer

2375—After Dinner Cup
2375—After Dinner Saucer

2375—Footed Bouillon
2375—Saucer

2375—5 in. Fruit
2375—6 in. Cereal
2375—7 in. Soup
2375—7 in. Round Nappy
2375—8 in. Round Nappy

2375—Cream Soup
2375—Cream Soup Plate

2375— 9 in. Oval Baker
2375—10½ in. Oval Baker

2375—10½ in. Oval Platter
2375—12 in. Oval Platter
2375—15 in. Oval Platter

2375—8½ in. Pickle
2375—8½ in. Relish—Same as Pickle,
but with 1 partition

2375—11½ in. Relish
2375—11½ in. Celery—Same as Relish,
but without partitions

2440—5 in. Handled Lemon

2440—8½ in. Oval Tray

2440—Oval Cake Plate,
2 Hdles. Length 10½ in.

2440—6½ in. Oval Sauce Dish

2440—2 Part Handled Relish
Diameter 6½ in.

2440—6½ in. 2 Part Mayonnaise

2440—3 Part Handled Relish
Diameter 7½ in.

2440—7 in. Bowl "D"

2440—10 in. Bowl "B"

2440—12 in. Salad Bowl

2440—7 in. Vase

PIONEER PATTERN #2350

2350½ Footed Cup
2350   Saucer
Also made in Ebony

2350½ Footed Cream Soup
2350   Cream Soup Plate

2350   Cream Soup
2350   Cream Soup Plate
Cream Soup also made in Ebony

2350½ Footed Bouillon
2350   Saucer

2350   8-in. Pickle
2350   11-in. Celery

2350   5-in. Fruit
2350   6-in. Cereal
2350   7-in. Soup

2350½ Footed Cream
Also made in Ro-Eb

2350   After Dinner Cup
2350   After Dinner Saucer
Also made in Ebony

2350½ Footed Sugar
Also made in Ro-Eb

2350   Bouillon
2350   Saucer

2350   Egg Cup
Also made in Ro-Az

2350   Cup
2350   Saucer
Saucer also made in Ebony

BIBLIOGRAPHY AND SUGGESTED READING

Fostoria, Its First Fifty Years, written by Hazel Marie Weatherman and published in 1972, introduced collectible Fostoria Glass to today's glass enthusiasts. It remains the most complete assemblage of information covering that period in Fostoria production. Mrs. Weatherman added color and date information to the pictorial coverage of these important early lines. Her subsequent price guides added more information, including important data on late stems.

Fostoria, The Popular Years, first published in 1982 by Patrick McGrain and subsequently copyrighted by Park Avenue Publications, highlights production during the 1940-1960 time span. With emphasis on Fostoria's late production, it adds to the body of information which collectors find important.

Coin Glass Hand Crafted by Fostoria 1958 – 1982, written by Ronald and Sunny Stinson in 1988 and copyrighted by the Fostoria Glass Society of North Texas, has pictures and presents anecdotal information about the popular Coin line made over the 24 years during which Fostoria produced it. You may order it from Ronald Stinson, 16 West Ave. C, San Angelo, TX 76903.

Facets of Fostoria, the monthly publication mailed to members of the Fostoria Glass Society of America, regularly presents information on company production. Older company catalogs are advertised in the *Facets* and back issues are available from the Society at Box 826, Moundsville, WV 26041.

Fostoria, An Identification and Value Guide of Pressed, Blown and Hand Molded Shapes, by Ann Kerr, 1994, published by Collector Books, P.O. Box 3009, Paducah, KY 42002. It shows shapes, lists items made in those shapes, and presents suggested pricing for them.

Fostoria Master Etchings 1936 – 1972, written by Juanita Williams, Therese McIlrath, and Maryann Roberts, Copies may be ordered from the Fostoria Glass Collectors, 21901 Lassen St. #112, Chatsworth, CA 91311.

Fostoria Stemware, The Crystal for America, by Milbra Long and Emily Seate, written in 1994, published by Collector Books. A comprehensive, illustrated listing of Fostoria's stem production with suggested pricing. This comprehensive writing presents Fostoria's complete stemware production and adds to our understanding of that body of work. It may be ordered from Collector Books, P.O. Box 3009, Paducah, KY 42002.

Heather, A Study Guide, by Maryann Roberts, published in 1993, presents a detailed overview of this very popular Fostoria Etched pattern. It may be ordered from the Fostoria Glass Collectors, 21901 Lassen St. #112, Chatsworth, CA 91311.

Fostoria Reflections, a newsletter published monthly by the Fostoria Glass Collectors, 21901 Lassen St. #112, Chatsworth, CA 91311, contains specific information about Fostoria and other hand made glass. This active study and social group invites membership from across the country.

Various articles written by Virginia Scott, Glenita Stearns, and Ann Kerr in *The Glass Review*, no longer published; edited and published by Barbara Shaeffer. Also, articles written by the late Ed Trindle, published in the *Depression Glass Daze*, 275 S. State Rd., Box 57, Otisville, MI.

Henry J. Liebman is writing twelve accounts covering different aspects of Fostoria Glass Company production. These specialized works are informative, well documented and illustrated. They offer important data, adding to that which has not been presented before. This writing refers, in particular, to the *Carving* issue. These publications may be ordered from the author at 758 Colony Circle, Pittsburgh, PA 15241.

COLLECTOR BOOKS

Informing Today's Collector

For over two decades we have been keeping collectors informed on trends and values in all fields of antiques and collectibles.

DOLLS, FIGURES & TEDDY BEARS

4707	A Decade of **Barbie** Dolls & Collectibles, 1981–1991, Summers	$19.95
4631	**Barbie** Doll Boom, 1986–1995, Augustyniak	$18.95
2079	**Barbie** Doll Fashions, Volume I, Eames	$24.95
3957	**Barbie** Exclusives, Rana	$18.95
4632	**Barbie** Exclusives, Book II, Rana	$18.95
4557	**Barbie,** The First 30 Years, Deutsch	$24.95
4657	**Barbie** Years, 1959–1995, Olds	$16.95
3310	**Black Dolls,** 1820–1991, Perkins	$17.95
3873	**Black Dolls,** Book II, Perkins	$17.95
1529	Collector's Encyclopedia of **Barbie** Dolls, DeWein	$19.95
4506	Collector's Guide to **Dolls in Uniform,** Bourgeois	$18.95
3727	Collector's Guide to **Ideal Dolls,** Izen	$18.95
3728	Collector's Guide to Miniature **Teddy Bears,** Powell	$17.95
3967	Collector's Guide to **Trolls,** Peterson	$19.95
4571	**Liddle Kiddles,** Identification & Value Guide, Langford	$18.95
4645	**Madame Alexander** Dolls Price Guide #21, Smith	$9.95
3733	**Modern Collector's** Dolls, Sixth Series, Smith	$24.95
3991	**Modern Collector's** Dolls, Seventh Series, Smith	$24.95
4647	**Modern Collector's** Dolls, Eighth Series, Smith	$24.95
4640	Patricia Smith's **Doll Values,** Antique to Modern, 12th Edition	$12.95
3826	Story of **Barbie,** Westenhouser	$19.95
1513	**Teddy Bears & Steiff** Animals, Mandel	$9.95
1817	**Teddy Bears & Steiff** Animals, 2nd Series, Mandel	$19.95
2084	**Teddy Bears, Annalee's & Steiff** Animals, 3rd Series, Mandel	$19.95
1808	Wonder of **Barbie,** Manos	$9.95
1430	World of **Barbie** Dolls, Manos	$9.95

FURNITURE

1457	American **Oak** Furniture, McNerney	$9.95
3716	American **Oak** Furniture, Book II, McNerney	$12.95
1118	Antique **Oak** Furniture, Hill	$7.95
2132	Collector's Encyclopedia of **American** Furniture, Vol. I, Swedberg	$24.95
2271	Collector's Encyclopedia of **American** Furniture, Vol. II, Swedberg	$24.95
3720	Collector's Encyclopedia of **American** Furniture, Vol. III, Swedberg	$24.95
3878	Collector's Guide to **Oak** Furniture, George	$12.95
1755	Furniture of the **Depression Era,** Swedberg	$19.95
3906	**Heywood-Wakefield** Modern Furniture, Rouland	$18.95
1885	**Victorian** Furniture, Our American Heritage, McNerney	$9.95
3829	**Victorian** Furniture, Our American Heritage, Book II, McNerney	$9.95
3869	**Victorian** Furniture books, 2 volume set, McNerney	$19.90

JEWELRY, HATPINS, WATCHES & PURSES

1712	Antique & Collector's **Thimbles** & Accessories, Mathis	$19.95
1748	Antique **Purses,** Revised Second Ed., Holiner	$19.95
1278	Art Nouveau & Art Deco **Jewelry,** Baker	$9.95
4558	**Christmas Pins,** Past and Present, Gallina	$18.95
3875	Collecting Antique **Stickpins,** Kerins	$16.95
3722	Collector's Ency. of **Compacts, Carryalls & Face Powder Boxes,** Mueller	$24.95
4655	Complete Price Guide to **Watches,** #16, Shugart	$26.95
1716	Fifty Years of Collectible **Fashion Jewelry,** 1925-1975, Baker	$19.95
1424	**Hatpins** & Hatpin Holders, Baker	$9.95
4570	Ladies' **Compacts,** Gerson	$24.95
1181	100 Years of Collectible **Jewelry,** 1850-1950, Baker	$9.95
2348	20th Century Fashionable Plastic **Jewelry,** Baker	$19.95
3830	Vintage **Vanity Bags & Purses,** Gerson	$24.95

TOYS, MARBLES & CHRISTMAS COLLECTIBLES

3427	**Advertising Character** Collectibles, Dotz	$17.95
2333	Antique & Collector's **Marbles,** 3rd Ed., Grist	$9.95
3827	Antique & Collector's **Toys,** 1870–1950, Longest	$24.95
3956	Baby Boomer **Games,** Identification & Value Guide, Polizzi	$24.95
3717	**Christmas** Collectibles, 2nd Edition, Whitmyer	$24.95
1752	**Christmas** Ornaments, Lights & Decorations, Johnson	$19.95
4649	Classic Plastic **Model Kits,** Polizzi	$24.95

4559	Collectible **Action Figures,** 2nd Ed., Manos	$17.95
3874	Collectible Coca-Cola Toy **Trucks,** deCourtivron	$24.95
2338	Collector's Encyclopedia of **Disneyana,** Longest, Stern	$24.95
4639	Collector's Guide to **Diecast Toys & Scale Models,** Johnson	$19.95
4651	Collector's Guide to **Tinker Toys,** Strange	$18.95
4566	Collector's Guide to **Tootsietoys,** 2nd Ed., Richter	$19.95
3436	Grist's Big Book of **Marbles**	$19.95
3970	Grist's Machine-Made & Contemporary **Marbles,** 2nd Ed.	$9.95
4569	**Howdy Doody,** Collector's Reference and Trivia Guide, Koch	$16.95
4723	**Matchbox®** Toys, 1948 to 1993, Johnson, 2nd Ed.	$18.95
3823	**Mego** Toys, An Illustrated Value Guide, Chrouch	15.95
1540	**Modern Toys** 1930–1980, Baker	$19.95
3888	**Motorcycle** Toys, Antique & Contemporary, Gentry/Downs	$18.95
4728	Schroeder's Collectible **Toys,** Antique to Modern Price Guide, 3rd Ed.	$17.95
1886	Stern's Guide to **Disney** Collectibles	$14.95
2139	Stern's Guide to **Disney** Collectibles, 2nd Series	$14.95
3975	Stern's Guide to **Disney** Collectibles, 3rd Series	$18.95
2028	**Toys,** Antique & Collectible, Longest	$14.95
3979	**Zany Characters** of the Ad World, Lamphier	$16.95

INDIANS, GUNS, KNIVES, TOOLS, PRIMITIVES

1868	Antique **Tools,** Our American Heritage, McNerney	$9.95
2015	Archaic **Indian** Points & Knives, Edler	$14.95
1426	**Arrowheads** & Projectile Points, Hothem	$7.95
4633	**Big Little Books,** Jacobs	$18.95
2279	**Indian** Artifacts of the Midwest, Hothem	$14.95
3885	**Indian** Artifacts of the Midwest, Book II, Hothem	$16.95
1964	**Indian** Axes & Related Stone Artifacts, Hothem	$14.95
2023	**Keen Kutter** Collectibles, Heuring	$14.95
4724	Modern **Guns,** Identification & Values, 11th Ed., Quertermous	$12.95
4505	Standard Guide to **Razors,** Ritchie & Stewart	$9.95
4730	Standard **Knife** Collector's Guide, 3rd Ed., Ritchie & Stewart	$12.95

PAPER COLLECTIBLES & BOOKS

4633	**Big Little Books,** Jacobs	$18.95
1441	Collector's Guide to **Post Cards,** Wood	$9.95
2081	Guide to Collecting **Cookbooks,** Allen	$14.95
4648	Huxford's **Old Book** Value Guide, 8th Ed.	$19.95
2080	Price Guide to **Cookbooks & Recipe Leaflets,** Dickinson	$9.95
2346	**Sheet Music** Reference & Price Guide, 2nd Ed., Pafik & Guiheen	$18.95
4654	**Victorian Trading Cards,** Historical Reference & Value Guide, Cheadle	$19.95

GLASSWARE

1006	**Cambridge Glass** Reprint 1930–1934	$14.95
1007	**Cambridge Glass** Reprint 1949–1953	$14.95
4561	Collectible **Drinking Glasses,** Chase & Kelly	$17.95
4642	Collectible **Glass Shoes,** Wheatley	$19.95
4553	Coll. **Glassware** from the 40's, 50's & 60's, 3rd Ed., Florence	$19.95
2352	Collector's Encyclopedia of **Akro Agate Glassware,** Florence	$14.95
1810	Collector's Encyclopedia of **American Art Glass,** Shuman	$29.95
3312	Collector's Encyclopedia of **Children's Dishes,** Whitmyer	$19.95
4552	Collector's Encyclopedia of **Depression Glass,** 12th Ed., Florence	$19.95
1664	Collector's Encyclopedia of **Heisey Glass,** 1925–1938, Bredehoft	$24.95
3905	Collector's Encyclopedia of **Milk Glass,** Newbound	$24.95
1523	Colors In **Cambridge Glass,** National Cambridge Society	$19.95
4564	**Crackle Glass,** Weitman	$19.95
2275	**Czechoslovakian Glass** and Collectibles, Barta/Rose	$16.95
4714	**Czechoslovakian Glass** and Collectibles, Book II, Barta/Rose	$16.95
4716	**Elegant Glassware** of the Depression Era, 7th Ed., Florence	$19.95
1380	Encyclopedia of **Pattern Glass,** McClain	$12.95
3981	Ever's Standard **Cut Glass** Value Guide	$12.95
4659	**Fenton** Art Glass, 1907–1939, Whitmyer	$24.95
3725	**Fostoria,** Pressed, Blown & Hand Molded Shapes, Kerr	$24.95
3883	**Fostoria Stemware,** The Crystal for America, Long & Seate	$24.95
3318	**Glass Animals** of the Depression Era, Garmon & Spencer	$19.95
4644	**Imperial Carnival Glass,** Burns	$18.95

3886	**Kitchen Glassware** of the Depression Years, 5th Ed., Florence	$19.95
2394	**Oil Lamps II**, Glass Kerosene Lamps, Thuro	$24.95
4725	Pocket Guide to **Depression Glass**, 10th Ed., Florence	$9.95
4634	Standard Encyclopedia of **Carnival Glass**, 5th Ed., Edwards	$24.95
4635	Standard **Carnival Glass** Price Guide, 10th Ed.	$9.95
3974	Standard Encylopedia of **Opalescent Glass**, Edwards	$19.95
4731	**Stemware Identification**, Featuring Cordials with Values, Florence	$24.95
3326	**Very Rare Glassware** of the Depression Years, 3rd Series, Florence	$24.95
3909	**Very Rare Glassware** of the Depression Years, 4th Series, Florence	$24.95
4732	**Very Rare Glassware** of the Depression Years, 5th Series, Florence	$24.95
4656	**Westmoreland Glass**, Wilson	$24.95
2224	World of **Salt Shakers**, 2nd Ed., Lechner	$24.95

POTTERY

4630	**American Limoges**, Limoges	$24.95
1312	**Blue & White Stoneware**, McNerney	$9.95
1958	So. Potteries **Blue Ridge Dinnerware**, 3rd Ed., Newbound	$14.95
1959	**Blue Willow**, 2nd Ed., Gaston	$14.95
3816	Collectible **Vernon Kilns**, Nelson	$24.95
3311	Collecting **Yellow Ware** – Id. & Value Guide, McAllister	$16.95
1373	Collector's Encyclopedia of **American Dinnerware**, Cunningham	$24.95
3815	Collector's Encyclopedia of **Blue Ridge Dinnerware**, Newbound	$19.95
4658	Collector's Encyclopedia of **Brush-McCoy Pottery**, Huxford	$24.95
2272	Collector's Encyclopedia of **California Pottery**, Chipman	$24.95
3811	Collector's Encyclopedia of **Colorado Pottery**, Carlton	$24.95
2133	Collector's Encyclopedia of **Cookie Jars**, Roerig	$24.95
3723	Collector's Encyclopedia of **Cookie Jars**, Volume II, Roerig	$24.95
3429	Collector's Encyclopedia of **Cowan Pottery**, Saloff	$24.95
4638	Collector's Encyclopedia of **Dakota Potteries**, Dommel	$24.95
2209	Collector's Encyclopedia of **Fiesta**, 7th Ed., Huxford	$19.95
4718	Collector's Encyclopedia of **Figural Planters & Vases**, Newbound	$19.95
3961	Collector's Encyclopedia of **Early Noritake**, Alden	$24.95
1439	Collector's Encyclopedia of **Flow Blue China**, Gaston	$19.95
3812	Collector's Encyclopedia of **Flow Blue China**, 2nd Ed., Gaston	$24.95
3813	Collector's Encyclopedia of **Hall China**, 2nd Ed., Whitmyer	$24.95
3431	Collector's Encyclopedia of **Homer Laughlin China**, Jasper	$24.95
1276	Collector's Encyclopedia of **Hull Pottery**, Roberts	$19.95
4573	Collector's Encyclopedia of **Knowles, Taylor & Knowles**, Gaston	$24.95
3962	Collector's Encyclopedia of **Lefton China**, DeLozier	$19.95
2210	Collector's Encyclopedia of **Limoges Porcelain**, 2nd Ed., Gaston	$24.95
2334	Collector's Encyclopedia of **Majolica Pottery**, Katz-Marks	$19.95
1358	Collector's Encyclopedia of **McCoy Pottery**, Huxford	$19.95
3963	Collector's Encyclopedia of **Metlox Potteries**, Gibbs Jr.	$24.95
3313	Collector's Encyclopedia of **Niloak**, Gifford	$19.95
3837	Collector's Encyclopedia of **Nippon Porcelain I**, Van Patten	$24.95
2089	Collector's Ency. of **Nippon Porcelain**, 2nd Series, Van Patten	$24.95
1665	Collector's Ency. of **Nippon Porcelain**, 3rd Series, Van Patten	$24.95
3836	**Nippon Porcelain** Price Guide, Van Patten	$9.95
1447	Collector's Encyclopedia of **Noritake**, Van Patten	$19.95
3432	Collector's Encyclopedia of **Noritake**, 2nd Series, Van Patten	$24.95
1037	Collector's Encyclopedia of **Occupied Japan**, Vol. I, Florence	$14.95
1038	Collector's Encyclopedia of **Occupied Japan**, Vol. II, Florence	$14.95
2088	Collector's Encyclopedia of **Occupied Japan**, Vol. III, Florence	$14.95
2019	Collector's Encyclopedia of **Occupied Japan**, Vol. IV, Florence	$14.95
2335	Collector's Encyclopedia of **Occupied Japan**, Vol. V, Florence	$14.95
3964	Collector's Encyclopedia of **Pickard China**, Reed	$24.95
1311	Collector's Encyclopedia of **R.S. Prussia**, 1st Series, Gaston	$24.95
1715	Collector's Encyclopedia of **R.S. Prussia**, 2nd Series, Gaston	$24.95
3726	Collector's Encyclopedia of **R.S. Prussia**, 3rd Series, Gaston	$24.95
3877	Collector's Encyclopedia of **R.S. Prussia**, 4th Series, Gaston	$24.95
1034	Collector's Encyclopedia of **Roseville Pottery**, Huxford	$19.95
1035	Collector's Encyclopedia of **Roseville Pottery**, 2nd Ed., Huxford	$19.95
3357	**Roseville** Price Guide No. 10	$9.95
3965	Collector's Encyclopedia of **Sascha Brastoff**, Conti, Bethany & Seay	$24.95
3314	Collector's Encyclopedia of **Van Briggle** Art Pottery, Sasicki	$24.95
4563	Collector's Encyclopedia of **Wall Pockets**, Newbound	$19.95
2111	Collector's Encyclopedia of **Weller Pottery**, Huxford	$29.95
3452	Coll. Guide to **Country Stoneware & Pottery**, Raycraft	$11.95
2077	Coll. Guide to **Country Stoneware & Pottery**, 2nd Series, Raycraft	$14.95
3434	Coll. Guide to **Hull Pottery**, The Dinnerware Line, Gick-Burke	$16.95

3876	Collector's Guide to **Lu-Ray Pastels**, Meehan	$18.95
3814	Collector's Guide to **Made in Japan** Ceramics, White	$18.95
4646	Collector's Guide to **Made in Japan** Ceramics, Book II, White	$18.95
4565	Collector's Guide to **Rockingham**, The Enduring Ware, Brewer	$14.95
2339	Collector's Guide to **Shawnee Pottery**, Vanderbilt	$19.95
1425	**Cookie Jars**, Westfall	$9.95
3440	**Cookie Jars**, Book II, Westfall	$19.95
3435	Debolt's Dictionary of **American Pottery Marks**	$17.95
2379	Lehner's Ency. of **U.S. Marks** on Pottery, Porcelain & China	$24.95
4722	**McCoy Pottery**, Collector's Reference & Value Guide, Hanson/Nissen	$19.95
3825	**Puritan Pottery**, Morris	$24.95
4726	**Red Wing Art Pottery**, 1920s–1960s, Dollen	$19.95
1670	**Red Wing Collectibles**, DePasquale	$9.95
1440	**Red Wing Stoneware**, DePasquale	$9.95
3738	**Shawnee Pottery**, Mangus	$24.95
4629	Turn of the Century **American Dinnerware**, 1880s–1920s, Jasper	$24.95
4572	**Wall Pockets** of the Past, Perkins	$17.95
3327	**Watt Pottery** – Identification & Value Guide, Morris	$19.95

OTHER COLLECTIBLES

4704	Antique & Collectible **Buttons**, Wisniewski	$19.95
2269	Antique **Brass & Copper** Collectibles, Gaston	$16.95
1880	Antique **Iron**, McNerney	$9.95
3872	Antique **Tins**, Dodge	$24.95
1714	**Black** Collectibles, Gibbs	$19.95
1128	**Bottle** Pricing Guide, 3rd Ed., Cleveland	$7.95
4636	**Celluloid Collectibles**, Dunn	$14.95
3959	**Cereal Box** Bonanza, The 1950's, Bruce	$19.95
3718	Collectible **Aluminum**, Grist	$16.95
3445	Collectible **Cats**, An Identification & Value Guide, Fyke	$18.95
4560	Collectible **Cats**, An Identification & Value Guide, Book II, Fyke	$19.95
1634	Collector's Ency. of Figural & Novelty **Salt & Pepper Shakers**, Davern	$19.95
2020	Collector's Ency. of Figural & Novelty **Salt & Pepper Shakers**, Vol. II, Davern	$19.95
2018	Collector's Encyclopedia of **Granite Ware**, Greguire	$24.95
3430	Collector's Encyclopedia of **Granite Ware**, Book II, Greguire	$24.95
4705	Collector's Guide to **Antique Radios**, 4th Ed., Bunis	$18.95
1916	Collector's Guide to **Art Deco**, Gaston	$14.95
3880	Collector's Guide to **Cigarette Lighters**, Flanagan	$17.95
4637	Collector's Guide to **Cigarette Lighters**, Book II, Flanagan	$17.95
1537	Collector's Guide to **Country Baskets**, Raycraft	$9.95
3966	Collector's Guide to **Inkwells**, Identification & Values, Badders	$18.95
3881	Collector's Guide to **Novelty Radios**, Bunis/Breed	$18.95
4652	Collector's Guide to **Transistor Radios**, 2nd Ed., Bunis	$16.95
4653	Collector's Guide to **TV Memorabilia**, 1960s–1970s, Davis/Morgan	$24.95
2276	**Decoys**, Kangas	$24.95
1629	**Doorstops**, Identification & Values, Bertoia	$9.95
4567	Figural **Napkin Rings**, Gottschalk & Whitson	$18.95
3968	**Fishing Lure** Collectibles, Murphy/Edmisten	$24.95
4568	**Flea Market Trader**, 10th Ed., Huxford	$12.95
3976	Foremost Guide to **Uncle Sam** Collectibles, Czulewicz	$24.95
4641	**Garage Sale & Flea Market Annual**, 4th Ed.	$19.95
3819	**General Store Collectibles**, Wilson	$24.95
4643	**Great American West** Collectibles, Wilson	$24.95
2215	Goldstein's **Coca-Cola** Collectibles	$16.95
3884	Huxford's Collectible **Advertising**, 2nd Ed.	$24.95
2216	**Kitchen Antiques**, 1790–1940, McNerney	$14.95
3321	Ornamental & Figural **Nutcrackers**, Rittenhouse	$16.95
2026	**Railroad** Collectibles, 4th Ed., Baker	$14.95
1632	**Salt & Pepper Shakers**, Guarnaccia	$9.95
1888	**Salt & Pepper Shakers** II, Identification & Value Guide, Book II, Guarnaccia	$14.95
2220	**Salt & Pepper Shakers** III, Guarnaccia	$14.95
3443	**Salt & Pepper Shakers** IV, Guarnaccia	$18.95
4727	**Schroeder's Antiques** Price Guide, 15th Ed., Huxford	$12.95
2096	**Silverplated Flatware**, Revised 4th Edition, Hagan	$14.95
1922	Standard **Old Bottle** Price Guide, Sellari	$14.95
4708	Summers' Guide to **Coca-Cola**	$19.95
3892	**Toy & Miniature Sewing Machines**, Thomas	$18.95
3828	Value Guide to **Advertising Memorabilia**, Summers	$18.95
3977	Value Guide to **Gas Station** Memorabilia, Summers & Priddy	$24.95
3978	**Wanted to Buy**, 5th Edition	$9.95